TRUST AND GOVERNANCE

TRUST AND GOVERNANCE

VALERIE BRAITHWAITE AND MARGARET LEVI

EDITORS

VOLUME I IN THE RUSSELL SAGE FOUNDATION SERIES ON TRUST

Russell Sage Foundation • New York

The Russell Sage Foundation

The Russell Sage Foundation, one of the oldest of America's general purpose foundations, was established in 1907 by Mrs. Margaret Olivia Sage for "the improvement of social and living conditions in the United States." The Foundation seeks to fulfill this mandate by fostering the development and dissemination of knowledge about the country's political, social, and economic problems. While the Foundation endeavors to assure the accuracy and objectivity of each book it publishes, the conclusions and interpretations in Russell Sage Foundation publications are those of the authors and not of the Foundation, its Trustees, or its staff. Publication by Russell Sage, therefore, does not imply Foundation endorsement.

Library of Congress Cataloging-in-Publication Data

Trust and governance / Valerie Braithwaite and Margaret Levi, eds.
    p.   cm.
    Includes bibliographical references and index.
    ISBN 0-87154-134-3
    1. Political ethics.   2. Political sociology.   3. Democracy.
    I. Braithwaite, V. A. (Valerie A.), 1951–   . II. Levi, Margaret.
    JA79.T78   1998   98-2935
    306.2—dc21   CIP

The paper used in this publication meets the minimum requirements of American National Standard for Information Sciences—Permanence of Paper for Printed Library Materials. ANSI Z39.48-1992.

RUSSELL SAGE FOUNDATION
112 East 64th Street, New York, New York 10021
10 9 8 7 6 5 4 3 2 1

To Patrick N. Troy

Contents

Contributors

Valerie Braithwaite is associate director of the Research School of Social Sciences at the Australian National University, Canberra, Australia. She is also coordinator of the Trust Strand of the Reshaping Australian Institutions Project in the Research School of Social Sciences.

Margaret Levi is professor of political science and Harry Bridges Chair in Labor Studies, University of Washington, Seattle. She is also director of the University of Washington Center for Labor Studies.

William T. Bianco is associate professor of political science at The Pennsylvania State University. In 1998 to 1999 he will be visiting associate professor of political science at Harvard University.

Simon Blackburn is Edna J. Koury Professor of Philosophy at the University of North Carolina, Chapel Hill.

John Braithwaite is professor of law in the Research School of Social Sciences at the Australian National University, Canberra, Australia.

Geoffrey Brennan is professor of economics in the Social and Political Theory Group within the Research School of Social Sciences at the Australian National University, Canberra, Australia.

Martin Daunton is professor of economic history at the University of Cambridge.

Russell Hardin is professor of politics at New York University.

M. Kent Jennings is professor emeritus, University of Michigan, and professor of political science, University of California, Santa Barbara.

Mark Peel is a lecturer in history at Monash University, Melbourne.

Philip Pettit is professor of social and political theory in the Research School of Social Sciences at the Australian National University, Canberra, Australia. He also serves as a visiting professor in the Department of Philosophy, Columbia University.

John T. Scholz is professor of political science at the State University of New York, Stony Brook.

Tom R. Tyler is professor of psychology at New York University.

Susan H. Whiting is assistant professor of political science and international studies at the University of Washington, Seattle.

Introduction

MARGARET LEVI AND VALERIE BRAITHWAITE

O N THE walls of the *Sala della Pace*, Hall of Peace, of Siena's City Hall are some glorious fourteenth-century frescoes illustrating the effects of good and evil government. The first depicts a form of heaven; the other is clearly hell. These are not, however, religious paintings. The character of one's government is neither a consequence of fate nor a reward for a life well led. Rather, the quality of governance reflects the quality of one's leaders and one's laws. Both the people and the rulers of this city of good government appear serene, even happy; they exit and enter their walls without fear; they engage in exchange and cooperative ventures with ease. There is no evidence of either policing or venality, the images that dominate the paintings of evil government. The viewer can only assume that good governance implies a mutual trust between citizens and governors and among the citizens themselves.

It may seem intuitively obvious that good governance requires trust, but is this in fact the case? Is the social trust that occurs among individuals the cause or the effect of good government? If trust is indeed a necessary feature of good government, what kinds of trust are essential? When does good governance depend on strong laws strongly enforced, and when does it depend on trust? Are the two mutually exclusive? Does one drive the other out, or do they reinforce each other? For that matter, is trust even a goal worth seeking? Theorists often write of the healthy mistrust that maintains democracies; checks and balances are a major credo of democratic government.

These are among the questions that shape the essays in this volume. In particular, the authors provide arguments and evidence for several very different perspectives on trust, especially as it relates to

1

governance. Some of the differences reflect disagreements, but some are more reflections of the range of disciplines represented in the discussion. This book grows out of a workshop and two conferences held at the Research School of Social Sciences (RSSS) of the Australian National University under the combined auspices of the Program on Administration, Compliance and Governability, the Program in Social Theory, and the Reshaping Australian Institutions Project, with some additional support from the Russell Sage Foundation. Another conference, cosponsored by the Russell Sage Foundation and the Department of Political Science, University of Washington, was a further source of papers and comments. The participants in this collaborative book come from the fields of psychology, political science, philosophy, history, sociology, economics, and law. They bring to these papers the particularities—and often peculiarities—of their academic branches as well as their own personal approaches, perspectives, beliefs, and findings.

The book is organized around four questions crucial to an understanding of the relationship between trust and governance. The first concerns the grounds on which someone might trust government. Russell Hardin claims that the logic of rational choice reveals the impossibility of a meaningful account of trust in government since most citizens do not have the information they need to decide to trust. Hardin argues for institutional designs that encapsulate the self-interest of officials and thus safeguard citizens against enticements to malfeasance.

Simon Blackburn does not deny the importance of institutional structures, but he argues that trust is both essential and achievable. Blackburn claims that being trusting and trustworthy are socially valued attributes and that their very desirability motivates trusting and trustworthy behavior.

Valerie Braithwaite pursues the normative argument by demonstrating that the conditions for trusting government and its agents are expressions of shared social values. Braithwaite identifies two sets of trust norms that are brought into play in different institutional contexts, one concerned with the regularity and predictability of action, the other concerned with an awareness of and capacity to act in the interests of the other.

The second question has to do with the evidence for the effects of trustworthy governments on both governance and the economy. Margaret Levi provides an overview of the existing literature, details the institutional arrangements that make government agents trustworthy, and elaborates some of the implications for democracy. Instituting fair procedures and ensuring credible commitments enhance a government's trustworthiness, which in turn contributes to citizen compliance and ethical reciprocity. Levi's model highlights the dynamic nature of trust and reveals the role of democratic institutions in providing corrections when breaches of trust occur.

Martin Daunton provides a historical account of how British politicians extended the extractive capacity of the state by means of rules, regulations, and institutions that assured citizens of the limits on government power. The British government won legitimacy for and compliance with its tax system by means of credible commitments to curtail government spending, bring equity into the tax system, and increase accountability and transparency.

John Scholz presents findings from three studies that demonstrate the limited utility of deterrence for tax compliance and the more significant role of trust and duty heuristics. Scholz offers empirical evidence for his claim that changes to the tax law that favor the taxpayer produce a higher sense of duty than changes that are unfavorable to the taxpayer.

Susan Whiting examines the relationship between trust and economic development in two provinces in China. Whiting uses the notion of encapsulated self-interest to explain why more private investment flourishes in the region with the weaker legacy of public enterprise development. Reliance on private capital for economic development means that local officials are motivated to work through the complexities posed by the political-legal framework of the central government to provide credible commitments to investors seeking security for their enterprises.

The third section of the book focuses more specifically on issues of democratic governance. Geoffrey Brennan explains how consideration of the subjective payoffs of guilt and loss of esteem over and above objective payoffs turns the reliance game into a trust game. Brennan argues that it is rational for us to adopt a trustworthy disposition when our guilt and shame exceed the benefits of defecting and when the other party communicates a judgment of us as trustworthy. Brennan concludes that when officials are elected for their trustworthiness, when expectations of trustworthiness are communicated, and when officials value the esteem in which they are held, rational actor theory offers a plausible account of how representative democracy can produce elected officials who are trustworthy and a citizenry that can trust its officials.

Kent Jennings and William Bianco explore the role that trust actually seems to play in U.S. democratic government. Jennings uses survey data over a thirty-year period to show how trust in the national government has been eroded through a failure to meet performance expectations. In contrast, trust in local and state governments has not suffered. He argues that on the subnational level trust is based less on criteria of performance than on criteria of linkage—that is, the capacity to convince constituents that government officials care about and represent the concerns of ordinary people. Jennings concludes that loss of confidence in government at the national level has helped popularize the move toward devolution of responsibility for service provision to the local level.

Bianco models the interplay of constituent trust and legislator response with the Evaluation Game and finds that constituent trust and distrust of legislators may play a greater constraining role on representatives than current critics of democratic institutions seem to credit. Bianco shows the importance to legislators of having their constituents believe that they share the constituents' interests. Once beliefs of common interest are established, constituents will trust legislators, regardless of the extent of their own knowledge about particular issues.

The final section turns to the way in which trusting and trustworthiness are mutually reinforcing. Tom Tyler uses the findings from a series of studies to build a model of social as opposed to instrumental trust. Tyler argues that governments that are regarded as trustworthy, procedurally fair, and respectful of citizens generate social trust through establishing a social bond or a shared identity. Citizens derive a sense of pride and respect from their identification with their government. This sense in turn enhances the legitimacy of the authorities as well as a willingness to defer to the authorities.

Examining trust from a republican perspective, Philip Pettit points out that institutional constraints can go only so far to ensure freedom from the domination of others. Pettit argues that in addition to external constraints that institutionalize impersonal trust, a mechanism is required to reinvigorate trustworthiness as a civic virtue. The mechanism Pettit proposes is trust responsiveness, triggering trustworthiness by trusting. For the nonvirtuous reasons of esteem and love of glory, individuals will desire to be seen as trustworthy. Communicating personal trust in another who desires to be thought trustworthy gives that person a powerful incentive to act in a trustworthy way in the republican state where vigilance through impersonal trust is high.

Mark Peel uses case studies of four disadvantaged Australian communities to tell the reverse story of spirals of reciprocal distrust. Peel details the way in which the imposition of control mechanisms of accountability and surveillance by government has communicated lack of confidence in both the competence and integrity of citizens to design community services to meet their needs. Peel describes a citizenry that has disengaged from government and views government assistance with cynicism and distrust.

Finally, John Braithwaite presents a defense of the proposition that trust is a virtue and is the most important resource available for combating breaches of trust. Braithwaite argues that trust as confidence increases efficiency, while trust as obligation protects against the abuse of power, and that both types of trust are mutually reinforcing. Institutional safeguards against exploitation of this culture of trust are provided by republican circles of guardianship in which each community of dialogue is accountable to each other, with draconian strategies of distrust waiting in the wings for use with rational calculators who persistently breach the trust that has been placed in them.

The chapters in this volume offer a variety of claims for the kind of work that trust can do for governance. Trust may ease coordination among citizens and with government actors, reduce transaction costs, increase the probability of citizen compliance with government demands, and contribute to political support of the government. Most of the authors concur that trust may do these things but disagree over the mechanisms by which trust brings about these desiderata and the extent to which trust is even necessary for their achievement. Underlying the claims of nearly all the authors, however, is the assumption that rules and institutions are necessary to protect citizens from the worst effects of misplaced trust. The best design of those rules and institutions remains a subject of scholarly and political debate.

PART I

THE BASIS FOR TRUSTING THE STATE
AND ITS AGENTS

Chapter 1

Trust in Government

RUSSELL HARDIN

T HERE ARE two senses in which trust has long been associated
with government. One tradition is stated well in the ancient
Greek "Anonymous Iamblichi": "The first result of lawfulness
is trust, which greatly benefits all people and is among the greatest
goods. The result of trust is that property has common benefits, so
that even just a little property suffices, since it is circulated, whereas
without this even a great amount does not suffice" (294). In essence,
law enables people to trust and therefore to exchange, to their great
benefit. The context of the remark is a list of the benefits of lawfulness. Clearly, the anonymous author shared the central vision of
Thomas Hobbes.

The more common association in modern discussions is stated
early by John Locke ([1690]1988), who held that society turns power
over to its governors, "whom society hath set over it self, with this
express or tacit Trust, That it shall be imployed for their good, and the
preservation of their Property" (§171:381). The political philosopher
John Dunn (1988, 1984) has suggested that this is the core of Locke's
political philosophy, that the relationship of citizens to government is
one of trust, not one of contract. It is the possibility of this relationship and its working that are to be explained (see also Laslett 1988,
114–17). There are surely at least two elements at the core of governing a "working" society. One is some variant of Hobbes's concern
with obedience motivated by compelling incentives of self-interest
even when there is no trust. The other is Locke's trust, which itself is
grounded in relevant judgments of government agents' incentives to
serve the interests of citizens.

I wish to argue that the older Greek insight into the relationship

9

between trust and government is the better one. Trust in government is not a major consideration in the working of a modern society, but the trust among themselves that a good government enables its citizens to have is very important in their lives. I will not attempt to establish the latter claim here but will focus on the coherence of the claim that citizens can or should trust government. My conclusion will be that a claim that one trusts government is not closely analogous to a claim that one trusts another person. One might still wish to say that a citizen can trust government, but this "trust" is different from the trust that I might have in you. The seeming goodness and importance of ordinary interpersonal trust does not clearly transfer to any nonanalogous notion of trust in government.

The standard contemporary argument for the *importance* of trust in government is related to the commonplace view that without normative commitments by citizens, government cannot gain obedience from citizens. The English legal theorist H. L. A. Hart (1961, 196) argued that the Hobbesian vision of using coercion to motivate obedience depends on the fact that most people comply willingly, perhaps for normative reasons. It is their compliance that makes it possible for the state to focus its limited resources for coercion on the potentially disobedient.

But Hart's conclusion can be true only in relatively benign contexts. In Nazi-ruled Czechoslovakia, obedience out of fear of severe reprisal seems likely to have been virtually the whole story for a very large segment of the population. Not many non-Fascist Slavs in Czechoslovakia can have been willingly obedient, in Hart's sense, to their Nazi regime. The Czechoslovak case, while extreme, is not as rare as one might wish. Spanish rule of southern Italy, medieval rule of randomly conquered regions, and the rule of various Chinese empires and many colonial governments have had little more than the acquiescence of large parts of the relevant population. Similarly, for many partial rules, such as white rule over blacks in the United States, acquiescence of many was the most that could be claimed.

One might make an argument for trust in government that is analogous to Hart's argument for obedience to government: Because enough people do trust, government can work well despite the lack of trust or even the active distrust of others. But, again, not many non-Fascist Slavs in Czechoslovakia can have trusted their Nazi regime. My concern here will be with benign cases in which trust is more nearly plausible than in Nazi Czechoslovakia and in which its plausibility is to be explained.

Any claim that government requires citizen trust is conspicuously false. A claim that *is* worthy of investigation is whether government that depends on extensive reciprocal participation by citizens requires trust in order to work well. Largely for empirical reasons, I will argue that even such a claim cannot be sustained. Or, rather, it cannot be sustained if what we mean by trust when we speak of trust in government is conceptually the same as what we mean when we speak of trust in another individual. Very often, all that is needed for government to work is for citizens not actively to distrust it. In general, it is important to note that contrary to the vernacular sense of not trusting, one may neither trust nor distrust another or a government with respect to some issue. If someone says, "I do not trust him," she very likely means she actively *distrusts* him. But very often we are ignorant of another's intentions or likely behavior and therefore we are in a state of neither trust nor distrust toward that other.

Trust is a fundamentally cognitive notion. To trust or to distrust others is to have some presumption of knowledge about them. For the vast majority of people in the world, including those whom we are likely to encounter, we know essentially nothing about their specific motivations toward us. The same is true of most of the people in our government: We do not know whether to trust them. If we are confident of their behavior in some context, that is because we generalize inductively from the behaviors of many of their peers or because we infer from the organizational incentives they face that they are more than likely to be trustworthy in that context.

A common claim about trust is that it is inherently normative. Unless it is merely an abstruse definitional move, this claim is not well grounded and even appears to be false (Hardin 1992, 1991). Although trust can well stand on the interest of the person trusted to live up to the trust placed in her, there may often be a tendency to associate the plausible normativity of trustworthiness with the notion of trust (Hardin 1996). In the encapsulated-interest account of trust summarized in the following section, my trust is grounded in my assessment of your interest in fulfilling my trust. I question any account of trust in government as similarly based on the truster's assessment of the trusted's incentive to be trustworthy.

Advocates of moralized conceptions of trust at the individual level argue that trust is inherently a two-part relation, that it is not merely rational expectations about the behavior of others. Sociological accounts of trust, such as that of Bernard Barber (1983), however, seem to account for trust as simple expectation grounded in large-number regularities. Barber's interest in trust grows in large part out of his more general concern with the role of professionalism in our lives. We cannot know enough to judge the competence of the professionals who serve us; therefore, we must essentially trust them to some extent.

To bring trust into political theory requires a micro-level account of how government works at the macro level. This will largely be an account of rational expectations of what government and its agents are likely to do. But the expectations will be rational not because they extrapolate from current and past actions, as might be adequate for a sociological account of credible, inductive expectations. Merely institutionalizing government and the implementation of policies should lead to greater stability of citizens' expectations and hence to greater trust in this limited sociological sense. To reach Dunn's concern of putting trust at the core of the relation between citizens and government, however, citizens' expectations must also be rational in the sense of depending on the rational commitments of officials. Rationally grounded trust in officials therefore requires that the officials be responsive to popular needs and desires. To have incentive to be responsive, they must be somehow accountable—most plausibly, perhaps, through competitive elections or some other form of public oversight.

To give an account of trust in government on analogy with trust in individuals requires two classes of argument. First, we must give an account of the *trustworthiness of government agents*. Second, we must account for the *knowledge citizens are likely to have* of such trustworthiness. In both accounts, the central problem is the translation from individual-to-individual relationships to individual-to-group or individual-to-institution relationships.

Trust as Encapsulated Interest

At the individual level, trust is a three-part relation: A trusts B to do x (or with respect to matters x). If, in the vernacular, I merely say that I trust you, it is commonly understood that there are limits to my trust of you. I might trust you to keep various promises or to act as an agent on my behalf on certain matters even though I might not trust you to repay a very large unsecured loan or to avoid romantic entanglements with my spouse. I wish further to stipulate that it is trust I have and not merely inductive expectations *if* I think you have a reason in some way grounded in me for fulfilling my trust. For example, I might well expect you to rise every morning at 7:00 because I know your habits very well, but I do not trust you to do so if I have no reason to suppose you do so somehow on my behalf. I can further say I trust you with respect to some action if your reason for doing it is to take me into account in some relevant way. Typically your reason will be that it is in your interest to maintain our relationship. Hence, my trust in you is typically encapsulated in your interest in fulfilling my trust.

Locke and others clearly were speaking of trust even in large contexts, such as political relationships. There is a substantial literature that supposes trust is out of place in the individual's relations to large groups and, therefore, to government. Against this view, it is clear that in principle—that is to say, conceptually—individuals can trust government, or at least parts of it or some of its agents, even under the relatively demanding notion of trust as encapsulated interest. Thus Locke's position is possible in principle. Unfortunately, in practice few people may genuinely be in a position to trust government in this sense. Trust is therefore largely irrelevant for the loyalties of most citizens. Hence, the metaphorical model of the social contract cannot be rescued by recourse to citizen trust.[1]

Many recent treatments of trust suppose it to be inherently restricted to small-number, even dyadic, relationships. Some of these accounts are compelling, but, oddly, the generalization from them that trust is irrelevant to large-number interactions is misguided. Consider two classes of accounts—one based on arguments from the iterated prisoner's dilemma and one based on familiarity of the trusted to the truster. These are both essentially grounded in a vision of trust as dependent on thick (or close, ongoing) relationships.

The sociologist Niklas Luhmann (1980) and the philosopher Bernard Williams (1988) have supposed that trust applies *only* to small-number contexts. Their view seems to rest on the model of cooperation in iterated prisoner's dilemma: I have an interest in cooperating with you now because I want you to cooperate with me in future interactions. The interest one has in cooperating in a two-person iterated prisoner's dilemma interaction does not generalize to large-number prisoner's dilemma interactions (Hardin 1982, 145–50; 1991). Hence, Luhmann says, trust is vital in personal relations, but participation in functional systems such as the economy is not a matter of personal relations. It requires confidence, but not trust (Luhmann 1980, 102).[2]

Surely the central issue in the thick-relationships account of the trusted's interest in fulfilling a trust is not that it is grounded specifically in iterated prisoner's dilemma incentives. Rather, the central issue is that the trusted have an interest in fulfilling a trust at all. Because iterated prisoner's dilemma provides such an interest, it makes interpersonal trust work in many contexts of ongoing relationships—in essence, it makes for trustworthiness. If public officials and their institutions are to be trusted, they must have interests in fulfilling the trust placed in them just as I have an interest in fulfilling trusts placed in me by family, friends, colleagues, and neighbors with whom I expect to have long associations. Their interests need not—indeed cannot be—dependent on iterated prisoner's-dilemma interactions with each particular individual who might trust them; there are other devices for giving them relevant incentives.

Locke was concerned with trust in those who govern. Some of his own discussion seems to mirror the Luhmann-Williams account. Arguably, the more complex and the more economically differentiated the society in question, the more likely trust is to be absent. (Certainly the less likely it is that trust grounded in the incentives of the iterated prisoner's dilemma will fit all relationships.) Locke supposed that the best condition for humans is an environment in which they are fortunate enough to have well-founded confidence (Dunn 1988, 83–4). Much of Locke's view seems to imply a need for something like face-to-face interactions, thus a small society.

In the second class of small-number accounts, those based on familiarity of the trusted to the truster, consider two visions of trust at the small scale of a particular community, those of the Anti-Federalists and of the anthropologist F. G. Bailey. The central appeal of the Anti-Federalist vision during the constitutional era of the United States was to representation by one's own kind. Why? They can be trusted to share one's interests on various legislative matters. In this respect, today's communitarians agree with the Anti-Federalists and with part of Locke's account.

Bailey (1988, 85) more generally argues that people are better inclined to like those whom they see as similar to themselves. This is evidently an armchair judgment rather than a hard empirical claim. Nevertheless, it might be a reasonable claim in many contexts. For example, one might generally expect to be better at predicting the behavior of those like oneself, and one might therefore find them more reliable. Still, the claim might be incoherent in many contexts. If I am to like others, must they be similar to me in intellect, sense of humor, ethnicity, religion, gender, interests, upbringing, or what?

The Anti-Federalists were not actually concerned with whether they liked one another. They were concerned with whether their local interests were to be the determinants of government policy. No doubt the typical small-town individual in upstate New York in 1788 was just as likely to dislike a fellow local citizen as the typical Manhattan pluralist was to dislike a fellow city-dweller. But the small-town individual may have had interests that significantly differed from those of the urban pluralist. Anyone who greatly values life in a pluralist community with its interestingly different people has an interest in maintaining liberal pluralist institutions, just as actual (as opposed to academic) communitarians have an interest in maintaining their communities.

Bailey's comment on liking those who are similar is made along the way in a discussion of trust in political leaders. In his context of small anthropological societies, he said such trust is achieved through devices of familial style plus unique capacities, such as intuition (1988, 85–6, 91). Oddly, however, he notes that to be leader of everybody requires marginality in the form of a lack of identification with any particular group (87).

Consider several examples of this observation in larger societies with great potential for divisive group conflict. Marshall Broz Tito was of mixed ethnic background and could not readily be seen as partial to Croats or Serbs. He was therefore an ideal leader of the multiethnic Yugoslav Republic. Similarly, Siad Barre was of mixed-clan background and was naturally nationalist in his leadership of Somalia. These men could be trusted by varied groups just because they could not be trusted by any one group to take its side. Alas, such leaders cannot easily be elected over locals if political careers are backed by group loyalties. For most of three decades Canadian prime ministers have been Québecois. A Québecois who is nationalist can be trusted by both anglophone and francophone citizens. In many mixed societies, such as Yugoslavia today and Rwanda and Burundi since their independence more than thirty years ago, political leaders whose careers have been grounded in ethnic loyalties have produced destructive government, because they cannot be trusted by those of other ethnic backgrounds (Hardin 1995, ch. 6).

In these contexts, political leaders can be widely trusted only if they are, as Bailey says, marginal and therefore different from others, not similar to them. One who is of mixed background is likely to have an interest in maintaining reasonable relations between the groups. Having that interest makes the marginal leader trustworthy to more than a single group. The small towns of upstate New York in 1788 could plausibly have been better served by one of their own than by representatives from across the land. Hence, because of the very different circumstances of Bailey's society and the Anti-Federalists' society, there were clearly different principles for securing interests. In both cases, however, it was not small scale in principle and therefore not thick relationships that defined interests.

The Problem of Institutional Trustworthiness

Many plausible psychological and normative accounts of individual behavior may be hard to generalize to apply to institutional behavior. If trust does not generalize to institutions, it is of limited interest in political theory and international relations. Observers of politics often speak in analogies that may be fallacies of composition. For example, one might try to explain peaceful Anglo-American relations by saying that England and the United States trust each other, but this would, however, be a loose claim that one might be hard-pressed to articulate beyond its seeming metaphor.

In vernacular usage the term *trust* is readily applied to many institutions and institutional actors, such as banks, nations, and political leaders. As with individuals, the question of whether we can reasonably trust institutions reduces to the question of whether institutions can be trustworthy. As a matter of simple descriptive fact, it appears that many institutions can be reliably expected to fulfill their missions. It would be odd if this were merely a regularity or if it were a hard law of nature. Our task, therefore, is to unpack our sometimes reliable expectations to find out why they are reliable.

If our notion of trust comes from understandings of individual behavior and character, the term may be entirely out of place in application to a nation, group, or institution. There may be ways to interpret the notion to apply it to such actors, but it is not likely to be prima facie applicable without interpretation. It is now a commonplace understanding that interest does not readily generalize from individual to group or national levels. It should not surprise us to find that trust, which is commonly at issue just because interests are at stake, does not readily generalize either. Nevertheless, the encapsulated-interest conception of trust can be generalized to fit institutions.

Suppose one has no prior experience of institutions but only of individuals, and one now wonders whether a particular institution is trustworthy. This question is not strictly analogous to the problem of the infant and child who must learn from experience whether to trust, but it is somewhat similar. If I have a long history of relatively benign and even beneficial dealings with certain organizations, I can plausibly suppose they are trustworthy with respect to relevant matters. Alternatively, if my dealings have been bad, I can meaningfully say those organizations are not trustworthy. But when I have no experience and no reputational evidence from the experience of others in dealing with those organizations, I cannot say very confidently one way or the other whether they are trustworthy.

At first thought, this statement sounds like only part of an account of trust as encapsulated interest. I can predict from a lot of data, but I have no reason to think the organization especially takes my interests somehow into consideration. If we cannot add the latter, we can only say we have a regularity from which we infer a tendency, as we infer that the sun will rise tomorrow from the fact that it seemingly always has done so every day. This problem is often resolved by fiat. It is merely assumed that the officials in an organization act from the desire to accomplish some organizational goal of service.

Against this resolution by fiat, it would be odd if we found that individuals in organizational contexts had motivations for action that were significantly different from their usual motivations. They typically do have different incentives; that is how organizations work, by giving role holders incentives, negative and positive, for and against various actions, and by coordinating people acting from varied incentives. If individual trustworthiness correlates strongly with encapsulated interest in individual-to-individual relations, it seems likely that it must do so as well in intraorganizational relations that are, at times, individual-to-individual. If so, then the question whether role holders in an organization will be trustworthy will tend to correlate with whether it is in their interest to do what they are expected or trusted to do.

Endemic Distrust

When distrust in government is endemic, as in the East European and Soviet worlds at the end of the 1980s, there may be no better move than to weaken government substantially (Hardin forthcoming). Elimination of agencies and powerful bureaus and bureaucrats will eliminate the objects of distrust. "Strong" leadership is precisely what is not wanted when strong leaders have been the problem. Weak leaders unable to intervene capriciously are what is wanted to make the society develop successful trusting relationships. As it happens, the only economic system that works without leadership is the market, and even it requires stable law enforcement in certain realms if firms are to be trusted, either by workers, customers, or other firms.

Still, creating trustworthy institutional supports for legal and economic relations may be difficult even when the institutions are created de novo. The staff of any new organization or of any massively reformed organization is likely to come from the staff of prior organizations. If one created a new agency in New York City to handle some problem in a fresh and innovative way but hired staff from the extant pool of seemingly qualified people, one might discover that the new agency almost immediately fell into the usual New York malaise in which all supplicants are forced to invest in massive, wasteful hassling to get routine, reasonable things done. To create a genuinely new agency, it might be better to recruit staff from Texas, Wyoming, and scattered other places.

This potentially grievous problem stands in the way of simply changing policies in Russia and expecting to get the desired results. The distrust of Russian state agencies that oversaw the economy during its woeful years includes, rightly, distrust of many of the officers of those agencies. To give them proper incentives for behaving constructively might require massive organizational redesign. When New

York officials tell me something cannot be done or cannot be done in less than some large number of months, I openly disbelieve them. I am virtually sure that, if they were merely willing to do what they ostensibly are supposed to do (sometimes merely to sign a form lying before them), it could be done immediately, reasonably, correctly, and competently. As is often true, they seem to have come to view their interests as tied to the interests of their organization rather than to the interests of their clientele. This can happen simply because it is within the organization that they are rewarded, so that it is their organization and not their clientele who give them their incentives for action or inaction. They suffer something akin to the professional deformation that corrupted the French military establishment in defense of its honor even at the cost of punishing the innocent Dreyfus. Hence, they cannot be trusted in the compelling sense that their interests do not encapsulate mine.

At the most extreme change in government, such as after a major social revolution, the problem of establishing stable expectations may make trust nearly impossible for a while. Many people might have faith in the new regime because they think it represents their interests. And they might therefore say they trust the regime. They might continue to have such faith even after arduous years of failure, as in the Stalinist years in the Soviet Union, when the virtual deification of Stalin was evidently effective in many parts of the population. This trust would not be grounded, although it might be an unusual case of what some philosophers call trust as blind faith. It is hard to see how such trust can be good except by blind fortune.

It may be nearly impossible to avoid endemic distrust in much of politics without simultaneously avoiding clear positions on issues. Perhaps the most striking difference between leaders of many non-governmental organizations, such as business firms, and elected officials is that the former typically must live up to relatively clear expectations, while the latter often can attempt to make expectations vague and the judgment of achievements therefore pliable. The difference is not stark. For example, in the so-called cola wars, Pepsi engaged not in defining its product but in identifying its potential consumers, the Pepsi generation.[3] Much of the appeal to voters is similarly directed at their identifications, not at the programs they might like to see implemented. In politics, it is often a drastic mistake to be very specific, because most people must necessarily have preferences that fall some distance away from any proposed policy.

There are, of course, many issues for which this may not be true. For example, preferences on abortion policy in the contemporary United States are very nearly bimodal, with very sharply defined pro and con positions. The arguments of such writers as the lawyers

Ronald Dworkin (1993) and Laurence Tribe (1990) that the two sides are not so far apart are prima facie unconvincing.[4] Some candidates attempt to straddle this divide by being vague about how they would handle abortion policy or by passing the issue off to an alternative decision arena such as the courts or a possible constitutional amendment.

But for issues that have a more or less normal distribution of preferences, staking oneself to a precise position is tantamount to putting distance between oneself and most voters. The task of gaining the trust of constituents, then, is complicated by the virtual certainty that effectiveness in office will correlate strongly with disappointing or even offending large numbers of constituents on particular issues. Ronald Reagan, the best president the American Right has ever had, was reviled by much of that Right soon after he entered office. Dwight Eisenhower had the nearly unique advantage of being elected by a populace ignorant of any of his views, if he had any. And the first president, George Washington, was reviled at the end of his tenure by Thomas Paine for his compromises.[5] From Washington's time forward, American presidents could be trusted—if that is not a distortion of the term—to change their stripes while in office. This might merely be an instance of Burkean representation that takes positions not according to constituents' positions but according to their supposed interests. Again, however, this stance is apt to require faith rather than trust.

The Possibility of Governmental Trustworthiness

In the encapsulated interest account, trust and cooperation are related problems, but they are not always the same problem. Cooperation may generally require conditions that make for trust, but not all trusting relationships are sensibly grounded in ongoing cooperation. Some trusting relationships depend on love or altruism from the trusted, and some involve only a loose concatenation of interests, nothing like direct exchange or pursuit of common goals. The latter may be especially typical of political life, where it may be vital to establish something analogous to trustworthiness for institutions, so that citizens may prosper and institutions and nations may cooperate. The trustworthiness of institutions need not, however, entail that they be trusted.

Some political philosophers, including the usually very sensible Hume ([1739 to 1740] 1978, 537), have supposed that government requires public-spirited people to make it work well. In practice most political institutions are staffed by people whose motives are heavily, if not entirely, self-interested. To gain our trust, they have to work in our interest. Hence, the general problem is to make it the interest of various officials to work in our interest. We do this in part by making some officials directly answerable to citizens and in part by making other officials answerable to these. Both of these controls are likely to be very loose, but the latter seems especially weak. What is needed to complete the picture is a theory of how the general interest can be served by a government of millions of bureaucrats who are fundamentally self-interested, who are motivated not by unusual public spirit but primarily by income and career.

In crude outline, the most plausible theory is one that takes James Madison's analysis down to the level of individual officials. In defense of the U.S. Constitution, he wrote, "In framing a government which is to be administered by men over men, the great difficulty lies in this: you must first enable the government to control the governed; and in the next place oblige it to control itself" (*Federalist* no. 51, 322). He recommended, "Ambition must be made to counter ambition. How? If I violate the norms determined by our bureaucratic mission, you and others are likely to find it in your interest to oppose me (Hardin 1988, 526–7). Sometimes the enticements to malfeasance are so great that they infect almost everyone in a relevant agency, as we often hear of whole governmental structures (as in Italy) or entire police units (as in the United States) that succumb to bribery or even to direct involvement in profitable relations with the Mafia or illegal drug traders. But commonly, even in such extreme cases, someone will have a strong career interest in bringing them to account. Strong moral commitment beyond interest may help and may be common, but it may also lead officials into taking the law into their own hands, and it cannot be reliable.

Often we expect institutions to be more stable than individuals. Many institutional promises and threats are more reliable than their individual equivalents. Consider some examples. The nuclear deterrent threat was credible because it did not depend on a particular individual's commitment to act in the relevant moment. The individual might choose, once deterrence had failed, to act as a humanitarian rather than as an avenger or as an automaton programmed to retaliate. The reliability of retaliation approaches near certainty if it is institutionalized in the form of many actors prepared to act in related but not entirely centrally controlled ways. (The success of a deterrent strategy may not require anything approaching near certainty of retaliation, because even a small risk is too much to invite.) Similarly, many of us might trust our fortunes to a bank more readily than to most individuals, perhaps even to close friends and relatives with whom we expect our relationships to last our lifetimes. Those relationships have a better chance of lifetime survival if they are not strained by excessive demands for trustworthiness.

Aristotle argued that the best of all governments would be a good monarchy and the worst would be a bad monarchy, or tyranny. The differences between a good and a bad democracy would be less great. To reduce variance, we might choose democracy as the preferred form of government in general. There may be little or no empirical study of Aristotle's factual claims, but they sound sensible. Government by the many may induce a kind of regression toward the mean and hence much greater predictability.

Seldom in history has anyone gone so far toward establishing institutional trust as did Soviet President Mikhail Gorbachev, head of a system that, throughout its seven decades, had exhibited extraordinary variance. He made some previously possible Soviet threats virtually impossible by putting institutional barriers in their way. For example, in inviting the reformation of the East European regimes and the dismantling of the iron curtain, he greatly reduced the possibility of a sudden Soviet conventional attack on West Europe. By withdrawing troops and certain materiel, he made it virtually impossible to launch a secret attack, without first visibly warning of attack during the necessary restoration of troops and equipment to the European theater. The obstacles he created consist of institutional structures that can impede individual audacity. Such institutional arrangements are appealing partly because they stabilize our expectations. Institutional behavior regresses toward the mean to average out the variance of individual behavior.

Our expectations may not be grounded in any theory or explanation of why they are justified, but simply in experience. For example, political trust of many kinds may be easier in the Soviet Union now than it was a generation ago, although many of the older generation may still be reticent in trusting others with their opinions. And such trust must be harder in China now than it was shortly before the June 1989 massacre in Tiananmen Square.

One might suppose that trustworthy (that is, reliable) institutions are reliable because the right people are in the right places in them. But banks and many other institutions do not use great rigor in selecting people for their roles, and it seems unlikely that reliability emerges from simple goodwill on the part of individuals in those roles. Most of us are somewhat like bank tellers: We are secured in our normal honesty by institutional arrangements that make significant dishonesty risky, even difficult. Much of what looks like honesty is essentially self-interest at work.

Institutional arrangements may secure our expectations, and hence our trust, with the devices of self-interest, just as our own individual arrangements do. I become trustworthy by establishing a reputation and by setting myself up for real losses if I betray a trust. If I betray your trust, I may lose the opportunity not only to have you depend on me again but also to have others depend on me. Those who fail to learn such lessons are seen as capricious and adolescent. Public officials and institutions are like individuals in that they also must often live by the reputations they establish. But, as is argued in the following section, they might well be trustworthy even though citizens do not generally trust them.

The Epistemology of Trusting Institutions

How can we make sense of trusting an institution if trust must be grounded in the interests of the institution and its agents? There are at least two ways we might unpack our trust of an institution. First, we could trust every individual in the organization, each in the relevant ways, to do what each must do if the organization is to fulfill our trust. Second, we could trust the design of the roles and their related incentives to get role holders to do what they must do if the organization is to fulfill our trust. In this case, the individual role holders might be broadly interchangeable, and we need to know few if any of them.

Neither of these visions is plausible for citizen trust of modern governmental institutions. Virtually no one can know enough of the large number of individual role holders to claim to trust them in the strong sense of seeing that they have interests in fulfilling trust placed in them. And few people can have an articulate understanding either of the structures of various agencies and the roles within them or of the government overall to be confident of the incentives that role holders have to be trustworthy. As a matter of actual practice, it is utterly implausible that trust underlies most citizens' views and expectations of government.

In actual life we might not trust an organization but might merely depend on its apparent predictability by induction from its past behavior. Then we have merely an expectations account of the organization's behavior. Inductive knowledge in some contexts seems very compelling. Most of us expect the sun to rise tomorrow just because that is what has always happened so far as we know. For many people, that expectation is reinforced by the belief that there are physical laws to govern the sun's rising. Their expectations are Newtonian and not merely inductive.

Expectations of human behavior are much less reliable than the merely inductive expectations about the sun's behavior. Indeed, their unreliability is the central driving force of most great literature. In a cute moment, one might say that one of the strongest expectations we must have of people in the long run is that they will defy our expectations. (On a recent flight, a pilot told us, "We are now experiencing the unexpected turbulence I mentioned earlier.") While there is no analog of Newtonian physics to reinforce our expectations of human behavior, there is a consideration that is arguably far more widely understood than is Newtonian physics. We base many of our expectations of people's actions on beliefs about human psychology. Among the most compelling and generalizable of psychological traits is that people are motivated by their interests. Hence, trust—expectations grounded in encapsulated interest—may be more widely motivated than are beliefs about physical relationships that are grounded in nothing more than induction.

Of a large part of the population perhaps we can claim no more than that they have inductive expectations about government, not that they have grounds for trust as encapsulated interest. That an agency or its role holders are trustworthy might matter to some people, but to most there is nothing beyond expectations. Immanuel Kant's neighbors may have relied on his punctuality in his morning walk to set their own schedules. To trust requires more: that they rely on his having their interests at heart in deciding when to take his walk. If they could not think he did, they could not be said to trust him (Baier 1986, 234). Like Kant's neighbors, those people who merely have inductive expectations cannot be said to trust government. Inductive expectations that government will be capricious might be sufficient to ground distrust, but for most people there might be neither trust nor distrust of a reliable government or agency.

The trustworthiness of government might matter enormously to some citizens, but it might count only by default for many other citizens. Distrust comes easily; trust requires too rich an understanding of the other's incentives to come easily to many people. If Locke's understanding of government is that it must be grounded in trust to be legitimate, then no major government of modern times is likely to be legitimate for more than passing moments. For example, the government of the Czech Republic in its early days or the governments of England and the United States during the Second World War might have been legitimate in the eyes of most citizens, but the government of the United States since the Second World War cannot have counted as legitimate in Locke's demanding sense. Evidently, however, government need not be legitimate in Locke's sense to survive and even to manage a nation through major difficulties and into prosperity. It may suffice that government not be generally distrusted. If some core of the populace genuinely does trust a government and not too many of the rest of the populace distrust it, then it has likely done well by historical standards for governments of large states.

In the end, trust may still be crucial to the success of government. Those most attentive to government will also be those most likely to know enough about governmental actions and structures to know whether at least parts of the government and some of its agents are trustworthy. If they are also the people most likely to oppose government effectively in response to its failings, then the possibility of trustworthiness and the epistemological possibility of trust could be fundamentally important to the stability of government. The significance of their role in support of government might be ramified by the implicit support of those who act from mere expectations without articulate knowledge of the trustworthiness of government. The expectations of the latter group might be based in large part on the expectations of others, just as most of us know many of the things we know only in the sense that we gather that others think those things are true. Our crippled epistemology is little more than mimicry.

Low voter turnouts in many nations, including, notoriously, the United States, are commonly taken as evidence that government has failed to elicit support. But, prima facie, an equally or even more plausible conclusion may be that such turnouts are evidence that government has not engendered grievous distrust and opposition. Silence cannot unambiguously prove the case for or against government. If mimicry very much underpins our expectations of government, then the limited commitment of most people to try to change or affect government makes epistemologically good sense.

Concluding Remarks

Some, perhaps most, of the contributions to this volume suppose that there is more at stake in relationships of trust than mere expectations grounded in the interests of the trusted to fulfill the trust. That is, they suppose that trust is not encapsulated in the interests of the trusted, as I assume for most trusting relations. For example, John Braithwaite, Simon Blackburn, and Martin Daunton argue in effect that trusting people can motivate them to be trustworthy. In Braithwaite's account, this appears to be an inherently moral claim. But James Coleman (1988) argued that when someone asks a favor from another, "he does so because it brings him a needed benefit; he does not consider that *it does the other a benefit as well* by adding to a drawing fund of social capital available in a time of need" (P. S117, emphasis added). Coleman's claim is, of course, often false, and his addendum is true only if there is reason to expect the relationship to be ongoing, so that there is an incentive to each party to repay the trust-worthiness of the other. It follows naturally that this would also be true in the relations between public agents, such as welfare workers, and their clients, who will continue to depend on the agents well beyond their current interaction.

A reviewer of this volume asserted that "these are relationship-generated motivations that are outside the received tradition in rational choice." This conclusion is simply false, nor need we "stretch rational choice theory to encompass [these motivations]," as the reviewer claims. Indeed, it can be argued that the largest body of contemporary rational choice work in sociology is work on *ongoing relationships* that involve iterated interactions, as in the vast literature on the iterated prisoner's dilemma. That is to say, "relationship-generated motivations" are at the heart of rational-choice understanding of social and interpersonal interactions. Indeed, it is ongoing relationships that make it meaningful for us to speak of society rather than merely of an aggregation of individuals. If there is a lesson to be learned from the rich findings of Braithwaite and others on (supposedly) one side and rational-choice theorists on (supposedly) the other side, it is how much we have in common in our understanding, not how far apart we are. We would all benefit if the rhetoric of pro- and anti-rational-choice theory could be less heated and if our arguments could focus, rather, on the power of our particular explanations.[6]

Earlier versions of this paper were presented at the Pacific Division meeting of the American Philosophical Association, San Francisco, April 1 1995, and at the conference Trust in Government, Australian National University, Canberra, Australia, February 2–3, 1996. The paper has benefited from commentary at these sessions and, especially, from extensive written commentary by Margaret Levi and two anonymous reviewers. I am grateful to these colleagues and others for their comments. These comments included occasional looks of disbelief from those who finally came to believe the argument was intended. The writing of the paper has been supported by New York University and by the Russell Sage Foundation.

Notes

1. More generally, it cannot be rescued at all. See Hardin 1990.

2. As his subtitle suggests, Luhmann focuses on our need to trust (that is, to have stable expectations about) large institutional aspects of life, such as the stability of our currency or the reliability of our political leaders during crises that could lead to foolish war.

3. This move began as early as the 1940s. By now, in a trick of marketing, virtually every living American is in "the" Pepsi generation. See Schuessler 1997; Tedlow 1990.

4. See Davis 1993, a critical review of Tribe's book.

5. Washington's character, Paine said, was a "non-describable, chameleon-colored thing called prudence," which was "in many cases a substitute for principle [and] so nearly allied to hypocrisy that it easily slides into it" (*New York Times*, 19 February 1995, 4.1). Paine was a master of invective, and he resented Washington's treatment of him during his presidency. But his remarks are well grounded in Washington's gift for opportunism, such as in his preferring English monarchy to French revolutionary democracy. From long before his presidency, Washington seemed to value successful personal achievement well above principle. See Ayer [1988] 1990, 159, 164.

6. I am perhaps forced to be more alert to this possibility than are many scholars on these issues. I regularly participate in conferences dominated by anti–rational-choice theorists and also in conferences dominated by pro–rational-choice theorists. At both kinds of conference, I am regularly pilloried as the person most out of touch with social reality.

References

"The Anonymous Iamblichi." 1995. In *Early Greek Political Thought from Homer to the Sophists*, edited by Michael Gagarin and Paul Woodruff. Cambridge: Cambridge University Press.

Ayer, A. J. 1990 [1988] *Thomas Paine*. Chicago: University of Chicago Press.

Baier, Annette. 1986. "Trust and Antitrust," *Ethics* 96 (January): 231–260.

Bailey, F. G. 1988. "The Creation of Trust." In Bailey, *Humbuggery and Manipulation*, Ithaca, N.Y.: Cornell University Press.

Barber, Bernard. 1983. *The Logic and Limits of Trust*. New Brunswick, N.J.: Rutgers University Press.

Coleman, James S. 1988. "Social Capital in the Creation of Human Capital." *American Journal of Sociology* 94 (Supplement): S95–S120.

Davis, Nancy (Ann). 1993. "The Abortion Debate: The Search for Common Ground, Part II." *Ethics* 103 (July): 731–78.

Dunn, John. 1984. "The Concept of 'Trust' in the Politics of John Locke." In *Philosophy in History*, edited by Richard Rorty, J. B. Schneewind, and Quentin Skinner. Cambridge: Cambridge University Press.

———. 1988. "Trust and Political Agency." In *Trust: Making and Breaking Cooperative Relations*, edited by Diego Gambetta. Oxford: Basil Blackwell.

Dworkin, Ronald. 1993. *Life's Dominion: An Argument about Abortion, Euthanasia, and Individual Freedom*. New York: Knopf.

Hardin, Russell. 1982. *Collective Action*. Baltimore, Md.: Johns Hopkins University Press for Resources for the Future.

———. 1988. "Constitutional Political Economy: Agreement on Rules." *British Journal of Political Science* 18 (October): 513–30.

———. 1990. "Contractarianism: Wistful Thinking." *Constitutional Political Economy* 1: 35–52.

———. 1991. "Trusting Persons, Trusting Institutions." In *The Strategy of Choice*, edited by Richard J. Zeckhauser. Cambridge, Mass.: MIT Press.

———. 1992. "The Street-Level Epistemology of Trust," *Analyse und Kritik* 14 (December): 152–76. Reprinted: *Politics and Society* 21 (December 1993): 505–29.

———. 1995. *One for All: The Logic of Group Conflict*. Princeton, N.J.: Princeton University Press.

———. 1996. "Trustworthiness," *Ethics* 107 (October): 26–42.

———. Forthcoming. "Constitutional Economic Transition," chapter 6 of *Liberalism, Constitutionalism, and Democracy*. Oxford: Oxford University Press.

Hart, H. L. A. 1961. *The Concept of Law*. Oxford: Oxford University Press.

Hume, David. [1739–40] 1978. *A Treatise of Human Nature*, ed. L. A. Selby-Bigge and P. H. Nidditch. Oxford: Oxford University Press.

Laslett, Peter. 1988. "Introduction to *Two Treatises of Government by John Locke*, edited by Peter Laslett. Cambridge: Cambridge University Press, [1690] 1988.

Locke, John. [1690] 1988. *Two Treatises of Government*, edited by Peter Laslett. Cambridge: Cambridge University Press.

Luhmann, Niklas. 1980. *Trust: A Mechanism for the Reduction of Social Complexity*. In Luhmann, *Trust and Power*. New York: Wiley.

Madison, James G. [1788] 1961. *Federalist*, no. 51. In *The Federalist Papers*, edited by Clinton Rossiter. New York: New American Library.

Schuessler, Alexander. 1997. "Soft Drinks and Presidents." New York University, New York. Unpublished paper.

Tedlow, Richard S. 1990. *New and Improved: The Story of Mass Marketing in America*. New York: Basic Books.

Tribe, Laurence H. 1990. *Abortion: The Clash of Absolutes*. New York: Norton.

Williams, Bernard. 1988. "Formal Structres and Social Reality." In *Trust: Making and Breaking Social Relations*, edited by Diego Gambetta. Oxford: Basil Blackwell.

Chapter 2

Trust, Cooperation, and Human Psychology

SIMON BLACKBURN

There is, I admit, the obligation of the Treaty . . . but I am not able to subscribe to the doctrine of those who have held in this House what plainly amounts to an assertion, that the simple fact of the existence of a guarantee is binding on every party to it, irrespectively altogether of the particular position in which it may find itself at the time when the occasion for acting on the guarantee arises.

—W. E. Gladstone[1]

TRUST AND cooperation concern everyone. A search in the major journals database under the two words gives results from journals of architecture, dentistry, economics, education, law, and music, as well as politics, psychology, and philosophy. Why philosophy? It may not at first be clear what specifically philosophical questions such concepts raise. In thinking about them we seem to be in the domain of the social psychologist, who can do empirical research on the existence of trust, or the economist, who can measure its effects, for instance, on the costs of making various transactions. But there are deep currents in the modern world that suggest that cooperative relations are in some way surprising, unnatural, and in need of explanation, whereas there is nothing surprising or difficult to understand about adversarial relations. Part of this sense, of course, is the legacy of a century of the mutual interaction of popular Darwinism, with its metaphors of competition and struggle, and neoclassical economics, with its model of the self-interested consumer. But part is the result of a certain conception of rationality. This conception may, indeed, grow only in the soil of the Darwinian ideology, but it then exerts its own authority. The psychologist Kresten Monroe characterizes it, at its most bare, as follows (1995):

1. Actors pursue goals.

2. These goals reflect the actor's perceived self-interest.

3. Behavior results from a process that involves, or functions as if it entails, conscious choice.

4. The individual is the basic agent in society.

5. Actors have preferences that are consistent and stable.

6. If given options, actors will choose the alternative with the highest expected utility.

7. Actors possess extensive information on both the available alternatives and the likely consequences of their choices.

There is room for debate about what these mean, of course. Number 6, for example, can veer critically between being substantial and false or true but a tautology, a piece of bookkeeping for interpreting an agent within the grid of maximizing expected utility, whatever that agent's actual concerns; it is not clear how it expresses a substantial truth (Blackburn 1995). But at face value, what is intended is indeed a conception of the rational agent as both entirely forward-looking and entirely self-interested. If such agents look back, it is only to make strategic calculations for the future. If they forgo immediate advantage, it is only for the sake of deferred gains in the future. If they pay regard to the interests of others, it is so that the others will be more likely to benefit them sometime in the future. Henceforth, when I talk of rational-actor theory, it is this full-blown interpretation that I have in mind.

It is, I think, a remarkable fact, and a fact for philosophers, that this paradigm still dominates the social sciences. We have been through a quarter of a century when the humanities have been swept by a sense of untranslatability, of difference, of incommensurability, and by a resulting politics of identity devoted to stressing and celebrating the differences in the cognitive and emotional contours of different people, whether in different groups or of different genders. Many people question whether we understand each other well enough that women can be taught by men, or vice versa, or people of one ethnic background by people of another. Yet amidst all this difference, the paradigm of homo economicus still reigns supreme. It provides the spectacles through which diversity itself is brought into view.

Uncovering the presuppositions on which this view depends is a philosophical task. In this chapter I clear some of the ground for such a task, first by reflecting on what it is for a disposition to trust to be embedded in a human psychology. As we shall see, trust is easier to understand than cooperation. This may enable us to draw some morals for the analysis of social and political cooperation, perhaps rather different from those generally drawn from reflection on nonco-operative situations.

The Austere Basis of Trust

First of all, what is our concept of trust, and what are its principal divisions? I think the obvious point of entry is a tripartite relation-ship: One person trusts another to do something (X trusts Y to do Z). This formula allows, rightly, that one might trust one person to do things that one would not trust another to do. And it allows, equally rightly, that one might trust a person to do some things but not others; for instance, one can trust Vronsky to pay his gambling debts but not to keep his hands off one's wife.

The tripartite formula allows for expansion. There are cases where Y refers not to another person but to an institution or a government, and possibly even to an inanimate thing; we talk, for example, of trusting the rope to bear our weight, or trusting the old car to keep going for a while. We even trust to luck, rather too often in some cases. It is also possible, antecedently, that X need not be a person. One insurance company, for instance, may trust its policyholders more than a rival does. We do not always talk of trusting someone *to do* something; we sometimes trust people *with* things and people. Sometimes the equivalence is fairly obvious. If I trust you with my child, it means that I trust you to do a fairly wide but reasonably well-understood range of things and not to do various others. But sometimes the context is less clear, and there is scope for misunder-standing. If we talk just of whether we trust the government, for in-stance, we may easily get at cross purposes. I may trust the govern-ment to collect its revenues without trusting it to spend them wisely.

We can also speak of trusting someone not only to do something but to do it in a certain way, or we can trust someone to be in a certain state: to be at home, for instance, or to be cheerful at the party. So although we start with the simple tripartite form, we should ap-proach it with more than half an eye on the various expansions that we might want to accommodate. If any analysis rules out these ex-pansions or is forced to talk about "different senses" of the term, that will be a cost.

There is one expansion that is absolutely critical. We must bring into view cases where we trust someone or some corporate entity not so much to do a certain thing Z but to act *from* a certain motivation, whatever is done. In Kantian terms, we might trust someone to act on certain *maxims* and not to act on others. In more sentimentalist terms (in the sense of Hutcheson, Hume, or Smith), I may, for instance, trust someone to be, revolted by some fact, or I may trust that person to recoil from some project. I shall speak simply of trusting someone to act from a concern, where *concern* is a very broad portmanteau term covering any of the factors that influence an agent. A concern influences an agent when, if he is aware of it, his practical reasoning takes it into account. The measure of this will be her stronger disposition to seek or avoid the object of concern. Here we may not have a particular action Z in mind. We might trust, say, a guru to act out of wisdom and benevolence, without knowing what his wisdom and benevolence will lead him to do. We may even look forward to being surprised.[2]

Although the interests of the rational actor, homo economicus, are always forward-looking, concerns by contrast may be backward-looking ("She was kind to me when I was ill, so I can't just leave her in the lurch"). They may not even be keyed to the past or the future but derived purely from our conception of our role ("They're my children, so I have to look after them"). They may even be purely counterfactual ("Imagine what someone would say if they saw me do that"). This point becomes extremely important and merits some elaboration. Nobody sane denies that on the surface we have such susceptibilities and that they can influence us. The proponents of the rational actor either have to say that when we have them we are irrational or that when we have them they are a kind of disguise for an underlying calculus of self-interest (in the neo-Darwinian version popularized by the biologist Richard Dawkins [1976], a disguise for an unconscious calculus of genetic advantage). Thus apparent altruism is diagnosed as disguised expectation of reciprocal advantage; apparent trustworthiness is diagnosed as disguised desire to reap the benefits of appearing trustworthy, and so on.

Now, the first option—claiming that agents with plural sensibilities are irrational—is surely completely untenable. "Rational" is an endorsement. It claims that being some way, and only being that way, makes sense (Gibbard 1990). But why should anyone suppose that it makes no sense to think in terms of the past, or what one's role demands, or what people would think if they knew what one was doing—and all regardless of whatever light the past casts on the future? Furthermore, it is well known that only if we have these dispositions that we can solve the problem of collective action, and there is nothing attractive, let alone normatively compelling, in the psychology of any protohuman agents who cannot manage that (Hardin 1982; Kraus 1993; Olson 1963). I will return to this point later in the chapter.

As for the second option—that the superficial thoughts disguise the rational actor beneath—my immediate point is that it is importantly unmotivated. Talk of an unconscious calculus suggests that the surface disguises the "real" psychology underneath. But there is no reason to think that. Even if we like adaptive evolutionary stories, according to which the surface psychology is as it is because it benefited the individuals who have it, they give us no reason to deny that this *is* the psychology, and it is the beginning and end of it as well. The mother who cares for her baby may be like that because it is an adaptation to be like that. That is, single individuals or groups of individuals who were programmed not to be like that would have lost out in the evolutionary struggle to people who are like that, and this explains why we are. But it does not follow, and there is not the slightest reason for believing, that the evolutionary advantage is *implemented* anywhere in the individual's psychology. The mother does not think, at some deep, unconscious level, that it will benefit her, or her genes, if she looks after her baby (after all, she might know that the former is not true, if she is sacrificing herself for the baby in some obvious way, and she might be quite unable to think the latter, since the concept of a gene is hardly common property). She has only to think that it will benefit the baby, and this is what she does think, period.

What, then, is true when X trusts Y to do Z? The neutral core on which to build is simply that X relies on Y to do Z. This is all that there is to it when, for instance, I trust the rope to bear my weight. I rely on it to do so and show my trust by climbing on it. As the philosopher Richard Holton (1994) has stressed, it may even be that I do not fully believe that the rope will bear my weight. All that seems necessary is that I incorporate the supposition that it will bear my weight into my actions or plans for the future. I can do this while lacking at least some of the dispositions that would be part of really *believing* that the rope will bear my weight, and a fortiori without being certain that it will do so. This lack of confidence would be shown, for instance, by my eagerness to use another aid as soon as I can do so, or my relief at getting into the position where I no longer have to rely on it. "Relying on the rope" is a matter of acting or planning for action rather than one of being confident or believing. So I may have no option but to rely on the rope, or trust myself to it. Similarly, in a large range of social circumstances, I may have no option but to trust the post office, or my insurance company, or the government, at least with respect to some actions and policies.

So why do we rely upon people to do some things and not others? Again, the fundamental case is where we rely on them to do what they have always done. We may rely upon birds to fly south in winter and to return in the spring. It is said that the people of Königsberg trusted Kant to provide the time for them by taking his walk every afternoon at exactly the same hour, and their reliance was justified because this is what he always did. Bare inductive cases are rare. Still, once Kant understood that the people had this reliance, it could in turn have acted as a motive to keep up his habit. He might have begun to feel that he ought to take his walk at a precise time, just because they relied on him to do so. In my terms, the other people's expectation would have become one of his concerns. It might be so even if he regretted accidentally getting into such a position. And a less benevolent person might take no account of their reliance, not allowing it to influence them in any way, while a mischievous person might even regard it as good fun to let them down.

Once civil society is up and running, there are devices for stabilizing Kant's habit, making it independent of his benevolence at the moment. Kant can *promise* the townspeople to take his walk on time, or he can *contract* with them to do so for a consideration. These performances are designed to make him more reliable, for reliability is the essential function of the practices of promising and contracting. I will return to this point later in the chapter.

If Kant reneges on a promise or contract, then moral emotions come into play. But at the first level, when we just rely on him because it is what he always does, then a failure need not justify any such reaction. I may, for instance, rely on a child to perform some errand, perhaps as part of an overall project of giving her practice in the ways of trusting and being trusted. If she fails through intention or recklessness or a variety of mens rea, I cannot feel resentment or indignation or anger, although I might just feel a bit stupid for having treated her as more mature than she is. The moral reaction would be possible but inappropriate, and I need not be disposed to it.

To sum up, then, reliance on Y to do Z may be sustained by a variety of causes or reasons, but the simple case is just that Z is what Y does. It is not necessary that Y know of the reliance; not necessary that Y be motivated by such knowledge; not necessary that Y feel altruistic or bound by principle or any other particular concern. Y's own psychological state is not necessarily implicated, although frequently it will be beliefs about that state that justify the other party's reliance.

So far we have been talking of reliance rather than trust. But by keeping the core concept extremely general, we are able to say that children become trusting and trustworthy by practice. We rely on them in little things and reward them when the reliance is well placed, and success builds on success until a habit is generated. When it has done so, the mere fact that she is being relied upon becomes a concern of the child. She finds it difficult or impossible to let someone down, and in turn she finds it confusing and flattening to be let down. What is practiced is just reliability, and what is discovered is the importance people put on it. It is important to this process that a decision to trust can be made in advance, before there is a long history of trustworthiness.

The austere basis of trust, I am suggesting, is just reliance. This of course does not imply cooperation, because it does not imply the mutual awareness or common knowledge that are necessarily involved in cooperating with someone.

Backwards Concerns and Forward Goals

When I rely on other people, it may be because I have little option, or it may be because I have reason to be confident in them. Technologists of trust can work both ends. When people join a regiment or a cult, they are systematically, even brutally, stripped of their other resources and so put in a position where they have nowhere else to turn. They are made vulnerable, and then their loyalty to the regiment or the cult is built upon its being their only lifeline: If they cannot rely on their fellows for various things, then they cannot rely on anyone or anything. But in a decent childhood, in which life is moderately stable, the child, although completely vulnerable, is constantly given reason to rely on his parents and those who care for him to do a whole variety of things he needs.

Reliance may be merely inductively based, as in the Kant case. But humans behave differently from one another. The child can rely on his mother to feed him, but not on a passing stranger. So we need communication. Just as a bird or a monkey can signal a danger to other birds and monkeys, so we can signal a future action of our own. And if things go well, there is a high correlation between people giving such signals and then acting as signaled, and this too is an inductive reliability that we can learn to depend upon.

Here we have the essence not only of devices such as giving promises or writing contracts but also of putting on uniforms or otherwise displaying the roles we are acting in. I do not think there is a general term covering what I have in mind, so I shall say that by displaying to others that we are prepared to perform some action, so that they may rely upon us, we submit to what I call *typecasting*. Being typecast I define as being put, either voluntarily or not, and either truly or not, into a class whose performance statistics for doing a certain kind of thing or acting from a certain kind of concern are better than average, or indeed anything up to perfect. If you are typecast, it is as if you have announced what you will do, or what concerns will motivate you. What is the advantage of being typecast? A person who is typecast is in a state in which the audience has more reason to rely upon that person to perform some action than to rely upon anyone at random to do so. For an audience, it is obviously often a benefit when people can be typecast, for it allows more refined and reliable predictions about their future behavior. But also consider the matter from the standpoint of the agent. Getting typecast is a matter of a relationship to the expectations of others. As such it may be either a cost or a benefit to the agent. It will be a benefit if the others' reliance on the agent to do something is likely to prompt them to behave in a way that is advantageous to the agent. So, for instance, getting typecast as friendly (likely to perform friendly actions and avoid aggressive ones) is advantageous to the agent if an audience who so casts him is more likely to behave in a friendly manner than if he is not so regarded. So even among animals it can be advantageous to be able to give a submissive signal, or an aggressive one, precisely when the reaction to such signals brings more good than when no signal is given.

In human beings, once a basic inductive correlation exists, we can rapidly ascend the kind of hierarchies of psychological state made familiar by the philosophers H. Paul Grice (1957) and David Lewis (1969). We can signal our future actions intentionally, and we can intend that the audience recognize our intent. And of course once devices for signaling future action are under intentional control, they can be exploited in a variety of ways, leading to stratagems of deception. But for the moment I will stay with cases where everything is above board: where there is no failure of the "common knowledge" condition.

Now suppose an audience A needs to be able to rely upon agent B to do something C. Then A can ask how much it will cost to ensure that B is in a class of agents, β, such that members of β frequently, or invariably, or almost invariably, do C (that is, actions corresponding to C). A can typically get B into such a class in a variety of ways. She can cajole, or threaten harm, or promise reward. In other words, she can work on B's other concerns, trying to align them with performance of C. In turn, if it is to B's benefit to be relied upon—that is, to be typecast as someone who does C—B may be willing to work reciprocally on A in order to persuade A to typecast him, and if it is not to his benefit, he may be willing to be put in the performing class β only if in turn A pays him. Why might it be to B's benefit to be typecast? Because, as has been shown, if she has a definite expectation of him she may modify her own behavior in ways that are mutually advantageous.

Suppose now that you have made no signal, but I decide to rely upon you to perform a task, and I communicate that I do so. This communication may become a concern of yours. You may be motivated by my trust and perform accordingly. If I hadn't trusted you to perform the task, and told you that I was doing so, perhaps you would not have done it. If I know that this is a causal chain that is very likely to be in place, there becomes an element of self-fulfillment about my trust: Given that I trust you and communicate my trust, I can be sure that my trust is not misplaced. A part of the mechanism may be showing that I trust you, and part of your mechanism for assuring me that the trust is not misplaced will be to announce that I can trust you. Mutual reassurances have this point, and their purpose is confirmed rather than refuted by the fact that one of the first things a con artist may want to do is to announce that you can trust him.

Now normativity enters. People are *supposed* to find it salient that they are being relied upon by others. If someone communicates to me that she expects me to do something, then, other things being equal, that is supposed to influence my decision. It is supposed to be a concern. In the simplest case I may be subject to criticism and penalty if I do not do what she expects. And if I have played a role in creating that expectation, encouraging typecasting, then the criticism and penalties are likely to be all the greater. This is no more surprising than my becoming a nuisance and liable to be treated as such if I give signals that are usually correlated with some state, such as the arrival of a predator, when in fact this state is lacking. It is thus that the normative practices of promise and contract come to life.

Of course, whether getting someone into the high performance class β actually works may be contingent on how it is done. That is, although by definition the performance statistics of β are good, the class may divide into those who are in it from one cause and those who are in it from another. If I have exacted a promise from you under duress, then in addition to being in the high performance class of those who have promised, you are in what may be the much lower-performing subset of the class, namely, those who gave a promise reluctantly, or who resent having had to give it, or who are professional diplomats, or who are members of clan X hoping to get members of clan Y to drop their guard, and these are possibilities I have to take into account.

That being trusted or still more having deliberately encouraged trust sometimes motivates us is simply beyond dispute. It is one of the platitudes of human life that takes no empirical research to discover, like "people make friends" or "people sometimes speak languages" or "mothers sometimes love their children."

Notice how natural it has been to slip from the language of reliance toward the language of trust, once the mechanisms of motivation I have described come into being. This means that the discussion so far is slightly orthogonal to a claim often made in the literature. Karen

Jones (1996), for example, has written, "Trust is an attitude of optimism that the goodwill and competence of another will extend to cover the domain of our interaction with her, together with the expectation that the one trusted will be directly and favorably moved by the thought that we are counting on her."

I have not wanted to be so specific. Another's goodwill is, of course, frequently and sometimes centrally involved in trusting that person; we trust other people to care for us and our concerns, and if they know we are counting on them, we trust them to be concerned by that. And central cases–indeed, in human terms, the *best* cases—of trust are ones that might equally be called love, in which there is not only optimism but certainty that however vulnerable you are to another, you are at the same time perfectly safe. But I want to include other cases. I do not, for instance, want to exclude the idea of trusting someone to do something because it is his duty to do it quite regardless of whether he bears any goodwill towards me. Consider, too, third-party cases. One of an estranged couple may trust the other to look after the children but not be pretending that the other bears the trusting party any goodwill. And in institutional cases, there is typically no presumption of altruistic motivation. You trust the postal carrier to bring you the mail, but not because you think she wishes you well. You trust her to do it because that is her job. Associated with that may be the confidence that she will believe there are penalties if she does not bring it. But you may not even believe that this bothers her. You may just think she is conscientious, at least to the extent of thinking of herself as a postal carrier–and delivering the mail is what postal carriers do. So trusting someone to do something because of good will toward you is only one particular case, even if it is the best case.

Deciding to Trust

Before approaching the richer phenomenon of cooperation, I will take a small detour through the phenomenon of deciding to trust someone. There is nothing surprising about deciding to trust—that is, to rely upon—a rope or the post office. The more interesting phenomenon is that we can decide to trust an informant, such as one witness to some event, rather than another. This decision is puzzling, for it sounds very like deciding to believe one thing rather than another, and philosophers have frequently held that belief is not and cannot be directly under the control of the will. For a state to be a belief state, it should be open to evidence, and I cannot will evidence away or will it to point in directions other than those in which it actually points.

There are complexities here, for we all know that beliefs are influenced by our emotions and concerns. We can also deceive ourselves, or so it seems, and we can set about courses of action with the intention that at the end we shall actually have come to believe something, although we cannot see our way to believing it now. These are what we can call Pascal cases, since the famous wager is an example. In Pascal's wager you decide to get yourself to believe in God, even when the belief is unsupported by reason, since you regard it as a "can win, can't lose" gamble. But the case of deciding to trust a witness is not straightforwardly a Pascal case. The problem can be put in the form of a threatened contradiction:

1. Starting from a state of agnosticism, I cannot decide directly to believe a proposition P.

2. Starting from a state of agnosticism, I can decide to trust a witness who testifies that P.

3. If I decide to trust a witness who testifies that P, then I believe P.

A Pascal case might seem to be of the same structure:

1'. Starting from a state of agnosticism, I cannot decide directly to believe in God.

2'. Starting from a state of agnosticism, I can decide to stupefy myself.

3'. If I decide to stupefy myself, then I will believe in God.

Pascal cases are not contradictory. They show that I can adopt means with foreseeable ends that involve acquisitions of belief that I do not at present have. So should we say that the same point defuses the threat of paradox in deciding to trust a witness? Not immediately. The difference is that in Pascal cases stupefying yourself (associating with the faithful, going through the motions) is a causal *antecedent* to belief. So 3' represents a causal conditional; this is why I put the future tense *will* in it. It is just a brute fact that it is effective, and indeed there may be psychologies in which it is not—people whose doubts cannot be put to sleep by these means. But the first case is different; trusting the witness and believing what he says are not distinct events related as means to an end. There is apparently no trusting the witness without believing what he says; the two are logically related rather than causally related, and I therefore put no future tense in 3.

But is the conditional logical rather than causal? We saw earlier that trusting the rope is not quite the same as believing that the rope is safe. So let us interpret 2 with this in mind. Discussing these cases, Holton (1994) says that we can trust a friend to speak knowledgeably and sincerely without believing that they will. The idea is that this trust, like trust in the rope, can be manifested in just some of the dispositions that would be necessary for full belief. We rely on the witness, in the same sense as we rely on the rope. It may be that typically full belief follows on causally, just as in the Pascal case or any other case of coming to acquire a new belief as a result of our decisions. So the air of paradox is dispelled if we back away from belief. We may decide to rely upon a witness, but insofar as it is a decision (because his testimony does not compel conviction), we only rely pro tem. If we decide to trust him, we decide to rely on him, but we don't really believe him.

In some cases this may be the full story. But I think it is important that there are others. Suppose a witness has just told her version of events. I decide to trust her at least to have spoken knowledgeably and sincerely. But this trust surely does involve *believing* her to have spoken knowledgeably and sincerely. Here, it seems to me, there is not the same gap between reliance and belief. I may rely on someone to do something, although I do not fully believe that she will. But the gap between reliance and belief only opens when things are hostage to fortune: to accidents and chances over which she, the subject, has no control. But she does have control over whether she speaks knowledgeably and sincerely.[3] So if I am relying on her to have done so, must I not thereby believe her version of events? And in that case, deciding to trust her does sound like deciding to believe some particular thing.

If this is right, then the witness case cannot simply be solved by interpreting it as a Pascal case. For when I decide to trust the witness to be speaking knowledgeably and sincerely, there is not a core that I genuinely believe about the witness, and another part that is hostage to fortune, about which I may have hopes but no confidence. This is why to trust a witness to be speaking knowledgeably seems to entail believing her; it is not a preliminary to belief but equivalent to it. And I think it is not accidental that in these cases, just as naturally as saying that we decided to trust one witness, we can also say that we *decided* to believe her (just as we say that the jury *preferred* to believe one side or another). We should also notice this. Suppose trust in this case does fall short of confidence; suppose it is better described as mere *acceptance*, a state with only some of the marks of full belief. Then it would seem that the only natural concomitant would be similar acceptance of the proposition to which the witness testifies: perhaps a recognition that this is the version we have to record or the version of events we must adopt in reaching our verdict, but without any confidence that it is true. Now if acceptance is the starting point, it is not clear what takes the place of the Pascal process, the causal process supposed to turn this state into one of full belief. I don't think there is usually a chemistry that turns this kind of nominal acceptance into true belief; indeed, if we start by distinctly withholding belief from what the witness says, I think we shall end up by doing so as well. In this case we would not be trusting the witness but mistrusting her, and mistrust does not evaporate easily. Pascal processes are quite difficult, at least for most of us, most of the time.

So how should we conceptualize deciding to trust, or deciding to believe? What best resolves the threat of contradiction contained in 1 to 3? One can restore a similarity to Pascal cases by thinking about the problem in terms of seduction and surrender. It has often been noticed that testimony is typically infectious (Coady 1992). Arguably, when one hears someone say something, the default is belief. It takes active suspicion to overcome this default. There is a philosophical issue here into which we need not go: Is this default belief just a fact about most of us in most circumstances, or is it somehow integral to sharing a language at all? Either way, it is clear that people can start off pretty skeptical about what a witness says but let themselves be won over. As I listen, I find myself drawn to the witness or to his version of events. I could resist the process, but often I don't; I allow myself to surrender to him and to believe what he says. If we let this process happen too quickly and easily, then we are gullible and lack judgment. The reverse is to be stubborn or even countersuggestible. It may be wrong to think of this allowing oneself to surrender as something one *decides* to do. But it happens, and it is within our control, in the sense that we can, when we are so minded, resist it.

Although I can let myself be influenced or seduced in this way, it does not follow that I can do it all by myself. I cannot succumb to the atmosphere of the party if there is no party and no atmosphere. So indeed I cannot directly and immediately decide to like an ice cream or to believe that aliens have landed in Arkansas. Neither the ice cream nor the proposition have any charms for me. But I can—or some people can—let themselves be influenced by people who are ice-cream lovers or flying-saucer enthusiasts. This is a process within our control, and one that ends up with belief or desire. For some people it may take only the briefest push for full surrender. The push might even be self-generated; sometimes people can be said to have made up their minds to believe some proposition, even without the exposure to outside testimony or other evidence. They make up a story, and the story becomes the way they take things to be.

Pascal's process takes practice and a long time. I am suggesting that it is the drawn-out version of a process that can happen quite easily and take very little time. We can succumb to the witness's story even as it is being told, if it is told seductively enough. It is in this sense that we decide to trust, and equally that we decide to believe.

Decide, however, is not exactly the word to stress, better is the idea of *letting oneself believe* or *letting oneself trust*, which nods in the right way to the passive elements of the process, which it would take resistance to oppose.

It might be thought that even if the process just described is psychologically accurate, it must be a manifestation of irrationality, and a paradox may reappear: I cannot rationally decide to believe something, because trusting a witness entails believing what she said, and hence I cannot rationally decide to trust a witness. The right reaction to this formulation is to reverse it. By surrendering to a witness one is not flying in the face of evidence; one is deeming her testimony to be evidence, just by deciding that she is knowledgeable and sincere. It is exactly as if two instruments give different readings of a physical quantity; by deciding that one instrument is functioning as it should, one would be treating that reading as evidence. Such a decision may be unfounded and irrational, but it may be quite appropriate and well judged.

Of course, some surrenders are indeed irrational: wishful thinking, self-deception, gullibility, and plain bad judgment. But there are also rigid thinking, unimaginative application of rules, and unwarranted skepticism. So in fact I can rationally decide to believe some things and in some circumstances. These will be circumstances in which, if someone comes along and testifies P, it would be rational to trust him.

It is well to remember, too, that the air of paradox may partly depend upon treating belief (and trust) too much as all-or-nothing states and forgetting the varying amounts of credence that may be involved in a real case. Even while I let myself be seduced by the witness's version of events, I may still retain some self-control; I wouldn't bet my life on it. Even when I avow my belief, and avow it to myself, it may be that in truth I would not feel nearly as surprised if it turns out to be a fiction as I would have expected it to be. I wouldn't be flabbergasted, as I would be if it turns out that Queen Elizabeth II is male. Moreover, my belief may be real but surprisingly fragile; seduction is fraught, and the witness may have only to put one foot wrong to destroy the mood.

Cooperation

The chapter so far has considered regularities of action and motivation, and has showed how they can be relied upon and then reinforced by signals from the actor that they can be relied upon, or from the agent that they are being relied upon. Normativity can then be associated with such signals, eventually resulting in a fully cemented practice of promising and trusting in promises. When mutual assurances can be given and relied upon, we have the possibility of cooperation exists. It is integral to the account that the facts put in place at each stage of signaling and reliance can act as concerns. They motivate people, and they are supposed to do so.

In this story, someone else's legitimate expectation is a feature of the situation that has a positive affect of its own. Feeling this affect is not the same as altruism or benevolence. It is closest to Adam Smith's [1759] 1976, III, 2, 3, mechanism of an internal voice whose sound we shy away from, a voice representing the potentially hostile and critical voices of others whom we would let down if we failed to fulfill their trust. We can find avoiding this voice to be one of our concerns even when we do not care about the persons who are relying on us to act. Standard examples show the difference. Suppose others trusted me, and I let them down. Happily, events intervened so that it did them no harm, and they never learned of it. But I still feel bad about it. Or, they trusted me, and I did my bit. Unhappily, events intervened so that harm happened, and they never learned that I did my bit. But my self-respect is intact.

Many features of actions have their own affect—that is, make their own contribution to the dynamic field of forces that sway decisions (Damasio 1994). It is not just the thought that something is in my interests that sways me but other simple thoughts as well: It is my job, It would not be fair, It would disappoint Grandma, It would reduce the rainforests, It would not be doing my bit, This would embarrass her, Parents do not do that, It is not the action of a gentleman, How could I face her, and so on and so on. P. G. Wodehouse got his letters into the mail in London in the 1930s by the simple expedient of tossing them out of his hotel window, trusting that the average British pedestrian, seeing a stamped letter on the pavement, would pop it into the nearest mailbox. He did not suppose that the strangers expected him to do them good in the future, nor that they had indirect expectations—for example, that if they acted well in this respect then, by some chain of causes, letters they tossed on the pavement would get mailed. They would just think, Someone needs this letter to be mailed, and then they would do it. Similarly, if I trust someone to do something, I do not necessarily suppose that he is motivated by any expectation of reciprocal favors. I trust the stranger from whom I ask the way to be telling the truth, but not because I impute any such expectation to him. I just suppose he has enough of the heterogeneous, self-effacing crowd of everyday concerns into which even the rational actors of game theory will have been inducted. And among these concerns can be numbered a distaste for noncooperative options. One of our concerns can be to cooperate, and good for us.

As was noted earlier in the chapter, the strategy for the rational-actor theorist is either to condemn such facts as irrational or to make them epiphenomenal, superficial skin over a forward-looking and self-interested core. But it is, in effect, provable that this approach cannot be right. As I have already mentioned, one can appeal here to the literature that takes a bare competitive situation, most notably the prisoner's dilemma, and points out that for rational actors it is insoluble (that is, they end up in the socially worst corner). One can take the state of nature, characterized as in Hobbes, and ask whether rational actors, put in that situation, could ever decide upon the mechanisms that turn it into civil society. The difficulty is obvious: They cannot make promises when there is no reason to trust anyone to take them seriously; they cannot sensibly turn over power to a sovereign when there is no reason to suppose that she will do anything except use those powers against them. So we are left with the melancholy thought that the rational actors are those that do badly; they stay in the state of war of all against all, or they continually fail to achieve the socially optimal outcome in prisoners' dilemmas. And they cannot give each other trustworthy signs and signals that they are willing to move to a cooperative stance, since no sign or signal could induce any other rational actor, who also knows their rationality, to expect them to forgo their advantage when the time comes.

So the puzzle of how rational actors ever come to do better seems to present a kind of miracle, for people do manage to find themselves in cooperative relations with each other. But one person's modus ponens is another's modus tollens, as philosophers like to say. It is perfectly proper to point out that since people sometimes manage to achieve cooperative relations, utilizing others' willingness to act in some way because they are trusted to act in that way, and for no other reason, then any picture of human psychology that makes it impossible to do such a thing is false. The right response is not to deny the phenomenon, but to save the phenomenon and deny the picture that made it seem impossible.

So I believe it is necessary to reject the conceptualization of social situations that goes with the picture of the self-interested, forward-looking economic agent. A more organic model is needed in which, rather than designing a way out of the war of all against all, we are seen as growing out of it, or rather, growing so that it never occurs. As Hume saw, we need not so much contract as convention, and convention can just grow. A parent and child do not have to lever themselves miraculously into a relationship of trust by getting away from a "natural" situation of war with each other. Neither do other kinfolk, these being people with whom you share rather than those with whom you compete. Our social relations are not all born from situations in which we fight competitively for limited resources, so that if one wins another loses.

One does not have to go all the way with Rousseau to realize that the Hobbesian miracle that transmutes war into cooperation never had to happen, for the actors that Hobbes imagined never existed. But of course there are social situations in which a version of the miracle is needed. These are cases where there is no history of trust, no loyalty to a shared pattern of action that has stood each agent in good stead. It is then indeed hard to find a strategy that would, for instance, change the Balkans into something more like the United States. And in our pessimistic moments we can all be aware of the fragility of cooperation: the tendency, as it were, of the United States to turn into something more like the Balkans. Parents can nurture trusting and trustworthy stances in their children, and politics can nurture similar stances in the relations citizens and states bear to each other, but only by fomenting a culture of trustworthiness and relying on others to catch on. There is no shortcut. But the solution works.[4]

And here it may be worthwhile to reflect for a moment on the importance of the task. Some of our propensities may be hardwired. In that case, theorizing about them will not disturb them. But our propensities to trust, to act from various motivations, and to attribute them to others are not so robust. Theory can disturb them. So rational-actor theory is self-verifying in the sense that if we believe that others are untrustworthy, and if we ourselves feel we cannot afford to be better than they are, then we create a world in which there is no trust in people to act *because* they are trusted or even because they have deliberately encouraged trust. And having created that world, we would be foolish to do anything except look out for ourselves. We will have reintroduced the war of all against all. The agents we would then have become would not be able to lever themselves out of the war, but the theorists can in principle push us down into it.

So it may be appropriate to end with the following melancholy fact. The remark by Gladstone that is quoted in the epigraph was well known to European diplomats. In the fifty years after he made it, German foreign policy was progressively contoured around the belief that Britain would not stand by guarantees, such as those she had given to Belgium, if push came to shove. Without that belief, push might never have come to shove, for many of the events that precipitated the First World War might never have occurred.

Notes

1. Hansard, 10 August 1870. I owe the reference to *Decisions for War, 1914*, edited by Keith Wilson, UCL Press, 1995, p. 189. Gladstone cites as like-minded authorities Lords Aberdeen and Palmerston.

2. I thank Keith Lehrer for drawing my attention to this case.

3. This statement overgeneralizes somewhat. "Externalists" about knowledge construct cases in which someone may speak knowledgeably without knowing whether or not she is doing so, because an element of luck is involved, the situation may not be one in which there is indeed knowledge. But for the purpose of this chapter, such examples can safely be set aside. The basic and normal case is one in which a witness knows whether she did or did not perceive what she says she did.

4. See, for instance, empirical studies such as Braithwaite and Makkai 1993.

References

Blackburn, Simon. 1995. "Practical Tortoise Raising," *Mind* 104(3): 695–710.

Coady, A. J. 1992. *Testimony*. Oxford: Oxford University Press.

Damasio, Antonio R. 1994. *Descartes' Error: Emotion, Reason and the Human Brain*. New York: Grosset/Putnam.

Dawkins, Richard. 1976. *The Selfish Gene*. Oxford: Oxford University Press.

Gibbard, Allan. 1990. *Wise Choices, Apt Feelings*. Cambridge: Harvard University Press.

Grice, H. P. 1957. "Meaning," *Philosophical Review* 66.

Hardin, Russell. 1982. *Collective Action*. Baltimore: Johns Hopkins Press.

Holton, Richard. 1994. "Deciding to Trust, Coming to Believe," *Australasian Journal of Philosophy* 72(1): 63–76.

Jones, Karen. 1996. "Trust as an Affective Attitude," *Ethics* 107, 4–25.

Kraus, Jody. 1993. *The Limits of Hobbesian Contractarianism*. Cambridge: Cambridge University Press

Lewis, D. K. 1969. *Convention*. Cambridge: Harvard University Press.

Monroe, Kresten Renwick, with Kristen Hill Marher. 1995. "Psychology and Rational Actor Theory," *Political Psychology* 16(1): 1–21.

Olson, M. 1963. *The Logic of Collective Action*. Cambridge: Harvard University Press.

Smith, Adam. [1759] 1976. *The Theory of Moral Sentiments*, edited by D. D. Raphael and I. MacFie. Oxford: Oxford University Press.

Chapter 3

Communal and Exchange Trust Norms: Their Value Base and Relevance to Institutional Trust

VALERIE BRAITHWAITE

I N THE PREVIOUS chapters, Russell Hardin and Simon Blackburn have given two different accounts of how people come to trust government. For Hardin, trust is based on knowledge, knowledge that allows good predictions about how one party will respond to the expectations placed on it by another. For Blackburn, such an informational base contributes to trust but is not sufficient; trust comes with a shared understanding that one is relying on the other. Trust in the Blackburn sense transcends information and has its source in the social bond.

The purpose of this chapter is to show that both conceptions of trust not only have theoretical roots in the social sciences but have empirical counterparts within the belief systems of individuals. The criteria that individuals use to arrive at judgments about the trustworthiness of government and its agents align with the notions of trust as knowledge about others and trust as social connectedness to others. From the perspective of citizens, the two types of trust are not mutually exclusive, although they are based on different social values, and they come into play in different institutional settings.

The chapter is organized into four sections. First, different understandings of the social world and collective action are analyzed through the concept of values—specifically, value systems that further the ends of security and harmony. The second section argues that these values shape expectations of others and are linked to the criteria used to identify others as trustworthy. These criteria, as Kent Jennings shows later in this volume, are used consistently by individuals, and can be regarded as trust norms. Trust norms, along with values, play a role in determining the degree to which citizens trust government and its branches. The third section presents data demonstrating that security values are linked with trust norms based on exchange principles and harmony values with trust norms based on communal principles. It also brings data to bear on the relationship between values, trust norms, and trust in institutions. The importance that individuals place on security values and institutional compliance with exchange trust norms are hypothesized as predictive of trust in security-based institutions. The importance placed on harmony values and the extent to which harmony-based institutions comply with communal trust norms are hypothesized as predictive of the trust they are accorded by citizens. In the final section, I argue that different trust norms can work in a symbiotic relationship in a democratic society, mutually reinforcing each other, with one type counterbalancing the inherent weaknesses of the other.

Values as a Key to Understanding Trust Relations

Trust defines a relationship between actors or groups in which one party adopts the position, expressed either verbally or behaviorally, that the other will pursue a course of action that is considered preferable to alternative courses of action. The alternatives are plausible options that may benefit the holder of trust or harm the giver of trust, yet trust is expected to be honored and often is. Explaining this phenomenon involves a broad range of social science concepts of both an individual and a societal kind. On the individual side are self-interest, motives, needs, and attitudes; on the societal side, cooperation, norms, laws, and institutions.

In general, analyses of trust focus on the tension between individual and collective interests. As important and interesting as such conflicts are, they constitute a relatively small proportion of the socially coordinated activities of daily life. Resolution of much self/collective conflict occurs spontaneously and effortlessly. Socialization ensures that individuals are well practiced in juggling their own needs and the expectations of others, a process that is greatly facilitated by the internalization of shared conceptions of how things should be done. Knowledge of this kind, acquired throughout life, becomes part of the individual's belief system used to interpret future events and guide decision making (Rokeach 1973). Beliefs may be specific and tightly organized, as with a decision heuristic (see Scholz, chapter 6), or complex and multifaceted, as with an ideology (Rose and McAllister 1986), or universal and overarching, as with a value system (Kluckhohn 1951; Rokeach 1973; Schwartz 1992, 1994).

Values are enduring, abstract, and socially shared principles that regulate action (Kluckhohn 1951; Scott 1965; Williams 1968). They incorporate goals toward which individuals and groups should strive, as well as standards for how humans should interact with each other (Rokeach 1973). Value studies show that most people believe that they should be both trusting and reliable in their relationships with others (Braithwaite 1979; Rokeach 1973; Scott 1965). Yet experience tells us that trust can be breached, often with dire consequences. Given that honoring and breaching trust feature so prominently in human consciousness, one might expect to find that individuals hold coherent sets of beliefs about the criteria that should be used to gauge the trustworthiness of the other. Furthermore, such criteria, like the values themselves, are likely to be shared in the community, assuming the status of trust norms and not simply individually tailored trust beliefs.

Belief systems are widely recognized for their interconnectedness; attitudes, values, needs, and interests often show high levels of cognitive consistency with each other (Abelson 1983; Rokeach 1973). Thus, it is unlikely that trust norms exist in isolation from the other beliefs that individuals hold, particularly those representing a person's understanding of the social world and how it operates. Value systems capture such world views and therefore should be linked with the criteria that individuals prefer to use in assessing trustworthiness.

The hypothesized relationship between value systems and trust norms requires that a theoretical distinction be made between these concepts at the outset. A value is defined as an enduring belief that a certain mode of conduct or goal in life is personally and socially preferable to the converse mode of conduct or goal in life across specific objects and situations (Rokeach 1973). For example, honesty would be a value if a person believed this mode of conduct to be personally and socially preferable to dishonesty, regardless of context. Similarly, economic prosperity would be a value if a person believed this goal in life to be personally and socially preferable to poverty, regardless of context. As principles with a personal and social "oughtness" that transcends situations, values differ from the more context-sensitive concepts of attitudes and norms. Attitudes are clusters of beliefs that focus on a particular object or situation and give rise to a favorable or unfavorable response predisposition on the part of the individual. Norms, like attitudes, are more commonly observed within particular contexts but are less individualistic phenomena. Norms represent socially defined and enforced standards of behavior (Deaux and Wrightsman 1988). Norms need not be conscious beliefs spontaneously articulated by individuals. The current analysis, however, assumes that individuals can recognize trust norms as criteria to which they attach varying levels of importance in assessing trustworthiness.

Values are interconnected and organized into value systems (Braithwaite and Law 1985; Braithwaite and Scott 1991; Rokeach 1973; Schwartz and Bilsky 1987; Scott 1960). In previous work, I have drawn a distinction between security and harmony values (Braithwaite 1982, 1994, 1997, 1998). The security value system brings together personal and social goals and modes of conduct that are considered important for protecting oneself or one's group from oppression by others. At a social level, values such as national economic development, the rule of law, and national greatness are socially sanctioned goals for ensuring the safety of one's group and individuals within it. At a personal level, security values include having social recognition, economic prosperity, authority, and competitiveness. These goals and modes of conduct ensure that one is well positioned to protect one's interests and further them within the existing social order (see appendix to this chapter for sample items).

In contrast, the harmony value system brings together social and personal values with goals of furthering peaceful coexistence through a social order that shares resources, communicates mutual respect, and cooperates to allow individuals to develop their potential to the full. Harmony values for society include a good life for others, rule by the people, international cooperation, a world at peace, human dignity, greater economic equality, and the preservation of the natural environment. Harmony values for the individual include self-insight, inner harmony, the pursuit of knowledge, self-respect, and wisdom, as well as being tolerant, generous, forgiving, helpful, and loving (see appendix to this chapter for sample items).

The security and harmony systems are stable, enduring, and valued at some level by the vast majority of the population (Blamey and Braithwaite 1997a; Braithwaite and Blamey forthcoming). In spite of very high levels of acceptance of these values in the community, individuals differ in the way in which they prioritize them (Braithwaite 1994, 1997, 1998). They are useful, therefore, for explaining how individuals see their obligations to the collectivity (Blamey and Braithwaite 1997b; Dryzek and Braithwaite 1997). Of particular interest are those who rate security and harmony values equally as either high in importance (*dualists*) or low in importance (*moral relativists*). Compared with dualists, moral relativists are less engaged with the political system, more cynical about those with power, more likely to take context into account in their decision making, and more self-interested. Those whose security and harmony values are in a state of imbalance have familiar profiles reflecting the typical conservative and the typical progressive. The security-oriented (high security, low harmony) support the political right, deregulation, tougher law enforcement, and the death penalty; they are opposed to political protests, welfare, high taxes, and programs to assist women and minority groups. The harmony-oriented (high harmony, low security) support the political left, political activism, wealth redistribution, the protection of wilderness areas, and affirmative-action programs; they oppose increases in police power and stiffer sentencing practices (Blamey and Braithwaite 1997a, 1997b; Braithwaite 1982, 1994, 1997, 1998; Heaven 1990, 1991; Thannhauser and Caird 1990).

The value orientations of harmony and security bear a theoretical resemblance to other two-dimensional value models that have appeared in the social science literature. William Scott (1960) distinguished competitive and cooperative goals and modes of engagement; Seymour Lipset (1963) identified achievement and equality as core American values; Milton Rokeach (1973) argued for a modified version comprising freedom and equality; Irwin Katz and R. Glen Hass (1988) elaborated on these themes with the value orientations of individualism and communalism; Kenneth Rasinski (1987) contrasted principles of justice in terms of proportionality and egalitarianism; Ronald Inglehart (1971, 1977) coined the terms *materialism* and *postmaterialism*; Pitirim Sorokin (1962) postulated sensate and ideational cultural mentalities; Max Weber (1946) contrasted the ethic of ultimate ends with the ethic of responsibility; and Erich Fromm (1949) theorized about the individual's engagement with society in terms of the authoritarian conscience and humanistic conscience. All described their two value systems in terms of distinctive dimensions that are not necessarily conflictual, oftentimes existing side by side.

Despite differences in emphasis and the breadth of territory covered, commonality can be found across these models in the principles being articulated. One ethical system legitimates competition for resources of a material and social kind, expresses reservations about the capacity of humans to restrain their antisocial impulses, and advocates reliance on authority and externally imposed rules to establish order. Those for whom security values dominate can be expected to see societal relationships in terms of winning and losing and a need for enforceable rules to ensure that the competitive game does not lead to social destruction.

The second ethical system represents the humanistic expression of integrity, placing supreme importance on finding inner harmony and harmony with the external world and on having knowledge and understanding of one's moral principles, the strength of character to act on these principles, and the realization of human potential in relation to others as well as to the self. Those for whom harmony values dominate can be expected to see relationships in less adversarial terms than do the security-oriented. For the harmony-oriented, what is at stake is not finite external resources for which one must compete but rather inner experience and feelings of spiritual well-being achieved through personal integrity.

Four Theoretical Perspectives on Trust Norms

The key to linking value systems and trust norms lies in the way in which "the other" is construed. By definition, the construction of the other is central to both the concept of trust and that of values. From the perspective of security values, the other is a competitor. Harm rendered by this competitor can be minimized through rules and laws that structure the other's actions (at the value level) and through the ability to predict the other's actions (at the trust level). Thus, it is hypothesized that those who are predominantly security-oriented will express a greater likelihood of trusting when they are in a position to know the other's competence, commitments, track record, and competing interests. For the security-oriented, knowledge increases predictability and minimizes risk, making trust possible.

For those who favor harmony values, the relationship between self and other is not conflictual but mutually reinforcing. Rewards are internal and spiritual and therefore not dependent on the external resources for which individuals must compete. Furthermore, the other is seen as an equal, worthy of the respect and opportunities one wishes for oneself. Harmony is sought through sharing resources and understanding and accommodating the needs of others. From the perspective of the harmony-oriented, giving the gift of trust (Pettit 1995) is part of establishing social connectedness and reinforcing shared identities, and trustworthiness is built through respecting others, sharing resources, and meeting others' needs.

Thus the two value systems point to different bases for inferring trustworthiness; the former emphasizes information about likely outcomes and constraints, while the latter relies on social connectedness. This distinction has parallels in other literatures, most notably typologies of trust, theories of social cooperation, and justice norms.

The multidimensional nature of trust is widely recognized and variously represented (Barber 1983; Butler 1991; Cummings and Bromiley 1996; Deutsch 1973; Lewicki and Bunker 1996; Mishra 1996; Shapiro, Sheppard, and Cheraskin 1992; Sheppard and Tuchinsky 1996; Sitkin and Roth 1993; Tyler and Degoey 1996). Three recurring themes can be extracted from the typologies proposed. The first involves inferences of trustworthiness from openness, concern, not taking advantage of others, identification, value congruence, and respect for others. These behaviors reveal commonalities between actors and enhance perceptions of similarity. As such, they are consistent with a harmony perspective on trust: Trust is a by-product of shared understandings, goals, and social responsibility. A second theme associates trust with calculation of risk, knowledge, and the capacity to control and predict outcomes to achieve a desired benefit. This basis for trust is consistent with a security-oriented perspective. The third theme is the notion of trust as performance, captured by such concepts as commitment, competence, reliability, meeting obligations, and civic order. Trust based on performance has elements in common with both a harmony orientation (responsibility for others) and a security orientation (consistency of performance), although it might be expected to have stronger connections with security. Security-based trust depends on a detailed knowledge of what might happen and the capacity to constrain and predict outcomes. Performance by another that entails consistency, competence, and reliability is likely to enhance greatly the likelihood of the development of a relationship of trust. In contrast, where trust emanates from a harmony base, performance is not essential to the trust relationship. Good intentions and confirmation of shared goals and understandings are a sufficient basis for trust.

Theories of cooperation can also be divided along the axis of how the other is conceptualized—that is, whether in terms of individual/ other exchange (see, for example, Williamson 1993) or in terms of shared social identity (for example, Tyler, Degoey, and Smith 1996). From the exchange perspective, the key explanatory concept is motivational interdependence, the idea that individuals cooperate because they expect such cooperation to result in the satisfaction of individual needs or the achievement of rewarding outcomes at some time in the future. When applied to relationships of trust, exchange theories focus attention on utilities—material, social, or psychic—evaluated and weighed by the actor in deciding whether it is in the actor's interest to give or honor trust. Unlike this perspective, the social-identity perspective does not start from the position of the individual distinct from the social group. In this view, there can be no individual identity without identification with social groups and therefore "acting in terms of self" must incorporate both group and individual behavior (Turner 1987). From this perspective, trust is a by-product of shared social identity. Once the collective "we" and "I" have merged—that is, once an actor has identified with a group because of some perceived salient similarity—trusting others in the group to pursue the group's interest is little different from trusting oneself to do so. Giving and honoring trust is a function of how well actors have been imbued with norms and values furthering collective interests, how well they see others in the group sharing these same norms and values, and how resistant they are to adopting alternative identities that compete for salience as the social context changes.

The importance of the distinction between exchange- and identity-based trust in explaining deference to authority is illustrated by Tom Tyler in chapter 11 of the present volume. A related example of why these types of trust should be distinguished has been provided by the social psychologist Roderick Kramer (1996), who showed that individuals with different levels of power in an organization use different frames of reference in assessing trustworthiness. Those with power were more likely to adopt a perspective that fits the exchange model of trust, while those without power were more likely to adopt a shared social identity perspective. Kramer's work suggests that naive theories of trust are not idiosyncratic but constitute shared understandings among different subcultures within the society.

A major goal of this chapter is to provide a fuller appreciation of the cultural underpinnings of different expressions of trust. Trust based on knowledge and exchange and trust based on oneness and connectedness are institutionalized in our society. Both types of trust can be expressed as beliefs that are widely shared and prescriptive, so much so that they constitute trust norms that are tied to our major value systems. Furthermore, security- and harmony-based trust norms are brought into play in different institutional settings.

Conceiving of security- and harmony-based trust as two sets of institutionalized norms owes much to the work of the psychologist Margaret Clark and her colleagues (Clark 1984, 1986; Clark and Mills 1979; Clark, Mills, and Powell 1986; Williamson and Clark 1989). They have identified two types of justice norms regulating social relationships among families, friends, and acquaintances: communal norms and exchange norms. Harmony-based trust is consistent with Clark's conception of communal norms, which define relationships in which there are mutual feelings of responsibility for the other's well-being. Benefits are given in response to the other's needs or simply to please the other with no expectation of repayment. Behaviors that reflect special obligations for others include giving help, feeling good about helping and bad about not helping, keeping track of others' needs and allocating resources on this basis, and being sensitive to others' emotions. Security-based trust is compatible with Clark's exchange norms. Exchange norms do not involve feeling a special responsibility for the well-being of another. Benefits are given to repay debts created by benefits previously received or in anticipation of receiving payment in the future. Behaviors that reflect exchange norms include prompt repayment for social benefits, giving and receiving comparable benefits, requesting payment for benefits, and keeping track of individual inputs into joint ventures.

Williamson and Clark (1989) have argued that experimental manipulations of the social context can determine which type of norm is activated but that at the same time, there are individual differences in preferences for one kind of relationship over the other. Some people prefer to operate under principles of exchange, while others favor communal norms.

The work of Clark and her colleagues on justice in personal settings (Clark 1984, 1986; Clark and Mills 1979; Clark, Mills, and Powell 1986; Williamson and Clark, 1989) can be extended to clarify the bases of trust between government and its citizens. In general, exchange norms are based on knowledge of the performance of the other and the benefits the other has delivered reliably and consistently in the past. They allow for security in relationships of trust. For the purposes of understanding trust in government, exchange trust norms can be defined as shared beliefs that government and its branches are trustworthy if they act in ways that are predictable, consistent, orderly, and competent, and if they deliver on promises in a timely fashion. They are hypothesized as the expression of security values geared to safeguarding the individual or group against the exploitation and domination of others. Communal norms in general are based on perceptions of need and feelings of responsibility for others. They promote trust through harmony in social relationships. In relation to citizens and government, communal trust norms are defined as shared beliefs that government and its branches are trustworthy if they act in ways to uncover the needs of citizens, show concern for their well-being, foresee their difficulties, share their aspirations, respect them, and treat them with dignity. They are hypothesized as the expression of harmony values that prescribe service to the other as a social ideal.

The association between exchange trust norms and the security value system, on the one hand, and communal trust norms and the harmony value system on the other are examined empirically in the next section. As figure 3.1 suggests, those more committed to security values are hypothesized to place greater reliance on exchange trust norms to assess trustworthiness. Those who are more strongly predisposed to harmony values are expected to attach more importance to communal trust norms in deciding who should be trusted.

At the same time different sets of trust norms are hypothesized as operating in different domains of governance. For instance, exchange trust norms might be expected to guide judgments of the trustworthiness of tax collectors, in questions about whether they have acted

Figure 3.1   Values and Their Relationship to Trust Norms

| security values | ⟶ | exchange trust norms |
| harmony values | ⟶ | communal trust norms |

Notes: The theoretical model postulates values as causally prior to trust norms. The present study, however, provides only an empirical test of association.

competently, consistently, and reliably as keepers of the public purse. In contrast, when disasters strike communities, citizens may be more likely to look for understanding and concern when deciding whether to trust rescue workers to help them out of their predicament. In a later chapter, Kent Jennings suggests that communal trust norms may be more important locally, exchange trust norms nationally.

It is tempting to infer from the discussion in this chapter that institutions with security objectives rely on exchange trust, while those with harmony objectives rely on communal trust. This need not be the case. When national security is addressed through the raising of an army in time of war, appeals can be made both to communal and to exchange trust. Similarly, in pursuing the harmony objective of a democratically elected government, the outcome is safeguarded through an electoral process that stringently adheres to norms of exchange trust. The congruence between security values and exchange trust and between harmony values and communal trust within the belief systems of citizens is based on "psycho-logic" or the need for cognitive consistency. Such a principle should not be extended from the individual to the institutional level.

Nevertheless, to simplify the research question, this study analyzed institutions where objectives and trust norms are aligned in a way that matches the belief systems of individuals. Security institutions were defined as those that pursue security objectives and that rely on exchange norms to build trust. Harmony institutions, on the other hand, were defined as those that pursue harmony goals and rely on communal norms to win the trust of their consituents.

Four institutions were selected for empirical analysis. The High Court of Australia and Australia's central bank, the Reserve Bank, were judged to be examples of institutions that advance security values at the levels of law and order and economic development and that rely most heavily on exchange trust norms in their relations with citizens. Representing the peak bodies of law and monetary policy, both institutions are remote from citizens. They steadfastly proclaim freedom from interference from either private interests or government; justify their operations in terms of precedent and tradition; are judged on outcomes, since processes are hidden from view; and value consistency, experience, and ability in appointees. The behaviors that can be witnessed by citizens are behaviors that fit exchange trust norms rather than communal trust norms.

Institutions that contrast with the Reserve Bank and High Court in their advancement of harmony values and advocacy of communal trust are the Family Court and charities. Charities in Australia are increasingly coming under the scrutiny of the Australian government as they take on more of the welfare role of the state (Industry Commission, 1995). The Family Court and charities focus on reconstructing family relations and assisting those in need of support, thereby reversing injustices and reestablishing harmonious relationships. The trademark of both the Family Court and charities is their ability and willingness to understand the difficulties facing individuals, to act responsively to their needs, to avoid blame and punishment where possible, and to provide the support necessary to empower clients to resolve their conflicts and problems through processes of conciliation. These ways of doing business rely for their success on the operation of communal trust norms.

The values that individuals hold and their perceptions of compliance with trust norms by institutions are expected to contribute to how much trust they place in public institutions. These expectations are formalized as hypotheses in figure 3.2. Trust in security institutions should be highest among those who value the institutional mission (that is, who have a high commitment to security values) and perceive the institution as complying with exchange trust norms. Trust in harmony institutions should be highest among those who value the institutional mission (that is, who have a high commitment to harmony values) and who rely on communal trust norms.

These hypotheses are based on the notion of congruence in objectives and expectations between individuals and institutions. Value congruence refers to the degree to which there is a good fit between the interests of the individual and those of the institution. Value congruence is an integral part of an individual's adaptation to any social system (Feather 1972, 1979; Hofstede 1980, 1994) and, more specifically, of trusting relationships (Bianco, this volume; Shapiro, Sheppard, and Cheraskin 1992).

Congruence in trustworthiness norms between institutions and individuals means that institutions provide the feedback necessary for citizens to reaffirm their trust in the institution. A common language of trust must be developed if there is to be meaningful engagement

Figure 3.2   Values and Norm Adherence as Predictors of Institutional Trust

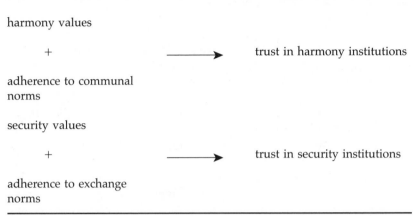

harmony values

+

adherence to communal
norms   ⟶   trust in harmony institutions

security values

+

adherence to exchange
norms   ⟶   trust in security institutions

Notes: The theoretical model postulates a causal relationship. The present study, however, provides only an empirical test of association.

across the micro/macro divide. Once institutions and citizens agree on relevant trust norms, citizens can evaluate the extent to which institutions have complied with them. If institutions fail to comply, or if they switch trust norms, the trust relationship is likely to suffer. Institutional signals seeking to establish communal trust will be wasted on a citizenry focusing on exchange trust, and, conversely, institutional expressions of exchange trust will do little to impress when citizens expect signs of communal trust.

An Empirical Analysis of Values, Trust Norms, and Institutional Trust

The Data Base

Questionnaire data from 504 respondents were used to test the hypotheses represented in figures 3.1 and 3.2. The sample was nonrandom, obtained through a snowball strategy whereby undergraduate students recruited family and friends to take part in the study.

Measures

Values   The security value system was represented by four scales measuring the value accorded to (*a*) national strength and order, (*b*) propriety in dress and manners, (*c*) social standing and getting ahead, and (*d*) competence and effectiveness. The harmony value system was represented by three scales measuring the value accorded to (a) international harmony and equality, (b) personal growth and inner harmony, and (c) a positive orientation to others. These multi-item scales are part of the *Goal, Mode, and Social Values Inventories* (Braithwaite and Law 1985; Braithwaite and Scott 1991). Respondents are asked to rate each item in terms of its importance as a guiding principle in life, using a seven-point scale where 1 = "I reject this," 2 = "I am inclined to reject this," 3 = "I neither reject nor accept this," 4 = "I am inclined to accept this," 5 = "I accept this as important," 6 = "I accept this as very important," 7 = "I accept this as of the utmost importance."

Item responses were summed to produce a scale score for each of the seven scales. To aid interpretation and comparison, total scores were divided by the number of items in the scale, so that the possible range for scale means was 1 to 7. The descriptive statistics for these scales (means, standard deviations, and alpha reliability coefficients) are given in table 3.1. The identification of each value scale as part of the security or harmony system has been established in previous work (Braithwaite 1997). The principal components analysis with varimax rotation reported in table 3.1 confirms the distinctiveness of the security and harmony value scales in the present data set.

Trust Norms   Trust norms were represented by thirteen behaviors, and respondents were asked how important each was for bringing about and maintaining trust in society's institutions. Five behaviors represented exchange trust norms of predictability, orderliness, consistency, and sound performance: (a) not taking risks, (b) acting in a predictable fashion, (c) being consistent in decision making, (d) having a track record of getting things done, and (e) showing strong leadership. Eight behaviors represented communal trust norms of respecting, protecting, sharing, and representing the collective identity: (a) treating people with respect, (b) having insight into future problems, (c) having an interest in the lives of ordinary Australians, (d) consulting widely with different groups, (e) keeping citizens fully informed, (f) being accountable for own actions, (g) sharing the goals of the people, and (h) understanding the position of others. Each item was rated on a five-point scale from "not at all important" to "very important."

A principal components analysis with an oblique rotation reduced the data set to two factors, one corresponding to exchange trust, the other to communal trust (see table 3.2). The two factors accounted for 43 percent of the variance in the item set. The factors were correlated positively (r = .34). Scales to measure the importance of exchange trust and communal trust were constructed by

Table 3.1   The Security and Harmony Components Underlying the Personal and Social Values Scales

Value Scales	M (SD) α	Factor 1 Security	Factor 2 Har- mony
Security values			
National strength and order	5.02 (1.07) .80	.82	.02
Propriety in dress and manners	4.88 (.96) .83	.73	.23
Social standing and getting ahead	4.15 (1.04) .78	.78	.03
Competence and effectiveness	5.34 (.74) .73	.74	.39
Harmony values			
International harmony and equality	5.64 (.68) .79	.07	.76
Personal growth and inner harmony	5.71 (.79) .77	.27	.74
Positive orientation to others	5.39 (.84) .78	.06	.83
Percentage of variance (before rotation)		43.7	20.1

Notes: This table features means, standard deviations, and alpha reliability coefficients for the personal and social values scales. The factor loadings were derived from a principal components analysis and variant rotation of the personal and social values scales.

summing the responses to relevant items and dividing by the number of items in the scale. With regard to exchange trust, the majority considered these behaviors as important indicators of trust ($M = 3.63$, $SD = .64$), with 80 percent scoring above the midpoint on the "not at all important" to "very important" rating scale. Endorsement rates were even higher for communal trust ($M = 4.37$, $SD = .49$), with 98 percent locating themselves above the midpoint. Thus, exchange trust and communal trust, like values, enjoy a high degree of support within the community, suggesting that they are not individualistic variables but widely shared societal norms. The alpha reliability coefficient for the exchange trust norm scale was .68, and for the communal trust norm scale it was .79. The scales were positively correlated ($r = .48$, $p < .01$), indicating that support for exchange trust norms and support for communal trust norms go hand in hand in society.

Compliance with Trust Norms   Respondents were required to indicate whether or not they thought the thirteen behaviors were characteristic

Table 3.2   The Components of Communal and Exchange Trust

Trust Items	Factor 1 Communal	Factor 2 Exchange
Exchange trust		
Not taking risks	−.13 (.12)	.73 (.68)
Acting in a predictable fashion	.10 (.36)	.75 (.79)
Being consistent in decision making	.05 (.30)	.75 (.76)
Having a track record of getting things done[a]	.40 (.51)	.32 (.46)
Showing strong leadership[a]	.37 (.47)	.29 (.42)
Communal trust		
Treating the people with respect	.80 (.74)	−.16 (.12)
Having an interest in the lives of ordinary Australians	.73 (.72)	−.03 (.22)
Consulting widely with different groups	.69 (.67)	−.05 (.18)
Keeping citizens fully informed	.64 (.64)	.00 (.22)
Having insight into future problems	.62 (.59)	−.09 (.12)
Being accountable for own actions	.53 (.54)	.04 (.22)
Sharing the goals of the people	.51 (.54)	.11 (.28)
Understanding the position of others	.52 (.58)	.17 (.35)
Percentage of variance (before rotation)	32.2	11.1

Notes: This table features factor pattern (structure) loadings from principal components analysis and oblimin rotation of the exchange trust and communal trust items.
[a]These items were retained as exchange items, in spite of the higher pattern matrix loadings on communal trust, because of their theoretical importance to the exchange concept and because of the structure matrix loadings, which show that both types of trust are present in the item in this data set. To take account of this finding, exchange trust is used as a statistical control in analyses involving communal trust and vice versa.

of each of four institutions: (*a*) the High Court, (*b*) the Reserve Bank, (*c*) charities, and (*d*) the Family Court (1 = "yes," 0 = "no"). For each institution, responses were summed over relevant behaviors to give a score of perceived compliance with exchange trust norms and perceived compliance with communal trust norms. Total scores were divided by the number of behaviors making up the scale. Mean scores and standard deviations for each institution are presented in table 3.3. The High Court was regarded as showing strongest adherence to exchange trust norms and the Family Court weakest. Charities showed strongest adherence to communal trust norms and the Reserve Bank weakest. The differences between communal and exchange trust norms in adherence by the four institutions were in the expected directions but were not substantial.

Table 3.3   **Levels of Compliance with Exchange and Communal Trust Norms in the High Court, the Reserve Bank, the Family Court, and Charities**

Norms	High Court	Reserve Bank	Family Court	Charities
Exchange trust	.46 (.32)	.38 (.31)	.36 (.31)	.39 (.31)
Communal trust	.32 (.31)	.24 (.26)	.37 (.32)	.56 (.30)

Notes: This table features means and standard deviations for levels of compliance. Scores can range from 0 (no compliance) to 1 (compliance on all criteria).

Institutional Trust   Institutional trust was indexed through single-item measures asking respondents to indicate how much personal trust they were prepared to place in the High Court of Australia, the Reserve Bank, the Family Court, and Australian charities (for example, the St. Vincent de Paul Society and the Smith family). Responses were made on a five-point rating scale from "very little trust" to "a great deal of trust." For each institution, the mean score was above the midpoint ($M = 3.57$, $SD = .96$ for the High Court, $M = 3.12$, $SD = .99$ for the Reserve Bank, $M = 3.12$, $SD = .97$ for the Family Court, $M = 4.09$, $SD = .94$ for charities), suggesting all enjoyed a reasonable degree of trust within the community.

Findings

Values and Trust Norms   The hypotheses in figure 3.1 linking the security value system to exchange trust and the harmony value system to communal trust were tested using ordinary least squares (OLS) regression analysis. Placing importance on trust norms was predicted for exchange trust norms in the first analysis and for communal trust norms in the second analysis from the seven value scales and one control variable. The importance placed on communal trust norms was used as a control variable in predicting exchange trust norm preference, and the importance of exchange trust norms was used as a control in predicting communal trust norm preference. This step was taken because of the strong positive correlation between the two trust scales, possibly reflecting the individual difference variable of a generalized willingness to trust (Rotter 1980; Stack 1978). The intention was to use the seven value scales to explain the portion of trust uniquely related to exchange and, similarly, the uniquely communal portion of trust.

Table 3.4   The Prediction of Exchange Trust Norms from Security and Harmony Values Scales

Controls and Values	r	β
Communal trust norms	.48**	.38**
National strength and order	.39**	.15**
Propriety in dress and manners	.46**	.22**
Social standing and getting ahead	.27**	.04
Competence and effectiveness	.38**	.09
International harmony and equality	.22**	.00
Personal growth and inner harmony	.17**	−.12*
Positive orientation to others	.22**	.01
Adjusted R^2		.36**

Notes: This table features Pearson product-moment correlation coefficients between the values scales and exchange trust norms, and the standardized regression coefficients for the values scales when used to predict exchange trust norms in an ordinary least squares regression analysis. Communal trust norms appear in the regression analysis as a control variable.
* $p < .05$ ** $p < .01$

The results of the OLS regression analysis predicting the importance of exchange trust norms appear in table 3.4. The predictors together accounted for 36 percent of the variance in the outcome variable. The standardized regression coefficients reported in table 3.4 indicate that the major value predictors were the security value scales for national strength and order and propriety in dress and manners. The social standing and getting ahead and competence and effectiveness scales did not have significant beta coefficients because of their strong correlation with the other security value scales (Braithwaite 1997). A significant negative beta coefficient for the personal growth and inner harmony scale from the harmony system showed that those who value the search for self-knowledge, wisdom, personal development, and inner tranquillity are less likely to rely on exchange principles for inferring trust.

The OLS regression analysis demonstrating that communal trust norms are more strongly endorsed by those with harmony values is reported in table 3.5. Together the predictors accounted for 40 percent of the variance in the outcome variable. International harmony and equality, personal growth and inner harmony, and a positive orientation to others had significant and positive standardized regression coefficients in predicting communal trust.

These analyses confirm predictions about the different bases for exchange and communal trust norms. Both flourish in the community

Table 3.5   The Prediction of Communal Trust Norms from Security and Harmony Values Scales

Controls and Values	r	β
Exchange trust norms	.48**	.36**
National strength and order	.22**	−.02
Propriety in dress and manners	.29**	.05
Social standing and getting ahead	.13**	−.06
Competence and effectiveness	.30**	.01
International harmony and equality	.47**	.29**
Personal growth and inner harmony	.38**	.14**
Positive orientation to others	.40**	.11*
Adjusted R^2		.40**

Notes: The table features Pearson product-moment correlation coefficients between the values scales and communal trust norms, and the standardized regression coefficients for the values scales when used to predict communal trust norms in an ordinary least squares regression analysis. Exchange trust norms appear in the regression analysis as a control variable.
* $p < .05$ ** $p < .01$

in that the majority of citizens consider them to be important behaviors for inferring the trustworthiness of society's major institutions. At the same time, they are expressions of two different value orientations, both of which are widely endorsed in the society. Exchange trust norms are found to be linked to a constellation of values that reflect concern for security. Exchange trust norms have most appeal to those who view themselves and their groups as engaging in a competitive struggle for social and material resources; who value the standards of propriety that society imposes on individuals to ensure that behavior is regulated and civility is maintained; and who are less preoccupied with the pursuit of inner peace and harmony. Communal trust norms are most enthusiastically endorsed by those who favor harmony-oriented societal goals such as international cooperation, equality, rule by the people, and a good life for others; who pursue inner peace and personal development at an individual level; and who value a positive attitude to others (being loving, understanding, helpful, forgiving). Communal trust norms rest on a philosophy that seeks well-being through harmonious social bonds between self and other.

Values, Compliance with Trust Norms and Institutional Trust   OLS regression analyses were used to test the hypotheses in figure 3.2 for each of the four institutions separately. An overall security system

Table 3.6   The Prediction of Trust in the Reserve Bank and the High
Court from Value Orientations and Perceived Use of Trust
Norms, Using OLS Regression Analysis

	Reserve Bank		High Court	
Predictors	r	β	r	β
Security value orientation	.10*	.11*	.12**	.09
Harmony value orientation	−.03	−.08	.11*	.05
Perceived use of exchange norms	.28**	.26**	.22**	.12*
Perceived use of communal norms	.20**	.04	.23**	.14*
Adjusted R^2		.09**		.07**

Note: The table features Pearson product-moment correlation coefficients and standardized regression coefficients.
* $p < .05$ ** $p < .01$

score was calculated through summing scores on national strength
and order, propriety in dress and manners, social standing and getting ahead, and competence and effectiveness. The harmony system
score was an aggregate of international harmony and equality, personal growth and inner harmony, and a positive orientation to others.
Thus, for each institution, the independent variables were the importance that individuals attached to the two value systems—security
and harmony—and the degree to which they believed the institution
adhered to exchange and communal trust norms. Institutional trust
was the dependent variable. The results are reported in tables 3.6 and
3.7.

In the case of the Reserve Bank, the hypothesis was confirmed,
with trust being higher among those who valued security and observed exchange trust norms operating in the institution (see table
3.6). The findings in relation to the High Court, however, differed
from expectations in important ways. Trust in the High Court was
determined by the degree to which the institution projected an image
of compliance with both exchange and communal trust norms (see
table 3.6). The importance of communal trust norms above and beyond exchange trust norms is a revealing finding, since the High
Court is not an institution that is readily accessible to ordinary Australians. Most interestingly, trust in the High Court was not dependent on an individual's basic value orientation.

The findings for the Family Court and charities, presented in table
3.7, were in keeping with expectations. Trust in these institutions was
higher for those who were more strongly oriented to harmony values

Table 3.7   The Prediction of Trust in the Family Court and Charities from Value Orientations and Perceived Use of Trust Norms, Using OLS Regression Analysis

	Family Court		Charities	
Predictors	r	β	r	β
Security value orientation	−.02	−.07	.04	.00
Harmony value orientation	.09	.10*	.17**	.17**
Perceived use of exchange norms	.25**	.08	.19**	.08
Perceived use of communal norms	.33**	.28**	.23**	.17**
Adjusted R^2		.12**		.07**

Notes: The table features Pearson product-moment correlation coefficients and standardized regression coefficients.
* $p < .05$ ** $p < .01$

and who perceived the institutions as abiding by the rules of communal trust.

Summary of Findings and Implications for Governance

This chapter has identified two sets of trust norms that vary in importance across institutions and individuals. Exchange trust norms are built on behaviors that reflect competence, predictability, consistency, and cautious decision making. They are important in predicting trust in institutions such as the High Court and the Reserve Bank, which base their reputations on meeting high performance standards and on procedural correctness, consistency, and predictability. Exchange trust norms are endorsed most strongly as the basis for assessing trustworthiness by those who are strong supporters of security values at both a social and a personal level. Such people endorse competitive values, aspiring to positions of status at a national and a personal level. They believe in the rule of law, and they endorse traditional standards of behavior such as being polite, reliable, prompt, and neat.

Communal trust norms exist comfortably alongside exchange trust norms as a basis for judging trustworthiness. They are influential, however, in different institutional settings. Communal trust norms, with their emphasis on communicating with others, understanding and responding to the needs of others, and treating others with respect are important in predicting trust in the Family Court and charities, institutions that are designed to be flexible and adaptable to meet the demands of the people they serve. In terms of the individual difference dimension, communal trust norms are more likely to be used by those who are harmony-oriented, believing in such values as equality, rule by the people, wisdom, the pursuit of knowledge, tolerance, and helpfulness.

Any supposed cleavage between harmony- and security-oriented individuals and institutions was disrupted by the findings associated with the High Court, which was postulated as an institution that pursued security values and relied predominantly on exchange norms. Trust in the High Court, however, was related to neither value orientation but to both sets of trust norms. Thus, even institutions that are structured such that they are distant from the people and not directly accountable to them can engender perceptions of adherence to communal trust norms. The High Court, through its decisions and the conduct of its judges, had given the message of a commitment to, an understanding of, and a concern for the well-being of ordinary Australians.

The last and most important finding from these data is that perceptions of adherence to trust norms influence trust regardless of the individual's basic value orientation. Trust can be cultivated, it seems, even by institutions whose agenda does not coincide with that of citizens.

This chapter presents data showing that both communal and exchange trust norms flourish in the community and are relevant to understanding trust in government. How important they are remains unclear from this study alone. The R^2 values are small, suggesting that other factors may shape institutional trust. On the other hand, the trust data are derived from single-item measures, and such items are notorious for large proportions of unexplained variation. These methodological issues will be resolved through further research. In the meantime, the findings signal some important principles for designing institutions that will deliver effective and popular governance in a democratic society.

Both exchange and communal trust norms are important in the community, and social problems are more likely to be created than solved by a failure to recognize the role each may play in any institutional context. To illustrate the risks, a recent government inquiry has focused considerable attention on the efficiency, financial accountability, and management of charitable organizations in Australia (Industry Commission 1995). This inquiry has been endeavoring to build a base for stronger exchange trust norms in this sector in anticipation of the increased involvement of charities in delivering welfare services. In itself, the goal is reasonable, but the wisdom of redesigning charitable institutions in this way needs to be assessed more broadly, given the findings presented in this chapter. In Australia, charities are dependent for their survival on community trust—the trust of clients who come to seek help and the trust of donors and volunteers who keep services going. The findings reported here show that trust in charities stems from compliance with communal norms. If the increased attention that is given to exchange trust norms undermines the capacity to operate under communal trust norms, the future of charitable institutions may be seriously threatened. They may be efficiently run and well-funded organizations, but they may lose the confidence of the constituencies that they were originally designed to serve and that have traditionally supported them. This story is illustrated later in this volume in Mark Peel's case studies of how disadvantaged communities have resisted or disengaged from government agencies because public officials are seen to operate on exchange trust norms that suit political masters and to fail to respect the communal trust norms that could earn them credibility in the eyes of the disadvantaged groups they are trying to serve.

The importance of looking at questions of institutional design from the perspective of both exchange and communal trust norms is the primary message to emerge from this research. Changing one set of norms without considering the effects on the other can destroy established bases of trust in society. This is not to suggest that exchange and communal trust norms function in a hydraulic relationship; they can flourish simultaneously and, as was evident in the case of the High Court, have an additive effect on levels of trust in institutions.

Clearly, the structures and functions of institutions can lend themselves to the implementation of one set of trust norms more readily than the other. Yet the findings in relation to the High Court demonstrate that structures that are distant, hierarchical, and closed from public scrutiny nevertheless are capable of adhering to trust norms that one might expect were possible only in open, flat, and consultative structures. How this state of affairs has actually come about in the case of the High Court of Australia is beyond the scope of this chapter, although one possibility might be that the historic Mabo decision, giving land rights to Aboriginal communities and reducing the security of land tenure for white interest groups, has played a significant role. At this point, the important finding is that trust in the High Court is not a function of the value congruence of individuals and their institution but rather of compliance with both types of trust norms. The political ramifications of this result provide an interesting basis for future work. Values represent goals, goals that traditionally separate those on the right from those on the left of the political spectrum (Braithwaite 1994). In cases where bipartisan support for an institution is sought, or in cases where neither the right nor the left can be satisfied, promotion of both exchange and communal trust norms may be useful for building trust.

In addition to finding that different trust norms are influential in different institutions, this study has shown that individuals vary in the degree to which they infer trust on the basis of seeing communal trust norms or exchange trust norms in action. Social actors who seek security, order, and stability prefer to rely on exchange trust norms, while those seeking cooperation and harmony prefer to rely on communal trust norms. This finding reinforces the case for the nurturance of both sets of trust norms in society wherever possible. A high-trust society would best be supported through encouraging the operation of both sets of trust norms. For one to prosper at the expense of the other is to deny one part of the polity the conditions of social life necessary for their engagement with society.

Finally, both exchange and communal trust norms have socially maladaptive faces, creating an institutional design challenge of maximizing the benefits of each while minimizing the risks. Trust based on exchange norms is inherently conservative in that it favors those whose reputations provide capital to trade for being a trust recipient. Exchange trust norms emphasize the importance of knowledge, of being able to predict future actions, of being sure the other will deliver on commitments, and of seeing consistency in the actions of the other. Without information of this kind, there can be little trust. As such, exchange trust works against newcomers or marginalized groups who have not had the opportunity to earn what Geoffrey Brennan and Philip Pettit refer to in this volume as the status that goes with being considered trustworthy. Exchange trust, therefore, might be expected to privilege past leaders who have done their job steadfastly and reliably but not necessarily with the imagination or energy to find new modes of adaptation to meet the challenges of the future. Exchange trust is likely to entrench power in the hands of elites until breaches of trust are discovered by citizens.

When citizens are not well served through trusting those with established track records, communal trust norms provide an avenue for adaptation. A chance can be taken with those who offer innovative ideas, promising an unconventional and untried approach to society's problems. Where little knowledge is available, trust can be placed on the belief that the other understands needs, has insight and commitment to the group, and will not act in a way that will hurt the group. The trust is based on shared identity without a knowledge of the specific actions that the other is likely to take in particular circumstances. Trust based on communal norms can be a gift enjoyed by anyone who captures the identity of the other. As such, communal trust can undermine elite power cliques who are in a position to protect their reputational capital against assaults by the less powerful. At the same time, communal trust offers no performance guarantees. The factors that lead to the establishment of a shared identity may have nothing to do with the personal qualities necessary for effective leadership. Electing a leader on the basis of shared identity may lead to surprises that seriously jeopardize the stability of government.

Exchange trust and communal trust are dynamic qualities in a well-functioning society, and both need to be strong to check the weaknesses of the other. Democracy is an institution that allows citizens to make judgments not only about political platforms but also about the trustworthiness of leaders and to signal the type of trust that they believe is necessary for good governance at any particular point in a nation's political history. At times, exchange and communal trust are closely tied to each other in leadership contests, but not always. Exchange trust depends on a track record. It follows that those holding office and seeking reelection, be they of the left or of the right, can be judged in terms of their compliance with exchange trust norms: Did they do what they promised? Have they been consistent and sound in their decision making? Have they avoided making mistakes? In contrast, those seeking election for the first time have less of a track record and therefore are less likely to have recourse to exchange trust as a means of establishing trustworthiness. In such situations, communal trust norms provide a useful vehicle for building support. One possible model of the workings of exchange and communal trust in the political sphere is that incumbents need to attend more to their adherence to exchange trust norms, while challengers need to be conscious of building communal trust. Winning elections depends on more than the attractiveness of political platforms (Dalton and Wattenberg 1993). Knowing the type of trust norms relevant in different situations as well as having the capacity to deliver on these expectations may be central dimensions in campaign planning.

Theoretically, this chapter strengthens the argument for a multidimensional conceptualization of trust relationships. Communal and exchange trust are seen to have their origins in different psychological processes, to be cultivated through different actions, and to have different consequences for the quality of democratic governance. Their importance varies across individuals and across institutional contexts, but at the same time they are interdependent. In adopting a pluralist perspective on trust, this chapter purposefully avoids entering a debate that pits self-interest and exchange-based theories against procedural fairness and identity-based theories. As proponents of each continue to vie for the theoretical crown of providing the most fundamental explanation of human cooperation, this chapter is intended to demonstrate that institutions of democratic governance may be sufficiently complex to accommodate both world views. Debate focused on fundamental processes of human cooperation may be well complemented by theory that delineates the sequencing and interdependencies of exchange and communal trust and that explains when and why citizens expect different norms to operate and when good governance depends on their operation.

Appendix

Table 3A.1   Sample Items from the Goal, Mode and Social Values Inventories

Security: societal
  National strength and order
    National greatness (being a united, strong, independent, and powerful nation)
    National economic development (greater economic progress and prosperity for the nation)
    The rule of law (punishing the guilty and protecting the innocent)
    National security (protection of the nation from enemies)

Security: personal
  Propriety in dress and manners
    Politeness (being well-mannered)
    Neatness (being tidy)
    Promptness (being on time)
    Reliability (being dependable)
  Social standing and getting ahead
    Economic prosperity (being financially well off)
    Authority (having power to influence others and control decisions)
    Ambition (being eager to do well)
    Competitiveness (always trying to do better than others)
  Competence and effectiveness
    Competence (being capable)
    Resourcefulness (being clever at finding ways to achieve a goal)
    Self-discipline (being self-controlled)
    Logicalness (being rational)

Harmony: societal
  International harmony and equality
    A good life for others (improving the welfare of all people in need)
    Rule by the people (involvement by all citizens in decisions that affect their community)
    International cooperation (having all nations working together to help each other)

Table 3A.1 *Continued*

Greater economic equality (lessening the gap between the rich and the poor)

Harmony: personal
  Personal growth and inner harmony
    The pursuit of knowledge (always trying to find out new things about the world we live in)
    Wisdom (having a mature understanding of life)
    Self-knowledge or self-insight (being more aware of what sort of person one is)
    Inner harmony (feeling free of conflict within oneself)
  A positive orientation to others
    Tolerance (accepting others even though they are different)
    Helpfulness (always ready to assist others)
    Generosity (sharing what one has with others)
    Forgiveness (willing to pardon others)

References

Abelson, Robert P. 1983. "Whatever Became of Consistency Theory?" *Personality and Social Psychology Bulletin* 9(1): 37–54.

Barber, B. 1983. *The Logic and Limits of Trust*. New Brunswick, N.J.: Rutgers University Press.

Blamey, Russell, and Valerie Braithwaite. 1997a. "The Validity of the Security-Harmony Social Values Model in the General Population." *Australian Journal of Psychology* 49(2): 71–77.

———. 1997b. "A Social Values Segmentation of the Potential Ecotourism Market." *Journal of Sustainable Tourism* 5(1): 29–45.

Braithwaite, Valerie. 1979. "Exploring Value Structure: An Empirical Investigation." Ph.D. diss., University of Queensland.

———. 1982. "The Structure of Social Values: Validation of Rokeach's Two Value Model." *British Journal of Social Psychology* 21: 203–11.

———. 1994. "Beyond Rokeach's Equality-Freedom Model: Two-Dimensional Values in a One-Dimensional World." *Journal of Social Issues* 50: 67–94.

———. 1997. "Harmony and Security Value Orientations in Political Evaluation." *Personality and Social Psychology Bulletin* 23(4): 401–14.

———. 1998. "The Value Balance Model of Political Evaluations." *British Journal of Psychology*. Forthcoming.

Braithwaite, Valerie, and Russell Blamey. Forthcoming. "Consensus and Meaning in Abstract Social Values." Submitted for publication.

Braithwaite, V. A., and H. G. Law. 1985. "Structure of Human Values: Testing the Adequacy of the Rokeach Value Survey." *Journal of Personality and Social Psychology* 49: 250–63.

Braithwaite, V. A., and W. A. Scott. 1991. "Values." In *Measures of Personality and Social Psychological Attitudes,* edited by J. P. Robinson, P. R. Shaver, and L. S. Wrightsman. San Diego: Academic Press.

Butler, J. 1991. "Toward Understanding and Measuring Conditions of Trust: Evolution of a Conditions of Trust Inventory." *Journal of Management* 17: 643–63.

Clark, M. S. 1984. "Record Keeping in Two Types of Relationships." *Journal of Personality and Social Psychology* 47: 549–57.

———. 1986. "Evidence for the Effectiveness of Manipulations of Communal and Exchange Relationships." *Personality and Social Psychology Bulletin* 12: 414–25.

Clark, M. S., and J. Mills. 1979. "Interpersonal Attraction in Exchange and Communal Relationships." *Journal of Personality and Social Psychology* 37: 12–24.

Clark, M. S., J. Mills, and M. C. Powell. 1986. "Keeping Track of Needs in Communal and Exchange Relationships." *Journal of Personality and Social Psychology* 51: 333–38.

Cummings, L. L., and Philip Bromiley. 1996. "The Organizational Trust Inventory (OTI): Development and Validation." In *Trust in Organizations: Frontiers of Theory and Research,* edited by Roderick M. Kramer and Tom R. Tyler. Thousand Oaks, Calif.: Sage.

Dalton, R. J., and M. P. Wattenberg. 1993. "The Not So Simple Act of Voting." In *Political Science: The State of the Discipline II,* edited by A. Finifter. Washington, D.C.: American Political Science Association.

Deaux, K., and L. S. Wrightsman. 1988. *Social Psychology.* Pacific Grove, Calif.: Brooks/Cole.

Deutsch, M. 1973. *The Resolution of Conflict.* New Haven, Conn.: Yale University Press.

Dryzek, John, and Valerie Braithwaite. 1997. "Inclusive Republicanism and Its Discontents: Insights from Values Analysis." Paper presented to the Social and Political Theory Seminar Series, Research School of Social Sciences, Australian National University (July 16, 1997).

Feather, N. 1972. "Value Similarity and School Adjustment." *Australian Journal of Psychology* 24: 193–208.

———. 1979. "Human Values and the Work Situation: Two Studies." *Australian Psychologist* 14: 131–41.

Fromm, E. 1949. *Man for Himself: An Enquiry into the Psychology of Ethics.* London: Routledge and Kegan Paul.

Heaven, P. C. L. 1990. "Economic Beliefs and Human Values: Further Evidence of the Two-Value Model?" *The Journal of Social Psychology* 130: 583–89.

———. 1991. "Voting Intention and the Two-Value Model: A Further Investigation." *Australian Journal of Psychology* 43: 75–77.

Hofstede, G. 1980. *Culture's Consequences: International Differences in Work-Related Values.* Beverly Hills, Calif.: Sage.

———. 1994. *Cultures and Organizations.* London: HarperCollins.

Industry Commission. 1995. *Charitable Organisations in Australia.* Report No. 45. Melbourne: Australian Government Publishing Service.

Inglehart, R. 1971. "The Silent Revolution in Europe: Intergenerational Change in Post-Industrial Societies." *American Political Science Review* 65: 991–1017.

———. 1977. *The Silent Revolution*. Princeton, N.J.: Princeton University Press.

Katz, I., and R. G. Hass. 1988. "Racial Ambivalence and American Value Conflict: Correlational and Priming Studies of Dual Cognitive Structures. *Journal of Personality and Social Psychology* 55: 893–905.

Kluckhohn, C. K. M. 1951. "Values and Value Orientations in the Theory of Action." In *Toward a General Theory of Action*, edited by T. Parsons and E. Shils. Cambridge: Harvard University Press.

Kramer, Roderick M. 1996. "Divergent Realities and Convergent Disappointments in the Hierarchic Relation: Trust and the Intuitive Auditor at Work." In *Trust in Organizations*. *See* Cummings and Bromiley 1996.

Lewicki, Roy J., and Barbara Benedict Bunker. 1996. "Developing and Maintaining Trust in Work Relationships." In *Trust in Organizations*. *See* Cummings and Bromiley 1996.

Lipset, S. M. 1963. *The First New Nation: The United States in Historical and Comparative Perspective*. New York: Basic Books.

Mishra, Aneil K. 1996. "Organizational Responses to Crisis: The Centrality of Trust." In *Trust in Organizations*. *See* Cummings and Bromiley 1996.

Pettit, Philip. 1995. "The Cunning of Trust." *Philosophy and Public Affairs* 24: 202–25.

Rasinski, K. A. 1987. "What's Fair Is Fair—Or Is It? Value Differences Underlying Public Views About Social Justice." *Journal of Personality and Social Psychology* 53: 201–11.

Rokeach, M. 1973. *The Nature of Human Values*. New York: Free Press.

Rose, R., and I. McAllister. 1986. *Voters Begin to Choose*. London: Sage.

Rotter, J. B. 1980. "Interpersonal Trust, Trustworthiness, and Gullibility." *American Psychologist* 35: 1–7.

Schwartz, S. H. 1992. "Universals in the Content and Structure of Values: Theoretical Advances and Empirical Tests in 20 Countries." *Advances in Experimental Social Psychology* 25: 1–65.

———. 1994. "Are There Universal Aspects in the Structure and Contents of Human Values?" *Journal of Social Issues* 50: 19–45.

Schwartz, S. H., and W. Bilsky. 1987. "Toward a Universal Psychological Structure of Human Values." *Journal of Personality and Social Psychology* 53: 550–62.

Scott, W. A. 1960. "International Ideology and Interpersonal Ideology." *Public Opinion Quarterly* 24: 419–35.

———. 1965. *Values and Organizations: A Study of Fraternities and Sororities*. Chicago: Rand McNally.

Shapiro, D., B. H. Sheppard, and L. Cheraskin. 1992. "Business on a Handshake." *Negotiation Journal* 8: 365–77.

Sheppard, Blair H., and Marla Tuchinsky. 1996. "Micro-OB and the Network Organization." In *Trust in Organizations*. *See* Cummings and Bromiley 1996.

Sitkin, S. B., and N. L. Roth. 1993. "Explaining the Limited Effectiveness of Legalistic 'Remedies' for Trust/distrust." *Organization Science* 4: 367–92.

Sorokin, P.A. 1962. *Social and Cultural Dynamics*, vol. 1. New York: Bedminster Press.

Stack, L. C. 1978. "Trust." In *Dimensions of Personality*, edited by H. London and J. E. Exner, Jr. New York: Wiley.

Thannhauser, D., and D. Caird. 1990. "Politics and Values in Australia: Testing Rokeach's Two-Value Model of Politics—A Research Note." *Australian Journal of Psychology* 42: 57–61.

Turner, John C. 1987. *Rediscovering the Social Group: A Self-Categorization Theory*. Oxford: Basil Blackwell.

Tyler, Tom R., and Peter Degoey. 1996. "Trust in Organizational Authorities: The Influence of Motive Attributions on Willingness to Accept Decisions." In *Trust in Organizations. See* Cummings and Bromiley 1996.

Tyler, Tom, Peter Degoey, and Heather Smith. 1996. "Understanding Why the Justice of Group Procedures Matters: A Test of the Psychological Dynamics of the Group-Value Model." *Journal of Personality and Social Psychology* 20: 913–29.

Weber, M. 1946. "Politics as a Vocation." In *From Max Weber: Essays in Sociology*, edited by H. H. Gerth and C. Wright Mills. New York: Oxford University Press.

Williams, R. M. 1968. "Values." In *International Encyclopedia of the Social Sciences*, edited by E. Sills. New York: Macmillan.

Williamson, Gail M., and Margaret S. Clark. 1989. "The Communal/Exchange Distinction and Some Implications for Understanding Justice in Families." *Social Justice Research* 3: 77–103.

Williamson, O. E. 1993. "Calculativeness, Trust, and Economic Organization." *Journal of Law and Economics* 34: 453–500.

PART II

WHAT DIFFERENCE DOES A TRUSTWORTHY STATE MAKE?

Chapter 4

A State of Trust

MARGARET LEVI

T HE TOPIC of trust has recently inspired a host of books and conferences. This is in part because of recent events. The overturning of the communist regimes in Eastern Europe and the emergence of democratization movements in other parts of the world raise questions about how to institute trust in an unaccustomed state and government. The creation of new institutions to manage the European Union seems also to depend on the development of trust, this time among both member states and their citizens. The intensity of ethnic and religious conflicts generates concern about what fuels and maintains distrust. The relative success of the Japanese economy and of Korean immigrants to the United States suggests the importance of small-group trust in generating productive and efficient economic organization.

Of equal importance in explaining the focus on trust is the need for some such concept in social science research dedicated to the explanation or design of institutions. Many economists and political economists who spent most of the 1980s working on models aimed at "getting the incentives right" are now recognizing that they need something more than incentives if they are to have better models of internal relationships within the firm (see, for example, Kreps 1990; Miller 1992; Williamson 1993), of organizations more generally (Kramer and Tyler 1996); of collective action and cooperation (see, for example, Gambetta 1988; North 1990; Orbell and Dawes 1991, 1993), of negotiation of government policies (Scharpf 1994), or of compliance with government regulations (see, for example, Ayres and Braithwaite 1992; Levi 1988, 1997). Further contributing to this preoccupation with trust is the attractiveness of the idea of social capital, a concept popularized by Robert Putnam (1993) but drawing on the work of the economist Glen Loury and the sociologist James Coleman, as a means to produce better polities and economies.

Trust is, in fact, a holding word for a variety of phenomena that enable individuals to take risks in dealing with others, solve collective action problems, or act in ways that seem contrary to standard definitions of self-interest. What it is, what work it does in improving governance, and what accounts for its variation, however, are only beginning to be the subjects of serious theoretical and empirical investigations. Thus, the first part of this chapter attempts to clarify the concept and clear away some of the theoretical and empirical misconceptions. The following sections evaluate the literature on how the state affects interpersonal trust. The final parts explore the relationship between trust—among citizens and of government—and effective governance. The emphasis in these last sections is on citizen compliance with and consent to governmental demands and draws heavily on my own recent research (Levi 1997) and work done under the aegis of the Program in Administration, Compliance and Governability.[1]

What Is Trust?

Trust has three parts: A trusts B to do X. The act of trust is the knowledge or belief that the trusted will have an incentive to do what she engages to do. As Hardin (1993, this volume) has argued, trust is a form of encapsulated interest. A trusts B because he presumes it is in B's interest to act in a way consistent with A's interest. Further, trust is relational. The initial grant of trust depends on one person's evaluation that another will be trustworthy. Its maintenance requires confirmation of that trustworthiness, or else trust will be withdrawn. Trust by this definition is not equivalent to cooperation, a common conflation, although it may facilitate cooperation..

Behaviorally, the more trusting an individual is the lower the personal investment she will make in learning about the trustworthiness of the trusted and in monitoring and enforcing his compliance in a cooperative venture. Notice that each clause is important here. The investigation is of trusting behavior, not its outcome. In other words, someone can trust mistakenly. The measurement is of personal investment in monitoring and enforcement and not of the cost of institutional arrangements that lower that investment. At issue is a cooperative venture, which implies that the truster possesses a reasonable belief that well-placed trust will yield positive returns and is willing to act upon that belief. Thus, the observer can tell if an individual is trusting by noting whether a transaction took place,[2] determining what kind of transaction it was, and measuring the truster's investment in learning about potential partners in cooperation and in monitoring them and enforcing their behavior once the bargain has been struck. The absence of a transaction indicates the absence of trust. A transaction that depends on the institutionalization of assurances and commitments reflects less trust than one that requires only a handshake. The higher the investment in information gathering, monitoring, and so on, the less trust.

Trust implies a risk to the truster. In some instances the risk may be so low that we tend to use the label *confidence* instead of *trust*. In other instances the risk is so high that we consider the truster gullible. In certain cases, the risk is worth the payoff; this seems to be the estimate of the Persian rug salesperson who offers to let someone take a valuable rug home, often to another state or country, and try it out before paying a cent. In other cases, the possible risk is so considerable that no trust is given. The overguarding of children by their parents is an example.

The actual extent of risk and the extent to which the truster is taking a "sensible" risk are variables. They are always partially and often largely functions of the trustworthiness not only of the trustee but also of those on whom the truster relies for information and for punishments against a trust-breaker. Sometimes this actor is the truster himself; this is the case when he relies on his own assessments of character. More often, there is a third party who either has vetted the trustee, will sanction the trustee if necessary, or both. Trust is, therefore, a relational and rational, although not always fully calculated, action. In many if not most cases, it depends upon confidence in institutions that back up the trustee.

Trust is not one thing and does not have one source; it has a variety of forms and causes. Although a reasonable belief that the trustee will act consistently with the truster's interests depends on knowledge of the trustee, this can be, but need not be, detailed personal knowledge. Arrangements that both lower personal investment and reinforce reasonable beliefs are diverse, ranging from an individual's capacity to make sound character assessments to his embeddedness in thick networks of interaction that make knowledge of others easy to acquire and to reliance on institutions that do the work of information-gathering and monitoring.

All such arrangements have in common their capacity to solve information problems and provide credible assurances that the trustee will follow through on her obligation. The major distinction between them is the extent to which they rely on individual assessments or personal relationships rather than impersonal but institutionalized interactions. No other obvious factors distinguish them, however. Computer technology may offer a more detailed account of an individual's history of promise-keeping than does living next door or being her cousin, but sometimes it does not. For example, someone who always pays her bills on time will find herself in the perverse situation of having difficulty getting a bank loan because of her lack of credit history. In this case, personal knowledge may be a better source of information.[3] The relative costs of bringing punitive measures to bear if need be may be extremely high in a close-knit community where the truster may feel ashamed of his bad judgment or where he must bring evidence to bear against a popular and important member of the group. It is also extremely costly, in time, money, and reputation, for a citizen to bring or defend a harassment suit, despite (and sometimes because of) all the protections and procedures under law. Many communities have elders, pastors, and other influential community members to bring pressure to bear on trust-breakers, and a phone call to the police or one's attorney—and often only the threat—can be a relatively low-cost way to enforce an agreement.

This discussion begins to clarify another significant analytical distinction: between trust and trustworthiness. Only persons can trust or be trusting, but trustworthiness can attach to either individuals or institutions. In everyday language and in the contemporary media, there are innumerable expressions of concern about the loss of trust in institutions generally and in government specifically. These concerns make sense if what is meant is a decline in the trustworthiness of these institutions and governments. Institutional trustworthiness implies procedures for selecting and constraining the agents of institutions so that they are competent, credible, and likely to act in the interests of those being asked to trust the institution. Thus, it is not actually the institution or government that is being trusted or is acting in a trustworthy manner. Rather, when citizens and clients say they trust an institution, they are declaring a belief that, on average, its agents will prove to be trustworthy. In this chapter, the terminology of trusting the state or another institution carries this meaning.[4]

Trust has a multiplicity of forms as well as a multiplicity of mechanisms that evoke and secure it. Trust can result from closely knit networks of individuals who are dependent on each other and engage in iterated interactions that promote loyalty even when alternative options may appear preferable; this is what Karen S. Cook and Richard M. Emerson (1978) have termed *commitment*.[5] Despite the insistence of Cook and Toshio Yamagishi (forthcoming) that trust and commitment are different mechanisms for resolving uncertainty, commitment is one of the means to create trust.[6] It produces what Toshio Yamagishi and Midori Yamagishi (1994) have labeled *assurance* and what Fukuyama (1995) seemed to mean by *familial trust*. *Generalized trust* (for which Cook and Yamagishi reserved the label *trust*) may result from a web of associational memberships, as Robert Putnam (1993) argued,[7] or it may depend on institutional arrangements that increase confidence in contracting. Sources of generalized trust may be morality, habit, or encapsulated interest.

This approach has several implications. First, trust is neither normatively good nor bad; it is neither a virtue nor a vice.[8] Ordinary usage treats trust as a virtue (as do several authors in this volume), but on close inspection it is not at all apparent why this should be the case. The act of trusting may have consequences productive for the individual or not, and beneficial to her society or not. Equivalently, distrust lacks normative connotations. In fact, active distrust, as opposed to trust or simple lack of trust, may be the normatively appropriate response, depending on the situation. When some fundamental interests are divergent—as between workers and management or between competing ethnic, religious, or racial groups—or when citizens are concerned about protecting themselves from incursions of state power or from intolerant majorities, there is good reason for the parties to be wary of each other. For example, recent republican arguments about the importance for democracy of a participatory and vigilant citizenry rest on distrust as the normatively correct stance (see, for example, Braithwaite and Pettit 1990). In other cases, distrust may obstruct coordination necessary for ethnic cleansing or some other such offense (Hardin 1995, this volume). Indeed, distrust may even be the basis for efficient organization. Gambetta's (1993) masterful account of the Mafia demonstrated the role of distrust in creating and maintaining a powerful and effective economic organization. The U.S. Constitution produced a lasting government organized around distrust of both factions and centralized power.

Second, trust—at least interpersonal trust—may be "a fragile commodity" (Dasgupta 1988, 50),[9] hard to construct and easy to destroy. Consequently, individuals may invest a great deal in establishing the relationships or institutions that create and maintain the possibility for trust. For example, managers and constitution-makers put large amounts of time and energy into designing institutions that promote trust, and some people take considerable care in choosing marriage partners or invest quite a lot in their marriages. The effect of these investments, intentional or not, is the establishment of trust when there is a real risk of betrayal involved.

How the State Affects Interpersonal Trust

A commonly accepted conclusion of the anthropological and theoretical literature is that centralized states destroy the social cohesion of traditional communities, undermine cooperation, and destroy trust among individuals (Gellner 1988; Taylor 1982). There is little real question about the first, considerable question about the second (from Hobbes on), and, until recently, no serious consideration of the third. It must certainly be the case that government agencies, depending on their nature and their personnel, are at times among the major forces for destroying interpersonal trust, either directly or by means of destruction of other institutions that support trust. Yet government is sometimes crucial in establishing levels of trust among citizens that make possible a whole range of social, political, and economic transactions that would otherwise not be possible. Critical to this task is its use of coercion, rightly understood and used. Moreover, there is some reason to believe that democratic institutions may be even better at producing generalized trust than are nondemocratic institutions—in part because they are better at restricting the use of coercion to tasks that enhance rather than undermine trust.

States potentially influence the construction, maintenance, and destruction of two kinds of interpersonal trust: communal and familial trust and generalized trust within a society. Both of these kinds of interpersonal trust facilitate cooperation (which sometimes appears to be spontaneous cooperation), while destruction of such trust can, at its limit, lead to anomie.

Communal and Familial Trust

Two lines of argument paint the growth of the state as a major cause of the decline in communal and familial trust. The first is anti-Hobbesian, and the second is anti-Marxist. Often the two combine, as in certain strains of libertarian communitarianism. The very development of a state may have negative effects for trust, initiative, incentives, community, and so on, or such negative effects may result from massive governmental intervention in people's lives. The extent to which the state actually has these effects, particularly on the construction of trust, remains an empirical question and one that is far from resolved. While Michael Taylor (1982) argued that the centralized state drives out spontaneous coordination that depends on small groups and thick networks of interaction, Francis Fukuyama (1995, 62–3 and *passim*) has claimed there is a correlation between precisely these kinds of organizations and a large state.

Moreover, normative communitarians tend to neglect the destructive distrust that can exist within families, villages, and small towns. Feuds within families and feuds among families suggest that intimate knowledge does not always produce either trust or cooperation and in fact can produce just the opposite. Edward Banfield's (1958) concept of "amoral familism," whether or not descriptive of the actual village he studied, remains a powerful indictment of societies in which trust extends only to insiders and distrust reigns outside.

In such cases, a government that reduces personal dependencies and resolves conflicts may actually enhance familial trust. By increasing social rights, the state plays an important role in eliminating risky personal reliance on another. For example, government-provided welfare or health care reduces the range of services that the needy must otherwise trust—or coerce—their families or community to provide.

Generalized Trust

James S. Coleman (1990), Robert Putnam (1993), and most recently Francis Fukuyama (1995) have conceptualized trust as one component of social capital, that is, "features of social organization, such as trust, norms, and networks, that can improve the efficiency of society by facilitating coordinated action" (Putnam 1993, 167). They have argued that a society with considerable social capital in the form of intermediary groups is more likely to produce the large-scale organization that is often correlated with development and the vibrant civic life associated with political democracy than a society with hierarchical, familial, or no social capital. Putnam (1993) has made the case that the alternative is a vicious cycle of distrust, with negative consequences of economic backwardness and ineffective government. His arguments are consistent with those of the historian Anthony Pagden (1988) and the political philosopher Russell Hardin (1993), who has shown how distrust breeds distrust with negative consequences for those who distrust.

There is relatively little attention in the recent literatures on either "social capital" or the firm, however, concerning the role of the state in influencing generalized trust. Coleman (1990) has emphasized the family, Putnam (1993) intermediate associations, Miller (1992) leadership, and Kreps (1990) a corporate principle. Only Fukuyama (1995) seems to take the state seriously in his analysis, for it is one source of social capital for him. Much of his argument is consistent with a tradition in political philosophy as well as more recent research, particularly in economic history, that affirms an important role for government institutions in lowering the personal investments and providing the assurances that make possible the trust that lubricates cooperation.

The absence of an effective state can lead to the Hobbesian world of the "war of all against all"–although, of course, there are other means to avoid such catastrophes than reliance on a centralized, coercive power. Nor does a centralized state necessarily ensure against the descent into violence; the U.S. Civil War is a case in point. None-theless, states often reduce the need for citizens to trust each other, or they may facilitate trust by solving the essential information, monitoring, and enforcement problems, or both. One of the major arguments in the work of the economic historian Douglass North (1981, 1990) has to do with the role of the state as enforcer of contracts. Efficient markets, in the Northian account, depend on state actions; with state enforcement of contracts, sellers and buyers have more reason to trust each other.

States enforce rights and rules other than those associated with economic and real property contracts. By protecting minority rights, states facilitate cooperation among individuals who have reason to be wary of each other. By legalizing trade unions or enforcing child labor laws, states reduce the costs to workers of monitoring and bringing sanctions against employers—and thus may increase the likelihood of trust.

On the other hand, the substitution of state institutions for other social arrangements for reducing personal investments carries an-other set of costs. John Wallis and Douglass North (1986) illustrated how transaction costs have actually risen over time in the United States and expected that they would find the same result in other advanced industrial economies. They conjectured that a decline in trust between workers and management is one cause of the rising transaction costs that are reducing labor productivity. There is also independent evidence that social distrust is increasing (Putnam 1995; Yamagishi and Yamagishi 1994).

Coleman (1990, 180–96) has elaborated other possible mechanisms for transferring trust and ensuring that it is widespread throughout a society: reliance on third parties. If a friend tells you to trust a friend of hers whom you have never met, you are likely to do so. If trust-worthy agents of government vet an individual or institution as trust-worthy, your trust is facilitated. The obverse is obviously also the case. Because of your confidence in your friend or the government agents, you rely on their information about the other party. Should the information prove false, you are likely to reevaluate the trust-worthiness of the initial party.

When government agents play these roles, they may facilitate the transference of trust from one domain to another. For example, citizens who trust the government or a major agent as a protector of legal rights may also trust the government as a fair conscripter for the military. This mechanism seems to lay at the heart of Albert Hirsch-man's (1984) claim that use of trust increases trust, and its nonuse diminishes it. It is certainly at the heart of Putnam's (1993, 1995) claims that those who learn to trust individuals in their soccer clubs, bird-watching societies, or bowling leagues may find themselves more willing to trust strangers. The logic behind this claim is that individuals learn that cooperation pays and thus choose to cooperate in other spheres in which they have little information—at least until proved wrong. Finding themselves in an iterated prisoner's dilemma, they refer to past experience and choose the "nice" strategy. There are, of course, other possible explanations, such as shared beliefs and social bonds (V. Braithwaite this volume; Dawes, Van de Kragt, and Orbell 1990; Tyler this volume) or satsificing with heuristics (Orbell and Dawes 1991, 1993; Pinney and Scholz 1995; Scholz 1994).

There seems to be as much evidence for the nontransference as for the transference of trust, however. Kent Jennings (this volume), for example, has found that Americans trust local government more than state government and state government more than federal government. Citizens in the Anglo-Saxon democracies, at least at the start of World War I, seemed to trust their governments to enforce property rights but were not so willing to trust them with the power to conscript (Levi 1997). A citizen may reasonably trust a government taxing authority to be honest and fair but not trust the tax policy–making of government actors; one can trust one's neighbors but not one's state, or vice versa; one can trust banks to safeguard one's money but not oil companies to safeguard one's environment.

How the State Creates Interpersonal Trust

If, as seems to be the case, states influence levels of socially productive interpersonal trust within a society, the next step is to investigate the characteristics of a state capable of producing such trust. The most important attributes would seem to be the capacity to monitor laws, bring sanctions against lawbreakers, and provide information and guarantees about those seeking to be trusted.

The first requirement is the ability to observe the behavior of those subject to the laws and regulations of the government. Small countries, whose inhabitants are well integrated in the community, will have such an ability, but almost no states small enough for such integration have survived into the modern world. The more likely basis for monitoring and information gathering is a well-developed infrastructure, but bureaucracies, policing, punishing, and information dissemination call for additional resources to cover their costs. This is not the place to rehearse the vast literature on the presuppositions for or variations in state capability to develop the necessary apparatus and resources; suffice it to say that monitoring, enforcing, and informing capacities can be greater or lesser and can take a wide variety of forms.

Infrastructure and resources are necessary but not sufficient conditions. If citizens doubt the state's commitment to enforce the laws and if its information and guarantees are not credible, then the state's capacity to generate interpersonal trust will diminish. If the state is one of the institutions—and, in many cases, the most important institution—for promoting generalized trust, it can play this role only if the recipients of these services consider the state itself to be trustworthy. Subjects and citizens must trust the competence of the state to perform its trust-producing roles.

Personal Trust of Political Leaders

Political entrepreneurs can affect the capacity of a group to trust government. By reminding citizens of past broken promises by government, opposition leaders can feed distrust. On the other hand, government leaders who wish to maintain or regain the trust of the people can sometimes do so—even, it seems, when they have failed to deliver on their policy promises (see Stokes 1998). Doing so usually requires making themselves personally and politically vulnerable; historically, this often meant quite literally leading battles. In modern times, trustworthy leadership is an effect of charisma, the demonstration of effectiveness, and the willingness to take an ethical stance in spite of determined and vocal opposition and potential costs. Examples of this last include Dwight Eisenhower's willingness to send federal troops to Arkansas and Mackenzie King's willingness to reconsider his promise not to impose conscription by running a plebiscite asking the public to release him from his earlier pledge.

Government actors are like other actors in that the major means for establishing their trustworthiness are proven character, demonstrated consistency of trustworthiness, and encapsulated interest. The first requires a presentation of self that includes a demonstrated willingness to act for principle and against self-interest. Consistency is an inductive measurement of trustworthiness, based on the track record of the actor. Both of these bases of trustworthiness are problematic, however. They can be indicators of a sophisticated opportunism, or the strategies of con men who forgo short-term interest in order to win a trust they then betray. Politicians and bureaucrats have certainly been known to play such a game.

Credible Commitments

Another basis of trustworthiness is the encapsulated interest of the government actor to honor her agreements or to act according to a certain standard. Credible commitments and self-enforcing institutions significantly reduce the citizen's need to make a personal investment in monitoring and enforcing government and thus enhance citizen trust of government. Credible commitments, reputational effects, and other such self-enforcement mechanisms that encapsulate interest, however, require institutional arrangements that will produce the feared sanctions if need be. Thus, trustworthy government actors are generally those who are embedded in trustworthy institutions. These institutions can take the form of the rules and norms of professional societies, the grievance procedures available to their clients and subordinates, or legal proceedings.

The existence of such institutions does not in itself ensure the trust of citizens in government actors.[10] The literature on credible commitments explicates and illustrates the origins and maintenance of institutional arrangements that effectively punish short-term opportunistic behavior by rulers and thereby promote the public welfare and, often, the rulers' long-term interests (see, for example, Greif, Milgrom, and Weingast 1990; North and Weingast 1989). Punishment is a step toward gaining trust, but not yet enough. To earn the trust of the citizens, government actors place themselves in institutional arrangements that structure their incentives so as to make their best options those in which their individual benefits depend on the provision of the collective benefit.

A concrete example of how government institutions build trust is the creation of bureaucratic arrangements that reward competence and relative honesty by bureaucratic agents (Levi and Sherman 1997). A competent and relatively honest bureaucracy not only reduces the incentives for corruption and inefficient rent-seeking but also increases the probability of cooperation and compliance, on the one hand, and of economic growth, on the other. To the extent that citizens and groups recognize that bureaucrats gain reputational benefits from competence and honesty, those regulated will expect bureaucrats to be trustworthy and will act accordingly. To the extent that bureaucracies can arrange long-term benefits for compliance by those regulated (in the form of reputation that is fungible or side payments in the form of less intervention), the regulated are more likely to cooperate. Together these factors may create a sense of obligation to cooperate, a belief in the trustworthiness and public-spiritedness of both the bureaucrats and the regulated, and thus a greater potential for wealth-producing contracting. The development of a bureaucracy is one of the factors that made politically possible the imposition of the initial income tax in 1799 in England (Levi 1988, 122–44).

How Trust Affects Governance Through Contingent Consent

The trustworthiness of the state influences its capacity to generate interpersonal trust, and the amount of socially and economically productive cooperation in the society in turn affects the state's capacity to govern. Trust of the state has additional consequences for governance:

It affects both the level of citizens' tolerance of the regime and their degree of compliance with governmental demands and regulations. Destruction of trust may lead to widespread antagonism to government policy and even active resistance, and it may be one source of increased social distrust. Legitimate (and "virtuous") government may depend on leaders' keeping faith with the citizens who have given them authority to act on the public's behalf (see, for example, Dunn 1988 and Pagden 1988). Failures of government representatives to uphold policy compacts, to achieve stated ends, or to treat potentially trustworthy citizens as trustworthy can have disastrous effects on the extent to which citizens trust government and trust each other.

The major sources of distrust in government are promise breaking, incompetence, and the antagonism of government actors toward those they are supposed to serve. Citizens are likely to trust government only to the extent that they believe that it will act in their interests, that its procedures are fair, and that their trust of the state and of others is reciprocated. These are the conditions of *contingent consent,* behavioral compliance with government demands even when an individual's costs somewhat exceed her individual benefits and even in the absence of strong ideological convictions that make costs totally irrelevant. Contingent consent is a citizen's decision to comply or volunteer in response to demands from a government only if she perceives government as trustworthy and she is satisfied that other citizens are also engaging in ethical reciprocity (see figure 4.1).

A trustworthy government is one that has procedures for making and implementing policy that meet prevailing standards of fairness, and it is a government that is capable of credible commitments. In both contingent consent and contingent refusal to consent, the assessment of the actual policy can make a difference. In most cases, however, citizens are willing to go along with a policy they do not prefer as long as it made according to a process they deem legitimate, and they are less willing to comply with a policy they like if the process was problematic.[11] As figure 4.1 indicates, institutions that make commitments credible (as discussed in the last section), ensure fair procedures, and improve mutual trust between government and citizen meet the requirements of contingent consent.

A trustworthy government is a necessary but insufficient condition for large-scale contingent consent. Although the perception of a trustworthy government might explain the choices of some individuals, its effects will be significantly enhanced by the additional presence of ethical reciprocity. If most other citizens are nonreciprocal, even though government appears trustworthy, then the possibility of contingent consent is remote. Ethical reciprocity refers to the norm of contributing one's fair share as long as others are also doing their

Figure 4.1   Model of Contingent Consent

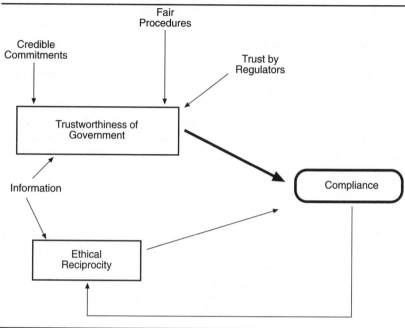

part. Contingent consenters are strategic but ethical actors; they want to cooperate if others are also cooperating. They have a prior commitment to an ethical position of fair play combined with a perception of the extent to which others who presumably share that position are cooperating with each other or free riding. Thus, ethical reciprocity is distinct from both normal reciprocity, a matter only of tit-for-tat, and social pressure, a question of selective incentives.

An assessment of costs and benefits also influences the decision to comply, but they are not the only consideration of contingent consenters. Even when short-term material self-interest would make free riding the individually best option, the contingently consenting citizen still prefers to cooperate.[12] If the costs of compliance become too high, however, then a cost-benefit calculation will probably trump other considerations. Contingent consent is reducible to neither material self-interest nor normative and moral considerations. Contingent consenters fit Laura Stoker's (1992) account of "citizens as ethical actors" with "each citizen as an individual with her own unique hopes and desires who is at the same time joined with others, part of and continually giving shape to a common social and political life" (p. 376). Given a set of ethical standards about what makes a government just and what is involved in being fair, contingent consenters are those individuals who want to act ethically, who would like to contribute to the collective good, all things being equal, but who will do so only under certain contingencies.

Contingent refusal to consent is abstention from or withdrawal of behavioral consent upon violation of either government trustworthiness or ethical reciprocity, but in this chapter the emphasis will be on government trustworthiness. Evidence of discriminatory government practices, violations of policy promises, or government distrust of citizens are likely to provoke this form of citizen noncompliance. So will indications of considerable citizen free riding that government could be but is not controlling.

Fair Procedures

Institutions make actors relatively predictable, but not necessarily fair or concerned with promoting the interests of others. Individuals need to have evidence that government is relatively fair and not just credible if they are to have confidence that the state will harmonize the interests of otherwise competitive parties. The belief in government fairness requires the perception that all relevant interests have been considered, that the game is not rigged.[13] Young men who volunteer to go to war or submit willingly to conscription generally trust government's claims that the war is justified, their service necessary, and the military apparatus relatively efficient (Levi 1997). Both historically and contemporarily, citizens who quasi-voluntarily pay taxes credit government with generally doing the right thing with their monies (Levi 1988; Scholz 1994). On the other hand, those asked to comply with affirmative action regulations often doubt the goodwill of government and consider its goals as different from their own (V. Braithwaite 1995); consequently, they cannot be trusted to comply.

There are at least four important and quite different ways in which a state signals its fairness: coercion of those who are not compliant, universalistic policies, establishment of credible courts and other impartial institutions for arbitrating disputes and ensuring that those who lose can sometimes win, and the involvement of the citizens in the actual making of policy. Some of these are potentially in the toolbag of any kind of government; others are clearly democratic devices.

Coercion   One of the major findings in both of my investigations of revenue and conscription systems over time and across place (Levi 1988; 1997) is that citizens are more likely to trust a government that ensures that others do their part. Those who choose not to be free riders are eager not to become suckers. Thus, the willingness to pay taxes quasi-voluntarily or to give one's contingent consent to conscription often rests on the existence of the state's capacity and demonstrated readiness to secure the compliance of the otherwise noncompliant.

Universalism   A second signal is the reliance of government on universalistic criteria in recruitment and promotion of its agents and in regulating the institutions of both government and civil society. In an earlier section I discussed the advantages of a relatively honest and competent bureaucracy, but the selection of its personnel on the basis of merit is yet another indicator of its relative impartiality, as Weber (1968) clearly recognized. The privatization of social services and the consequent nonuniversalism and nonstandardization in provision (Smith and Lipsky 1993) is likely to increase distrust in government as an institution that enforces impartiality.

Impartial Institutions   As Barry (1995) argues, as Tyler (1990) documents by investigating the responses of citizens to legal proceedings, and as Frohlich and Oppenheimer (1992) demonstrate with experimental evidence, those who believe the process was fair and just are much more likely to accept individually unfavorable outcomes.

Recurring, competitive elections in which the outcome is never an absolute certainty are another signal that the state does not rig the game (Przeworski 1991). Citizens feel that they may lose on some issues but win on others and that they will always get the chance to try again on those questions about which they feel strongly—and with some probability of success. The effect is trust in the institution combined with the continuing rehearsal of the same issues over and over. Thus, in the United States, abortion, states' rights, and many other questions keep coming up again and again. This, I suggest, is a sign of strong institutions in which the population has a deep trust.

On the other hand, apparently impartial electoral institutions, such as majority rule, are not a sufficient condition of trust in government. The fear of the tyranny of the majority is a recurring theme, and protection of minority interests through means of a unanimity rule or even a veto are among the solutions. There is the danger, however, that institutions meant to protect minorities are perceived by majorities as discriminatory against the majority.

Instructive is the consideration of cases where trust has broken down or is extremely fragile. This was the situation confronted by James Madison when he introduced mechanisms into the U.S. Constitution to limit majority rule and permit minorities to obstruct legislation that would harm their interests. The balance rule in the pre–Civil

War era is a later example.[14] By ensuring that for each non-slave state permitted into the Union there would be a slave state, the government ensured that the slave issue would not become the primary one in Congress. When the balance rule broke down, so did the Union. Although the absence of such institutions does not always lead to a major conflagration, it can perpetuate distrust of the central state. For example, the Quebecois know they will always lose on any issue in which there is a francophone-anglophone divide; they will always be outvoted and have no veto to prevent the imposition of a policy they strongly resent. Thus, it is not surprising that the Quebecois tend to distrust not only the Canadian federal government but also anglophone Canadians who persist in imposing such policies. The Canadian conscription crises during both world wars reflected exactly this kind of distrust of government (Levi 1997).

What these findings suggest is that impartial institutions that include some means to protect minority interests without unduly offending majority concepts of fairness are a necessary but not sufficient condition for the perception of fairness.[15] There must also be some trust built up among conflicting groups. Whether such interpersonal trust is prior or whether it is a consequence of the institutional arrangements is an empirical question still to be explored.

Participation   A state can further enhance its reputation of fairness by involving citizens in the policy-making process itself, so that they become aware of what is at issue and are included in the give and take that leads to compromise. There is, of course, always the danger that they will come to distrust government, particularly if government proves itself untrustworthy. A situation in which trust in government was recreated is instructive. In Australia in the 1970s, evidence of considerable tax evasion undermined tax compliance and evoked tax revolts. To reconstruct contingent consent with the tax system, Prime Minister Robert Hawke held what amounted to a mini-constitutional convention to renegotiate the government-citizen tax policy (Levi 1988, 158–72).

Once trust has been destroyed, its rebuilding may require extraordinary efforts—often even greater than that described in the Australian tax case. The francophones in Canada, the Irish in Britain, the blacks in the United States, the Aborigines in Australia, and many others who have experienced discrimination (or worse) require compensatory programs and iron-clad commitments to assure them that—this time—policy promises will be upheld. The effects may be counterproductive, however. Affirmative action programs and special dispensations may inflame those who do not receive the benefits and who consequently believe government is acting unfairly toward them.

Reciprocating Citizen Trust

Reciprocity is the last of the factors that enhance government trustworthiness. Citizens are likely to perceive government as reciprocating their trust when they can articulate a return for their compliance and, when they feel they are being treated with respect. When government has a good track record of delivering on its promises, especially those for which its commitments are not credible, citizens are more likely to trust the government and respond with trustworthiness—even in situations where it is extremely difficult to monitor them. Richard Weatherley (1991) has offered a very interesting account of beneficiaries of unemployment insurance who reported earned income over $100 because they felt that they should honor their part of their contract with a government that had acted in a trustworthy fashion to them. Not all citizens have such confidence in their governments, however. The experience of the francophones with broken promises by the Canadian federal government leads them to resist a large range of federal policy initiatives.

Perception that a government is untrustworthy is a function not only of its failure to fulfill promises but also of evidence that government agents distrust those from whom they are demanding cooperation and compliance. The hostility of street-level bureaucrats toward clients (Lipsky 1980) and of regulators toward the regulated (Ayres and Braithwaite 1992) can be extremely counterproductive. Mark Peel's account of the Australian community of Elizabeth (1995) offers a striking case of how a neighborhood that is badly treated by government comes to resent and distrust all agents of government. There is considerable evidence that reliance on sanctions tends to breed the opposite of the result intended; instead of deference and compliance, there is nonconformity with the rules and even resistance (J. Braithwaite 1989; J. Braithwaite and Makkai 1994; V. Braithwaite 1995). The alternative is cooperative regulation in which there is a pyramid of strategies, beginning with treating the regulated as equals and trusting them and becoming increasingly interventionist and punitive in response to failures to comply (see especially, J. Braithwaite 1989; Scholz 1984).

By contrast, being trusted may make citizens trust-responsive[16] and therefore more trustworthy. This is the philosophical (Pettit this volume) and empirical (Braithwaite 1989) claim that lies at the basis of republican theory. It is also the foundation of recent policy prescriptions that involve community shaming and reintegration of criminal offenders (J. Braithwaite this volume), of revised urban and poverty programs (Peel 1995), and of contingent consent.

Democracy and Trust

Although a state able to produce interpersonal trust may be a just state in the sense that it enforces contracts made under its laws, it is not necessarily a democratic state. The defining aspects of democracy are effective enfranchisement, civil liberties, and the right of citizens to influence governmental decision making through political parties, corporatist arrangements, and other forms of legal pressure. Democracy, so defined, influences the behavior of citizens in at least five important ways.

First, protection of civil liberties, free speech, free assembly, and free press expedite access to information that enables citizens to assess the actions of government officials and of other citizens. Second, these same democratic protections facilitate the ability of citizens to act on stable preferences. For example, the American subjects of George III of England wanted a voice in the imposition of taxes; witness the behavior of the participants in the Boston Tea Party. Only with the advent of democratic institutions, however, did some of the subjects (white, male, and propertied) become citizens with representation in taxation decisions. They acquired an active participatory role in the choice of representatives who determined the taxes that affected them.

Third, democracy can actually change preferences. By delimiting behavioral choices, institutions—democratic or not—reveal what actions the collectivity believes are acceptable. They set new standards of behavior for both government and citizens. The institutions may, in such cases, be simply constraints, but they may also change what people want. A predilection that may initially result from cognitive dissonance becomes the preference over time. For example, once-common American practices such as slavery, discrimination against women, and smoking have become either beyond the pale or, at the least, socially questionable. The fungibility of certain values becomes unthinkable; there develop what Philip Tetlock (pers. comm.) labels "taboo tradeoffs" (see Tetlock, Peterson, and Lerner 1996). For example, the sale of human beings, the sale of offices, and the purchase of substitutes for military service or jail time are no longer within the realm of legal, ethical, or even cognitive (except possibly for economists) possibility. The democratic element in democratic institutions may have the effect of changing preferences regarding to what constitutes fair influence over government, equitable policies, or standards of behavior for governmental actors (see Frohlich and Oppenheimer 1992). What begins as a norm of the few becomes the norm for the many. What is becomes what ought.

Fourth, democracy fundamentally changes the behavior of governmental actors. By providing citizens with a variety of effective means for punishing government actors, for interacting with them in the creation of policy, and for reducing the costs of citizen monitoring of governance, democratic institutions create a basis for cooperation between government officials and citizens. They make possible credible commitments by government actors and legitimate certain exercises of coercion.

Fifth, democracy increases the probability of contingent consent. To the extent that democracy ensures impartial institutions, policy-making processes that take into adequate consideration the concerns of all those with a stake in the outcome, and respect for the recipients of government services, it increases the trustworthiness of government. The effect is to increase the probability that citizens will approve governmental regulations and obey them.

Trustworthiness of government involves several levels of trust, however. Those whose trust is being elicited may trust the actors but not the institutions, or the institutions and not the actors. The democratic rules of the game make it difficult to trust both. If bureaucrats are maximizing budgets or power and if politicians are maximizing votes, their individual interests may trump their public interests.[17] In other ways as well, democratic institutions may undermine citizen trust in government. The free press and oversight institutions of democracies put government actors under extraordinary scrutiny. Open discussion about government actions contributes to its trustworthiness by providing a check on obfuscation and secret promises (or promise breaking). Free speech permits a level of public and scientific debate that eliminates certain abuses by lowering the costs to the normal citizen of both information gathering and monitoring. It is impossible in this day and age, for example, to hide nuclear testing or to make the claim that it is safe.

Revelations of falsifications, incompetence, corruption, or promise breaking may erode citizen confidence in government, or at least in politicians. Thus, the very institutions that reduce monitoring costs may increase distrust. Government actors walk a thin line in publicizing their actions. For example, revelation of tax-evasion schemes may convince the public of government's commitment to equitable enforcement or it may induce more noncompliance by providing evidence of the extent to which government has permitted exceptions.[18]

Distrust, when it reflects the failure of the state to meet the requirements of trustworthiness, is more salutary than harmful to democracies. The noncompliance or even active protest generated by distrust can reveal government lies and illegalities and stimulate institutional correctives. Distrust is a problem for democracies only when it leads to a nonproductive increase of government regulations and bureaucracy as a means to build or regain trust or when it translates into noncompliance with legitimate policies or into bellicose cleavages. Giandomenico Majone (1995) has discussed some of the problems with the European Community in light of this first negative effect of distrust. The current spate of terrorist acts and resistance by the fringe militias, Freemen, and other such groups in the United States exemplifies the second, for the antipathy of these groups to government seems to rest on misinformation and misunderstandings about what government is doing.

Trust and distrust both have their roles in democracy, and so does lack of trust in the sense of standing back and failing to trust until given sufficient evidence or reasons for trusting. The healthy skepticism of citizens is a prerequisite of democracy. Citizen trust of government should be and is conditional. The very trust of government in democracies is grounded in institutions that are constantly scrutinizing the performance of government actors and that permit punishment if necessary. This means that at times there will be a very high personal investment in monitoring and controlling, in the form of active political participation. In fact, the very nature of democratic governance suggests there should always be at least some personal investment in keeping up with the news or in making a decision to comply, cooperate, or consent with government demands.

Democratic institutions have enabled citizens to trust government by making government more trustworthy,[19] and they permit citizens to be skeptical and even distrustful in ways that may lead to even better democratic institutions (see also Sztompka forthcoming). The existence of a greater societal capacity for trust has all the positive implications so well described in the literatures on both social capital and trust, but equally important are the political advantages of distrust and the lack of trust. A trusting citizenry and a trustworthy government are the sine qua non of contingent consent (see, for example, Dunn 1988; Pagden 1988; Putnam 1993), democracy may well be a prerequisite of an appropriately trusting citizenry and of trustworthy government and is certainly essential for providing institutional protections to citizens whose expressions of skepticism and distrust may be the major engine for an even more democratic state.

I benefited from the comments of participants at the conferences and workshops at which I gave earlier versions of this chapter, but I wish especially to thank Karen Cook, Tony Gill, Russell Hardin, Jon Mercer, John Scholz, Patrick Troy, and two anonymous reviewers for their careful readings and helpful corrections.

Notes

1. This was a research program directed by Professor P. N. Troy at the Research School of Social Sciences, Australian National University.

2. I wish to thank Daniel Verdier for helping me to see this component of the behavioral indicator of trust.

3. Pat Troy offered me this example.

4. Claus Offe (1996) elaborates a somewhat similar argument, but he is ambivalent about whether it is meaningful to say that a citizen trusts government. Both Geoffrey Brennan and Philip Pettit (this volume) believe it is possible to make such a statement, but they both claim that such trust has at least as much, if not more, basis in the mechanisms for selecting virtuous office-holders than it does in the incentives and sanctions that constrain them.

5. Although trust in closely knit networks seems to involve no risk, there is always the possibility of defection. The risk may be low, but it exists.

6. They made these points in discussion during the Russell Sage Foundation–University of Washington Conference on Trust and Social Structure (September 8–9, 1995).

7. I am not exactly sure, however, about the mechanism by which such associations produce trust. (See Levi 1996).

8. Trustworthiness, on the other hand, may be a virtue, as the Boy Scouts claim and as Russell Hardin (this volume) argues.

9. As Jean Blondel noted in discussion at the European University Institute, sometimes trust in government is quite durable. As I found in the study of contemporary Australian taxes (Levi 1988), however, trust in the fairness of the tax system can be quite fragile.

10. For interesting and important developments of this kind of argument as applied to the management of firms and organizations, see especially, Kramer and Tyler 1996; Kreps 1990; and Miller 1992.

11. This statement is, of course, consistent with Tom Tyler's arguments and findings (1990).

12. For the moment, I will avoid the debate about whether such actors are "quasi-rational" (Thaler 1991) or acting out of enlightened self-interest (see for example, Binmore 1994). Clearly, however, I am dealing with issues in which moral choice and egoistic choice sometimes conflict (see especially, Hardin 1988).

13. The discussion in this section seems to provide empirical evidence for the arguments made by Brian Barry (1995). The perception of fairness may also, however, depend on the existence of a shared set of values, as some psychologists claim (V. Braithwaite 1995, this volume; Tyler this volume), but my intuition is that psychological issues belong at a later point in the argument.

14. Barry Weingast (1994, in progress) has written a series of papers in which he considers governmental arrangements that prevented conflicts among groups by structuring decision processes so that each had an effective veto against policies they would find particularly harmful (see also Scharpf 1997).

15. Fritz Scharpf pointed this out in a personal conversation.

16. This lovely term is Philip Pettit's (this volume).

17. Michael Smith made this interesting point at a conference at the Australian National University.

18. This is a case I have explored in some detail (Levi 1988, 158–72).

19. See Hardin 1993, 512–13, for an elaboration of this distinction.

References

Ayres, Ian, and John Braithwaite. 1992. *Responsive Regulation.* Oxford: Oxford University Press.
Banfield, Edward. 1958. *The Moral Basis of a Backward Society.* Glencoe, Ill.: Free Press.
Barry, Brian. 1995. *Justice as Impartiality.* Oxford: Oxford University Press.
Bianco, William. 1994. *Trust: Representatives and Constituents.* Ann Arbor: University of Michigan Press.
Binmore, Ken. 1994. *Game Theory and the Social Contract: Playing Fair.* Vol. I. Cambridge, Mass., and London: MIT Press.
Braithwaite, John. 1985. *To Punish or Persuade.* Albany: State University of New York.
———. 1989. *Crime, Shame, and Reintegration.* Sydney: Cambridge University Press.
Braithwaite, John, and Toni Makkai. 1994. "Trust and Compliance." *Policing and Society* 4: 1–12.
Braithwaite, John, and Philip Pettit. 1990. *Not Just Deserts: A Republican Theory of Criminal Justice.* Oxford: Oxford University Press.
Braithwaite, Valerie. 1995. "Games of Engagement: Postures Within the Regulatory Community." Working Paper 26. Canberra: Administration, Compliance, and Governability Program, Research School of Social Sciences, Australian National University.
Coleman, James S. 1990. *Foundations of Social Theory.* Cambridge, Mass.: The Belknap Press of Harvard University Press.
Cook, Karen S., ed. 1987. *Social Exchange Theory.* Beverly Hills, Calif.: Sage Publications.
Cook, Karen S., and Richard M. Emerson. 1978. "Power, Equity and Commitment in Exchange Networks." *American Sociological Review* 43: 721–39.
Cook, Karen S., and Toshio Yamagishi. Forthcoming. "Uncertainty, Trust and Commitment Formation in the United States and Japan," *American Journal of Sociology.*
Dasgupta, Partha. 1988. "Trust as a Commodity." In *Trust: Making and Breaking*

Cooperative Relations, edited by Diego Gambetta. Cambridge, Mass.: Basil Blackwell: 49–72

Dawes, Robyn, Alphons J.C. van de Kragt, and John Orbell. 1990. "Cooperation for the Benefit of Us—Not Me, Or My Conscience." In *Beyond Self-Interest*, edited by Jane Mansbridge. Chicago: University of Chicago Press.

Dunn, John. 1988. "Trust and Political Agency." In *Trust: Making and Breaking Cooperative Relations*, edited by Diego Gambetta. Cambridge, Mass.: Basil Blackwell.

Frohlich, Norman, and Joe A. Oppenheimer. 1992. *Choosing Justice*. Berkeley: University of California Press.

Fukuyama, Francis. 1995. *Trust*. New York: Basic Books.

Gambetta, Diego. 1993. *The Sicilian Mafia: The Business of Private Protection*. Cambridge: Harvard University Press.

Gambetta, Diego, ed. 1988. *Trust: Making and Breaking Cooperative Relations*. New York: Basil Blackwell.

Gellner, Ernest. 1988. "Trust, Cohesion, and the Social Order." In *Trust: Making and Breaking Cooperative Relations*, edited by Diego Gambetta. New York: Basil Blackwell.

Greif, Avner, Paul Milgrom, and Barry R. Weingast. 1994. "Coordination, Commitment and Enforcement: The Case of the Merchant Guild." *Journal of Political Economy* 102 (4): 745–76.

Hardin, Russell. 1988. *Morality Within the Limits of Reason*. Chicago: University of Chicago Press.

———. 1993. "The Street Level Epistemology of Trust." *Politics and Society* 21 (4): 505–29.

———. 1995. *One for All*. Princeton: Princeton University Press.

Hirschman, Albert. 1984. "Against Parsimony: Three Easy Ways of Complicating Some Categories of Economic Discourse." *American Economic Review* 74(2): 89–96.

Kramer, Roderick M., and Tom R. Tyler, eds. 1996. *Trust in Organization: Frontiers of Theory and Research*. Thousand Oaks, Calif.: Sage.

Kreps, David M. 1990. "Corporate Culture and Economic Theory." In *Perspectives in Positive Political Economy*, edited by James Alt and Kenneth Shepsle. New York: Cambridge University Press.

Levi, Margaret. 1988. *Of Rule and Revenue*. Berkeley: The University of California Press.

———. 1996. "Social and Unsocial Capital: A Review Essay of Robert Putnam's Making Democracy Work." *Politics and Society* 24(1): 45–55.

———. 1997. *Consent, Dissent and Patriotism*. New York: Cambridge University Press.

Levi, Margaret, and Richard Sherman. 1997. "Rationalized Bureaucracies and Rational Compliance." In *Institutions and Economic Development*, edited by Christopher Clague. Baltimore: Johns Hopkins University Press.

Lipsky, Michael. 1980. *Street-Level Bureaucracy*. New York: Russell Sage Foundation.

Majone, Giandomenico. 1995. "Mutual Trust, Credible Commitments and the Evolution of Rules for a Single European Market." Florence, Italy: EUI Working Paper, Robert Schuman Center 95/1.

Miller, Gary. 1992. *Managerial Dilemmas*. New York: Cambridge University Press.

North, Douglass C. 1981. *Structure and Change in Economic History*. New York: Norton.

———. 1990. *Institutions, Institutional Change, and Economic Performance*. New York: Cambridge University Press.

North, Douglass C., and Barry R. Weingast. 1989. "Constitutions and Commitment: The Evolution of Institutions Governing Public Choice in Seventeenth Century England." *Journal of Economic History* 49(4): 803–32.

Offe, Claus. 1996. "Trusts and Beliefs, Rules and Decisions: Exploring a Difficult Conceptual Terrain." Paper presented to conference on "Trust and Democracy" at Georgetown University, fall 1996.

Orbell, John, and Robyn M. Dawes. 1991. "A 'Cognitive Miser' Theory of Cooperators' Advantage." *American Political Science Review* 85(2): 515–28.

———. 1993. "Social Welfare, Cooperators' Advantage, and the Option of Not Playing the Game." *American Sociological Review* 58 (December): 787–800.

Pagden, Anthony. 1988. "The Destruction of Trust and Its Economic Consequences in Eighteenth Century Naples." In *Trust: Making and Breaking Cooperative Relations*, edited by Diego Gambetta. New York: Basil Blackwell.

Peel, Mark. 1995. *Good Times, Hard Times*. Melbourne: Melbourne University Press.

Pinney, Neil, and John T. Scholz. 1995. "Duty, Fear, and Tax Compliance: The Heuristic Basis of Citizenship Behavior." *American Journal of Political Science* 39: 490–512.

Przeworski, Adam. 1991. *Democracy and the Market*. New York: Cambridge University Press.

Putnam, Robert. 1993. *Making Democracy Work: Civic Traditions in Modern Italy*. Princeton, N.J.: Princeton University Press.

———. 1995. "Bowling Alone: America's Declining Social Capital." *Journal of Democracy* 6 (1): 65–78.

Scharpf, Fritz. 1994. "Games Real Actors Could Play: Positive and Negative Coordination in Embedded Negotiations." *Journal of Theoretical Politics* 6(1): 27–53.

———. 1997. *Games Real Actors Play*. Boulder, Colo.: Westview Press.

Scholz, John T. 1984. "Cooperation, Deterrence, and the Ecology of Regulatory Enforcement." *Law and Society Review* 18(2): 179–224.

———. 1994. "The Adaptive Compliance of Citizens: Tax Compliance as Contingent Consent." Working Paper 21. Canberra: Administration, Compliance and Governability Program, Research School of Social Sciences, Australian National University.

Smith, Steven Rathgeb, and Michael Lipsky. 1993. *Nonprofits for Hire: The Welfare State in the Age of Contracting*. Cambridge: Harvard University Press.

Stoker, Laura. 1992. "Interests and Ethics in Politics." *American Political Science Review* 86(2): 369–80.

Stokes, Susan. 1998. "Pathologies of Deliberation." In *Deliberative Democracy*, edited by Jon Elster. New York: Cambridge University Press.

Sztompka, Piotr. Forthcoming. "Trust, Distrust, and Two Paradoxes of Democracy," *The European Journal of Social Theory*.

Taylor, Michael. 1982. *Community, Anarchy and Liberty*. Cambridge, Eng.: Cambridge University Press.

Tetlock, Philip E., Randall Peterson, and Jenninfer Lerner. 1996. "Revising the Pluralism Model: Incorporating Social Content and Context Postulates." In *The Psychology of Values*, edited by Clive Seligman, James D. Olson, and Mark P. Zanna. Hillsdale, N.J.: Erlbaum.

Thaler, Richard H., ed. 1991. *Quasi-Rational Economics*. New York: Russell Sage Foundation.

Tyler, Tom R. 1990. *Why People Obey the Law*. New Haven: Yale University Press.

Wallis, John J., and Douglass C. North. 1986. "Measuring the Transaction Sector in the American Economy, 1870–1970." In *Long-Term Factors in American Economic Growth*, edited by S. L. Engerman, and R. E. Gallman. Chicago: University of Chicago Press.

Weatherley, Richard. 1991. "Doing the Right Thing: How Social Security Clients View Compliance." Working Paper 3. Canberra: Administration, Compliance, and Governability Program, Research School of Social Sciences, Australian National University.

Weber, Max. 1968. *Economy and Society*. Berkeley: University of California Press.

Weingast, Barry R. 1994. "Constructing Trust: The Political and Economic Roots of Ethnic and Regional Violence." Paper presented at the University of Maryland/NSF Conference on Institutions, College Park, Md. October 14–15, 1994.

———. in progress. *Institutions and Political Commitment: A New Political Economy of the American Civil War Era*.

Williamson, Oliver E. 1993. "Calculativeness, Trust, and Economic Organization." *Journal of Law and Economics* 34: 453–500.

Yamagishi, Toshio, and Karen S. Cook. 1993. "Generalized Exchange and Social Dilemmas." *Social Psychology Quarterly* 56: 235–48.

Yamagishi, Toshio, and Midori Yamagishi. 1994. "Trust and Commitment in the United States and Japan." *Motivation and Emotion* 18(2): 129–66.

Chapter 5

Trusting Leviathan: British Fiscal Administration from the Napoleonic Wars to the Second World War

MARTIN DAUNTON

I N 1829, William Heath published a cartoon that portrayed a common view of British society. At the top of the image was a wooden
beam, labeled "manufactures and commerce," that had snapped
under the weight of people dependent on it. Desperately clinging to
the beam were four tattered workmen. Hanging on to their legs were
two prosperous business men, and clutching in turn at their coat tails
was a plump individual, splendidly attired in the robes of a bishop
and peer. The caption spelled out the message "Manufactures and
commerce support the workmen, they the merchants and masters
who are the chief tax payers and thereby support the great tax eater
Church-and-State."

The notion of the state as a "tax eater" was stressed by radicals
such as William Cobbett and formed a central tenet in radical rhetoric
and in the formation of a middle-class identity (Wahrman 1995). As
an Anglican clergyman put it in 1809, "The middle order must be
supported, or the whole fabric will tumble in; if the higher ranks have
been oratorically termed 'the Corinthian capital of polished society,'
the middle class is the strong pillar that supports, and lifts it from the
dust. It forms that arch in our constitution, which springing from the
foundation, supports the superstructure" (Wahrman 1995, 52, 163).

Disaffection with the burden of taxation was crucial to the emergence of a middle-class identity.

During the eighteenth century, a powerful "fiscal-military state" emerged in Britain. It was able to extract higher levels of taxation than the French state, with less tension and resistance, and to use the revenue to fund loans for warfare and imperial expansion. A high level of consent was achieved, but trust in the tax system and the state started to weaken during the wars with revolutionary and Napoleonic France between 1793 and 1815 (Brewer 1989; Mathias and O'Brien 1976). During the war, taxes had an obvious justification in combating the menace of revolutionary ideology and Napoleonic ambitions and providing protection for English liberties. After 1815, the justification was no longer present, and the burden of the postwar debt meant that criticism of the state and the tax system did not disappear, despite the "peace dividend" of reduced defense expenditure. The threat to English liberties was now perceived as coming from within, in the costs of servicing the debt and the rentiers it sustained, the menace of militarism and a luxurious court, and the subversion of the social order by a class of rich financiers and mighty landowners benefiting from pensions and sinecures. Such concerns contributed to the failure of the government to renew the income tax in 1816, which resulted in a much more regressive tax system dependent on customs and excise duties that fell on domestic producers and working-class consumers (Hope-Jones 1939; ch. 7; O'Brien 1988).

The outcome was clear: The fiscal system lacked legitimacy, and the trust that had characterized eighteenth-century taxation had collapsed. There was a lack of trust that fellow taxpayers were making a reasonable contribution to the expenses of the state or that the state was spending its revenues in a way which was equitable between classes and interests. In Britain in the 1820s, the state was considered by many to be undemocratic, bloated, and inefficient. The issue facing politicians was how trust in the state and the tax system was to be reestablished and legitimacy restored. The process of reestablishing that trust was remarkably successful, so that in the second half of the nineteenth century the British state and the taxes that supported it were widely seen as neutral between classes and interests.[1]

One way of approaching the process of creating trust in the state and in taxation in Britain is by making comparisons with other countries in Europe, where taxation generated less trust in the state and between taxpayers in the second half of the nineteenth century. The burdens of the First World War exposed the flaws in the fiscal system of Italy and Germany (Ferguson 1995; Forsyth 1993). By contrast, the British state emerged from the First World War with a high degree of legitimacy and trustworthiness and without the crises experienced after 1815 (Daunton 1996a). Why was the British state able to achieve a high level of trustworthiness? When the British fiscal regime is placed within a European context, a number of divergences are apparent that point to the most significant factors. First, there were different trends in the level of taxation in relation to gross national product, so that the reduction in expenditure was longer and deeper than in other European countries. Secondly, the relative importance of direct and indirect taxes moved in opposite directions; while the importance of indirect taxes fell markedly in Britain, it rose in many European countries. Thirdly, there were clear divergences in the nature of fiscal administration. The interaction of these three variables led to the creation and maintenance of an unusually high level of trust in the British state and hence of consent to taxation, a trust that stands in striking contrast to the earlier widespread criticism of the "tax-eater state." The achievement of a high level of trust in the central state—and in fellow taxpayers— reduced the costs of collective action and created the opportunity for the British state to take on new functions in the early twentieth century.

Chaining Leviathan

A closer look at the difference in trends in taxation between Britain and other European states in the nineteenth century reveals how this trust came about. In Britain, the level of taxation fell from 1815 to the end of the century, when there was a modest increase; in continental Europe, the reduction in taxes at the end of the Napoleonic wars was modest and soon reversed. In Britain, state expenditure fell as a proportion of GNP between 1820 and 1914, in contrast to expenditures in France and Germany (Harling and Mandler 1993; Middleton 1996, 59, 90; Schremmer 1989, 362). The British state was thus more effectively constrained than its continental neighbors until the outbreak of the First World War. The economists Barry Baysinger and Robert Tollison posed this issue in their study of the fiscal policies of Gladstone (Baysinger and Tollison 1981): How was Leviathan chained, and how was the British state able to reduce its claims on GNP to a greater extent than were its European counterparts (see also Leathers 1986)? The process of containment was a precondition for accepting the trustworthiness of the state.

Public choice theory suggests that individuals making a private choice in the market weigh the cost of their decision against the benefits, whereas voters making a public choice are more aware of the benefits of any policy to themselves than they are of the costs and economic consequences of financing all policies supported by the electorate. Politicians in pursuit of votes are likely to compete in promising to spend money in a way that appeals to particular interests, and the cost of government escalates. According to such an account, the process is reinforced by the self-interest of bureaucrats who aim to maximize the expenditure of their own department, without adequate consideration of the total cost of all departments (Buchanan and Wagner 1977; Niskanen 1973; Olson 1965). Arguably, this interpretation is currently more applicable to the United States than to Britain, with its different bureaucratic structure, and to the recent past, when a larger proportion of state expenditure has been on welfare, than to the eighteenth and nineteenth centuries, when warfare dominated spending (Clarke 1990; Brewer 1989; Peacock 1979, ch. 17). It cannot be applied to Britain between the end of the Napoleonic wars and the outbreak of the First World War, when the processes of growth assumed by the model were consciously aborted by politicians and bureaucrats. The links of the chains that bound Leviathan were forged by politicians and bureaucrats who were well aware of the temptations to themselves and the electorate of allowing government expenditure to rise.

Forging Fiscal Restraint

The costs of the fiscal-military state had been high in the eighteenth century, rising from at most 4 percent of national income before 1688 to between 8 and 10 per cent in the 1700s and reaching a new peak of 20 percent during the Napoleonic wars (O'Brien and Hunt 1993). This increase threatened a loss of consent, most obviously with the return to peace and the removal of the external threat. The machinery of war, it seemed, had become too expensive and wasteful; it sustained parasitical loan contractors and rentiers who were sucking the lifeblood of the productive classes. Such a view could potentially bring together working-class and middle-class radicals in hostility to the "tax-eater" state, and it might also appeal to many with little sympathy for radicalism. The external threat from French absolutism and Catholicism, succeeded by the dangers of revolutionary ideology and Napoleonic ambition, had justified a fiscal-military state as a means of sustaining the social hierarchy, preserving English liberty, and securing commercial hegemony (Dickson 1967; Hoppit 1990; Pocock 1985). The removal of the external threat in 1815 changed the situation, for country gentlemen could now be more critical of the high costs of taxation that sustained rentiers and subverted the social hierarchy (Hilton 1977). Similarly, the achievement of industrial and commercial dominance meant that a policy of free trade had an increasing appeal to industrialists and merchants, who were inclined to overlook the role of state power in securing markets and protecting them from competition (O'Brien, Griffiths, and Hunt 1991; O'Brien and Pigman 1992).

Politicians came under criticism from a variety of sources: from radicals complaining about the subversion of the constitution, from disaffected farmers and gentry concerned about their position relative to the greater landowners and the monied class, and from evangelical critics of dissipation and luxury. The campaign was self-reinforcing, for the appointment of parliamentary inquiries to rectify one abuse placed more information in the public sphere on related issues and so led to renewed demands for reform. Historians have devoted much attention to these criticisms of "old corruption," the system of sinecures and pensions created by Tory ministers and their hangers-on. This emphasis on the language employed by the critics of "old corruption" may, however, obscure two other points.

The first point is that the actual scale of "old corruption" was less massive than is implied by radical language and rhetoric, which has misled some recent historians (Rubinstein 1983; Thompson 1963, 676). As the historian Philip Harling has remarked, there was a dramatic widening of the gap between radical perception and administrative reality beginning around 1806 and increasing after the war (Harling 1995, 1996, 137–9, 144–50). Of course, the pensions and sinecures attacked were symbols of the existence of privilege in an unreformed political and fiscal system, which was skewed against producers to the benefit of "parasites." The critics did have a point, for higher landed rents since the late eighteenth century had increased the wealth of great aristocratic landowners relative to small owners and tenant farmers; Cobbett's attack on "old corruption" was part of his wider campaign for a return to the social structure of the mid-eighteenth century (Daunton 1995, 52–6; Dyck 1992, 135; Harling 1996, 150). It would appear, therefore, that the reestablishment of trust in the state and taxation entailed more than a simple reduction in the level of extraction, for criticism mounted as the peace dividend allowed government expenditure to fall.

Secondly, more attention should be paid to the response of politicians to radical language, for they countered the rhetoric of their critics by articulating an image of probity, stressing office as a public trust and learning a new code of political manners. Between the end of the war and 1830, Tory ministers introduced precisely the measures of economic and administrative reform that radicals believed their greed made impossible. Their motivation was to isolate the radicals who demanded sweeping changes in the system of government. By convincing "respectable" critics that a narrow political elite was able to govern efficiently and cheaply, they could preserve its power and legitimate the existing political system, so that a widening of the franchise could be avoided. This response of Tory ministers to criticism reduced the threshold for venality and made the political elite eager to meet public expectations of "diligent and disinterested service." Ministers were eager to portray themselves as frugal and honest, basing their claim to authority on their dedication to public duties and their capacity as "men of business." The redefinition of the character projected by public men in the early nineteenth century was not entirely successful, however, for the Tories' attempt to avoid parliamentary reform eventually failed in the early 1830s in the face of continued demand for constitutional change as a means of removing a parasitical ruling elite. The massive tax concessions of 1830 left the government open to charges of financial irresponsibility and failed to contain pressures for parliamentary reform. The symbol of "old corruption" continued to represent biases in the political system, despite the widening gap between the rhetoric of the radicals and the reality of reduction in expenditure (Collini 1991, 104–12; Harling 1996, 138–9, 150–96).

The retrenchment of the Tory ministries between 1815 and 1830 and the export of some of the costs of the fiscal-military state to the empire did mark a turning point in the fiscal-military state, which reduced its claims on the economy below the levels of the eighteenth century (Bayly 1994a, 1994b; Harling 1996, 165, 177–8). But the shrinking state did not achieve legitimacy and trust as the Tory ministers hoped, in part because the strategy was designed to *prevent* a wider definition of citizenship and in part because the taxes levied to pay for the reduced level of public expenditure were widely (and correctly) perceived to be inequitable. At the end of the war, the ministry was forced—against its better judgment—to abandon the income tax, with the result that it was obliged to rely upon customs and excise duties that fell on working-class consumers and on domestic production (Hilton 1977; O'Brien 1988). By acceding to pressure for retrenchment through the abolition of the income tax, the ministry was contributing to criticism of the unfair incidence of taxation, to which the radical response was further cuts in expenditure. The attempt to create a sense of trust in a patrician elite and state failed, and the constitutional reform so assiduously opposed by the Tories was introduced by the Whigs in the early 1830s.

In 1832, the parliamentary franchise was extended and "rotten" boroughs were removed; in 1835, self-electing municipal corporations were replaced by elected councils; the judiciary was reformed; and the privileges of the Church were reduced. Such institutional reform was portrayed as an onslaught on the structure of old corruption and was linked with a further onslaught on expenditure. The legitimacy of the state was not reasserted, however, and in the 1830s public agitation mounted, with protests against the new poor law, pressure for the removal of agricultural protection, and demands for universal manhood suffrage to allow workers to take control of the state. The problem faced by the Whig government was that its policy of retrenchment left it open to charges of financial mismanagement, especially when a serious depression resulted in budget deficits. Although indirect taxes were reduced, the tax system was not reformed by introducing new taxes—and particularly the income tax, which was anathema to radicals as the engine of warfare and a bloated state (Harling 1996, 197–227). Despite the considerable reduction in its scale by 1840, the state was still far from achieving legitimacy and trust. Protection of landed interests through the corn laws suggested that policy was still biased, and the tax system was heavily dependent on indirect taxes that fell on working-class consumers and middle-class producers.

Peel, Gladstone, and Disinterest

The successful creation of legitimacy and trust in the state was the result of the measures of the Tory ministry of Sir Robert Peel, whose policies were continued within the Liberal party by William Gladstone. Peel and Gladstone were the heirs to the notion of public duty developed by Tory politicians after the Napoleonic wars, with the difference that it was now integral to their character as public men rather than a (possibly cynical) response to outside pressure. Above all, their devotion to public duty was linked to a claim that they—and the state—were disinterested. Their ambition was conservative, but in a different sense from the conservativism of the postwar Tory ministries, which aimed to preserve the rule of a narrow political elite within an unreformed constitution. Rather, Peel concluded that the best strategy for preserving the rule of the political elite and of protecting property was by adopting policies that treated evenhandedly the propertied and the nonpropertied and all types of property. By constraining state expenditure and as far as possible excluding the state from involvement with economic interests, he hoped to protect the political elite from challenge and to define the state as a neutral arbitrator between interests. Politicians must rise above personal greed and self-interest; they must also rise above any temptation to use the state to favor one interest against another, whether a trade group in search of protection or a social group seeking tax breaks.

In 1842, Peel reintroduced the income tax in an attempt to balance the budget, in two senses: first, by removing the deficit left by the Whigs and restoring order to government finances, and second, by establishing a sense of equity among different types of wealth and income. In 1846, he took a further step by abolishing agricultural protection. His policy was continued by Gladstone, most notably in his budget of 1853. Peel and Gladstone established the principle that the state should not appear to favor any particular economic interest and that taxes should be a carefully devised system of checks and balances. For example, any bias in the income tax against "industrial" or earned income (which was vulnerable to loss during ill health or trade depression) compared with "spontaneous" or unearned income (which was supported by capital assets producing income regardless of health or economic depression) should be balanced by taxation of property at death. Minimal state expenditures and the retrenchment proposed, as Gladstone argued in a manner appealing to radical assumptions, would remove the source of revenue that sustained parasitical hangers-on and warfare; retrenchment offered peace and liberty. Peel and Gladstone therefore articulated a language of public trust (Biagini 1991, 1992; Daunton 1996c; Harling 1996, 228–54; Harling and Mandler 1993; Hilton 1977; Matthew 1979 and 1986; McKibbin 1990). The creation of at least an *appearance* of neutrality was achieved more successfully in Britain than in other European countries and particularly in Germany (Eley and Blackbourn 1984). The willingess of the elite to shoulder the burdens of the income tax and to abandon the corn laws marked a triumph of "disinterestedness." The success of the policy was clear in 1848, when revolutions in the rest of Europe contrasted with the demise of Chartism as a movement. The radicals of mid-Victorian Britain were willing to trust elite politicians such as Peel and Gladstone and to accept the legitimacy of the state, rather than to castigate them as selfish and corrupt (Biagini 1992; Read 1987, 288–9, 319).

The ability to restrict the state and to create widespread acceptance that it and the political elite were trustworthy did not depend simply upon the assiduous cultivation of a sense of public duty and the creation of a class-neutral state. Both Gladstone and the officials at the Treasury who were reared in the stern tenets of Gladstonian financial orthodoxy were very conscious that there were new dangers arising from the pursuit of votes by competing politicians and the ambitions of spending departments, on the lines suggested by public-choice theory. They feared that retrenchment would be replaced by expenditure unless there were clearly established, rigid conventions; it was easier to bring down spending from the heights of the Napoleonic wars than to keep it at the new lower level. The rhetoric of the neutrality of the state and of public duty, and the appeal to retrenchment and liberty, were sustained by detailed technical accounting principles that the Tories started to formulate before 1830 but that became a well-defined system in the middle of the century. These principles formed the links in a chain forged by Gladstone and Treasury officials to constrain the state.

The first link in the chain was a rejection of hypothecation of tax revenue—that is, pledging particular revenues to particular purposes. In the eighteenth century, hypothecation had been used to create trust in the tax system by making it clear that certain taxes were earmarked to cover particular loans, thereby creating confidence that interest would be paid (Brewer 1989, 211). By the mid-nineteenth century, a different assumption applied. It was realized that hypothecation would contribute to an increase in the role of the state by treating it as a collection of services and functions, each individually desirable with a protected source of revenue. Revenue should therefore be unified, treated as a single pool of money or consolidated fund, separate from the purposes for which it was raised. No less important was the second link in the chain, the rejection of virement of funds. Although revenue was treated as a single sum without any ties to a specific purpose, expenditure was minutely subdivided by annual votes of the Commons. This system contributed to limits on government expenditure. A sum of, say, one thousand pounds might be voted for the construction of a new vessel for the Royal Navy and another of five hundred pounds for a post office in Aberdeen; a surplus of one hundred fifty pounds on the first could not be used to cover a deficiency on the second or diverted to some other purpose, such as building a new prison in Manchester or an army barracks in Sydney, which would need its own vote. The danger of virement was that spending would always rise to the available revenue and would ratchet up expenditure.

It followed that it was necessary to have annual votes by Parliament and that spending plans should not be carried over from year to year. There was a very strong emphasis on the need for constant vigilance by parliament, as a protection for the public against the spending plans of the executive. Radical reformers had argued for an extension of the franchise, less for its own sake in creating a more democratic political system than as a means of changing the composition of parliament, in order to purge the Commons of "interest" and to make parliamentary control more effective in eliminating militarism and waste. Indeed, between 1832 and 1867, parties had limited cohesion, and the Commons was seen as an autonomous arena from which the executive could be chosen and prevented from becoming overly powerful. Although the emphasis did shift in the 1870s with a greater stress on the role of strong and stable parties based upon programs and electoral supremacy, it was still assumed that the Commons would minutely scrutinize spending plans (Hawkins 1989; Taylor 1995, 30–2, 45, 135). The principle was clearly expressed by Gladstone when the Conservative chancellor, George Goschen, broke the principle that the spending plans of the year should be covered by a vote of the revenue of the year. In 1889, Goschen created a Naval Defence Fund to pay for the construction of battleships and borrowed money that would be repaid out of taxes over the next ten years. The proposal horrified Gladstone as a breach of the constitutional principle that the Commons should not pledge future revenue. Governments would, he feared, soon succumb to the temptation to cast burdens onto the future, thus storing up long-term financial difficulties in order to obtain a superficial, short-term popularity (Gladstone, speech at Hastings 19 March 1891, cited in Public Record Office, T168/22, *Financial Papers*, 1891–2). When Gladstone returned to power, he and his chancellor, William Harcourt, undid Goschen's "great constitutional innovation" (Daunton 1996c, 149–50). Asquith, the chancellor in the next Liberal government, reiterated Gladstonian principles in 1906. He insisted that loans should be limited to times of war and that using them for other purposes would lock up capital needed by trade and industry. Any capital expenditure for army and naval purposes should therefore be provided out of the revenue of the year rather than by borrowing, which "inevitably encourages in the spending departments crude, precipitate, and wasteful experiments" and removed expenditure from "effective Parliamentary supervision" (Parliamentary Debates 1906, cols. 289–91).

The ban on hypothecation and virement, along with the insistence on annual votes, meant that there was the possibility of a surplus at the end of the year as a result of buoyant tax revenues or underspending on any vote. A further financial convention was that this surplus should not be carried forward to the next year. Here again was a temptation that, it was feared, self-interested, ambitious politicians would not resist; a chancellor would be able to carry over surpluses in order to make a dramatic reduction in taxation in time for an election, which would turn the tax system into a "gigantic system of jobbery" (Blackett 1910). Since 1829, the convention had called for any surplus to be transferred to the sinking fund in order to reduce the national debt, thereby releasing funds that could be used more efficiently elsewhere. Repayment of the national debt would also create confidence that the state was trustworthy and thus maintain British credit and ensure that the public would lend to the state in times of war, when the revenue from annual tax revenues would need to be supplemented (Parliamentary Papers 1857, appen. 1, 25–53; 1828, 4–6; see also Blackett 1910; Daunton forthcoming).

By these means, barriers were constructed to the expansion of the state. These technical accounting procedures and the annual votes of the Commons were erected into matters of high constitutional principle, integral to English liberty and national identity. In the hands of Gladstone, the annual budget became a matter of high theatricality, or perhaps more accurately of religious ceremony. Instead of the established church providing the basis for a moral, organic state, as he had initially hoped, "fiscal probity became the new morality" (Matthew 1986, 76). The budget, along with the consolidated fund, which brought together all sources of revenue into a single entity, made government finances transparent; it was clear to the public and taxpayers where money came from and where it was going. Above all, spending was open to parliamentary scrutiny on an annual basis. Gladstone's speech of 1891 denouncing Goschen's breach of these principles was, appropriately, delivered at Hastings, a central site in the formation of English national identity. The battle fought there in 1066 was interpreted by late Victorian historians as a beneficial fusion of the democratic principles of the defeated Saxons and the centralizing tendencies of the victorious Normans (Burrow 1981, 143). The existence of one without the other would lead to a weak, fragmented polity or to autocracy; it was therefore considered a necessity to maintain the balance between the two elements by rigorous financial checks on the ambitions of the executive by local representatives gathered in the Commons. As Gladstone argued,

> The finance of the country is intimately associated with the liberties of the country. It is a powerful leverage by which liberty has been gradually acquired. Running back into the depths of antiquity for many centuries, it lies at the root of English liberty, and if the House of Commons can by any possibility lose the power of the control of the grants of public money, depend upon it your very liberty will be worth very little in comparison (Gladstone, speech of March 19, 1891, cited in Public Record Office, T168/22, *Financial Papers*, 1891-2).

The rhetoric of Gladstonian fiscal orthodoxy was reinforced by administrative checks, parliamentary procedures, and a vision of English history that constrained the temptation to spend.

These changes in procedure resulted in a reconfiguration of the central state. As the historian Joanna Innes (1994) has argued, in the late seventeenth and early eighteenth centuries "central government became increasingly polyarchic—multi-centred. Power was distributed among a number of institutions, which were coordinated by more or less informal co-operation between leading statesmen" (98-9) and the "cabinets" of leading ministers mainly dealt with diplomatic and military affairs. The reforms of government accounting procedures and budgetary controls in the second quarter of the nineteenth century meant that the business of the central state was much more coordinated, through the ability of the Treasury and the chancellor of the exchequer to control spending plans and of parliament to check the annual votes. The polyarchic structure of the eighteenth-century state gave way to a more unified system. Leviathan was, as a result, both chained and trusted.

The Fiscal Structure:
Direct Versus Indirect Taxes

At the same time that public expenditure was falling as a proportion of GDP, a transformation was taking place in the structure of taxation, away from indirect taxes (in particular, customs and excise taxes) to direct taxes. British experience ran counter to the pattern in France and Belgium (whose tax system was largely introduced by the French following their occupation of the country). Between 1842 and 1914, the share of direct taxes rose in Britain and fell in France and Belgium, where indirect taxes at the end of the period reached the level from which Britain had started. The British tax system in 1842 was extremely limited, for the wartime income tax had been abandoned in 1816 as part of the reaction against the fiscal-military state, and the government was left heavily dependent upon customs duties and a few excise duties. The result was a highly regressive fiscal regime, which was attacked both by working-class groups and by industrialists and traders. The reintroduction of the income tax in 1842 marked the start of a new trend, for direct taxes on wealth and income rose from 29.8 percent of central government revenue in 1852 to 58.6 percent in 1911; indirect taxes on consumption fell from 70.2 percent to 41.4 percent. In Belgium, direct taxes were initially more significant, accounting for 62.2 percent of central government revenue in 1840. Their proportion subsequently fell, reaching 41.0 percent in 1912, before the introduction of an income tax after the war; meanwhile, indirect taxes rose from 37.8 to 59.0 percent (Daunton and Janssens forthcoming). The comparative position of the two tax regimes was therefore reversed over the nineteenth century.

How can the change in the structure of taxation be related to the constraints imposed on the growth of the British state in the nineteenth century? At first sight, these two features might appear to be working in opposite directions, for it could reasonably be assumed that the introduction of the income tax was intended to raise more revenue for the state, so that containment of public expenditure occurred *despite* rather than *because of* the existence of an income tax. It would be more accurate, however, to argue that the reintroduction of an income tax in 1842 was a crucial link in the chains binding the British state. The income tax in Britain (and later in Belgium) was not intended as a means of increasing the revenue of the state but of removing political tensions and so improving governability and trust.

Peel's reintroduction of the income tax was designed to contribute to political and social stabilization by creating a tax system that would be neutral between interests and protect property in general. Care had to be taken, however, that it not be interpreted as a means of fueling the expansion of the state. Free traders who were initially suspicious of Peel's motives attacked the protection of the landed interest and demanded the liberalization of the economy, fearing that the income tax offered an alternative to retrenchment and would be used to finance war (Hilton 1977; Taylor 1995, 138). Acceptance of the income tax therefore rested upon the assumption that it would help to constrain the state, rather than provide it with additional resources. Peel and Gladstone argued—and their claims were not without foundation—that the tax was temporary and would be abolished as soon as retrenchment had done its work; it was simply a socially equitable means of covering expenditure in the interim, before economic growth in a free market led to higher tax revenues (*Parliamentary Debates* 1842, cols. 431, 437–9, 444; see also Biagini 1991, 156). It was also argued that the tax would create a sense of political responsibility by bringing the public choice of electors into line with their private choice. There was a close correlation between paying income tax and possessing a vote in parliamentary elections under the terms of the Reform Act of 1832, and it was believed that electors would therefore have an incentive to vote for cheap government, because their public choices would have immediate private consequences in their tax bills (Daunton 1996c, 149–50; Matthew 1986, 125–8). The income tax was therefore linked to the process of dismantling the fiscal-military state rather than to the provision of revenue for new functions.

Intention was one thing; outcomes in the longer term were another. In the course of the nineteenth century, the British state became more and more dependent on the income tax. Yet the constraints imposed on the state in the mid-Victorian period and the stress upon class neutrality created a high degree of legitimacy and trust, and the virulent attacks on the "tax-eater" state of the early Victorian period ceased. The success of Gladstonian financial reform created a high degree of acceptance of the tax system in general and of the income tax in particular, which increasingly became the crucial element in the finance of the British state, allowing the remission of indirect taxes and providing revenue in times of emergency. The contrast with countries where the role of indirect taxes increased is striking. A comparison with Belgium at least begins to suggest how this came about (Daunton and Janssens forthcoming).

The tax system in Belgium in the early nineteenth century had a wider base than that in Britain, for it was much less dependent on consumption taxes and had a variety of direct taxes. These took the form of the contribution foncière on real estate; the droits de patente on the presumed profits of trade, industry, and the professions according to the category of trade, the scale of the business, and its location; and the contribution personnelle, based on presumed income measured by conspicuous expenditure, above all on residences. The reintroduction of the income tax in Britain in 1842 should be seen as bringing the British fiscal system into line with Belgium's by taxing a similar range of incomes. It was not a modern "global" income tax so much as a collection of different "schedules" that taxed income from various sources, each with its own method of assessment and collection. Thus, schedule A covered income from real estate and was equivalent to the contribution foncière; schedule D taxed the profits of trade, industry, and the professions and was equivalent to the droits de patente. Although the British income tax was nominally at the same rate on all sources of income, unlike the various specific taxes in Belgium, there was again a certain similarity, for the real level of taxation of the different schedules varied. Collection of schedule A was made at the source from the tenant, on the gross rent before expenses, and therefore it was difficult to evade; by contrast, the income from schedule D taxes rested upon traders making returns of net profits to assessors who were drawn from the taxpaying class, with considerable scope for underassessment. The British income tax therefore resembled the Belgian system in seeking to extract revenue from the same range of activities, by a variety of methods, and at different effective rates.

The main difference between the direct tax systems in the two countries was that the Belgian tax system was less flexible than the British and less capable of extracting increases in the national income. The point may be made by a comparison between the droits de patente in Belgium and schedule D in Britain. The three criteria that determined the droits de patente created a mass of categories: the scale established in 1819, for example, ranged from a levy of 1.06 francs from a carpenter in the country working alone or with one assistant, to 423 francs from a shipowner in Antwerp. The complexity of the scale and the anomalies it threw up made any adjustment of the tax exceedingly difficult, for a multitude of trade and regional interests were affected. By contrast, despite the dangers of underassessment, schedule D was likely to produce more revenue in line with economic growth and increased profits, without the political ramifications found in Belgium and without creating serious tensions between classes and interests. The increase in the tax base, allied with restrictions on expenditure, made it possible to keep the income tax rate low, except in periods of war; indeed, the ability to raise large sums of money by a swift increase in the rate of income tax above normal peacetime levels was stressed as a vital element in Britain's armory (Public Record Office, T168/69, "Mr. Speyer on National Finance," E. W. Hamilton, 25 June 1905). Moreover, it was possible to manipulate the income tax in Britain to produce greater differences between classes than in Belgium. The British income tax had a relatively high threshold and was modified to create various allowances that offered "degression" for the lowest levels of taxable income; the trend was taken still further when the surtax and progression were added in 1909. Modest middle-class incomes therefore paid a lower effective rate of tax than the well-to-do (Daunton 1996c, 157–65; Murray 1980). In Belgium, the package of direct taxes was less flexible and the tax base less responsive to economic growth and its heavier burden on the middle class than on the rich reduced consent to taxation and eroded trust in the state.

The Belgian state became more dependent on indirect taxes as a result of the failure of direct taxes to rise in line with economic growth, and the difficulties of reform. A contrast may be drawn with the actions of the political elite in Britain in reforming the tax system and constraining the state. The group of landowners from whom many of the leading British politicians were drawn had a range of interests; some like Peel, came from a background in the cotton industry of Lancashire, while others, like Gladstone, came from Liverpool merchants and slave traders (Harling and Mandler 1993, 70). In Belgium, the political system limited the ability of politicians to stand— or create the appearance of standing—above interests as an independent propertied elite. Until 1893, the franchise was determined by the amount of direct taxes paid, and the upper chamber was not hereditary and was elected by the same people as the lower chamber. As a result, there was less possibility of an independent propertied elite than in Britain, and electors had a vested interest in limiting the amount of direct taxation, both to restrict the franchise and to limit their tax burden. The result was to constrain direct taxation without at the same time constraining the state, for the burden was shifted to indirect taxes. The result was the creation of political tensions and a lack of trust in the state. Although it seemed obvious to moderate reformers that the introduction of an income tax would offer a means of equalizing the incidence of taxation between classes, as it had in Britain in 1842, reform was delayed by a further political consideration: The income tax was also being advocated by socialists as a first step toward the abolition of private property, rather than—as in Britain in 1842—its preservation. Although the reformist wing of the labor movement within the Catholic party advocated an income tax without these ambitions, other members of the Catholic party were wary. Consequently, it was only in 1916 that the first serious discussion of the income tax took place in Belgium, in the wartime government of national unity.

Meanwhile, the British income tax was restructured between 1906 and 1914; a surtax was introduced to provide higher, graduated taxes on large incomes, and a differentiation was made between earned and unearned income. The result was to increase the ability of the income tax to raise revenue without alienating the crucial middle-class electorate. The strategy was to shift increases in the income tax to large incomes, especially to those with a large "socially created" element, and to reduce taxation on modest middle-class incomes, especially those of family men with dependent children. Such an approach provided a means for the Liberal party to contain the growth of a separate Labour party by offering increased social expenditure and at the same time to retain middle-class support by ensuring that the costs fell on the recipients of large unearned incomes rather than productive, morally superior, earned incomes. At the same time, Liberal fiscal policy offered a means of preserving free trade and limiting the appeal of tariff reform, which the Conservatives were proposing as a means of both providing revenue and solving the problems of poverty through a stable, protected imperial market (Green 1985; Murray 1980).

A combination of political factors and the nature of the tax system therefore led to a reversal of the proportions of direct and indirect taxes in the two countries. The income tax had been introduced into Britain as a part of the strategy designed to dismantle the fiscal-military state and to constrain expenditure, but it also contained within itself the possibility of providing a source of revenue that was widely accepted as legitimate, and whose yield rose with economic growth. Although the various taxes in Britain and Belgium were designed to extract revenue from the same source of income, they were connected with the underlying economic base in very different ways that made them more or less responsive to changes in the level of activity and more or less easily modified as a result of political contingencies. The result in Belgium was a rigidity in direct taxes that pushed the government towards indirect taxes, especially in view of the connection between payment of direct taxes and the franchise. In Britain, direct taxes were more flexible and responsive to economic growth, allowing a remission of indirect taxes and also allowing the rate of income tax to be held down. The high reliance on income tax for central government revenue, however, along with a widening of the franchise to non–income tax payers and the deliberate attempt to reduce the burden of direct taxation on modest middle-class family incomes, created the circumstances for a separation between public choices and private costs that threatened to slacken the chains binding Leviathan.

Delegation and the Effectiveness of the State

The British state in the nineteenth century has sometimes been characterized as weak because of its willingness to cede various functions to the market or to voluntary associations. It is more accurate to say that it was highly effective and able to rely upon dependable auxiliaries in civil society (Bulpitt 1983; Thane 1990). The state and tax system in nineteenth-century Britain operated on the basis of a high level of delegation, characterized by two features. First, functions were delegated both to voluntary associations (such as educational institutions, voluntary hospitals, orphanages, trade unions for unemployment insurance, and the mutual "friendly societies" for health insurance) and to agents of the local state such as the board of guardians, and school boards, as well as the municipal corporations. Until about 1860, these voluntary societies were largely distinct from public bodies and formed a part of civil society; for the rest of the nineteenth century, they drew together with the municipalities in a strong, localized associational and municipal culture. The result was to limit the growth of the central state (Morris forthcoming).

Tax reform was a significant component in the creation of a cheap, neutral state and in the legitimation of aristocratic governance. The creation of a sense of equity in taxation and of safeguards against political sinecures, made it possible to establish new government agencies without a fear of creating new opportunities for privilege and patronage. It was necessary for the state to be "cleansed" and curtailed before a more positive role was feasible. Tax reform and economy alone were not enough, for as Joanna Innes (1996) has remarked, "The experience of penny-pinching Prussian kings . . . suggests that economy—and bureaucratic impartiality—could only do so much to legitimate systems of government" (839). A willingness to provide a large measure of self-rule was a further requirement. The legitimation of aristocratic governance at the center rested not only on its cheapness and apparent impartiality but on its ability to shed large areas of responsibility. It was a process with antecedents in the eighteenth century and not simply the product of reappraisals of the British state after the Napoleonic wars. During the eighteenth century, the central government became more concerned with issues of war and empire and less involved with local initiatives and administration, which devolved to local authorities. Such a trend was less obvious in other European countries in the eighteenth century; in France and Prussia, for example, the central government increased its control over the localities in order to mobilize troops and obtain revenues (Innes 1994, 96, 101–2, 118–19). The reforms of the second quarter of the nineteenth century did not mark a shift in this process of devolution or "subsidiarity"; what the reforms *did* achieve was the imposition of greater constraints on spending at the local level, or at least a sense that local expenditure was cost-effective and economically desirable.

In the early nineteenth century, the largest element of local expenditure was the poor law, where costs seemed to be mounting inexorably as a result of supplements to wages of the "able-bodied" poor. These grants in aid of wages were denounced by many economists and politicians as counterproductive, weakening the need for "preventive" checks on population growth and therefore leading to a further reduction in wages and an ever-larger burden of poor relief. Further, it seemed in the early 1830s that the poor law was no longer preserving social order at a time of agrarian riots and discontent. The solution was to remove control of the poor law from individual parishes, where the vestries and overseers were largely coterminous with the beneficiaries of relief, and to group parishes in unions with boards of guardians elected on a property franchise. The right of appeal from the parish to any justice of the peace in the county was abolished. That procedure had made sense when it was assumed that social order rested upon the ability of the local governing elite to exercise discretion and therefore to command deference and respect; by the 1830s, it seemed that the result was instead to generate new demands rather than deference, and an alternative pattern of order was emerging based upon a professional police force, prisons, and workhouses. The elected guardians would bring the justices into line, and the new bodies would—at least in theory—obey codes laid down from the center. As a result, spending would be brought under control (Mandler 1987).

Although the central government became more coordinated and hypothecation was opposed, there was a different pattern at the local level, where government became *more* polyarchic, with specific property taxes imposed for various purposes. The guardians levied a poor rate; school boards were created in 1870 to provide elementary schools supported by a separate rate; and in addition, the town council levied its own rate. Not surprisingly, local taxation and expenditure increased more rapidly than central taxation. In 1840, local expenditure amounted to 21.9 percent of total government expenditure; in 1890 it was 38.4 percent and in 1910 47.9 percent. The annual growth rate of central government expenditure was 1.5 percent between 1850 and 1900, and of local government expenditure 2.9 percent; the elasticity of government expenditure in respect of GNP was low for the central state and higher for local government (Flora et al. 1983, 441; Middleton 1996, 90; Peacock and Wiseman 1967, 202). The devolution of spending to the localities had the advantage of removing contentious issues from the central state; for example, maintaining separate school boards allowed the deep religious division between Anglicans and nonconformists to be compartmentalized and so prevented it from disrupting other parts of the local and central state (Sutherland 1973). There was also a built-in mechanism to prevent a program of municipal extravagance from running out of control. The local tax base was extremely narrow, resting on a property-based rate; the result was that ratepayers were likely to remove spendthrift councils at elections. Also, a public meeting of owners and ratepayers was needed to approve private bills for major ventures (Bellamy 1988; Hennock 1973). Indeed, in the case of the poor law, large ratepayers were given additional votes, and recipients of relief were disenfranchised. When tussles did occur over the level of local expenditure, they were confined to the council chamber and did not threaten the central state. As one politician put it in 1850, "It is evidently wise to put as little on the Government whose overthrow causes a revolution as you can and to have as much as you can on the local bodies which may be overthrown a dozen times and nobody be the worse" (quoted in Waller 1983, 244–45). The result was that, at least until the last quarter of the nineteenth century, it was safe to delegate responsibilities to the localities without a fear that spending would run out of control and without disrupting the central state.

Not only did the central state delegate responsibilities for spending to voluntary associations and the localities; it did so for tax assessments and collection as well, out of caution about creating a strong central bureaucracy for the administration of the income tax. Both the assessment and collection of the income tax, which came to form an increasing share of government revenue, were delegated to members of the taxpaying public. The system was operated by lay commissioners chosen from the local business and professional community, with lay assessors to determine individuals' tax liability; the tax was then collected on a commission basis by collectors drawn from the ranks of local businessmen. As a result, the number of government officials was small, and these were mainly concerned with providing oversight and supplying information to the lay commissioners and assessors. Such an approach seemed curious to commentators from other countries, who preferred a more centralized and bureaucratic approach (Ingenbleek 1908, 309–10), but it did contribute to creating trust in the state.

The costs of collecting the income tax were minimized by avoiding as far as possible the need to assess total income. When the income tax was first introduced in 1799, an attempt was made to collect tax on global income from all sources, but the result was a low level of compliance and considerable tension. In 1803, the tax was transformed and was collected on each schedule without any effort to establish the individual's entire income. The result was a significant increase in compliance and in the yield of revenue. The new system rested upon the collection of as much tax as possible by deduction at the source, so that a tenant farmer paid his rent to the landowner net of tax and handed the balance to the tax collector. Similarly, tax was deducted from interest payments. The main difficulty came in schedule D profits from trade, industry, and the professions, where it was impossible to collect at source on a flow of earnings; it was necessary to wait until the end of the year when it was clear how much profit had been earned and whether it was above the tax threshold. The way around this difficulty was to delegate tax collection and assessment to lay commissioners, assessors and collectors, so that the role of official bureaucrats was relatively modest (Parliamentary Papers 1870, 101–7, 121; 1920). Further, it was left to the commissioners in each district to come to an agreement with organized trade associations on how to treat depreciation allowances in particular trades, a matter of interpretation of the legislation that was delegated to the localities (Parliamentary Papers 1905, appen. III–V).

The result was not necessarily to reduce the expenses of the state, for commissions paid to the assessors and collectors took the place of salaries for civil servants. The important consideration was not the relative costs of the two methods of assessment and collection, but the fact that lay commissioners, assessors, and collectors entrenched the income tax within civil society, through creating a high level of compliance, trust in the fairness of the tax, and widespread acceptance of the legitimacy of the state. In practice, the power of officials—the surveyors or inspectors of taxes—increased over time, as the system became more complicated with the addition of various allowances to personal income tax and a more sophisticated system of "degression" and progression. These modifications to the personal income tax meant that there was a trade-off between, on the one side, equity and balance, which were necessary to maintain consent to taxation, and, on the other side, higher costs of compliance and administration, with an increase in the power of state bureaucrats (Parliamentary Papers 1920, Part IV). Despite these strains in the system and the practical changes in the balance of power, the principle of lay control continued to sustain the widespread trust in the income tax.

As a result, the ground was prepared for a shift to central government responsibility for an increasing range of functions when both voluntary and local government bodies faced mounting financial crises in the early twentieth century. By about 1900, the voluntary hospitals were having problems securing sufficient donations and subscriptions to meet their rising costs; friendly societies that supplied sick pay and medical treatment to their members were facing mounting financial pressure as a result of actuarial miscalculations and competition for new members; and the local property tax proved to be inflexible and regressive in the face of the increased costs of urban government. As delegation to voluntary and local governmental bodies faltered, it proved possible to turn to the income tax and the central state for a solution (Daunton 1996b).

The greater reliance on central government taxation in the twentieth century, and the gradual atrophy of local government and voluntarism, were accompanied by considerable sensitivity about the need to maintain the trust of taxpayers in the tax system. Compliance with a tax system entails administrative costs for the authorities, which might cause resentment on the part of the taxpayers. These considerations were particularly important at the end of the First World War, which had resulted in massive increases in both debt services and the costs of social services. Could trust be maintained in the new circumstances? Officials at the Treasury, the Board of Inland Revenue, and the Board of Customs and Excise were well aware of the need to retain the consent of the taxpayers to the much higher levels of taxation. Certainly the postwar experience of other countries suggests that they had good reason to be concerned. In Italy, for example, the government was faced with large budget deficits and was unable to reform the tax system; to some extent, the rise of fascism was a revolt of taxpayers (Forsyth 1993). Similarly, the German state responded to the burden of the debt at the end of the war with a policy of hyperinflation that resulted in major shifts in the relative position of different social and economic interests and contributed to the erosion of trust in the state (Ferguson 1995, 1996). By contrast, in Britain the tax system retained a high level of trust and legitimacy, and the potential for a tax revolt was successfully contained (Daunton 1996a).

One feature of the maintenance of trust was the opposition of the Revenue Boards (Inland Revenue and Customs and Excise) to the introduction of a general sales or turnover tax after the First World War. Officials were concerned that the need to secure compliance from something like seven hundred thousand retailers would be administratively complex and costly, and that the resulting animosity to bureaucratic interference would generate hostility to the payment of income tax. Until the introduction of value-added tax (VAT), the British tax system was therefore marked by a structure that had low costs both of administration and of compliance for the revenue authorities; indirect taxes were dominated by a few excise duties that were relatively easy to collect from large concerns, and when the purchase tax was eventually introduced in the Second World War, it was confined to a relatively few large wholesalers. The authorities were also conscious that a shift to indirect taxes at the end of the war would alienate the working class, at a time of severe tension in labor relations and the introduction of universal manhood suffrage. The danger of increasing indirect taxes would be resentment from workers, who would feel they were providing revenue to sustain idle *rentiers* receiving interest on government loans. The result would be to undermine their trust in the state and the tax system; it would also increase support for a levy on capital to redeem the national debt, which would alarm property owners and make *them* fear the use of the tax system as a weapon against accumulated wealth. It was crucial, in the opinion of the Treasury and Board of Inland Revenue, that taxation should be kept above the tussle of interest groups and be seen as evenhanded and equitable. It was a task in which officials and politicians were largely successful, so that trust in the tax system was sustained at a much higher level of extraction (Daunton 1996a; Whiting 1987, 1990).

There was, however, some doubt whether the existing methods of administration could survive. By the First World War, Britain was starting to shift to a regime of high compliance costs and high complexity that threatened continued reliance on lay administration. Tensions arose with the proliferation of legal forms such as family settlements and private companies designed to avoid high levels of death duties. Further, the increase in the number of people paying income tax, most particularly in the lower middle class and well-paid working class, placed pressure on the system of delegation. Collection at source and the use of lay assessors, commissioners and collectors helped to build consent when the numbers of taxpayers were small and the social range narrow, but delegation was likely to cause difficulties when the assessors, commissioners and collectors were drawn from the taxpayers' employers (or their associates). In 1920, an attempt to increase the powers of the bureaucracy at a time of high postwar tax rates led to a backlash against an overly powerful, bloated state and a populist campaign against "waste." Although the role of lay assessors and collectors was eventually abolished, the ultimate appeal on tax liability still resided with the lay commissioners for each district (Daunton 1996a; Parliamentary Papers 1920, Part IV; Whiting 1990).

Increasingly, the smooth operation of the tax system as well as compliance came to rely on the relationship between the Board of Inland Revenue and the taxpayers' professional advisers, rather than on the existence of the lay assessors and commissioners in the locality. The process of reaching agreements and precedents in the interpretation of tax codes was more a matter of negotiation between autonomous professional bodies and tax officials than of formal administrative law. The relationship between these professional advisers and the tax authorities rested upon mutual support and respect, for the advisers needed a degree of confidence in the competence of the authorities in interpreting rules, and the authorities needed a degree of confidence in the integrity of the professionals. The nature of the relationship between professions and the state was another area of divergence between Britain and continental Europe.

Tax advice was provided by solicitors and accountants, whose professional status and integrity rested upon the Law Society and the Institute of Chartered Accountants. The emergence of these bodies should be seen in the context of two features of the formation of the English state that date from the seventeenth and eighteenth centuries. The first was the notion that the ideal form of law was precedent and immemorial custom, which guaranteed freedom and liberty. As the legal historian David Sugarman (1996) has suggested, the emphasis on freedom under the law linked "Englishness" with law and liberty and legitimated the state. The second feature was the emergence in the eighteenth century of a public sphere in the form of clubs, charities and commissions for a wide range of services and activities, which reconstituted civil society and often utilized private legislation (Brewer 1982; Langford 1991). The large measure of autonomy granted to professional bodies reinforced the wide discretion of the law. The combination of these two elements meant that the state was careful not to interfere with the professions, which had a high degree of autonomy at a time when self-governing professions in France and Germany were being subjected to state control (Burage 1989). The result was important not only for the professions but for the British state.

One example of the divergence between the British and the continental European experiences was the treatment of company accounts. In Britain, company legislation created a minimal need for financial reporting to a public body, and the role of accountants in auditing the books of companies was not strictly monitored by the state (Cottrell 1980, 39–79). This professional autonomy had an important effect on the operation of the tax system. For example, legislation gave little or no guidance on the definition of the phrase "an act done to further the purposes of trade," an omission that had major implications for tax liability. Until 1874, any dispute over the definition of such an act was left to the local commissioners, who were not necessarily legally trained; clear case law was lacking, and there was a potential for wide variation among districts. In 1874, the crown and the taxpayers were both given the right to contest a decision of the commissioners as erroneous in law and request that the commissioners "state a case" before the High Court; the issue could then be argued by barristers before a judge. Lawyers held considerable hostility to "officialism," which was seen as a threat to professional autonomy, and saw themselves in a strong professional ideology as the defenders of individual rights. These sentiments were linked to an ad hoc approach and a lack of general principles that gave considerable significance to informal understandings between the revenue authorities, accountants, and lawyers. The result, it has been suggested by the legal historian Raymond Cocks, was "massive problems" in tax law:

> Just because the interpretation of revenue statutes is a craft with its own, almost intuitive qualities, the drafting of revenue statutes is a nightmare. The possible responses of civil servants, accountants, tax advisers, solicitors, barristers and judges are so numerous that, with a view to eliminating uncertainty, the draftsman has to produce very detailed legislation indeed. And the result of course is the all but overwhelming weight and complexity of modern tax statutes. The strange legacy of the mid-Victorian determination to deal with revenue cases in what was seen as being a "common sense" manner is the creation of a body of law that is frequently far beyond the grasp of the most intelligent and "common sense" citizen. (Cocks 1984, 466; see also Sabine 1966, 106)

Cocks contended that the involvement of lay commissioners and lawyers in the definition of tax law led to a confused, diffuse, ad hoc body of case law, which parliamentary draftsmen sought to control through ever more complex and technical legislation. A vicious cycle emerged, of increasingly complicated law and methods of avoidance, with mounting costs of compliance. At the time, however, the process could be seen in a more positive light, as contributing to the acceptance of the tax system as legitimate and trustworthy.

The counterpart of delegation of administration and of interpretation was the exclusion of interest groups from any bargaining over tax rates and exemptions to be included in the legislation. The legislation was, as far as possible, general rather than particularistic, unlike tax law in the United States, which was written by Congress and was open to lobbying that resulted in thousands of exemptions, deductions, and credits for various activities, often in particular locations (Steinmo 1989). Such a pattern had applied in eighteenth-century Britain, when the fiscal regime was heavily dependent on indirect taxes negotiated in a complex pattern of power broking among trade interests—West Indian sugar planters, midlands iron-masters, West Country clothiers, and so on. The process of negotiation contributed to the formation of the British state by creating close connection between trade and regional interests, parliament, and the executive (Brewer 1989, 231–

49). In the nineteenth and twentieth centuries, consent was created by different methods through the *exclusion* of interest-group negotiation and the cultivation of an aura of independence. Unlike legislation in the United States, tax measures emanated from the executive, in circumstances of some secrecy. The budget was written by the Chancellor, often with minimal discussion with his colleagues in the cabinet, following the advice of a small group of Treasury officials with a strong commitment to general measures. The government rarely consulted even its own members, and the passage of the finance bill through the Commons was normally guaranteed as a result of the creation of party discipline from the 1870s (Steinmo 1989). This legislation might offer tax breaks to certain activities—for example, purchase of life insurance—or might grant allowances for children or dependent relatives. These concessions were of general application, however, and did not entail the exercise of any discretion by the tax authorities; there was strong opposition to allowing firms to apply for tax relief on, for example, the application of company reserves to productive investment. The authorities did not wish to become involved in the use of the tax system to encourage particular types of activity; to do so would simply exacerbate the problems already existing in defining the general principles in the courts. Their aim was, as far as possible, to write the tax law in such a way that there was no discretion in its implementation; if the government wished to encourage particular activities, it should be in the form of explicit grants, which were open to parliamentary scrutiny, rather than through "the jerrymandering of taxes" (Daunton 1996a, 899). As the Board of Inland Revenue argued during the First World War, "The object of taxation, as known in this country, is solely to provide money; taxes are of general application and, as equality of treatment between taxpayer and taxpayer is a cardinal principle, the scope and conditions of liability are closely defined by statute and discretionary powers are taboo" (quoted in Daunton 1996a).

The same sentiment contributed to the weakening of the associational voluntarism that was so strong in the nineteenth century. The hostility to discretion and the desire for general rules on the disbursement of public money meant that the Treasury was uneasy about allowing charities to have tax breaks; equality of treatment required all taxpayers to pay tax on their income rather than allowing them to set donations against tax; any grants for education or hospitals should be made by the government from its revenue, rather than by taxpayers who might want to divert their taxes from the state to objects of their own choosing (Daunton 1996b). Even when the state did delegate some authority for the disbursement of money to friendly societies and trade unions with the status of "approved" societies under the

National Insurance Acts of 1911, their autonomy was curtailed, and their authority to decide whether to spend their surpluses on, say, dental care was rescinded (Whiteside 1983). There was, therefore, a tension between the Treasury's concern for control of expenditure and the use of delegated bodies, which tended to be resolved in favor of centralization. Consequently, "the municipal culture of the local state with its associated agencies slowly disintegrated" (Morris forthcoming). In the nineteenth century, the central state shrank in the face of voluntarism and the local state; in the twentieth century, the process was reversed.

The fiscal system should therefore be located in the context of voluntarism and the strength of civil society, the role of municipal culture, and the relative autonomy of professional bodies. The British fiscal system combined a diffuse pattern of delegation or subsidiarity in the collection and administration of the tax, with an attempt to preserve generalized legislation that took discretionary power from the authorities. A comparison with other countries would suggest that Britain was unusual in this combination of features, which helped to create a high degree of acceptance of direct taxation. It would also appear that the balance that contributed to the chaining of the state in the nineteenth century was upset in the twentieth.

Unchaining Leviathan

The shackles on Leviathan were loosened by the First World War and the Second World War, both of which marked a displacement in the share of government revenue in GNP, without the subsequent reduction experienced after the Napoleonic wars. At the same time, the trend towards direct taxation was taken still further, and the central state increased at the expense of both voluntarism and municipal government. By the 1960s, these developments were contributing to a fiscal crisis, which was partially resolved by a shift to indirect taxes in the form of VAT and a renewed effort at delegation to voluntary and private provision for welfare, but without a reduction in the proportion of government revenue to national income. A number of factors contributed to the erosion of the constraints on the central state that had been effective during the nineteenth century.

The use of the income tax as a shackle on the state and the process of delegation in administration, combined with hostility to specific exemptions, created a very wide level of acceptance at an earlier date than occurred in most other European countries. The appearance of neutrality as part of the defense of property and the state created a greater willingness to use central, direct taxation to fund new welfare services than in other countries. At the same time that the central state and direct taxation were legitimated, the property rates that formed the basis of local government finance faced crisis (Offer 1981), and the process of devolution came under strain. Local taxation was restricted to a property-based rate, which encountered difficulties from the late nineteenth century as the costs of urban government increased much faster than rateable values, and the incidence of the rates was regressive. Radicals started to demand a reform of the system to pass the costs of local government onto landowners, which turned local government finance into a highly contentious issue. The problems of local tax revenues were exacerbated by various measures such as the derating of agricultural land in response to the agricultural depression of the late nineteenth century and the derating of industry in response to the industrial depression of the 1920s. There was also concern that local boards of guardians, which operated the poor law, would be captured by working-class interests. The removal of multiple votes from larger property owners in elections of guardians meant that the beneficiaries of relief could again threaten to take control, as they did before 1834. Similarly, problems in the running of education led to the abolition of the school boards in 1902 and a transfer of their powers to committees of borough or county councils. The change arose, at least in part, from the decision of the boards to provide postelementary education on parental demand, in a way that was not considered appropriate by metropolitan experts. By creating education committees within borough and county councils with wider responsibilities, the experts hoped to remove education from the hands of parents and to increase their own power and that of the council's finance committee in allocating resources between different functions (Sanderson 1987). The multifunctional borough councils were "safer" than single-purpose authorities, but even they were less constrained than in the past, and less dependable in the opinion of the Treasury. The ability of taxpayers to contain expenditure declined with a widening of the franchise and the growth of other interest groups such as trade unions and professional groups. "Peripheralization" no longer seemed such an attractive proposition to the Treasury and central government, and the state was less able to rely upon dependable local auxiliaries. The result was reform in 1929, when many of the functions of the poor law were transferred to multipurpose borough and county councils, where spending plans were more likely to be vetted by local bureaucrats and controlled by the ability of the finance committee to consider the budget as a whole. At the same time, the spending of local authorities was brought under greater central control by the devices of fixing the amount of central government subventions and removing central government's obligation to make grants from central taxation in line with local expenditure (Bradbury 1992; Bulpitt 1983).

Expenditure shifted from the localities to the center, where there was a further shift to reliance on direct taxes during and after the First World War. The chances of a fiscal revolt by the middle class against the increased burden of income tax were reduced by the careful attempt by Conservative chancellors between the world wars to follow the example of the prewar Liberal governments in reducing the burden of income tax on the middle-class family man (McKibbin 1990). The strategy succeeded until the 1970s, when inflation started to reduce the value of tax thresholds and higher marginal rates started to hit more people. At this stage, dependence on a narrow base of direct taxes became a source of political problems and contributed to the loss of legitimacy in collective action and the state that has been a theme of recent politics.

The process of establishing trust in the fiscal system is therefore complicated and contingent. It cannot be read simply from the level of extraction, for there was mounting criticism of taxation in the early nineteenth century as expenditure fell as a proportion of the gross national product. Moreover, a massive increase in the level of extraction was successfully negotiated between the wars without a serious loss of trust and consent. Of course, the way in which money was spent—or perceived to be spent—was clearly one important consideration, but this factor is not as simple as might at first appear. Expenditure on warfare might be tolerated at one period, when it is linked with patriotism and hostility to an external "other," but rejected at another period, when militarism is seen as in some sense "unBritish." The same point applies to expenditure on welfare, which might at one time be seen as a socially desirable pooling of risks and at another as the source of national decay. Clearly, other factors were at work, not least the ability of politicians, as a conscious act of policy, to foster a sense of "disinterestedness" and an image of the state as class neutral. This process was linked with carefully devised procedures to ensure that government finances were transparent and accountable, so that taxpayers were assured that the money was spent in the way that had been agreed on. Transparency in expenditure was complemented by opacity in the procedures by which the structure of taxes was adjusted. Alterations in taxes were excluded as far as possible from the interplay of interest groups, in order to prevent any suggestion that the fiscal system was open to special pleading. Further, the administration of taxes in Britain did not create the rigidities found in Belgium or France, where the system was more inflexible and adjustments created problems. The method of assessing and collecting taxes in Britain worked with civil society and limited hostility to bureaucratic intervention. By these means, the British state in the mid-nineteenth century was able, with a remarkable degree of success, to move from deep suspicion to widespread acceptance. Collective action and taxation were given a new legitimacy; Leviathan was chained and, perhaps more importantly, trusted.

Note

1. For a related argument, referring predominantly to labor legislation, see McKibbin 1990.

References

Bayly, Christopher A. 1994a. "The British Military-Fiscal State and Indigenous Resistance: India, 1750–1820." In *An Imperial State at War*, edited by Lawrence Stone. London: Routledge.

———. 1994b. "Returning the British to South Asian History: The Limits of Colonial Hegemony." *South Asia* 17.

Baysinger, Barry and Robert Tollison. 1981. "Chaining Leviathan: The Case of Gladstonian Finance." *History of Political Economy* 12(2): 206–13.

Bellamy, Christine. 1988. *Administering Central-Local Relations 1871–1919: The Local Government Board in its Fiscal and Political Context*. Manchester: Manchester University Press.

Biagini, Eugenio F. 1991. "Popular Liberals, Gladstonian Finance, and the Debate on Taxation, 1860–74." In *Currents of Radicalism: Popular Radicalism, Organized Labour and Party Politics in Britain, 1850–1914*, edited by Eugenio F. Biagini and Alistair J. Reid. Cambridge: Cambridge University Press.

———. 1992. *Liberty, Retrenchment and Reform: Popular Liberalism in the Age of Gladstone, 1860–1880*. Cambridge: Cambridge University Press.

Blackett, Basil. 1910. "Memorandum on the Finance Bill, 1909," November 22, 1910, Public Record Office, T171/9.

Bradbury, J. 1992. "The Making and Implementation of the 1929 Local Government Act." Ph.D. diss., University of Bristol.

Brewer, John. 1982. "Commercialisation and Politics." In *The Birth of a Consumer Society: The Commercialisation of Eighteenth-Century England*, edited by Neil McKendrick, John Brewer, and Jack Plumb. London: Hutchison.

———. 1989. *The Sinews of Power: War, Money and the English State, 1688–1783*. London: Unwin Hyman.

Buchanan, James M., and Richard E. Wagner. 1977. *Democracy in Deficit: The Political Legacy of Lord Keynes*. New York: Academic Press.

Bulpitt, James. G. 1983. *Territory and Power in the United Kingdom: An Interpretation*. Manchester: Manchester University Press.

Burage, M. 1989. "Revolution as a Starting Point for the Comparative Analysis of the French, American and English Legal Profession." In *Lawyers in*

Society, III, edited by Richard L. Abel and Philip S. C. Lewis. Berkeley: University of California Press.

Burrow, John W. 1981. *A Liberal Descent: Victorian Historians and the English Past*. Cambridge: Cambridge University Press.

Clarke, Peter F. 1990. "The Twentieth-Century Revolution in Government: The Case of the British Treasury." In *Ireland, England and Australia: Essays in Honour of Oliver MacDonagh*, edited by F. Barry Smith. Canberra and Cork: Australian National University and Cork University Press.

Cocks, Raymond. 1984. "Victorian Barristers, Judges and Taxation: A Study in the Expansion of Legal Work." In *Law, Economy and Society, 1750–1914: Essays in the History of English Law*, edited by Gerry R. Rubin and David Sugarman. London: Professional.

Collini, Stefan. 1991. *Public Moralists: Political Thought and Intellectual Life in Britain, 1850–1930*. Oxford: Clarendon Press.

Cottrell, Philip L. 1980. *Industrial Finance 1830–1914: The Finance and Organization of English Manufacturing Industry*. London and New York: Methuen.

Daunton, Martin J. 1995. *Progress and Poverty: An Economic and Social History of Britain, 1700–1850*. Oxford: Oxford University Press.

———. 1996a. "How To Pay For the War: State, Society and Taxation in Britain, 1917–24." *English Historical Review* 111(443): 882–919.

———. 1996b. "Payment and Participation: Welfare and State-Formation in Britain, 1900–51." *Past and Present* 150: 169–216.

———. 1996c. "The Political Economy of Death Duties: Harcourt's Budget of 1894." In *Land and Society in Britain, 1700–1914: Essays in Honour of F. M. L. Thompson*, edited by Negley Harte and Roland Quinault. Manchester: Manchester University Press.

———. Forthcoming. *The Ransom of Riches: Taxation and British Politics, 1842–1979*. London: Longmans.

Daunton, Martin J., and Paul Janssens. Forthcoming. "Distant Cousins or Blood Brothers? The British and Belgian Fiscal Systems in the Nineteenth Century." Working Paper. Cambridge: University of Cambridge.

Dickson, Peter G. M. 1967. *The Financial Revolution in England: A Study in the Development of Public Credit, 1688–1756*. London: Macmillan.

Dyck, Ian. 1992. *William Cobbett and Rural Popular Culture*. Cambridge: Cambridge University Press.

Eley, Geoffrey, and David Blackbourn. 1984. *The Peculiarities of German History: Bourgeois Society and Politics in Nineteenth-Century Germany*. Oxford: Oxford University Press.

Ferguson, Niall. 1995. *Paper and Iron: Hamburg Business and German Politics in the Era of Inflation, 1897–1927*. Cambridge: Cambridge University Press.

———. 1996. "Constraints and Room for Manoeuvre in the German Inflation of the Early 1920s." *Economic History Review* 49(4): 635–66.

Flora, Peter, Jens Alber, Richard Eichenberg, Jorgen Kohl, Franz Kraus, Winfried Pfenning, and Kurt Seebohm. 1983. *State, Economy and Society in Western Europe, 1815–1975, vol. 1. The Growth of Mass Democracies and Welfare States*. Frankfurt, London, and Chicago: Campus Verlag.

Forsyth, Douglas J. 1993. *The Crisis of Liberal Italy: Monetary and Financial Policy, 1914–22*. Cambridge: Cambridge University Press.

Green, Ewan H. H. 1985. "Radical Conservatism: The Electoral Genesis of Tariff Reform." *Historical Journal* 28(3): 667–92.

Harling, Philip. 1995. "Rethinking 'Old Corruption'." *Past and Present* 147: 127–58.

———. 1996. *The Waning of "Old Corruption": The Politics of Economical Reform in Britain, 1779–1846.* Oxford: Clarendon Press.

Harling, Philip, and Peter Mandler. 1993. "From 'Fiscal-Military' State to Laissez-Faire State, 1760–1850." *Journal of British Studies* 32(1): 44–70.

Hawkins, Angus. 1989. "'Parliamentary Government' and Victorian Political Parties, c. 1830–1880." *English Historical Review* 104(412): 638–69.

Hennock, E. Peter. 1973. *Fit and Proper Persons: Ideal and Reality in Nineteenth-Century Urban Government.* London: Edward Arnold.

Hilton, Boyd. 1977. *Corn, Cash and Commerce: The Economic Policies of the Tory Government, 1815–30.* Oxford: Oxford University Press.

Hope-Jones, Arthur. 1939. *Income Tax in the Napoleonic Wars.* Cambridge: Cambridge University Press.

Hoppit, Julian. 1990. "Attitudes to Credit in Britain, 1680–1790." *Historical Journal* 33(2): 305–22.

Ingenbleek, J. 1908. *Impots directs et indirects sur le revenue: La contribution personnelle en Belgique, l'Einkommensteuer en prusse, l'income tax en Angleterre.* Misch and Thron: Brusssels.

Innes, Joanna. 1994. "The Domestic Face of the Military-Fiscal State: Government and Society in Eighteenth-Century Britain." In *An Imperial State at War*, edited by Lawrence Stone. London: Routledge.

———. 1996. "Review: P. Harling, *The Waning of 'Old Corruption,'*" *Economic History Review* 49(4): 838–39.

Langford, Paul. 1991. *Public Life and the Propertied Englishman, 1689–1798.* Oxford: Oxford University Press.

Leathers, C. G. 1986. "Gladstonian Finance and the Virginia School of Public Finance." *History of Political Economy* 18(3): 515–21.

Mandler, Peter. 1987. "The Making of the New Poor Law *Redivivus*." *Past and Present* 117: 131–57.

Mathias, Peter, and Patrick O'Brien. 1976. "Taxation in Britain and France, 1715–1810: A Comparison of the Social and Economic Incidence of Taxes Collected for the Central Government." *Journal of European Economic History* 5(3): 601–50.

Matthew, H. Colin G. 1979. "Disraeli, Gladstone and the Politics of Mid-Victorian Budgets." *Historical Journal* 22(3): 615–43.

———. 1986. *Gladstone, 1809–1874.* Oxford: Oxford University Press.

McKibbin, Ross. 1990. *The Ideologies of Class: Social Relations in Britain, 1880–1950.* Oxford: Oxford University Press.

Middleton, Roger. 1996. *Government versus the Market: The Growth of the Public Sector, Economic Management and British Economic Performance, c.1890–1979.* Cheltenham: Edward Elgar.

Morris, Robert J. Forthcoming. "Structure, Culture and the Crucible of Civil Society: British Urban Places, 1840–1959." In *Cambridge Urban History of Britain, III*, edited by Martin J. Daunton. Cambridge: Cambridge University Press.

Murray, Bruce K. 1980. *The People's Budget 1909/10: Lloyd George and Liberal Politics*. Oxford: Oxford University Press.

Niskanen, William A. 1973. *Bureaucracy: Servant or Master?* London: Institute of Economic Affairs.

O'Brien, Patrick K. 1988. "The Political Economy of British Taxation, 1660–1815." *Economic History Review* 2nd ser. 41(1): 1–32.

O'Brien, Patrick K., Trevor Griffiths, and Philip Hunt. 1991. "Political Components of the Industrial Revolution: Parliament and the English Cotton Textile Industry, 1660–1774." *Economic History Review* 2nd ser. 44(3): 395–423.

O'Brien, Patrick K., and Philip Hunt. 1993. "The Rise of the Fiscal State in England, 1485–1815." *Historical Research* 66 (160): 129–76.

O'Brien, Patrick K., and Geoffrey A. Pigman. 1992. "Free Trade, British Hegemony and the International Economic Order in the Nineteenth Century." *Review of International Studies* 18(2): 89–113.

Offer, Avner. 1981. *Property and Politics, 1870–1914*. Cambridge: Cambridge University Press.

Olson, Mancur. 1965. *The Logic of Collective Action: Public Goods and the Theory of Groups*. Cambridge: Harvard University Press.

Parliamentary Debates. 1842. 3rd series 61, March 11.

———. 1906. 4th series 156, April 30).

Parliamentary Papers. 1828. V, *Second report from the Select Committee on Public Income and Expenditure of the United Kingdom. Ordnance Estimates.*

———. 1857. (2nd session). IX, *Report from the Select Committee on Public Monies, appendix I: Memorandum on Financial Control Put In By the Chancellor of the Exchequer, April.*

———. 1870. XX, *Report of the Commissioners of Inland Revenue on the Duties Under Their Management, for the Years 1856 to 1869, vol. 1.*

———. 1905. XLIV, *Report of the Departmental Committee on Income Tax, appendices III to V.*

———. 1920. XVIII, *Report of the Royal Commission on the Income Tax.*

Peacock, Alan. 1979. *The Economic Analysis of Government and Related Themes*. Oxford: Robertson.

Peacock, Alan, and Jack Wiseman. 1967. *The Growth of Public Expenditure in the United Kingdom*. London: George Allen and Unwin.

Pocock, John G. A. 1985. *Virtue, Commerce and History: Essays on Political Thought and History, Chiefly in the Eighteenth Century*. Cambridge: Cambridge University Press.

Read, Donald. 1987. *Peel and the Victorians*. Oxford: Basil Blackwell.

Rubinstein, William D. 1983. "The End of 'Old Corruption' in Britain, 1780–1860." *Past and Present* 101: 55–86.

Sabine, B. E. V. 1966. *A History of Income Tax*. London: George Allen and Unwin.

Sanderson, Michael. 1987. *Educational Opportunity and Social Opporiunity in England*. London: Faber and Faber

Schremmer, D. E. 1989. "Taxation and Public Finance: Britain, France and Germany." In *Cambridge Economic History of Europe, vol. 8, The Industrial Economies: The Development of Economic and Social Policies*, edited by Peter Mathias and Sidney Pollard. Cambridge: Cambridge University Press.

Steinmo, Sven. 1989. "Political Institutions and Tax Policy in the United States, Sweden and Britain." *World Politics* 41(4): 500–35.

Sugarman, David. 1996. "Bourgeois Collectivism, Professional Power, and the Boundaries of the State: The Private and Public Life of the Law Society, 1825–1914." *International Journal of the Legal Profession* 3(1/2): 81–135.

Sutherland, Gillian. 1973. *Policy-Making in Elementary Education, 1870–1895*. Oxford: Oxford University press.

Taylor, Miles. 1995. *The Decline of British Radicalism, 1847–1860*. Oxford: Clarendan Press.

Thane, Patricia. 1990. "Government and Society in England and Wales, 1750–1914." In *Cambridge Social History of Britain, III*, edited by F. Michael L. Thompson. Cambridge: Cambridge University Press.

Thompson, Edward P. 1963. *The Making of the English Working Class*. London: Gollancz.

Wahrman, Dror. 1995. *Imagining the Middle Class: The Political Representation of Class in Britain, c. 1780–1840*. Cambridge: Cambridge University Press.

Waller, Philip. 1983. *Town, City and Nation: England, 1850–1914*. Oxford: Oxford University Press.

Whiteside, Noelle. 1983. "Private Agencies for Public Purposes." *Journal of Social Policy* 12(2): 165–94.

Whiting, Richard C. 1987. "The Labour Party, Capitalism and the National Debt, 1918–24." In *Politics and Social Change in Modern Britain*, edited by Philip J. Waller. Brighton: Harvester Press.

———. 1990. "Taxation and the Working Class, 1915–24." *Historical Journal* 33(4): 895–916.

Chapter 6

Trust, Taxes, and Compliance

John T. Scholz

A DECADE ago compliance studies focused primarily on the coercive aspect of government. Citizens complied with the law out of fear of being caught, so government could enhance compliance by developing effective enforcement policies that deterred noncompliance. This Hobbesian perspective assumed that fear of detection and punishment were the primary incentives available to government to ensure that individuals would follow laws passed for the good of all. The rational-choice perspective and principal-agent models that stimulated research and policy designs for many other policy issues also stimulated innovations in enforcement policies based on the deterrence approach. Duty and shame were sometimes recognized as important motivations supporting compliance, but they were generally attributed to social conditions and childhood socialization that were not likely to be influenced by actions of government. Whether the government was "trustworthy" or not appeared to have little to do with compliance.

In the decade that followed, however, compliance studies have provided a richer view of compliance based upon the mutual interactions between the citizen and government. Two intellectual trends in particular have challenged and extended the basic assumptions of deterrence models of compliance, providing the same stimulation and innovation to compliance studies that was previously supplied by the rational-choice approach to deterrence.

First and most importantly, compliance has been analyzed as a collective action problem. Members of society gain if everyone complies with socially beneficial laws, but each member also faces strong incentives to free ride on the compliance of others while individually enjoying the benefits of noncompliance (Hardin 1982; Levi 1988, 1990; Margolis 1982). Since compliance is the equivalent of a cooperative solution to this collective action problem, the factors that maintain cooperative solutions have direct application to compliance issues.

Second, compliance is viewed from the standpoint of bounded or "low information" rationality. The decision aids or heuristics used by citizens facing compliance decisions may therefore play an important role in determining compliance (Smith 1990; Casey and Scholz 1991). If taxpayers have no idea what the likelihood is that they will get caught for not reporting some outside income, for example, how do they decide whether or not to report the income?

Trust and Compliance

This chapter analyzes compliance as a collective action problem in which heuristics shape compliance behavior; I argue that trust is a theoretically interesting and practically important factor influencing citizen compliance with state laws. Trusting relationships involve transactions in which the truster faces some risk of loss if the trustee does not live up to expectations and some loss of opportunity if the transaction is forgone for lack of trust. I extend and modify Russell Hardin's (1991, 187) account of trust as "encapsulated interest," an account in which the truster's expectations of the trusted's behavior depend on the rational assessment of the trusted's motivation. Potential club members, for example, pay initiation fees and dues in anticipation of the benefits that membership bestows. There is a risk, however, that other members may shirk their responsibilities or that club leaders may abscond with the club's funds. A potential member who joins therefore "trusts" the club members and leadership in the sense that she believes them to be sufficiently motivated to fulfill their expected roles in producing the expected benefits of club membership.

If this were simply a full-information, utility-maximizing decision in the rational choice perspective, trust would be a superfluous concept. But trusting situations involve guesses about the strategic behavior of others, which in turn rely on guesses about their motivations or payoffs as determined by encapsulated interests. In some instances the payoffs are clear, as in Hardin's (1991, 185–6) discussion of the failure of Dostoyevsky's merchant to return the final loan once a long-term relationship had ended. In fact, game theory is currently exploring an array of simple cases in which "credible commitments" can lead to trusting relationships, at least under certain assumptions about the rationality of the trustee.

Trust in everyday life, however, is less likely to reflect conscious, rational assessment and more likely to reflect heuristics developed to deal with the myriad trusting relationships encountered when dealing with other people in situations where encapsulated interests are less clear. Particularly in modern societies, people would have difficulty surviving without "trusting" a large number of relative strangers they encounter in various institutional settings. To cope with frequent decisions in these low-information settings, they develop "trust heuristics" that allow them to assess subconsciously the likelihood that the trustee will undertake expected actions if trusted. For example, the more frequently that trust is rewarded in a given situation, the greater the likelihood that the rewarded person will again trust others in similar situations (Hardin 1993). Like all heuristics, trust heuristics are subject to systematic errors, particularly when those that work reasonably well in one setting are extended to other settings; think, for example, of the gullibility of the proverbial "country bumpkin" in the big city.

This notion of trust heuristics is compatible with the political scientist Robert Putnam's (1993) thesis about trust as social capital. Citizens who develop the capacity to trust through social and civic engagement in church choirs, sports clubs, and other voluntary organizations can generalize this capacity to new situations. Societies whose citizens have developed trust heuristics can therefore enjoy the benefits of a broader range of transactions than other societies. The capacity to trust, combined with the institutional constraints on trustees that provide the basis for trust, enables people to gain the benefits of transactions that would be too expensive if fully rational principal-agent controls were required (Miller 1992).

Like other trusting relationships, compliance involves a risky transaction. Citizens undertake some immediate costly effort like paying taxes. In return for their compliance, they expect future benefits (tax-supported public goods for tax compliance, orderly traffic for compliance with traffic rules, reduced pollution for compliance with environmental laws) that may not materialize unless the government and other citizens maintain their side of the bargain. Any citizen not otherwise motivated by fear or duty to obey would be foolish to comply with a law if he did not "trust" the government and other citizens to meet his expectations, just as any potential club member would be foolish to join and pay membership dues if she did not trust club leaders and members to fulfill their obligations. Without trust, there is little basis for social cooperation and voluntary compliance with laws that could potentially benefit everyone. Without trust, deterrence theory provides a reasonable guide for governance.

But why should a trusting citizen comply if the same benefits are available even without compliance? Club members who don't pay their dues are easily discovered and readily excluded from the benefits provided by the club, but noncompliant citizens are neither easily discovered nor readily excluded. This temptation not to comply even if others comply defines the free-riding problem that is endemic in collective action situations in private as well as public institutions (Hardin 1982; Miller 1992). When free riding is possible, trust alone is not sufficient to ensure compliance. Whether or not taxpayers trust their fellow citizens to pay taxes and trust the government to collect and use the taxes wisely, why should the trusting taxpayer not take advantage of the opportunity to free ride?

Thus *trustworthiness* of the citizen, and not just trust, is necessary for trust-based compliance. Trustworthiness in the compliance context refers to a willingness of the citizen to obey laws despite the temptation to free ride. In the logic of collective action, even self-interested citizens who are not trustworthy would prefer to live in a society of trustworthy people who obey the laws and hence gain the advantages of social cooperation. As Hardin (1982, 173–87) notes, the interaction between networks and overlapping collective activities may provide a framework in which it is difficult to free ride without provoking punishments. In such a tight-knit society, each citizen must actually meet obligations (that is, be trustworthy) in order to avoid punishments meted out to defectors. In such societies, trust and trustworthiness are closely linked, since the incentives that convince one to be trustworthy imply that others facing the same incentives will also be trustworthy and hence can be trusted.

Of course, this enforced link between trust and trustworthiness is less plausible in the context of compliance with complex laws imposed and enforced by the array of public institutions in modern society. Noncompliance is seldom easy to detect and punish. Even when observed, noncompliance may not be construed by other citizens as untrustworthiness, and hence it is unlikely to trigger the dire consequences imposed on untrustworthy individuals in close-knit societies.

The primary argument in this chapter is that trust heuristics provide this otherwise missing link between trust and trustworthiness in explaining compliance with laws in large-scale societies. Citizens learn various heuristics for evaluating risk in small-group settings and generalize these same patterns of thought to compliance even in large-scale societies that lack external mechanisms to reinforce the link. I refer to this set of cognitive activities relating to trust as trust heuristics. The critical question in this argument is whether trust heuristics actually remain effective in contexts where they are not optimal to the individual. If heuristics accurately captured "embedded interests," taxpayers would quickly discover the advantages of free riding, and trust would have no impact on taxpaying behavior.

The remainder of this chapter explores this question in the context of federal income tax compliance—perhaps the least likely context for trust to influence citizenship behavior. The next section "Tax Compliance" introduces the tax context and the deterrence model of compliance that dominates research in this domain. I then summarize the findings of three empirical studies that illustrate the transition in compliance studies from deterrence models to models incorporating trust and cooperation as critical components of compliance theory. The first study (Scholz and Pinney 1995) emphasizes a major limitation of deterrence theory—the limited knowledge taxpayers have of their likelihood of being caught. The second study (Scholz and Lubell 1998b) directly documents the relevance of trust to compliance behavior. The third study (Scholz and Lubell 1998a) provides evidence that trust and duty respond to changes in the tax law as predicted by trust heuristics.

Taken together, the empirical evidence supports the view that cooperation plays a critical role in the collection of taxes and that trust heuristics provide mechanisms by which average citizens can support cooperative solutions to the collective problems of governance—solutions that are reasonably robust against exploitation by untrustworthy leaders and untrustworthy compatriots. Readers most interested in the theoretical argument can skip directly to the elaboration of the trust heuristic that follows the studies in the section entitled "Trust Heuristics."

The Deterrence Theory of Tax Compliance

Few arenas of modern governance impose more difficult problems of trust than the collection of income taxes. The incentives to cheat on taxes are immediate, concrete, and potentially quite large, while the public goods produced from tax revenues provide diffuse benefits that are often difficult to evaluate and are available whether or not one pays taxes. The advantages of not paying—or paying only what the IRS would catch if they were not paid—appear to far outweigh the infinitesimal drop in the provision of collective goods the individual would suffer if he alone evaded taxes.

Factors that encourage compliance with other laws are minimal for income tax laws. Compliance with laws encouraging energy conservation or the protection of the environment may provide direct satisfaction of personally contributing to the worthy cause of conserving the environment. Taxpaying, on the other hand, provides little psychic gratification beyond an often tacit, if sometimes reluctant, sense of doing one's duty to the state. Furthermore, reporting income for tax purposes is a private action generally unobserved by others and only partially observable even to tax collection authorities. These monitoring problems make it difficult to catch evaders and therefore to know over time whether other citizens are being trustworthy or not. The prospects for trust to play a major role in sustaining social cooperation appear at first glance to be bleak indeed.

Tax compliance not only provides a critical research site for investigating the issues of compliance and trust but is also an arena of considerable substantive concern for governance. Since its introduction in England two centuries ago, personal income tax has become the largest single source of revenue in most industrialized countries (Peters 1991), accounting for almost 90 percent of federal revenues in the United States when payroll taxes are included (IRS 1991). Tax compliance directly affects a large proportion of the citizens; in the United States, taxpayers have outnumbered voters in presidential elections since 1970. Furthermore, obtaining compliance with tax laws is problematic. Estimates of unpaid taxes in the United States generally range between $60 to $100 billion (IRS 1988; Roth, Scholz, and Witte 1989), or 10 to 20 percent of taxes due, with some assumptions leading to estimates as high as $200 billion (Feinstein 1991). IRS estimates suggest that about 40 to 50 percent of all tax returns involve at least some understatement of tax liability.

The empirical literature on tax compliance has been developed primarily by economists, who emphasize deterrence, and by sociologists, who emphasize social constraints as critical factors influencing tax-paying behavior (Roth, Scholz, and Witte 1989). In economic models, the coercive powers of government induce *fear* of detection and punishment that deters at least some tax evasion. This widely accepted deterrence concept assumes that self-interested taxpayers will comply as long as the expected penalties if they are caught exceed the expected savings in tax from underreporting income or overreporting deductions.

Sociological models, on the other hand, emphasize the importance of social constraints in controlling noncompliance with tax and other laws. The primary social constraints arise from internalized compliance norms developed from childhood socialization, which lead to psychological punishments of guilt for disobeying the law or rewards of positive self-esteem for fulfilling citizenship obligations and duties. Social constraints also include social punishments and rewards from fellow citizens who, for example, may ostracize tax evaders or give greater status to good citizens. I will refer to internalized compliance motivations as *duty* and to motivations from the action of others as *respect*.

The empirical literature on tax compliance generally confirms that the combined incentives of fear, duty, and respect inhibit taxpayers from the temptation to cheat on taxes (Roth, Scholz, and Witte 1989). The relationship between inhibition and cheating portrayed in figure 6.1 replicates the familiar results that groups with the highest total

Figure 6.1   Tax Cheating and Inhibitions

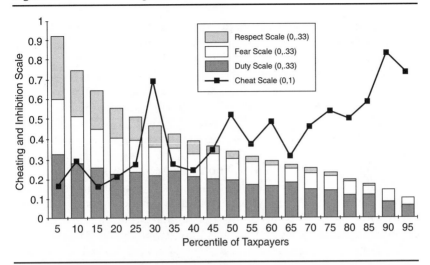

inhibition tend to cheat less. This figure is based on a sample of tax-payers and measures of compliance, fear, duty, and respect that are described later in this study (see Scholz and Pinney 1995). The height of the bar represents the mean inhibition score for each five-percentile group of the population, sorted in order of descending inhibition from left to right. The line indicates the mean score for each group on a cheat scale. The figure demonstrates that cheating goes up as inhibition decreases.

The relationship between inhibition and compliance behavior in this classic model of compliance is robust, but it ignores important aspects of the dynamic interactions between taxpayers and government. When applied simplistically in the tax context, the limitations to this approach can lead to mistaken theory with potentially disastrous policy implications. I first consider the limitations to the relationship between fear and compliance and then take up the more complex limitations to the relationships among duty, trust, and compliance.

Deterrence and Fear

Deterrence theory argues that compliance increases as the probability of detection and the size of penalties for noncompliance increase. As the expected penalty associated with cheating increases beyond the expected gain from cheating, rational individuals will forgo the temptation to cheat. Deterrence provides the philosophical basis for the Hobbesian Leviathan, a government with sufficient capacity to impose incentives to obey on a population expected to comply only out of self-interest.

No modern government could collect income tax without some form of a tax enforcement agency capable of detecting and punishing those who do not pay. Adam Smith's treatise on taxation argued against the feasibility of income tax in eighteenth-century England, in part, at least, because of the inability of tax collectors to monitor income accurately and catch noncompliers. The successful collection of taxes in the twentieth century is based to a considerable extent on the development of accounting practices that clearly define sources of income and on information reporting and tax withholding programs that inform tax agencies about who receives how much income. The most fully documented income sources include wages, interest, dividends, pensions, unemployment insurance payments, and social security payments, which accounted for 87 percent of all reportable income in estimates derived from the IRS's 1985 Taxpayer Compliance Measurement Program (TCMP). Robert Kagan (1989) used these estimates to demonstrate that the amount of cheating associated with a given income source is inversely proportional to the amount of income covered by such reporting and withholding programs. Similarly, tax cheating in countries with less-developed income reporting systems is more problematic in the private than in the public sector, since the wages of public sector employees are more accessible to government tax collectors. In this regard, the importance of the government's ability to detect noncompliance is not controversial.

Whether auditing and other enforcement activities play as direct a role in inducing compliance is less certain. After information reporting, audits are clearly the most important enforcement tool to the system, raising almost $5 billion in additional tax revenue in 1990. Yet audit rates in the United States have fallen from around 5 percent of all returns in the 1960s to well under 1 percent in the 1990s, with little evidence that compliance has deteriorated proportionately. Empirical tests have found some evidence that districts with higher audit rates have significantly higher compliance rates (Dubin, Graetz, and Wilde 1989; Erard and Feinstein 1994; Roth, Scholz, and Witte 1989), but the evidence is neither consistent nor fully convincing. Compliance in other legal arenas exhibits the same weak evidence relating compliance to the probability of detection and particularly to the size of expected punishments.

The Importance of Heuristics

The most evident weakness of deterrence theory is in the utility-maximizing and full-information assumptions on which the classic model is generally based. Laboratory experiments in social and cognitive psychology have documented numerous situations in which observed choice processes violate basic assumptions of expected utility theory (Kahnemann, Slovic, and Tversky 1982; for political science, see Quattrone and Tversky 1988; Sniderman, Brody and Tetlock 1991; for tax compliance, see Casey and Scholz 1991; Carroll 1989). These anomalies were initially assumed to describe limitations to human decision-making capabilities. Recent studies interpret them as low-information heuristics—that is, decision aids or cognitive shortcuts used to minimize cognitive effort for routine decision situations that may not merit the full cognitive effort assumed in normative decision theory (Payne, Bettman, and Johnson 1992, 1993).

Jeff Casey and I have demonstrated that taxpayers apply several heuristics to tax compliance decisions, at least in laboratory experiments (Casey and Scholz 1991). We noted that the context of the decision can determine whether the probability of being caught or the amount of fine imposed will be more influential in a decision. By varying the context, we showed that subjects reverse compliance decisions even when probability and fine remain unchanged. Thus the context of compliance decisions and the manner in which knowledge of probability and punishment are obtained play a critical and undeveloped role in the deterrence model.

Similarly, taxpayers focus on the most salient link in the chain of conditional probabilities that influence the likelihood of getting caught, rather than on the overall probability. Thus a 10 percent chance of getting caught and punished is treated as a lower risk than a combined 50 percent chance of getting caught and a 20 percent chance of being punished if caught, even though the actual risk in both situations is the same ($.5 \times .2 = .10$). The salience of the higher probabilities leads people to overcompensate in determining the joint effect on risk, a heuristic that has been called the "conjunctive effect." Given this effect, compliance levels increase when the salience of high probability links is increased, even when the underlying risk is unchanged.

People also treat low, ambiguous probabilities as equivalent to higher probabilities that are known for certain. That is, a taxpayer who would cheat if he knew for certain that the risk of getting caught is 10 percent may not cheat if he is not confident about that guess. This "ambiguity effect" was demonstrated to change the choice of tax professionals as well as the likelihood of noncompliance. Since the probabilities of detecting unreported income are quite low for income not directly reported to the IRS, this ambiguity aversion should reduce cheating for taxpayers who are not at all certain what the risk of getting caught might be. We argue that a systematic understanding of the conjunctive, ambiguity, and other relevant heuristics can enhance the relevance of deterrence theory to tax and other compliance domains (Casey and Scholz 1991). Heuristics can explain standard enforcement practices (like not revealing enforcement probabilities and practices to taxpayers) that make little sense from the deterrence perspective.

The Role of Heuristics in Tax Compliance: Three Studies

Study 1: Duty Heuristics Explain More Than Deterrence Does

Neil Pinney and I have extended the analysis of taxpayer heuristics one step further (Scholz and Pinney 1995). Deterrence theory is of little use in analyzing the behavior of average taxpayers, we argue, because taxpayers have little knowledge of the likelihood of being caught if they decide to cheat. The IRS policy of maintaining secrecy about enforcement activities, and the dearth of information about audit probabilities relevant to the individual taxpayer's circumstances, combined with the low-information heuristics discussed in the last section ensure that taxpayers do not know the likelihood of being audited.

The study demonstrated that the average person is unlikely to know the likelihood of getting caught or the penalty that would be imposed for failing to report some amount of their income. Likelihood and penalty are the two critical components of deterrence theory's compliance calculus. The evidence in the study is striking enough that the regression results are reported in table 6.1.

All three of the studies reported in this chapter are based on surveys and tax return data collected to examine the impact of the 1986 Tax Reform Act (TRA) on compliance behavior of sophisticated taxpayers most likely to be affected by the changes. The project surveyed middle- and upper-income taxpayers who itemized deductions, with an oversampling of those who filed the tax return without professional assistance and who filed schedule C for business income. Studies 1 and 2 were based on one-hour in-person interviews in one suburban location, while study 3 was based on a national telephone survey. Because of the selection criteria, the respondents were older, better educated, more often male, and better off than the average taxpayer. They also had a larger proportion of "temptation" income not covered by income-reporting programs and a greater likelihood of being audited. Further details are provided in the references to each study.

To probe beliefs about fear of getting caught, respondents were asked to estimate the probabilities of getting caught if they deliber-

Table 6.1   The Impact of Duty and Risk Factors on Subjective Probability
of Getting Caught for Tax Cheating

	OLS Regression Coefficient	t-statistic	Standardized Regression Coefficient
Risk factors			
Opportunity income (R)	−.05	−.34	−.05
Audit probability (R)	−.36	−1.44	−.07
Opportunity (R)	−.14	−1.26	−.07
Opportunity (S)	.79	.35	.02
Occupation	5.99	1.63	.08
Duty heuristic			
Tax duty	8.30*	4.36	.22
Tempted taxpayers			
Opportunity income (R)	−.03	−.17	−.03
Audit probability (R)	1.69*	3.12	.18
Opportunity (R)	.15	.78	.05
Opportunity (S)	−1.71	−.39	−.03
Occupation	6.19	.82	.05
Tax duty	−3.12	−.69	−.11
Constant	3.57	.29	.05
Control factors			
Knowledge	−3.03*	−4.34	−.22
IRS contact (R)	4.94	1.72	.08
IRS contact (S)	7.74*	2.56	.12
Female	7.15	2.46	.11
1987 income (R)	−.02	−.28	−.02
Age	.10	.83	.04
Bias test	−24.45	−.55	−.03
(Constant)	64.06*	4.76	
R^2	.25		
Adjusted R^2	.21		
$N = 439$			

Source: Table 2 in John T. Scholz and Neil Pinney, "Duty, Fear, and Tax Compliance: The Heuristic Basis of Citizenship Behavior," *American Journal of Political Science* 39: 490–512.
*$p < .01$, two-tailed test

ately and knowingly understated their income by $500 and $5,000 and to judge how severe a problem it would be for them to be caught. The probability questions provided a *subjective probability* scale, which was combined with the severity question to create a *subjective risk* scale. Since the results were very similar, table 6.1 reports just the subjective probability estimates.

Several factors that affect the objective risk of getting caught were measured for each taxpayer. *Opportunity income* measured the percentage of income on a tax return in categories not reported to the IRS by employers, banks, and others required to report payments to the IRS. *Audit probability* was calculated for the individual's tax return characteristics and IRS audit classification (or DIF score), on the basis of a large sample of returns with audit information. In addition, two other measures reflecting the *opportunity* to cheat were calculated on the basis of return characteristics (designated by "R") and on survey (S) responses about income sources. Finally, a dummy variable was included to designate taxpayers in *occupations* with high levels of noncompliance. None of these risk factors had a significant impact on subjective risk or subjective probability, as reported in table 6.1.

Given this lack of knowledge about risk, we argued that taxpayers rely on "duty heuristics" when required to make a compliance decision or to generate an estimate of the risk involved in cheating in order to answer a survey question. *Tax duty* was measured with a scale of five standard questions about moral obligation and guilt associated with both purposeful and inadvertent noncompliance. Taxpayers with a well-developed sense of duty to obey the law estimated that the likelihood of getting caught if they cheated was high, while those with a low sense of duty estimated that the likelihood was low. The results in table 6.1 support this duty hypothesis, since duty, not objective risk, predicts beliefs about the probability of getting caught.

We contend that this link between duty and fear maintains a comfortable cognitive consistency, since estimates of risk provide a calculated motivation to comply that is consistent with the sense of duty. More importantly, this link underscores the central role of duty in cognitive patterns associated with compliance behavior, which will be discussed later in the chapter. If individuals simultaneously develop a sense of trust and a sense of duty to meet obligations to specific collectives, then duty may provide the critical link between trust and trustworthiness that might otherwise be missing in large-scale collectives.

The influence of duty on fear is most plausible in the case of uninformed taxpayers with little relevant information on risk. The results in table 6.1 confirm that the duty heuristic affects subjective probability of more sophisticated taxpayers as well and thus provide a stronger demonstration of the cognitive centrality of duty. We identified tempted taxpayers as those in the top 20 percent of the sample facing the greatest temptation to cheat because of a combination of high marginal tax rates, high income, and the greatest opportunity to cheat. The *differences* in coefficients between 80 percent of average taxpayers and tempted taxpayers are listed the table.

The coefficient for tax duty did not significantly differ from that of the average taxpayer, indicating that duty played as strong a role in determining subjective risk of tempted taxpayers as it did for average taxpayers. Audit probability also played a significant role in determining subjective probability for this group, as would be expected of more sophisticated taxpayers, although other risk factors did not. For at least some small subgroups of taxpayers, IRS enforcement undoubtedly provided a critical motivation for compliance. The main point of this study is not that deterrence is unimportant for all taxpayers, but rather that enforcement cannot play the deterrence role expected in compliance models for the majority of taxpayers. I note in passing that two of the factors included to control for potentially relevant differences among all taxpayers were significant—prior contacts with the IRS, which increased subjective probability estimates, and knowledge about taxes, which decreased estimates. These will not be discussed further since they have little bearing on trust heuristics.

Study 2: Trust and Duty Increase Compliance

The second study tested the most critical prediction based on trust heuristics: that a taxpayer's attitudes toward trust in government and trust in other citizens will influence compliance even after controlling for duty and fear. To test this hypothesis, Mark Lubell and I analyzed a national survey of 299 taxpayers (Scholz and Lubell 1998b). The scale of noncompliance counted the number of question categories in which the respondent gave any answer other than "definitely did (report all income)." The resultant scale measured the intensity of the respondent's reported noncompliance activity on a scale from 0 (full compliance) to 4 (noncompliant responses in every possible category—income, deductions, other, and overall). A comparison with IRS audit-based estimates of noncompliance indicated that the frequency of noncompliance reported in the survey is very similar in all categories except for deductions, for which the rate is lower in self-reported data.

The two critical dimensions of trust expected to affect compliance are trust in government to use taxes to provide the expected benefits and trust in other citizens to pay their share of taxes. They reflect the two contingencies in Margaret Levi's (1988) quasi-voluntary taxpaying. They also correspond to the two critical factors affecting the gains from cooperation, since the expected benefits from taxes will decline if the government is untrustworthy or if other taxpayers don't pay their share of the taxes.

The measure *trust in government* summed responses to two standard questions used in National Election Studies (NES) to evaluate trust: "You can generally trust the government to do what is right" and "Dishonesty in government is pretty rare." To measure *trust in citizens*, respondents were asked, "What percentage of taxpayers at your income level . . . pay less taxes than they legally owe?" (Responses were recorded so high percentages corresponded to high trust.) The analysis also included direct measures of other perceptions relevant to the collective action analysis of the tax situation, including the relative value of public goods (*tax equity* and *tax fairness*) and measures of broader perceptions about the citizen's relationship to the collective (*civic duty* and *political efficacy*).

To test the contribution of trust over and above the inhibitors, we utilized several variables to control for the inhibiting influence of fear and duty on noncompliance. The *tax duty scale* was based on the same five questions about guilt and moral obligation mentioned in the description of study 1. Since subjective beliefs about *fear* would reflect duty more than objective risks of getting caught, as was discussed in the section on study 1, controls for differences in risk and detection were represented by two objective risk variables most robustly related to compliance in multiple tests—*opportunity* to cheat, based on categories of income reported on the tax return, and membership in an *occupation* with high noncompliance. Finally, an endogeneity control variable was included as part of the estimating procedure to control for the possibility of spurious or reverse causation between compliance, trust, and duty, as explained in Scholz and Lubell (1998b).

Table 6.2 reports the ordered probit estimates from the final model, which is highly significant ($p<.01$) with a chi-squared statistic of 81. As anticipated, two of the three inhibitor variables used to control for fear and duty were significant at the .01 level, while the third was more marginally significant. The likelihood that a taxpayer was noncompliant increases with greater opportunities to cheat and with employment in noncompliant occupations but decreases when individuals feel a duty to pay.

Controlling for these inhibitions, the critical test indicates that higher scores on both trust measures significantly decrease the likelihood of noncompliance. Using conservative two-tailed tests, trust in citizens is significant at the .01 level, while trust in government is significant at the .05 level. The magnitude of effects from both variables is also quite large. The impact of a full change from lowest to

Table 6.2   The Impact of Trust on Noncompliance, Controlling for Fear and Duty

	Coefficients	Standard Error	Impact of Full Change
Political factors			
Trust in government	-3.485**	(1.623)	.70
Trust in citizens	-.853***	(.260)	.31
Tax fairness	.478	(.372)	
Tax equity	-.159	(.378)	
Civic duty	-.247	(.384)	
Political efficacy	1.488***	(.372)	-.50
Inhibitors			
Tax duty	-1.279***	(.295)	.45
Opportunity	.340*	(.178)	-.13
Occupation	.524***	(.168)	-.19
Endogeneity control			
Government residual	3.004*	(1.65)	
Ancillary parameters			
Cut 1	-1.228	(.471)	
Cut 2	-.430	(.469)	
Cut 3	.199	(.468)	
Cut 4	.850	(.478)	

χ^2 Statistic = 81.25***
N = 299

Sources: Tables 1 and 2 in John T. Scholz and Mark Lubell, "Trust and Taxpaying: Testing the Heuristic Approach to Collective Action," *American Journal of Political Science,* 42: 398–417.
Notes: Table presents 2-Stage Conditional Maximum Likelihood Ordered Probit coefficients.
    *$p<.10$ **$p<.05$ ***$p<.01$

highest value in the significant variables is presented in the final column of table 6.2. As trust in government moves from its minimum to its maximum value, the probability of full compliance changes from .29 to .99, or almost unanimous compliance, for a remarkable change of .70 in the proportion of full compliers. This effect is even greater than the .45 change in probability that occurs in moving from the minimum to the maximum value on tax duty. Trust in citizens provides a slightly more modest change of .31.

The changes in compliance due to the self-interested, fear-related measures in our study, on the other hand, are of a considerably smaller magnitude. Thus deterrence does affect compliance but is by no means the most important factor. The other political factors have either insignificant effects or an intuitively implausible sign in the case of political efficacy.

In short, both trust measures appear to play a significant role in sustaining compliance at levels higher than would be expected if only inhibitions determined compliance. Compliance above and beyond the deterrence level indicates the willingness of the citizen to enter into a risky exchange that provides the defining characteristic of trust. This evidence confirms the link between the attitudinal measures of trust and the observed "trusting" behavior of trust-based compliance with tax laws. I turn next to the other link between the same attitudinal measures of trust and the notion of credible grounds for trust. Specifically, I consider whether attitudes of trust and duty adapt to changes in policy costs and benefits in a way that would emulate some aspect of Hardin's "encapsulated interest," as predicted by trust heuristics.

Study 3: Trust and Duty Adapt to Policy Changes

Do the attitudes of trust explored in study 2 behave as predicted by trust heuristics? Do they represent credible beliefs about the trusting relationship? As Hardin (1991) has noted, beliefs supportive of trusting relationships are likely to arise from many sources, including personal experiences with the objects of trust, indirect cues of trustworthiness, expectations about the incentives provided by the institutional context of the relationship, and beliefs of others about the object of trust. Taxpayers' attitudes of trust in government and trust in others will undoubtedly reflect complex and idiosyncratic beliefs. For trust to be instrumentally useful, however, trust must respond instrumentally to actions of others that affect the individual's well-being.

The purpose of study 3 (Scholz and Lubell 1998a) was to establish that trust responds to actions of government that affect benefits: The level of trust increases when government actions have positive consequences on the taxpayer and decreases when the consequences are negative. Given the importance of duty in both previous studies, we also tested the hypothesis that duty responds in a similar way to government actions. Since duty to obey is directly related to trustworthiness, evidence that trust and duty respond to similar changes would strongly suggest that duty provides a heuristic link between trust and trustworthiness that is otherwise not expected in large-scale collectives.

We expect trust and duty to respond adaptively over time with minor adjustments to normal legislative changes that have only small indirect effects on most citizens. Study 3 took advantage of the natural experiment provided by the Tax Reform Act (TRA) of 1986, an act that imposed substantial changes on a large number of taxpayers. If any single act of government can have a significant impact on trust and duty, the TRA is a most likely candidate (Slemrod 1990).

The magnitude of the changes in the TRA provided a particularly attractive natural experiment to test the trust heuristic hypothesis. Unlike most tax reforms, which either increase everyone's taxes or decrease taxes for a few special groups, the TRA decreased everyone's tax rate but increased taxable income by changes in over fifty-seven tax items, according to IRS calculations. Several items affected very large groups. Changes in deductions for sales taxes, credit card interest, and two-earner married couples, for example, adversely affected over 25 percent of all returns and increased tax liability by over $100 billion annually from affected groups. Other big-ticket items affected fewer taxpayers but imposed more concentrated losses. Restrictions on passive losses in tax shelters raised an estimated $36 billion from 4.2 percent of taxpayers. The elimination of investment tax credits increased taxes by $24 billion for 5.1 percent, restrictions on IRA deductions raised $24 billion from 7 percent, and restrictions on capital gains exemptions raised $22 billion from 8 percent. In sum, the impact on taxes were positive for some taxpayers and negative for others; in addition, the taxpayers affected in both directions belonged to diverse groups, and the changes were large and well-publicized.

To analyze the impact of TRA on trust and duty, we interviewed three hundred taxpayers from a national sample stratified to oversample high-income taxpayers most likely to be affected by the tax changes (Scholz and Lubell 1998a). Respondents were interviewed before and after the 1988 tax season in which they filed the first tax return fully affected by TRA. Using the respondents tax returns, we then calculated the change in taxes caused by the TRA and analyzed the impact of these changes on compliance-related attitudes. If taxpayers first learned the true personal consequences of TRA while filling out their returns during this period, as we assumed, then we hypothesized that a decrease (increase) in tax due to TRA would enhance (diminish) compliance-oriented attitudes of duty, trust, and fear in the post-filing period.

Our empirical study focused on changes in the three attitudes discussed for studies 1 and 2: tax duty, fear, and mistrust in others (reverse coded from the study 2 trust variable). We unfortunately did not repeat the trust-in-government questions in the second wave and therefore could not test for changes in that measure. Each attitude was measured before and after the tax season, with the same set of questions. By using the preseason attitude to predict the postseason attitude, we controlled for differences in the unmeasured characteristics that influenced preseason attitudes. We also included controls for the tax context that might explain changes occurring independently of the TRA. After controlling for prior attitudes and other factors that will be discussed later in the chapter, we expected *TRA change*, the measure of TRA impact, to have a significant influence on duty, trust, and fear, with reduced taxes increasing the level of duty, trust, and fear.

TRA change measures the dollar impact of the TRA on each taxpayer's tax payment for income reported on the TY1985 tax return. We used 1985 as a base year to capture the impact of the TRA based on tax behavior under the previous law. Two tax calculations were made with the National Bureau of Economic Research tax simulation model, one based on the law in effect in 1985 and the other based on the law after the passage of the TRA. The TRA calculation was subtracted from the 1985 law calculation, so positive values indicate a decrease in taxes under the TRA.

The broad range of items affected by TRA ensured that all taxpayers in our sample were affected by some changes, with the number of affected items ranging from eleven to twenty. The change in 1985 taxes if the TRA had been in effect in that year ranged from an increase of $650,000 to a decrease of $361,000, with a mean of $1,800-reduction and a median of zero change in taxes. Almost 15 percent of the sample suffered tax increases over $10,000, while 15 percent saw their taxes lowered by over $10,000. As a proportion of the tax actually paid in 1985, 42 percent experienced an increase of over 10 percent, while 33 percent experienced a reduction of over 10 percent due solely to the new tax law. If any law is expected to have the hypothesized impact on attitudes, these large positive and negative impacts should produce effects in observable quantity.

To ensure that observed relationships were not spurious, we included other factors likely to affect the attitudes under study. *TRA evaluation* measures preseason beliefs about the impacts of the TRA on the amount and fairness of taxes paid by the respondent and by other taxpayers, which formed a single-dimension scale. The intense media coverage of the TRA debates as well as preseason tax planning activities may have already exposed taxpayers to these impacts, since TRA evaluation and TRA change are significantly correlated (.13). The preseason variable controls for the impact of preseason subjective evaluations on attitude change occurring during the tax season.

The study investigated alternative cognitive theories about how policies might affect attitudes, which will be mentioned only in passing. *TRA items* is a count of the number of items on the 1985 return that were adversely affected by TRA. Taxpayers could readily track the number of adversely affected items that they encountered while preparing their return, since these items are more concrete, salient, and readily available than the overall impact of the TRA. *Tax change* calculates the actual difference between the taxes reported on the 1987 tax return—the first fully affected by the TRA—and the 1986 tax return. Note that this is not a good measure of TRA impact because it also reflects changes in taxpayers' income and deductions due to changes in personal finances. *Financial change* reports the respondents' self-evaluations of their general financial condition. Effort reports respondents' evaluations of the change in tax-filing effort attributable to the TRA. *Surprise* counts the positive and negative responses to an open-ended postseason question about surprises the respondents encountered while preparing their tax returns. *Expected refund* measures the difference between preseason expectations of refunds and the actual tax outcome.

As in any natural experiment, the primary effect we are investigating must be isolated from other factors that may be associated with changes in attitudes during the study period that were unrelated to TRA. We are not aware of other factors approaching the magnitude of the TRA that might influence our national sample. Even if these factors existed, they would pose a threat to validity only if they were also significantly correlated with the TRA impact yet not causally associated with the impact. I have already described the measure of individual financial change that is likely to alter attitudes, although it is not significantly correlated to tax change (Pearson coefficient = −.09) in any case. In addition, we include *income* and *audit threat* as important structural features of the tax situation, and *age* as a factor related in many studies to compliance attitudes. If non-TRA factors related to these structural features affected attitude changes, including these variables in our estimates will provide some control for those changes.

We use OLS regression to estimate the effect of TRA impact, alternative indicators, preseason compliance attitudes, and tax content on three dependent variables: postseason Tax duty, Mistrust, and Fear.

The primary hypothesis to be tested is that TRA change and/or TRA evaluation will have significant coefficients. Since preseason attitudes are included, the coefficients reflect the impact of each variable on the *change* in the attitude between preseason and postseason (Finkel 1995). Tax duty and fear are included in all three estimations to control for closely-related prior attitudes within the tax schema. Mis-

Table 6.3 The Impact of Policy Change on Duty, Fear, and Mistrust

	Tax Duty	Fear	Mistrust of Others
TRA impact			
TRA change	.029 (.013)***	.064 (.028)***	-.091 (.032)***
TRA evaluation	—	—	—
Alternative indicators			
TRA items	—	—	—
Tax change	—	—	—
Financial change	.081 (.041)**	-.122 (.082)	—
Effort	—	—	—
Surprise	—	—	—
Expected refund	—	—	—
Prior attitudes			
Tax duty	.560 (.036)***	.158 (.074)***	—
Mistrust of others	—	—	.523 (.066)***
Fear	—	.456 (.056)***	—
Tax context			
Income (1987)	-.004 (.016)***	—	—
Audit threat	—	—	—
Age	.002 (.0007)***	—	—
Constant	.305 (.047)***	.212 (.075)***	.253 (.027)***
R^2	.501	.286	.27
F	46.7***	23.20***	32.60***
N	237	235	176

Source: John T. Scholz and Mark Lubell, "Adaptive Political Attitudes: Duty, Trust, and Fear as Monitors of Tax Policy," *American Journal of Political Science*, 42: 903–20.
Notes: Table presents OLS coefficients of restricted models. Standard errors are given in parentheses.
*$p<.10$ **$p<.05$ ***$p<.01$

trust is not included in the estimations for duty and fear, however, because the number of missing cases reduces the sample to a much smaller size. Significant coefficients for any of the alternative indicators would suggest a particular cognitive mechanism through which changes are activated.

The regression coefficients and standard errors are reported in table 6.3 for the final models that include all significant variables from the full models. Because of the possibility of multicollinearity bias, alternative model specifications were checked to ensure that all significant relationships remain in the final models. All estimated models are highly significant, with explained variance (R^2) ranging from over .5 for Duty to slightly below .3 for Fear and Mistrust.

As hypothesized, favorable legislation leads to significant increases in compliance-related attitudes. In all restricted models, both the preseason attitude and TRA change are significant ($p<.01$). A TRA-induced reduction in taxes results in a significantly higher sense of duty, a greater fear of getting caught, and lower mistrust of other taxpayers, all of which are associated with higher levels of compliance in study 2.

It is interesting to note that the positive impact of TRA change on fear reinforces the conclusion that subjective estimates of the likelihood of being caught respond less to changes in objective risk than to the same experiences and information that affect duty, as was discussed for study 1. If TRA had any systematic impact on objective risk, it was to increase the risk for those facing tax increases, not tax decreases. Several deduction items affected by TRA (for example, medical expenses and work-related expenditures) were restricted in part because cheating was most prevalent on those items. Thus, taxpayers who were hurt by TRA should objectively be more likely to get caught. We observe instead that those who were hurt reported lower, not higher, fear of getting caught.

The large coefficients for preseason attitudes indicate considerable stability of attitudes during the period of study, while the magnitude of TRA impacts suggests that adaptation occurs in modest increments. The difference between the lowest to the highest possible score on the preseason attitude accounts for large postseason differences of .56 for Duty, .46 for Fear, and .52 for Mistrust (all three range from zero to one). Since TRA change is measured in $100,000 units, its coefficient indicates that a large change in tax produces a relatively minor adaptation in attitudes. According to the reduced model, a $100,000 reduction in taxes would increase the taxpayer's sense of Duty by less than 3 percent of the scale (.029). The same reduction would increase fear, the taxpayer's subjective estimate of the likelihood of getting caught, by 6.4 percentage points (.064). It would reduce mistrust by 9.1 percentage points (.091). Given that most tax-payers experienced much less than $100,000 in change, the impact is statistically significant but relatively small.

Small does not, however, mean unimportant. Judged in terms of the full range of TRA change, which varies in our sample from a loss of $650,000 to a gain of $361,000, the TRA effects are about half as large as the full-range change of the preseason variable for duty (.29 versus .56). They are greater than the full range for Fear (.64 versus .46) and considerably greater for mistrust (.91 versus .52). If we judge impact in terms of the change in attitudes in our sample, one standard deviation change in TRA change would account for 11 percent of one standard deviation in observed change in duty (duty1 − duty2), 13 percent for fear, and 25 percent for mistrust. Over 11 percent of our sample experienced TRA-induced changes of over $100,000. Even the more modest changes imposed on the average taxpayer take on practical significance, since every one-percent reduction in tax cheating erases over a billion dollars from the tax gap.

In order to observe relatively small effects in an affordable sample, study 3 focused on an unusually important change in tax laws, on taxpayers most affected by these changes, and on the kind of law with a clearly identifiable period in which compliance attitudes would be affected. Laws with lesser impact will undoubtedly produce less clear results, and attitude changes will generally be spread over longer periods of time. Furthermore, compliance attitudes undoubtedly adapt to a broad range of new laws and legal changes even in unrelated areas. These everyday changes in compliance attitudes will be more difficult to trace to a single event like the passage of the TRA, but the cumulative changes are likely to be greater in magnitude than those we observed.

Trust Heuristics

Taken together, the evidence supports the importance of trust and the related concept of duty in explaining taxpayer behavior. These studies have demonstrated that

- attitudes related to trust and duty adapt to policy changes in a way that reflects changes in expected payoffs for complying (study 3);
- changes in trust lead to changes in levels of compliance (study 2); and
- attitudes related to duty and trust play a central role in the heuristic processes involved in taxpaying (study 1).

I now piece these findings together to develop a more comprehensive perspective of trust heuristics. Specifically, trust heuristics

• provide cognitively simple mechanisms to monitor expected rewards and punishments;
• provide evolutionary advantages to individuals in collective action situations; and
• enhance "social capital" and democratic governance as a by-product of enhanced individual (bounded) rationality.

Trust Heuristics as Effective Monitors

Trust heuristics are first and foremost cognitive shortcuts developed to cope with everyday trust relations. In everyday situations, a number of attitudes toward potential "trustees" act as on-line processors that produce moving average measures of relevant information. Favorable information toward a category of trustees is stored as increases in affect and trust, while unfavorable information is stored as decreases in the same attitudes. If the moving average works accurately, individuals learn to trust more trustworthy individuals. Trust then becomes a reliable guide to behavior in trusting situations.

Trust in such situations provides an efficient cognitive device, providing "retrospective utilitarians" with a subconscious running estimate of the costs and benefits involved in risky relationships. Summary trust attitudes are much easier to store and retrieve when situations requiring choice are confronted than would be the case if all information had to be separately stored, retrieved, and processed when a choice was required. The social psychologist Anthony Pratkanis (1989) has argued that attitudes generally provide such cognitively efficient adaptive devices that guide behavior in most domains. The political scientists Michael Cohen and Robert Axelrod (1984) used computer simulation models to illustrate the advantage provided by adaptive preferences to boundedly rational Bayesian learners. Thus, trust is but one example of everyday adaptive heuristics.

Heuristics are most useful in low-information situations of the sort frequently confronting citizens in their relationship to government (Popkin 1991), where the potential complexity of information and difficulty in interpretation overwhelm the individual's capacity to process the information and interest in doing so. For example, the political scientists Milton Lodge, Kathleen McGraw and Pat Stroh (1989) show that voters simplify the task of remembering information about candidates in elections by adjusting their liking of a candidate to reflect new information and then voting according to their liking of each candidate. They demonstrate that after the vote subject's recollection of candidate positions reflect their liking and attitudes toward the candidates more closely than they reflect the actual positions of the candidates. This finding is strikingly similar to the finding in study 1 that taxpayer beliefs about getting caught reflect their basic attitudes toward duty rather than the objective risks of getting caught.

Reliable monitoring of the environment requires duplication and overlap of monitors (Landau 1969). A reliable trust heuristic would therefore utilize a range of related attitudes toward a range of potential trustees to record any given experience. Attitudes toward a specific trustee would be most strongly influenced by the most closely related experience and would subsequently influence behavior most closely related to those experiences (Ajzen and Fishbein 1980). Trustworthy acts by one trustee would affect attitudes toward similar trustees and similar trust relationship. Widespread exploitation may reduce trust toward everyone. The greater the number of attitudes used to monitor different trustees and relationships, the greater the potential accuracy of risk assessment for the heuristic process.

On the other hand, cognitive efficiency requires the use of fewer monitors and greater cognitive consistency (Festinger 1957). By imposing consistency on beliefs about broad categories of trustees and ignoring information that is only marginally relevant or that conflicts with current beliefs, on-line attitude adaptations can minimize the potential dissonance and discomfort from conflict that otherwise would occur in subsequent evaluations, judgments, or decisions.

The tradeoff between reliability and consistency—between complex versus simple accounting of trust—presumably reflects the relative value of trust relationships and the value of differentiating among different objects of trust in the individual's experience. Whether actual heuristics reflect some optimal tradeoff cannot be ascertained without more detailed observation and theoretical analyses of the attention, editing, and retention phases of information processing in observed trust heuristics.

Trust Heuristics as Effective Collective Action Strategies

Trust heuristics provide more than just efficient cognitive shortcuts in collective action situations. By monitoring the payoffs from the collective and adjusting the likelihood of cooperation accordingly, the trust heuristic can mimic the characteristics of "niceness" and "reciprocity" that Robert Axelrod (1984) identified and political scientists Jon Bendor and Piotre Swistak (1997) demonstrated to be the critical components of successful strategies in repeated prisoners' dilemmas. Prior experience in cooperative environments that establishes high trust would provide a reluctance to be the first to defect (niceness). Yet current experience with exploiters would reduce trust and hence lead to a proportionate decrease in cooperation (reciprocity). Niceness and reciprocity ensure cooperation with other cooperators, while reciprocity reduces the dangers of exploitation in noncooperative environments.

Thus, trust heuristics produce a pattern of behavior that is "better than rational" (Cosmedes and Tooby 1994)—that is, it generates a strategy that is more likely to gain the benefits of cooperation *for the individual* in a broad range of strategic environments than would a narrowly rational strategy of free riding. The political scientist John Orbell and psychologist Robyn Dawes (1991), for example, demonstrated that cooperative individuals tend to earn more than rational defectors in one-shot prisoners' dilemmas in which players can choose either to play or not to play. Cooperators are more willing to participate in prisoner's dilemmas because they trust others, leading to a greater proportion of cooperators among those choosing to play and hence a bonus to cooperators. Noncooperators who distrust others avoid these risky relationships and therefore lose the opportunity to gain from cooperation.

The degree of niceness and reciprocity in a given individual's trust heuristics is shaped not only by experiential learning of the individual (Coleman 1990) but also by the historical development process within a given culture (Putnam 1993) and the evolutionary development of "hard-wired" cognitive processes (Caporael et al. 1989; Cosmeides and Tooby 1994; Frank 1988). The mutual benefits of cooperation may be learned early in life. If the child learns to "trust" her mother by complying with the mother's command despite short-term temptations not to do so, and if the mother proves trustworthy by reciprocating benefits for obedience, trust may provide the basis for cooperative behavior within the family (Coleman 1990). When the child tries to exploit the mutual trusting relationship, she quickly learns the disadvantages of untrustworthiness in such closely monitored settings. Given the considerable advantage that cooperation could provide the family unit, cognitive structures that encourage the development of a capacity for trust and trustworthiness might indeed be the product of natural selection (Wilson 1993).

The capacity to trust might be further developed in a variety of kinship and neighborhood groups, where the thick web of interactions provides ample opportunities to observe and punish untrustworthy behavior, thereby reinforcing the link between trust and trustworthiness (Coleman 1990; Hardin 1982; Ostrom 1990). Of course, trust heuristics would be instrumentally dysfunctional to individuals if they were not capable of discriminating accurately between trustworthy and untrustworthy partners or groups. Furthermore, the capacity to trust may not develop at all for individuals growing up in environments dominated by untrustworthy partners (Hardin 1991) or in societies that provide few opportunities beyond the family for trusting relationships to be developed and tested (Fukuyama 1995; Putnam 1993).

Again, we need further theoretical and empirical studies to determine the extent to which observed trust heuristics mimic the most advantageous strategies for specified sets of collective action games. On the theoretical side, the evolutionary stability of strategies featuring niceness and reciprocity in two-person games needs further development in n-person games involving greater uncertainty, where the cues from other players are less clear and the ability to punish defectors is weaker. The nature of the strategic environment—the strategies played by the set of other potential players—becomes increasingly critical in n-person games. An ability to discriminate between different strategic environments may therefore become an important additional component of successful strategies. For example, simple strategies with the well-known characteristics of niceness and reciprocity ("tit-for-tat") were beaten by similar strategies that also analyzed the strategic environment in a computer simulation of three-person games (Fader and Hauser 1988). Trust heuristic observed of "nice" experimental subjects in eight-person social dilemmas were also found to be very sensitive to the strategic environment; nice subjects cooperated at significantly higher levels when the other (simulated) players also pursued nice and reciprocal strategies (Lubell and Scholz 1997).

Two lines of research appear most promising for understanding collective action heuristics. First, empirical observation of actual strategies in social dilemmas can clarify the strategic characteristics of trust heuristics across a range of socially interesting environmental conditions. Second, evolutionary game theory analysis and computer-simulated tournaments can analyze the strengths and weaknesses of observed characteristics of strategies within specified dilemma and environmental conditions. Together, these analyses can shed light on the stability and decay of trust. For example, how rapidly do individuals reduce trust in different strategic environments and different risk relationships? Do the different rates of change provide strategic advantages, and, if so, what do these different rates tell us about the kinds of social dilemmas most important to the individual?

Trust Heuristics and Social Capital

The two points about trust heuristics discussed in the preceding sections emphasize individual benefits. Effective trust heuristics can also provide social benefits beyond those direct individual benefits. In the example of the club discussed at the beginning of the chapter, joining or developing new clubs would face lower risks from exploitative members as the proportion of individuals utilizing effective trust heuristics increased, at least in societies with some minimal level of trustworthiness. By reducing risk and therefore increasing the range of potential cooperation in novel settings, the capacity to trust provides a valuable addition to the society's social capital and potential for economic development (Putnam 1993).

The trust heuristic can also contribute to democratic controls over governmental institutions. The three tax studies reviewed above suggest that trust heuristics are commonplace among citizens and are even relevant for large-scale collective problems associated with taxes and governance. Citizens experience the costs and benefits imposed by new policies when they comply and unconsciously encode these experiences in compliance-related attitudes. Beneficial laws that enhance general welfare through the resolution of collective action problems therefore enhance the likelihood of compliance. Conversely, exploitative laws diminish compliance.

Thus trust heuristics make compliance conditional on the action of governing elites and of other citizens. Conditional compliance helps to control the exploitative tendency of political elites and of other citizens (Levi 1988). Furthermore, competition across institutions in federalist structures should reward the most competent and least exploitative elites. Governing institutions that provide beneficial laws are rewarded with greater compliance at lower enforcement costs, and in turn trusted institutions are allowed to expand the scope of policies to resolve the constantly emerging collective problems endemic in modern societies. For example, if local governments provide a noticeably greater return on a given set of collective problems than state or federal policies, the gain in trust and hence compliance provide them with additional resources for extending solutions beyond the capacities of other levels of government.

Just as market institutions in modern economies have expanded the range of risky transactions that can be undertaken (Milgrom, North, and Weingast 1990; Schelling 1960; Williamson 1996), so also have democratic institutions enabled modern government institutions at all levels to expand the range of tax-supported activities and policy resolutions of collective action problems. The trust heuristic appears to play a significant yet poorly understood role in the ability of economic as well as political institutions to resolve the risks in collective action relationships. Although elections provide the best-understood process for democratic controls over the institutions of governance, the role of trust in maintaining compliance may be an equally important aspect of democratic control. The heuristics used by citizens to interpret, encode, and respond to government actions provide a poorly understood basis for the adaptive intelligence of democracy.

Are Trust Heuristics Individually and Socially Optimal?

Why would an individual apply the trust heuristic to large-group collectives, where free riding is always individually rational regardless of the level of trust? Particularly for the scale of collectives involved in institutions of governance, there are few rational grounds for believing that any individual's behavior will significantly affect the behavior of others. Why do we observe that trustworthiness is linked with trust even in federal taxpaying, where the temptation to free ride appears particularly strong?

Two conditions may explain the observed extension of the trust heuristic beyond its instrumentally useful range. First, the trust heuristic may be maintained because of the lack of sufficient disconfirming experiences in large-scale cooperative settings. As was noted in the first study, a primary reason that duty influences fear of being caught is the difficulty in knowing the objective risk of detection and punishment. The illusion of high risk among those with high trust is particularly unlikely to be tested, since trusters are unlikely to cheat. In short, the ambiguous consequences of an individual's actions in large-scale collectives may provide insufficient tests to challenge heuristics that have been tested in the less ambiguous crucibles of small-group actions.

Second, the cognitive costs of developing a more exploitative strategy for large-scale games may outweigh the potential gains. Economist Robert Frank (1988), for example, argues that the immediate temptation to exploit cooperative situations for short-term gains may be so powerful that "moral commitments" are necessary to enable individuals to maintain the long-term cooperative strategy that yields higher payoffs. This instrumental value of moral commitment in a broad range of collective settings may compensate sufficiently for the individual to retain moral commitments in large-scale settings rather than risk a corruption of commitments by engaging in untrustworthy behavior when moral commitments are not instrumentally useful.

The plausibility of a structural cognitive link is enhanced by a third consideration. When more prosperous early societies conquered less successful ones, cognitive traits that enhanced both individual and group gains from cooperation would have increased chances of survival (Caporeal et al. 1989). To the extent that selection pressures took place at the group as well as the individual level, the combined individual and social benefits of trust heuristics would have provided an evolutionary advantage to the cognitive architecture that supports the heuristics.

While such speculations are currently in their infancy, evolutionary analyses of simultaneous group and individual adaptive processes may help us understand the tradeoffs between political stability and change that are reflected in trust heuristics. For example, if citizens adapted too slowly to policy gains and losses, citizens would tempt elites to exploit them for short-term gains. If citizens adapted too fast, on the other hand, cooperation would collapse before trustworthy elites could detect and correct policy mistakes. Analyses that characterize the most advantageous rates of adaptation for given institutional settings could perhaps shed light on what rate of citizen adaptation is most effective for maintaining democratic institutions.

Conclusion

This chapter began with the question of why people comply with the laws of government. I have argued that trust and coercion are closely linked in the new perspective on compliance and governance. No law can reshape behavior without the backing of an effective enforcement agency. On the other hand, an effective agency does not try to deter each citizen from breaking the law but instead tries to provide a basis for trust by ensuring that untrustworthy citizens will be made to obey the law. For example, statutes and enforcement policies can reduce the temptation to cheat by providing clearly defined acts of noncompliance that are readily observed and immediately punished. Agencies can attack flagrant violations and tackle areas of suspected noncompliance that could erode confidence among complying citizens. Deterrence theory provides a particularly useful approach to this important but limited enforcement goal.

At the same time, agencies concerned with trust would minimize the use of obtrusive enforcement techniques on trustworthy citizens and ensure that enforcement procedures are perceived by the broader public as reasonable, fair, and in accordance with due process standards of the society. In the long run, trust-enhancing enforcement cannot be separated from the legal processes and contents of the law, since trust-based compliance is dependent on long-term social gains that offset compliance costs. Without trust in the broader set of political institutions, the narrower trust involving a given law and supported by a particular set of enforcement agencies is unlikely to be sustainable.

I gratefully acknowledge the many contributions made to the research reported in this chapter by Pat Troy of the Urban Research Program and by Valerie Braithwaite, Margaret Levi, and other participants in the February 1996 Seminar on Trust at the Research School of the Social Sciences, Australian National University. The research was partly funded by NSF grants SES8710891 and SBR9515344, and by the Russell Sage Foundation.

References

Ajzen, Icek and Martin Fishbein. 1980. *Understanding Attitudes and Predicting Social Behavior.* Englewood Cliffs, N.J.: Prentice Hall.

Axelrod, Robert. 1984. *The Evolution of Cooperation.* New York: Basic Books.

Bendor, Jonathon, and Piotr Swistak. 1997. "The Evolutionary Stability of Cooperation." *American Political Science Review* 91: 290–307.

Beron, Kurt J., Helen V. Tauchen, and Anne D. Witte. 1992. "The Effects of Audits and Socio-economic Variables on Compliance," In *Why People Pay Taxes: Tax Compliance and Enforcement,* edited by Joel Slemrod. Ann Arbor: University of Michigan Press.

Caporael, Linda R., Robyn Dawes, John Orbell, and Alphonse van de Kraft. 1989. "Selfishness Examined: Cooperation in the Absence of Egoistic Incentives." *Behavioral and Brain Sciences* 12: 683–739.

Carroll, John S. 1989. "A Cognitive-Process Analysis of Taxpayer Compliance." In *Taxpayer Compliance: Social Science Perspectives,* edited by Jeffrey A. Roth and John T. Scholz. Philadelphia: University of Pennsylvania Press.

Casey, Jeff T., and John T. Scholz. 1991. "Boundary Effects of Vague Risk Information on Taxpayer Decisions." *Organizational Behavior and Human Decision Processes* 50: 360–94.

Cohen, Michael, and Robert Axelrod. 1984. "Coping with Complexity: The Adaptive Value of Changing Utility." *American Economic Review* 74: 30–42.

Coleman, James. 1990. *Foundations of Social Theory.* Cambridge: Harvard University Press.

Cosmedes, Leda, and John Tooby. 1994. "Better than Rational: Evolutionary Psychology and the Invisible Hand." *American Economic Association: Papers and Proceedings* 84: 327–32.

Dubin, Jeffrey, Michael J. Graetz, and Louis L. Wilde. 1989. "The Effect of Audit Rates on the Federal Individual Income Tax, 1977–1986." *National Tax Journal* 43: 395–409.

Erard, Brian, and Jonathan S. Feinstein. 1994. "Honesty and Evasion in the Tax Compliance Game." *Rand Journal of Economics* 25: 1–19.

Fader, Peter S., and John R. Hauser. 1988. "Implicit Coalitions in a Generalized Prisoner's Dilemma." *Journal of Conflict Resolution* 32: 553–82.

Feinstein, Jonathan. 1991. "An Econometric Analysis of Income Tax Evasion and its Detection." *Rand Journal of Economics* 22: 14–35.

Festinger, Leon. 1957. *A Theory of Cognitive Dissonance.* Evanston, Ill.: Row, Peterson.

Frank, Robert. 1988. *Passions within Reason: The Strategic Role of the Emotions.* New York: W. W. Norton.

Fukuyama, Francis. 1995. *Trust: The Social Virtues and the Creation of Prosperity.* New York: Free Press.

Hardin, Russell. 1982. *Collective Action*. Washington, D.C.: Resources for the Future.

———. 1991. "Trusting Persons, Trusting Institutions." In *Strategy and Choice*, edited by Richard Zeckhauser. Cambridge: MIT Press.

———. 1993. "The Street-Level Epistemology of Trust." *Politics and Society* 21: 505–29.

Internal Revenue Service (IRS). 1988. *Income Tax Compliance Research: Gross Tax Gap Estimates and Projections for 1973–1992*. Publication 7285 (March 1988), United States Department of the Treasury, Washington, D.C.

———. 1991. *Annual Report 1990*. Publication 55 (Rev. 7–91), United States Department of the Treasury, Washington, D.C.

Kagan, Robert A. 1989. "On the Visibility of Income Tax Law Violations." In *Taxpayer Compliance: Social Science Perspectives*, edited by Jeffrey A. Roth and John T. Scholz. Philadelphia: University of Pennsylvania Press.

Kahneman, Daniel, P. Slovic, and A. Tversky, eds. 1982. *Judgment under Uncertainty: Heuristics and Biases*. Cambridge: Cambridge University Press.

Landau, Martin. 1969. "Redundancy, Rationality, and the Problem of Duplication and Overlap." *Public Administration Review* 29: 346–58.

Levi, Margaret. 1988. *Of Rule and Revenue*. Berkeley: University of California Press.

———. 1990. "A Logic of Institutional Change." In *The Limits of Rationality*, edited by Karen S. Cook and Margaret Levi. Chicago: University of Chicago Press.

Lodge, M., K. M. McGraw, and P. Stroh. 1989. "An Impression-driven Model of Candidate Evaluation." *American Political Science Review* 83: 399–419.

Lubell, Mark, and John T. Scholz. 1997. "Institutions and Heuristics as Social Capital in Experimental Social Dilemmas." Paper Presented at the 1997 Annual Meetings of the American Political Science Association, Washington, D.C. (1997).

Margolis, Howard. 1982. *Selfishness, Altruism, and Rationality*. Chicago: University of Chicago Press.

Milgrom, Paul R., Douglass C. North, and Barry R. Weingast. 1990. "The Role of Institutions in the Revival of Trade." *Economics and Politics* 2: 1–23.

Miller, Gary. 1992. *Managerial Dilemmas: The Political Economy of Hierarchy*. Cambridge: Cambridge University Press.

North, Douglass C. 1990. *Institutions, Institutional Change, and Economic Performance*. Cambridge: Cambridge University Press.

Orbell, John M., and Robyn M. Dawes. 1991. "A 'Cognitive Miser' Theory of Cooperators' Advantage." *American Political Science Review* 85: 515–28.

Ostrom, Elinor. 1990. *Governing the Commons: The Evolution of Institutions for Collective Action*. Cambridge: University of Cambridge Press.

Payne, J. W., J. R. Bettman, and E. J. Johnson. 1992. "Behavioral Decision Research: A Constructive Processing Perspective." *Annual Review of Psychology* 43: 87–131.

———. 1993. *The Adaptive Decision Maker*. Cambridge: Cambridge University Press.

Peters, B. Guy. 1991. *The Politics of Taxation: A Comparative Perspective*. Cambridge, Mass.: Blackwell.

Popkin, Samuel L. 1991. *The Reasoning Voter*. Chicago: University of Chicago Press.

Pratkanis, Anthony R. 1989. "The Cognitive Representation of Attitudes." In *Attitude Structure and Function*, edited by A. R. Pratkanis, S. J. Breckler, and A. G. Greenwald. Hillsdale, N.J.: Erlbaum.

Putnam, Robert. 1993. *Making Democracy Work: Civic Traditions in Modern Italy*. Princeton, N.J.: Princeton University Press.

Quattrone, George A., and Amos Tversky. 1988. "Contrasting Rational and Psychological Analyses of Political Choice." *American Political Science Review* 82: 719–36.

Roth, Jeffrey A., John T. Scholz, and Ann D. Witte. 1989. *Taxpayer Compliance: An Agenda for Research*. Philadelphia: University of Pennsylvania Press.

Schelling, Thomas C. 1960. *The Strategy of Conflict*. Cambridge: Harvard University Press.

Scholz, John T., and Mark Lubell. 1998a. "Adaptive Political Attitudes: Duty, Trust, and Fear as Monitors of Tax Policy." *American Journal of Political Science*, 42: 903–20.

———. 1998b. "Trust and Taxpaying: Testing the Heuristic Approach to Collective Action." *American Journal of Political Science*, 42: 398–417.

Scholz, John T., and Neil Pinney. 1995. "Duty, Fear, and Tax Compliance: The Heuristic Basis of Citizenship Behavior." *American Journal of Political Science* 39: 490–512.

Slemrod, Joel, ed. 1990. *Do Taxes Matter? The Impact of the Tax Reform of 1986*. Cambridge: Massachusetts Institute of Technology Press.

Smith, Kent W. 1990. "Integrating Three Perspectives of Noncompliance: A Sequential Decision Model." *Criminal Justice and Behavior*. 17: 350–69.

Sniderman, Paul M., Richard A. Brody, and Phillip Tetlock. 1991. *Reasoning and Choice: Explorations in Political Psychology*. Cambridge: Cambridge University Press.

Wilson, James Q. 1993. "The Moral Sense." *American Political Science Review* 87: 1–11.

Williamson, Oliver. 1996. *The Mechanisms of Governance*. New York: Oxford University Press.

Chapter 7

The Mobilization of Private Investment as a Problem of Trust in Local Governance Structures

SUSAN H. WHITING

T HE CONCEPT of trust is elusive; it is difficult to operationalize or measure and even more difficult to explain. The issue of trust arises in situations involving risk—specifically, "situations in which the risk one takes depends on the performance of another actor" (Coleman 1990, 91). The type of trust addressed in this chapter is specific as opposed to diffuse or general; in Russell Hardin's (1993) terms, "Trust is a three-part relation: A trusts B to do X" (506). In the context of trust in government, citizens either do or do not trust government agents to do X, where X may encompass a smaller or larger range of government commitments or responsibilities. This issue is distinct from the problem of generalized trust in government. Moreover, the type of trust addressed here is cognitive as opposed to noncognitive; cognitive trust involves employing available information to make intentionally rational assessments of risky situations. Thus, the term *trust* as used here is analogous to the terms *assurance* as employed by the sociologists Toshio Yamagishi and Midori Yamagishi (1994) and *credible commitment* as employed by the political scientist Barry Weingast (1995).[1]

Trust in Government

Operationalizing Trust

Attempts to operationalize the concept of trust in government fall into three main categories: surveys that elicit verbal expressions of trust in government,[2] experiments that elicit reactions indicative of trust in government (albeit in laboratory settings), and analyses of concrete actions or behaviors as indicators of trust in government. This chapter adopts the third approach; it focuses on a particular empirical phenomenon as an indicator of trust in government. It then considers four competing explanations of the phenomenon and evaluates their contributions to our understanding of the concept of trust in government.

The particular empirical phenomenon of interest involves private investment in fixed assets in industry in the People's Republic of China since the initiation of economic reforms in 1978. In theoretical terms this phenomenon stands as a useful proxy measure of trust in government. As numerous analysts of property rights have emphasized, private investors must "trust" the government to recognize and uphold their claims to their assets. Because the government apparatus as a whole enjoys a monopoly over the legitimate use of coercion, it is difficult to constrain its behavior. As the economic historian Douglass North (1990) has suggested, "If the state has coercive force, then those who run the state will use that force in their own interest at the expense of the rest of the society" (59). Indeed, if a private investor is not confident that he can reap the gains of his investment at some future point, then that assessment reduces the projected value of the investment and undermines the incentive to invest.

> For economic actors to undertake costly actions necessary for economic development, they must expect to garner the return of their efforts. The potential redistribution of these returns—whether through a substantial tax increase, a wholesale reversal of the reform process, or outright confiscation—reduces the expected private return to these actions (Weingast, 1993, 2).

Where positive expectations of reaping the returns from an investment are weak or absent, private investment tends to be on a smaller scale and for a shorter term than would otherwise be the case.

> We have only to contrast the organization of production in a Third World economy with that in an advanced industrial economy to be impressed by the consequences of poorly defined and/or ineffective prop-

erty rights. Not only will the institutional framework result in high costs of transacting in the former, but insecure property rights will result in using technologies that employ little fixed capital and do not entail long-term agreements. Firms will typically be small, except for those operated or protected by the government (North 1990, 64–5).

As these general treatments of property rights suggest, trust in the government is an important factor in the decisions of private investors to undertake the risk of investing—particularly in relatively immobile assets.[3]

Between 1956, when the Communist party abolished private industry as part of the socialist transformation, and 1978, which marked the initiation of reform, virtually no private industry existed in China. Since 1978, private industry has grown dramatically, but most private industrial enterprises are small compared with their publicly owned counterparts. The following discussion draws on data from China's rural industrial sector, where most private investment in industry is located.[4] By 1987, the first year for which comprehensive statistics are available at the national level, privately invested firms accounted for 86 percent of firms in the rural industrial sector, although they accounted for only 37 percent of employment and only 23 percent of output (see table 7.1).[5] By 1993, they accounted for 88 percent of firms, 42 percent of employment, and 28 percent of output. National statistics, however, mask tremendous regional variation in the significance of private industry.

Therefore, the focus here is on local governance structures.[6] The subsequent analysis draws on comparative case study research conducted in two counties in the wealthy southeastern coastal region of China during the early- to mid-1990s.[7] The two counties in Wenzhou and Shanghai differed dramatically in the roles played by private investment in the two local economies. The Wenzhou site (Yueqing County, Wenzhou Municipality, Zhejiang Province) was predominantly private; as can be seen in table 7.2, well over 90 percent of industrial enterprises were built with private investment and were privately owned. They provided most of the employment opportunities in industry (80 to 90 percent) and accounted for fully three-quarters of the gross value of industrial output. Thus, private industry played a much greater role in the economy of Yueqing County, Wenzhou, than in the national economy as a whole. In the Shanghai site (Songjiang County, Shanghai Municipality),[8] by contrast, privately invested firms accounted for less than 40 percent of industrial enterprises, less than 10 percent of employment in industry, and only 2 percent of the gross value of industrial output (see table 7.3). Thus, private industry played a much smaller role in the economy of Song-

Table 7.1 Comparison of Publicly and Privately Invested Industrial Firms in China, 1987 to 1993

	1987	1988	1989	1990	1991	1992	1993
Number of firms (million)							
Publicly invested	0.97	1.00	0.98	0.94	n/a	0.97	1.07
Privately invested	6.11	6.74	6.38	6.28		6.97	8.12
Total	7.08	7.74	7.36	7.22		7.94	9.18
Employment (million)							
Publicly invested	33.40	35.07	34.52	34.01		38.21	42.39
Privately invested	19.27	21.96	21.72	21.71		25.15	30.20
Total	52.67	57.03	56.24	55.72		63.36	72.60
Gross value of output (billion yuan)							
Publicly invested	261.05	322.67	461.36	524.06		985.28	1696.22
Privately invested	80.19	106.36	153.06	185.65		334.04	659.63
Total	341.24	429.02	614.42	709.70		1319.34	2355.86
Private share of total (%)							
Number of firms	86	87	87	87		88	88
Employment	37	39	39	39		40	42
Gross value of output	23	25	25	26		25	28

Sources: Zhongguo xiangzhen qiye nianjian (China's Township and Village Enterprise Yearbook) 1978 to 1987, 1989, 1990, 1991, 1993, 1994. Beijing: Agricultural Publishing House.
Note: The table includes all industrial firms at the township level and below.

Table 7.2 Comparison of Publicly and Privately Invested Industrial Firms, Yueqing County, Wenzhou, 1988 to 1994

	1988	1989	1990	1991	1992	1993	1994
Number of firms							
Publicly invested	217	181	164	144	125	91	77
Privately invested	2947	2959	2723	2770	2972	3636	4370
Total	3164	3140	2887	2914	3097	3727	4447
Employment							
Publicly invested	13294	10605	10360	9425	12907	7523	6976
Privately invested	64787	54248	50808	52088	60127	73185	n/a
Total	78081	64853	61168	61513	73034	80708	n/a
Gross value of output (million yuan)							
Publicly invested	188.07	175.23	174.87	250.62	358.41	548.07	524.92
Privately invested	487.77	575.22	524.99	712.18	1220.80	1970.15	n/a
Total	675.84	750.45	699.86	962.80	1579.21	2518.22	n/a
Private share of total (%)							
Number of firms	93	94	94	95	96	98	98
Total Employment	83	84	83	85	82	91	n/a
Gross value of output	72	77	75	74	77	78	n/a

Sources: Yueqing tongji nianjian (Yueqing Statistical Yearbook) 1990, 1991, 1993, 1994, 1995. Yueqing: Yueqing Statistical Bureau.
Notes: The table includes all industrial firms at the township level and below. Privately invested firms are in the form of gufen hezuo qiye.

Table 7.3 Comparison of Publicly and Privately Invested Industrial Firms, Songjiang County, Shanghai, 1989 to 1994

	1989	1990	1991	1992	1993	1994
Number of firms						
Publicly invested	1341	1300	1317	1359	1475	1352
Privately invested	173	267	349	555	711	826
Total	1514	1567	1666	1914	2186	2178
Employment						
Publicly invested	123992	124489	126551	127308	124297	115960
Privately invested	2427	3541	4947	8330	11893	12074
Total	126419	128030	131498	135638	136190	128034
Gross value of output (million yuan)						
Publicly invested	2110.82	2491.04	3127.44	4264.40	7027.22	11199.46
Privately invested	6.35	12.38	21.57	29.84	68.44	211.68
Total	2117.17	2503.42	3149.01	4294.24	7095.66	11411.14
Private share of total (%)						
Number of firms	11	17	21	29	33	38
Total employment	2	3	4	6	9	9
Gross value of output	0	0	1	1	1	2

Sources: Songjiang tongji nianjian (Songjiang Statistical Yearbook) 1989, 1991, 1992, 1993, 1994, 1995.
Notes: The table includes all industrial firms at the township level and below. Privately invested firms are in the form of siying qiye.

jiang County, Shanghai, than in the national economy as a whole. One of the challenges in analyzing private investment as a problem of trust in government is to explain these sharp regional variations.

Explaining Trust

Four distinct sets of competing explanations seek to account for the phenomenon of private investment in China: (1) the lure of huge potential gains in the marketplace even in the absence of trust in government, (2) trust in government stemming from third-party enforcement by the courts, (3) trust in government stemming from dense interpersonal networks that extend into the government apparatus, and (4) trust in government reflecting the institutionally defined interests of local officials.[9]

The first explanation for private investment in China suggests that the sheer magnitude of potential gains in the booming Chinese economy attracts private investment even in the absence of trust in government.[10] The notion of cognitive trust presented by the sociologist James Coleman (1990) holds that "individuals will rationally place trust if the ratio of the probability that the trustee will keep the trust to the probability that he will not is greater than the ratio of the potential loss to the potential gain, or if $p/(1-p)$ is greater than L/G" (p. 104). In other words, $p \times G$ must be greater than $(1-p) \times L$, where p is the probability that the trustee is trustworthy, L is the potential loss if the trustee is untrustworthy, and G is the potential gain if the trustee is trustworthy. Thus, when a small fixed investment (representing a small potential loss) can produce potentially huge gains, even a very low probability that government is trustworthy will motivate a rational investor to invest.

The second explanation focuses on the role of third-party enforcement by the courts in establishing trust in the government (Levi 1995; North 1990). China's Civil Procedure Law and Administrative Litigation Law include within their scope complaints against government organs regarding failure to protect property rights, unlawful denial or revocation of licenses, and infringement of lawful business autonomy, among other possible transgressions.[11] In theory, these laws offer protection to private investors against transgressions by government agents.

The third explanation centers on dense interpersonal networks that extend into the government apparatus. The sociologists Victor Nee and Sijin Su (1996) focused on "longstanding social ties based on frequent face-to-face interactions" (113) as an important basis for trust and cooperation between entrepreneurs and the government in the Chinese political economy. They emphasized that "transaction costs are lower in institutional settings where trust and cooperation flow from informal norms and established social relationships" (113). Dense interpersonal networks provide information as well as opportunities to impose sanctions that are important to the establishment of trust. Here it is important to note that the personal identities of those who staff the government apparatus and their membership in personal networks are key elements of the explanation. In a similar vein, the sociologists Nan Lin and Chih-jou Chen (1994) emphasized thick relationships based on familial ties. Finally, the sociologist David Wank (1995, 1996) considered thick-relationship trust in terms of patron-client ties. For Wank, "Long-term relations, by increasing the degree of trust and concern for mutual benefit, reduce the likelihood of opportunistic behavior by official-patrons vis-à-vis entrepreneur-clients" (178). He emphasized personal ties with government agents as a key source of protection for private investors in the absence of strong legal guarantees. Thus, dense interpersonal networks that reach into the government apparatus play a central role in generating trust in government. As the sociologist Ambrose King (1991, 79) noted, "Network building is used (consciously or unconsciously) by Chinese adults as a cultural strategy in mobilizing social resources for goal attainment in various spheres of social life. To a significant degree the cultural dynamic of guanxi building is a source of vitality in Chinese society" (79). As this statement suggests, the network explanation of trust in government is related to accounts of Chinese culture that emphasize the importance of networks of relations (guanxi) as a widespread sociocultural phenomenon.

The fourth explanation highlights the role of local officials embedded in local government institutions in China, who have an institutionally defined interest in protecting private investment in order to promote economic growth (Oi 1992, 1995; Whiting 1995; C. Wong 1991, 1992). In this approach to trust in government, unlike the approach based on interpersonal networks, the personal identities of those who staff the government apparatus are not central to the establishment of trust. Rather, the focus here is on the sources of *incentives* for government agents to be trustworthy in particular situations as shaped by the structure of governmental institutions. This approach is based on the notion of trust as encapsulated interest (Hardin 1993, 1995; Levi this volume). In theoretical terms, an encapsulated-interest account of trust in government involves several elements. First, as has been noted, the trustworthiness of government agents is evaluated in regard to *specific* government commitments and responsibilities (A trusts B to do X)—not in regard to the universe of possible government actions. Thus, the question of trust concerns a particular issue or set of issues. The second element concerns the trustworthiness of government agents; their trustworthiness is based on whether they have the incentive to fulfill citizen trust with respect to X. In other words, for government agents to be trustworthy, they must have an *interest* in doing X. This element of trust as encapsulated interest finds a direct parallel in the literature on credible commitment. For government commitments to be credible, they must be self-enforcing. Thus, it is necessary to "create a set of arrangements that alter incentives so that carrying out the original bargain—rather than behaving opportunistically ex post—is compatible with the incentives facing the actors after the fact" (Weingast 1993, 4). In the third element of the encapsulated interest approach to trust, citizens must be aware of the existence of incentives for government agents to be trustworthy in order for trust to operate. Hardin finds this element to be the most difficult to satisfy. Citizens may know enough to distrust government, but he finds it implausible in most cases that they will know enough to place their trust in government meaningfully. "Few people can have an articulate understanding of the structures of various agencies and the roles within them or of the government overall to be confident of the incentives that role-holders have to be trustworthy" (Hardin 1995, 23). Hardin does, however, allow that "those most attentive to government will also be those most likely to know enough about governmental actions and structures to know whether the government and its agents are trustworthy" (1995, 25). Finally, the assessment of the trustworthiness of government agents is informed by citizens' past experiences with government agents with respect to X.[12] In sum, the nature of government institutions and the institutionally defined interests of government officials, particularly at the local level, where citizens have rich knowledge of government, are key in this account.[13]

Without advocating either static or mono-causal explanations, this chapter seeks to establish the importance of the encapsulated-interest approach to trust in government, focusing on the key role played by local governance structures in the Chinese reform process. To foreshadow the conclusion, this type of explanation goes furthest in explaining the striking regional variation that has characterized private investment in China.

Encapsulated Interest in Local Governance Structures in China

The encapsulated-interest approach to trust in government focuses on the *interests of government agents* in being trustworthy with respect to the claims of potential private investors in industry. The discussion that follows will show that local officials across locales in China had varied interests with respect to the protection and promotion of private industry during the first decade and a half of reform.

Local government officials are key players in the highly decentralized Chinese political economy; their actions fundamentally shape property rights within their jurisdictions. The interests guiding their actions are determined by the incentives and constraints contained in their institutional environment.[14] The institutional environment during the reform era has provided all local officials with powerful incentives to promote economic—and particularly industrial—development. The initial choices of local officials about *how* to promote industrial development, however, were constrained by a number of factors, in particular by the nature of available resources and by the larger political-legal and market environments in which local communities were embedded. As a result, the interests of local officials in protecting and promoting private industry varied markedly depending on the nature of these constraints.

All local officials share an interest in promoting industrial development. This common interest derives from two characteristic features of their institutional environment: the appointment system for local officials and the fiscal system that finances their activities. Local officials in China are appointed by their superiors at the next higher level in the administrative hierarchy. Their superiors employ specific performance criteria (kaohe zhibiao) to determine each official's level of remuneration, tenure of office, and opportunities for advancement. The criteria are designed to make party and government leaders responsible for the performance of the local community in economic as well as in social and political terms. Interviews reveal that, in practice, industrial growth is the single most important element in assessing performance.[15] Yet in addition to economic performance, the provision of public goods, such as education, public health, and public order, is also considered in evaluating the overall performance of local leaders. Provision of these public goods is also linked to the success of industry in numerous ways. For example, local officials regard providing local residents with employment opportunities in industry as the primary means of maintaining public order. Moreover, industry is the main source of revenue for financing virtually all local government functions.

The incentives of local leaders are thus shaped by the nature of the fiscal system, since it determines the financial resources they can use to pursue their goals. Fiscal reforms initiated in 1980 created a revenue imperative for local officials by making local governments essentially self-financing at the same time that they increased the responsibility of local governments for financing public goods.[16] Township officials came to depend overwhelmingly on revenues generated in local industry to cover township expenditures, creating an industry-centered tax structure in which the burden of taxation fell most heavily on industrial enterprises. Data collected in Shanghai and

Wenzhou in 1992 demonstrate that close to 90 percent of total fiscal revenue at the township level derived from local enterprises—overwhelmingly from industry. Thus, the scale of financial resources at the disposal of local cadres was closely tied to the success of local industry. Given the incentives contained in both the appointment system and the fiscal system, local officials made the vigorous promotion of local industry one of their main objectives.

The types of property rights that local officials chose to support in promoting local industry at the beginning of the reform period differed markedly across regions, however. Choices were constrained by the resources available in the community.[17] In areas with a legacy of weak public enterprise development, such as Wenzhou, local cadres had a poor revenue base and little revenue to invest in publicly owned enterprises. When faced with the imperative of self-financing in the early 1980s, they responded by moving aggressively to support private property rights in order to encourage investment and develop the tax base.[18] By contrast, in areas with a legacy of strong public enterprise development, such as Shanghai, local cadres exercised direct control over capital and other resources that allowed them to invest further in public enterprise development. Local officials in Shanghai resisted the development of private enterprise and opted instead to protect and nurture public enterprises, greatly facilitating the rapid growth of these firms. The absence of secure private property rights stifled investment on the part of private entrepreneurs in Shanghai.

The broader political-legal environment also influenced the kinds of property rights that local officials were willing and able to support. Outright private ownership did not receive formal legal recognition from the central government until 1988, fully ten years after the initiation of reform. In that year, the National People's Congress revised the constitution to legitimate private ownership, and the State Council passed regulations governing private enterprise.[19] Nevertheless, even after the constitutional amendment and the passage of national regulations—both designed to legitimate private ownership—private enterprises continued to come under political attack at the central level. In particular, the economic rectification campaign of late 1988 through 1991, which targeted private enterprise, called into question the ability of local officials to protect investors from challenges from the center. The Fourth Plenum of the Thirteenth Central Committee in June 1989 led to an attack on "private entrepreneurs who use illegal methods to seek huge profits and thereby create great social disparity and contribute to discontent among the public." The Fifth Plenum of the Thirteenth Central Committee, held in November 1989, determined that unspecified aspects of private development were "not beneficial" to socialism and would be limited.[20] Even more recently, the Fifth Plenum of the Fourteenth Central Committee, held in September 1995, reiterated the position that "keeping the public sector of the economy as the dominant one . . . is the basic principle we have upheld for a long time. Any practice that shakes or forsakes the dominant position of the public sector is a departure from the socialist orientation."[21] As Margaret Levi (this volume, 88) has suggested, "antagonism of government actors toward those they are supposed to serve" is a major source of distrust in government. Policy statements like those cited above elicit distrust in the *central* government on the part of private investors. Such distrust has two implications. First, it reinforces the importance of trust in *local* government officials. Second, it generates a preference on the part of private investors for the protection offered by nominally public forms of investment.

Finally, choices about property rights are constrained by the market environment—by the nature of markets for capital, land, and other inputs into industry and by the nature of markets for industrial products. The extent to which goods are allocated by bureaucratic decisions rather than by prices limits the ability of private investors, who function for the most part outside of formal bureaucratic channels, to realize the full value of their investments.[22] As Victor Nee (1996) has noted, "In the state socialist redistributive economy officials act as monopolists who specify and enforce the rules of exchange by administrative fiat and exclude private entrepreneurs from taking part in legitimate economic activities. . . . The more developed the market economy, the greater the breadth and diversity of opportunities that develop outside the boundaries of the redistributive economy" (910–11). The perpetuation of bureaucratic control over the allocation of resources and the slow pace of marketization for land and capital constrain the effective exercise of private property rights over productive assets and shape the particular forms of property rights adopted in industry. In sum, choices about property rights are constrained by control over available resources as well as by the broader political and economic environments in which firms function. As a result of these constraints, the interests of local government officials in protecting private investments in industry have varied across locales.

Trust as Encapsulated Interest in Yueqing County, Wenzhou

The preceding discussion established that local officials in Wenzhou, unlike local officials in Shanghai, had an interest in mobilizing private capital for productive investment in rural industry. The development of public enterprise was relatively weak in Wenzhou during the Maoist era. This area, which is located directly across from Taiwan, received little central or provincial investment during the years of greatest tension between the mainland and Taiwan. Furthermore, it is surrounded by mountains and coastline and therefore was relatively isolated from the major industrial centers of the region. As of 1978, per capita industrial output in Yueqing County, Wenzhou, was approximately one hundred ten yuan, compared with approximately six hundred yuan in Songjiang County, Shanghai.

With relatively few resources under the direct control of county and township governments and with the presence of at least some capital resources in the hands of local residents, local officials in Wenzhou sought to mobilize alternative, private sources of investment by specifying private property rights. As one local official commented, "We must encourage investment on the part of individuals because the [government] doesn't have enough money itself" (Informant 167). Local officials in Wenzhou were, however, limited in their ability to specify and provide effective political support for private property rights within the existing political-legal framework. The relatively hostile political climate for private investment, described in the last section, tended to inhibit private investment. Nevertheless, as James Coleman (1990) has pointed out, "The trustee [here, the local government] may engage in actions explicitly designed to lead the potential trustor to place trust. . . . These actions . . . to be successful must be based on an understanding (intuitive or explicit) of the potential trustor's basis for deciding whether or not to place trust" (96). Local government officials in Wenzhou were keenly aware of the concerns of private investors. According to an official of the Wenzhou System Reform Commission, his office consulted directly with more than twenty actual and potential private investors in order to ascertain what would encourage them to invest more actively (Informant 171). He reported that they were most concerned about two issues: the determination of the "political nature" (dingxing) of the enterprise and the disposition of firm assets. Specifically, the entrepreneurs wanted their firms legitimately to be considered *socialist* in nature, and they wanted clear title to their firms' assets; the former was seen as essential to their political security as well as to their ability to participate in restricted factor and product markets. In response, local officials in Wenzhou sought to work within the existing political-legal framework to meet investors' demands.

The framework for private investment adopted in Wenzhou addressed the ongoing concerns of private investors about the political nature of their enterprises and official recognition of their claims to their assets. In the early 1980s, well before the promulgation of regulations governing outright private enterprise, local officials in Wenzhou began to encourage private investors to invest in privately formed cooperatives (gufen hezuo qiye). Such cooperatives were a response to both the discrimination against and the limitations on private investment (Informant 247). By 1987, the Wenzhou government had passed the first version of formal, *local* regulations governing shareholding cooperatives.[23] These regulations made clear that individuals who invested capital or other assets in such a cooperative venture retained private ownership of those assets. Moreover, the firm would be considered a part of the socialist economy; this determination was based on an implicit appeal to the precedent found in mutual aid teams and agricultural producers' cooperatives from the 1950s. As a recognized part of the socialist economy, private shareholding cooperatives would be taxed at the same rate as comparable public enterprises and would be eligible for tax breaks according to the guidelines governing comparable public enterprises. The regulations on private shareholding cooperatives not only encouraged private investment by legitimating it within the existing political-legal framework; they also enabled private investors to realize the full value of their assets, since the cooperatives were afforded better access to land and bank capital, which had yet to be fully marketized. For example, in 1987 local officials in Yueqing County began building an industrial park to accommodate the needs of investors in private shareholding cooperatives for land and factory space. With respect to capital resources, table 7.4 provides data on *average* bank loans outstanding for private shareholding cooperatives in Yueqing County. These statistics show that privately invested firms had access to the state-run banking system as early as 1985, and the size of loans grew dramatically in most years between 1985 and 1994. While the size of the average loan was relatively small, some loans to private investors were as large as two hundred fifty thousand yuan. Finally, private shareholding cooperatives also enjoyed access to bureaucratically controlled production permits that allowed firms to enter restricted product markets.

Private shareholding cooperatives whose status was based on locally promulgated regulations must be distinguished from private firms that registered *falsely* as public enterprises in Wenzhou and elsewhere. Like cooperatives, fake public enterprises emerged in response to the discrimination against and limitations on private investment. In practice, individual investors would pay local government officials a fee in return for nominal status as a public enterprise. Unlike cooperatives, however, fake public enterprises offered no official recognition of the claims of investors to their assets. On the contrary, the assets officially belonged to the local government. As both Chinese and Western scholars have pointed out, a change in the disposition of lo-

Table 7.4 Growth of Privately Invested Industrial Firms, Yueqing County, Wenzhou

	1985	1986	1987	1988	1989	1990	1991	1992	1993	1994
Level										
Average employment per firm	16	18	10	22	18	19	19	20	20	n/a
Average bank loans outstanding per firm	1177	4195	4980	8426	9605	8898	17628	30784	45547	45437
Total value of fixed assets (million yuan)	n/a	20.37	23.51	48.42	70.77	89.74	117.36	211.53	430.24	819.49
Average value of fixed assets per firm	n/a	9159	10398	16430	23917	32956	42368	71174	118328	187526
Increase over previous year (%)										
Average employment per firm		11.5	−46.3	130.7	−16.6	1.8	0.8	7.6	−0.5	n/a
Average bank loans outstanding per firm		256.4	18.7	69.2	14.0	−7.4	98.1	74.6	48.0	−0.2
Total value of fixed assets (million yuan)		n/a	15.4	106.0	46.2	26.8	30.8	80.2	103.4	90.5
Average value of fixed assets per firm		n/a	13.5	58.0	45.6	37.8	28.6	68.0	66.3	58.5

Sources: Yueqing tongji nianjiang (Yueqing Statistical Yearbook) 1990, 1991, 1992, 1993, 1994, 1995. Yueqing Statistical Bureau.
Notes: The table includes all industrial firms at the township level and below. Privately invested firms are in the form of gufen hezuo qiye.

cal officials toward these firms "could suddenly demote the founders and investors to mere employees with no right to a return on the capital that they had invested" (Clarke 1995, 305). Such occurrences were not unheard of—even in Wenzhou (Informants 146, 147). Moreover, fake public enterprises were particularly vulnerable to campaigns emanating from higher levels. For example, following the conservative line established at the Fourth Plenum of the Thirteenth Central Committee in 1989, the State Council launched a series of investigations into tax evasion in the private economy, targeting all private firms but focusing in particular on those firms that continued to register falsely as public enterprises.[24] This campaign extended even to Wenzhou, where fake public enterprises were targeted for rectification while shareholding cooperatives retained their status as legitimate members of the socialist economy.[25] Fake public enterprises were often established through personal ties between private investors and government officials; by contrast, private shareholding cooperatives were an institutionalized form of protection for private investors. Status as a private shareholding cooperative was based on guidelines set forth by the local government and not solely on the relationships between particular investors and particular officials.

Table 7.4 illustrates the growth of private shareholding cooperatives in Yueqing County since 1985. According to a representative of the Yueqing System Reform Commission, prior to 1985 only a few hundred private shareholding cooperatives existed in the county (Informant 247). While the number of enterprises has grown slowly since 1985 and fell slightly in 1990, the average value of fixed assets has increased steadily at double-digit rates—even during the years of economic rectification from 1989 through 1991. Moreover, with the greater perceived trust in local government officials' commitment to private shareholding cooperatives, this form of cooperative has become the dominant form of enterprise in many jurisdictions within Wenzhou. Table 7.2 highlights the predominant share of firms, employment, and industrial output accounted for by private shareholding cooperatives in Yueqing County between 1988 and 1994. Table 7.5 provides ownership breakdowns for number of firms, level of employment, and tax receipts for all industrial enterprises in one township in Yueqing County in 1991; shareholding cooperatives account for the largest share in every category.

Local officials in Wenzhou had an institutionally defined interest in promoting private industrial development. They furthered that interest by promulgating regulations designed to allay the fears of private investors and to create a local institutional environment conducive to private investment. Moreover, private investors in Wenzhou were

Table 7.5   **Industrial Enterprises by Ownership, Hualing Town, Yueqing County, Wenzhou, 1991**

	Firms (units)	Firms (% of total)	Employment (thousands)	Employment (% of total)	Tax Receipts (million yuan)	Tax Receipts (% of total)
Total	275	100	7.84	100	20.76	100
Publicly invested	24	9	1.69	21	8.51	41
Privately invested	251	91	6.15	79	12.26	59

Source: Informant 144.
Notes: Publicly invested firms are in the form of township and village enterprises (xiangban and cunban qiye), while privately invested firms are in the form of siying qiye and gufen hezuo qiye.

aware of the interests and actions of local officials on their behalf; indeed, they were consulted.

Trust as Encapsulated Interest in Songjiang County, Shanghai

While privately invested industrial enterprises developed ahead of national regulations in Wenzhou, private enterprises in industry did not emerge in Shanghai until the passage of national regulations in 1988.[26] Local officials regarded the development of private industry as a competitive threat to the public enterprises in Shanghai's suburban industrial sector. Given the area's strong endowment in public assets as of the early 1980s, the dependence of the local government on public enterprise for fiscal revenue, and the close ties between public enterprises and the local government, local officials in Shanghai had an interest in resisting the development of private enterprises, and they did so by creating barriers to entry and growth.

The constraints on private enterprise were of several kinds. Private firms were not granted licenses in any industrial sector or product line in which a publicly owned factory was already operating. Those private enterprises that did receive licenses were taxed aggressively. Limitations on access to land and credit were also major constraints on private enterprise development. Private enterprise owners in Songyang Town, Songjiang County in the early 1990s had to operate out of their own homes or rent abandoned buildings or sheds from the village. Even when private entrepreneurs won approval to expand existing workshops, their investments were minimal because of the belief that the government could repossess the land and buildings at any time, depriving the owners of their assets (Informants 89 and 94). Similarly, in principle neither the local state-run bank nor the state-sponsored credit cooperative granted loans to private enterprises; as a bank representative in Songjiang put it, "In general, we don't make loans to private enterprises" (Informant 111).[27] In practice, however, about half the private enterprises in the township had received small, short-term loans from the credit cooperative, none of them exceeding ten thousand yuan (Informants 96 and 99). According to a representative of the credit cooperative, total loans to private firms accounted for approximately 0.2 percent of the credit cooperative's loans outstanding in 1991 (Informant 99).[28] The institutionally defined interests of local officials in Songjiang contributed to their lack of support for private investors.

Nevertheless, the fact that private investors in Songjiang were not completely barred from the local economy or entirely shut out of the loan market demonstrates that institutionally defined interests are not completely determinate. Interpersonal networks operate even where the broader institutional environment is unsupportive of private investment. As the following section demonstrates, however, the impact of the institutional environment is significant nonetheless.

A Comparison of Yueqing and Songjiang

Tables 7.2 to 7.6 present contrasting pictures of private industrial development in Songjiang County, Shanghai, and Yueqing County, Wenzhou. In Wenzhou private investment in industry began earlier than in Shanghai. The average size of fixed asset investment was larger across the board, and the average size increased much faster in every year until 1994. In 1989, as private industry was just beginning to develop in Songjiang, the average output value of private industrial firms in Yueqing was more than five times that in Songjiang; as of 1994, the average value of industrial output was still twice that in Songjiang. The comparative strength of private industry in Wenzhou likely reflects the more supportive environment provided by trustworthy local officials who had an institutionally defined interest in promoting private industry. Private property rights (particularly in private shareholding cooperatives) were more secure, and investors enjoyed better access to land and capital. These factors underpinned the strength of private industry in Yueqing, Wenzhou. Private investment accounted for more than 90 percent of enterprises, 80 to 90 percent of employment, and three-quarters of industrial output in Yueqing. By contrast, private investors accounted for 10 to 40 percent of enterprises, less than 10 percent of employment, and only 2 percent of industrial output in Songjiang.

**Table 7.6   Growth of Privately Invested Industrial Firms, Songjiang
County, Shanghai, 1989 to 1994**

	1989	1990	1991	1992	1993	1994
Level						
Average employment per firm	14	13	14	15	17	15
Average bank loans outstanding per firm	n/a	n/a	n/a	n/a	n/a	n/a
Total registered capital (million yuan)	4.14	6.41	8.97	19.20	28.87	91.93
Average registered capital per firm	23913	24007	25702	34595	40605	111295
Increase over previous year (%)						
Average employment per firm		−5.5	6.9	5.9	11.4	−12.6
Average bank loans outstanding per firm		n/a	n/a	n/a	n/a	n/a
Total registered capital		54.9	39.9	114.0	50.4	218.4
Average registered capital per firm		0.4	7.1	34.6	17.4	174.1

Sources: Songjiang tongji nianjian (Songjiang Statistical Yearbook) 1989, 1991, 1992, 1993, 1994, 1995. Songjiang: Songjiang Statistical Bureau.
Notes: The table includes all industrial firms at the township level and below. Privately invested firms are in the form of siying qiye.

Conclusion

Each of the competing hypotheses regarding trust in government that were introduced at the beginning of this chapter contributes to a comprehensive explanation of the growth of private investment in China, where private investment stands as a proxy measure for trust in government at the local level. The first explanation suggests that the sheer magnitude of potential gains in the booming Chinese economy will attract private investment even in the absence of trust in local government. Private investment grew in Songjiang despite the relative lack of support on the part of local officials. Indeed, the burst of private investment in Songjiang in 1994 may reflect the increasing potential gains stemming from the overall economic development of the greater Shanghai area in the mid-1990s. The lure of potential gains does not, however, explain the contrasting growth paths in Songjiang and Yueqing up to 1994. By this account, virtually every feature of the marketplace in Shanghai suggests that it should have led Wenzhou in private investment. Proximity to market demand and development of transportation networks in particular suggest that the Shanghai region should consistently attract more investment. Wenzhou, surrounded by mountains and coastline, is relatively isolated, and there is no rail connection linking Wenzhou to the major industrial centers of the region. Yet in 1994 total private investment in fixed assets in industry was eight hundred twenty million yuan in Yueqing, compared with ninety-two million yuan in Songjiang. The greater (average and total) magnitude of investment in Yueqing County, Wenzhou, suggests that the lure of potential gains is not the whole story.

Second, while the political-legal environment for private enterprise is gradually improving, it is unlikely to provide an adequate basis for trust in government at present. The case studies of private enterprise development in Songjiang and Yueqing did not provide any evidence that courts were an important means of resolving disputes involving government agencies—despite the existence of the Administrative Litigation Law. Indeed, legal experts and others express skepticism about the willingness and ability of courts to enforce rulings against the interests of local government officials (Clarke 1995; Lyons 1994; Potter 1994a, 1994b). Local officials continue to exert influence over courts as over other government agencies within their jurisdiction. Thus, while third-party enforcement is an important theoretical possibility, there is little evidence that the court system has sufficient independence from the government and party apparatuses to perform this role in China. Moreover, the inability of the courts to enforce rulings against the interests of local officials highlights the significance of the institutionally defined interests of those officials.

Third, the importance of interpersonal networks that extend into the government apparatus in China is undeniable. For example, personal connections affected the ability of private investors to secure bank loans in Songjiang. Nevertheless, reliance on personal connections in Songjiang did not result in private sector development comparable to that in Yueqing. Moreover, there is no evidence to suggest that the density of personal networks linking private entrepreneurs to government officials varies systematically by region. Indeed, such networks seem to pervade every region and to pervade the public and the private sectors alike. An explanation based on widespread cultural practice is less useful in accounting for local variation, even though such practice may be an important factor in explaining business success in general.[29] Furthermore, enterprises require scores of approvals, forms, and licenses in order to function, and the cultivation of personal connections for each and every approval is costly.[30] The need to rely solely on personal connections to underpin the emergence and growth of private enterprise may hinder its development significantly. Finally, many analysts of Chinese business practices highlight that sociocultural factors alone cannot explain investment behavior; the political environment is a crucial variable (Hamilton and Biggart 1988; Hsiao 1991; Whyte 1995).

The pattern of regional variation in private investment suggests systematic differences across locales. This chapter has focused on the institutionally defined interests of local government officials. It has shown that local officials in Wenzhou, regardless of their personal identities and personal connections, had an institutionally defined interest in promoting private industry. By contrast, local officials in Shanghai had an interest in resisting the rapid development of private industry. These interests significantly shaped the development of private enterprise in the two communities. This analysis highlights the utility of the encapsulated interest approach to trust in government— at least at the local level. While this approach does not explain the presence or absence of generalized trust in government, it does provide an explanation for intentionally rational trust in government with respect to particular local commitments and responsibilities.

Fieldwork for this study was supported by grants from the Committee for Scholarly Communications with the People's Republic of China and from the Joint Committee on Chinese Studies of the American Council of Learned Societies and the Social Science Research Council with funds provided by the Chiang Ching-kuo Foundation. Additional support was provided by a Faculty Research Grant from the China Studies Program of the University of Washington. I benefited from comments and discussion at two seminars sponsored by the Russell Sage Foundation: the Russell Sage Workshop on Trust and Social Structure in Seattle, September 1995, and the Russell Sage Workshop on Trust, New York, April 1996.

Notes

1. One of the issues involved in the use of the term *trust* is the association of positive affect for the trustee associated with lay use of term. No such connotation is intended here.

2. See, for example, the four-question battery in the National Election Study survey that constitutes the index of trust in government.

3. Moreover, the role of the government is important in underpinning other kinds of contracts besides property rights in fixed assets. The government can facilitate trade by acting as a neutral third party that can and will enforce contracts between firms. If the government does not regard private firms as legitimate, however, it is less likely to play this role in enforcing contracts in which private firms are involved.

4. The rural industrial sector includes all industrial enterprises at the township level or below. The township is the lowest level in the government administrative hierarchy in China. The township is directly subordinate to county government, which in turn is typically subordinate to a hierarchy of municipal, provincial, and central government.

5. These national statistics on privately invested firms do not distinguish between household firms employing up to eight workers (known as *getihu*) and private enterprises employing more than eight employees. It is the latter category that is of particular interest here, since firms of this size bear significantly more risk.

6. In the context of the PRC, local governance structures refer to the government and party organizations that make up the local state apparatus. There is significant overlap between these two organizations. For simplicity, they will be referred to in the discussion as "local government."

7. As part of a larger research project, counties were selected for variation in the concentration of property-rights forms in rural industry. Interviews were conducted with enterprise owners and managers as well as with an array of officials representing various government bureaus and bank and credit cooperative offices at the county, township, and (where applicable) village levels. Approximately two hundred fifty interviews were conducted in 1991, 1992, and 1996; of these, forty-seven interviews were conducted in Yueqing County and fifty-seven interviews were conducted in Songjiang County. Adapted for the purpose of analyzing trust in the government (using private investment in fixed assets as a proxy measure), the case study data under examination suffer from the problem of selection on the dependent variable. Private investment in the case study sites spans a wide range of variation, however, varying from 0 to near 100 percent of industrial investment in the sites. Moreover, the key independent variable, the institutionally defined interests of local officials, varies as well. Nevertheless, the primary utility of this set of case study data is to establish the plausibility of the institutional approach to trust in the state (introduced later in the chapter), to be tested by subsequent research.

8. Shanghai Municipality enjoys the status of a province and is governed directly by the central government.

9. A fifth possible explanation has been put forth by the economists Martin Weitzman and Chenggang Xu (1994, 138). They seek to explain the success of non-state industry in China on the basis of the *assumption* of a high level of society-wide trust. Weitzman and Xu's assumption is that "East Asia is a high-lamda [that is, high trust] society relative to Europe," where lamda is defined as follows: "Let the outcome to a repeated non-cooperative prisoner's dilemma game be quantified by the parameter lamda, which is valued between 0 and 1. A high value of lamda near one means a non-cooperative solution that comes close to looking as if it were the outcome of cooperative collusion. . . . The parameter lamda stands for the ability of a group of people to resolve prisoner's dilemma type free-riding problems internally, without the imposition of explicit rules of behavior, other things, including the size of the group, being equal. With a value 1 of lamda, people in a group would be able to resolve completely free-riding problems internally" (138). The assumption of a high-trust society, however, begs the very question of interest in

this chapter; therefore, this approach will not receive further consideration here.

10. I thank Victor Nee for suggesting this approach.

11. See, for example, "Zhonghua renmin gongheguo xingzheng susong fa (Administrative Litigation Law of the PRC)," translated in *Chinese Law and Government* 24(3) (Fall 1991): 22–34, especially 23.

12. Hardin (1993) refers to this as "common sense Bayesianism" (517).

13. For another treatment of local industrial development in China that suggests that information problems are less severe in smaller, local jurisdictions, see (Walder 1995).

14. This analysis is based on the underlying assumption that local government officials seek to maintain their official positions in order to exercise the power and perquisites of office.

15. For example, according to representatives of the county office of management and administration in Songjiang County, Shanghai, 1995 bonuses for township leaders were determined by five key indicators: gross value of industrial output, industrial profits from collective enterprises, GDP, receipts of local taxes, and total new investment. For each indicator, both the level and the increase over the previous year were assessed. The highest-paid government executive and party secretary were from the town with the highest combined ranking, while the lowest-paid were from the town with the lowest combined ranking. Looking at the level of and increase in the gross value of industrial output alone produces a virtually identical ranking (Informant 214 and Songjiang County Statistical Bureau *Songjiang tongji nianjian 1996* [*Songjiang Statistical Yearbook 1996*]).

16. This situation has a parallel in "unfunded mandates" to state and local governments in the U.S. system. On the Chinese fiscal system, see Byrd and Gelb 1990; Oi 1992; Whiting 1995; and Wong 1992.

17. Under the incentive structure just outlined, local officials would be expected to prefer to promote publicly owned (collective) enterprises, other things being equal. The township government received taxes and fees from all enterprises, but as the owner of township-run collectives it also received profit remittances from these firms. Furthermore, as owner, the local government faced lower information costs in extracting revenue from these firms.

18. A vast secondary literature has emerged on the Wenzhou model; see, for example, Fei and Luo 1988; He 1987; Yuan 1987; and Zhang and Li 1990a, 1990b. In English, see A. Liu 1992; Y. Liu 1992; Nolan and Dong 1990; Parris 1993; and Young 1989.

19. For the revised text of the constitution, see "Zhonghua renmin gongheguo xianfa xiuzhengan," in *Zhongguo nongye nianjian, 1989* (*Agricultural Yearbook of China, 1989*) (Beijing: Nongye chubanshe, 1989), 538. For the regu-

lations, see "Zhonghua renmin gonghequo siying qiye zanxing tiaoli,"
"Zhonghua renmin gonghequo siying qiye suodeshui zanxing tiaoli,"
and "Guowuyuan Guanyu zhengshou siying qiye touzizhe geren shouru
tiaojie shui de guiding," *Jingji Ribao* (*Economic Daily*), June 29, 1988, 2.

20. See State Council document [1989] #60, August 30, 1989: "Guowuyuan
Guanyu dali jiaqiang chengxiang geti gongshanghu he siying qiye shuishou zhengguan gongzuo de jueding (State Council Decision Regarding
Vigorously Strengthening Tax Collection Work in Urban and Rural Individual Industrial and Commercial Enterprises and Private Enterprises),"
in *Guowuyuan gongbao* (*State Council Bulletin*) 16 (September 20, 1989),
626–29; and Central Party document [1989] 11, November 9, 1989,
"Zhonggong zhongyang guanyu jinyibu zhili zhengdun he shenhua
gaige de jueding," in State System Reform Commission Office, *Shiyijie
sanzhong quanhui yilai jingji tizhi gaige zhongyao wenjian huibian* (Beijing:
Gaige chubanshe, 1990), 598–99.

21. Yang Chungui, "Make an Effort to Grasp the Dialectics of Socialist Modernization—Studying Comrade Jiang Zemin's 'Correctly Handle Several
Major Relationships in the Socialist Modernization Drive,' *Renmin ribao*
(*People's Daily*), November 6, 1995, translated in Foreign Broadcast Information Service Daily Report—China, December 15, 1995, 17.

22. The economist Yoram Barzel (1989) has established that "the greater is
others' inclination to affect income from someone's asset without bearing
the full cost of their actions, the lower is the value of the asset" (5).

23. See, Wenzhou Municipality People's Government, "Guanyu nongcun
gufen hezou giyu rougan wenti de zanxing guiding (Provisional Regulations Regarding Several Questions on Shareholding Cooperatives),"
Mimeo, November 7, 1987.

24. "Guowuyuan Guanyu dali jiaqiang chengxiang geti gongshanghu he
siying qiye shuishou zhengguan gongzuo de jueding (State Council Decision Regarding Vigorously Strengthening Tax Collection Work in Urban and Rural Individual Industrial and Commercial Enterprises and
Private Enterprises)," in *Guowuyuan gongbao* (*State Council Bulletin*) 16
(September 20, 1989), 626–29.

25. "Zhejiangsheng gongshang xingzheng guanliju guanyu qingli 'jia jiti' he
dui hezuo jingying qiye ruhe dengji guanli de tongzhi ([1989] 21)," in
Yueqing County System Reform Committee, *Gufen hezuo jingji wenjian
huibian* (*A Collection of Documents on the Cooperative Stock Economy*) 1991.
no publisher: 52–54.

26. Note that this discussion excludes individual household firms (getihu).
This type of household firm is not considered a private enterprise in the
Chinese regulatory context. The distinction between getihu and other
private firms is based on the notion that owners of getihu are themselves
directly involved in labor, while owners of larger private firms—firms
that employ more than eight workers—are engaged in the exploitation
of labor. The cutoff at eight employees is derived from Marx. For a dis-

cussion of the ideological justification for distinguishing between getihu and other privately invested firms, see Wu 1994.

27. As is reflected in table 7.6, officials statistics for Songjiang County do not report bank loans to private enterprises.

28. A comparison of tables 7.4 and 7.6 shows that not only were there more privately invested firms in Yueqing that in Songjiang, but privately invested firms in Yeuqing embodied significantly more capital, on average.

29. The sociologists Gary Hamilton and Nicole Woolsey Biggart (1988) make a similar point in their treatment of cultural explanations of East Asian business organization.

30. The sociologist Siu-lun Wong (1991) makes this point as well. Some level of trust in the institutions of government is required to complement personal trust; without it, social investment in personal trust would be too costly for business.

References

Barzel, Yoram. 1989. *Economic Analysis of Property Rights*. New York: Cambridge University Press.

Byrd, William A., and Alan Gelb. 1990. "Why Industrialize?" In *China's Rural Industry: Structure, Development, and Reform*, edited by William A. Byrd and Lin Qingsong. New York: Oxford University Press.

Clarke, Donald C. 1995. "The Execution of Civil Judgments in China," *China Quarterly* 141: 65–81.

Coleman, James S. 1990. *Foundations of Social Theory*. Cambridge: Harvard Belknap Press.

Fei, Xiaotong, and Hanxian Luo, eds. 1988. *Xiangzhen jingji bijiao moshi (Comparative Rural Economic Models)*. Chongqing: Chongqing chubanshe.

Hamilton, Gary G., and Nicole Woolsey Biggart. 1988. "Market, Culture, and Authority: A Comparative Analysis of Management and Organization in the Far East." *American Journal of Sociology* 94 (Suppl.): S52–S94.

Hardin, Russell. 1993. "The Street-Level Epistemology of Trust." *Politics and Society* 21(4): 505–29.

———. 1995. "Trust in Government." Paper presented to the Russell Sage Foundation Workshop on Trust and Social Structure. Seattle (September 1995).

He, Rongfei, ed. 1987. *Wenzhou jingji geju — women de zuofa he tansuoxing yijian (The Structure of the Wenzhou Economy: Our Methods and Ideas*. Wenzhou: Zhejiang renmin chubanshe.

Hsiao, Michael Hsin-Huang. 1991. "An East Asian Development Model: Empirical Explorations." In *Business Networks and Economic Development in East and Southeast Asia*, edited by Gary G. Hamilton. Hong Kong: University of Hong Kong, Centre of Asian Studies.

King, Ambrose. 1991. "Kuan-hsi and Network Building: A Sociologial Interpretation." *Daedalus* 120(2): 63–84.

Levi, Margaret. 1995. "Trusting the State." Paper presented to the Russell Sage Foundation Workshop on Trust and Social Structure. Seattle (September 1995).

Lin, Nan, and Chih-jou Chen. 1994. "Local Initiatives in Institutional Transformation: The Nature and Emergence of Local Market Socialism in Jiangsu." Paper presented to the Annual Meeting of the Association of Asian Studies. Boston (March 24–27, 1994).

Liu, Alan. 1992. "The 'Wenzhou Model' of Development and China's Modernization." *Asian Survey* 32(8): 696–711.

Liu, Yia-ling. 1992. "Reform from Below: The Private Economy and Local Politics in the Rural Industrialization of Wenzhou." *China Quarterly* 130: 292–316.

Lyons, Thomas P. 1994. "Economic Reform in Fujian." In *The Economic Transformation of South China*, edited by Thomas P. Lyons and Victor Nee. Ithaca, N.Y.: Cornell University East Asia Program.

Nee, Victor. 1996. "The Emergence of a Market Society: Changing Mechanisms of Stratification in China." *American Journal of Sociology* 101(4): 908–49.

Nee, Victor, and Sijin Su. 1996. "Local Corporatism and Informal Privatization in China's Market Transition." In *Reforming Asian Socialism: The Growth of Market Institutions*, edited by John McMillan and Barry Naughton. Ann Arbor: University of Michigan Press.

Nolan, Peter, and Furen Dong. 1990. *Market Forces in China: Competition and Small Business — The Wenzhou Debate*. London: Zed Books.

North, Douglass C. 1981. *Structure and Change in Economic History*. New York: Norton.

———. 1990. *Institutions, Institutional Change and Economic Performance*. New York: Cambridge University Press.

Oi, Jean C. 1992. "Fiscal Reform and the Economic Foundations of Local State Corporatism in China." *World Politics* 45(1): 99–126.

———. 1995. "The Role of the Local State in China's Transitional Economy." *China Quarterly* 144: 1132–1149.

Parris, Kristen. 1993. "Local Initiative and National Reform: The Wenzhou Model of Development." *China Quarterly* 134: 242–63.

Potter, Pitman B. 1994a. "The Administrative Litigation Law of the PRC." In *Domestic Law Reforms in Post-Mao China*, edited by Pitman B. Potter. Armonk, N.Y.: M. E. Sharpe.

———. 1994b. "Riding the Tiger: Legitimacy and Legal Culture in Post-Mao China," *China Quarterly* 138: 325–58.

Walder, Andrew G. 1995. "Local Governments as Industrial Firms: An Organizational Analysis of China's Transitional Economy." *American Journal of Sociology* 101(2): 263–301.

Wank, David L. 1995. "Bureaucratic Patronage and Private Business: Changing Network of Power in Urban China." In *The Waning of the Communist State: Economic Origins of Political Decline in China and Hungary*, edited by Andrew G. Walder. Berkeley: University of California Press.

———. 1996. "The Institutional Process of Market Clientelism: Guanxi and Private Business in a South China City." *China Quarterly* 147: 820–38.

Weingast, Barry R. 1993. "The Economic Role of Political Institutions." Stanford University. Unpublished paper.

———. 1995. "The Economic Role of Political Institutions: Market-Preserving Federalism and Economic Development." *Journal of Law, Economics, & Organization* 11(1): 1–31.

Weitzman Martin L., and Chenggang Xu. 1994. "Chinese Township-Village Enterprises as Vaguely Defined Cooperatives." *Journal of Comparative Economics* 18(2): 121–46.

Whiting, Susan H. 1995. "The Micro-Foundations of Institutional Change in Reform China: Property Rights and Revenue Extraction in the Rural Industrial Sector." Ph.D. diss., University of Michigan.

Whyte, Martin King. 1995. "The Social Roots of China's Economic Development." *China Quarterly* 144: 999–1019.

Wong, Christine. 1991. "Central-Local Relations in an Era of Fiscal Decline: The Paradox of Fiscal Decentralization in Post-Mao China." *China Quarterly* 128: 691–715.

———. 1992. "Fiscal Reform and Local Industrialization: The Problematic Sequencing of Reform in Post-Mao China." *Modern China* 18(2): 197–227.

Wong, Siu-lun. 1991. "Chinese Entrepreneurs and Business Trust." In *Business Networks and Economic Development in East and Southeast Asia*, edited by Gary G. Hamilton. Hong Kong: University of Hong Kong, Centre of Asian Studies.

Wu, Yushan. 1994. *Comparative Economic Transformations: Mainland China, Hungary, the Soviet Union, and Taiwan*. Stanford: Stanford University Press.

Yamagishi, Toshio, and Midori Yamagishi. 1994. "Trust and Commitment in the United States and Japan." *Motivation and Emotion* 18(2): 129–66.

Young, Susan. 1989. "Policy, Practice and the Private Sector in China." *Australian Journal of Chinese Affairs* 21: 57–80.

Yuan, Enzhen, ed. 1987. *Wenzhou moshi yu fuyu zhi lu* (*The Wenzhou Model and the Road to Affluence*). Shanghai: Shanghai shehui kexueyuan chubanshe.

Zhang, Renshou, and Hong Li. 1990a. "Wenzhou moshi (The Wenzhou Model)." In *Zhongguo nongcun jingji fazhan tansuo* (*An Exploration of China's Rural Economic Development*), edited by Zhang Liuzheng. Beijing: Zhongguo jingji chubanshe.

———. 1990b. *Wenzhou moshi yanjiu* (*Research on the Wenzhou Model*). Beijing: Zhongguo shehui kexue chubanshe.

PART III

HOW TRUST AFFECTS
REPRESENTATIVE DEMOCRACY

Chapter 8

Democratic Trust: A Rational-Choice Theory View

GEOFFREY BRENNAN

W HAT MIGHT it mean to say that citizens rationally trust democracy—or for that matter, trust any particular political
order within which collective decisions are made? In this
chapter, I distinguish two possible answers to this question. One answer—the one that has been predominant in the rational-actor political theory tradition—is that citizens can trust democracy to the extent
that democratic arrangements structure incentives in such a way that
rational agents will be led to produce political outcomes that are in
the citizens' interests. Another possible answer—the one that will be
my chief concern in this chapter—is that democratic institutions serve
to select relatively trustworthy agents who can be relied on, within
broad limits, to pursue the interests of citizens because that is what
those agents have publicly undertaken to do. To make this second
answer plausible within a rational-actor framework, I must show,
first, why it may be rational for at least some agents to acquire the
motivational disposition to keep promises (to be trustworthy persons)
and then second, how democratic processes might plausibly serve to
select the relatively trustworthy to act as political decision makers on
the citizens' behalf.

Although the argument here is focused on democracy, it has more
general application within the rational-choice theory of institutional
design—or what has come to be called *institutional economics*. The
first aspect of this more general application involves the extension of
rational-choice methods to the metalevel of choice among dispositions
as distinct from the substantive level of choice among actions. The

second aspect attends to the selection properties of institutions, the manner in which institutional arrangements serve to allocate persons with differing dispositions across different activities. In fact, the account of democratic trust that I shall offer in this chapter can be seen as an illustration of this more general line of argument, as well as an engagement with an issue that is of much interest in its own right.

The argument is developed as follows. I first lay out the "reliance game," the social predicament that trust is seen to overcome. I then distinguish two broad types of solution to the reliance predicament: a directly "institutional" solution; and a "dispositional" solution. Both of these solutions are to be seen as rational responses to the reliance predicament, although the dispositional solution involves a (rational) suppression of the opportunistic aspect of rationality at the level of action. Although the dispositional solution is contrasted with an institutional solution, it is important to recognize that the dispositional solution to the trust predicament is also indirectly institutional, in that different institutional arrangements can affect both the incentive to acquire the trustworthy disposition and the allocation, across alternative employments, of such trustworthiness as there is. In the next section, I deal specifically with the issue of dispositional heterogeneity and the way in which institutions may allocate persons of different dispositions. The sections that follow address (briefly) the directly institutional version of "democratic trust" and offer a more detailed account of the dispositional (and indirectly institutional) version of democratic trust.

The Reliance Predicament and the Dependence Interaction

Discussion of trust in economics typically begins with a diagnosis of the social predicament that trust is required to overcome. This predicament is often referred to as the "trust," game: I shall here describe it as the "reliance game" for reasons to be elaborated later in the chapter. The game involves two players. A moves first and must choose whether or not to rely on B, the second mover; B likewise has two choices—to "exploit" A or to "fulfill." The objective payoffs are such that the exploit strategy is dominant for B but leaves A worse off than A would have been had A not relied on B. The fulfill outcome leaves both A and B better off than if A had not relied on B. Accordingly, if A believes that B is "rational," A will choose not to rely on B because A knows that a rational B will exploit him if given the opportunity. The interaction shares with the prisoner's dilemma the feature that it has an equilibrium outcome, N, which is not Pareto optimal: both

Figure 8.1   The Reliance Predicament

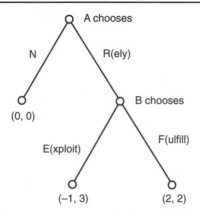

parties could be better off under the rely-fulfill outcome, but that outcome is made inaccessible jointly by B's rationality and the presence of B's option to exploit. The predicament facing both A and B is therefore how to secure the rely-fulfill outcome as the equilibrium outcome for rational players.

A particular example of such an interaction is depicted in figure 8.1. The number pair at the outcome nodes shows the payoffs to A (first number) and to B (second number). If A chooses N, the game concludes and both players receive zero. If A chooses R (to rely), B gets to choose between E (exploit) or F (fulfill). Under the former choice A gets −1 and B gets 3; under the latter option both get 2. Since B does better under E than under F, B will rationally choose E. But A knows this, and since A's payoff under E (−1) is less than A's payoff under N (0), A will choose N. That is, A cannot rationally rely on B, and hence both are worse off than they might have been under (the inaccessible) F.

As economists have come increasingly to realize, this predicament is one that is surprisingly common in ordinary two-person market exchanges. Since such exchanges constitute the foundation of the standard analysis of markets, both in its normative and explanatory variants, finding a solution to the reliance predicament is a major piece of basic economic theory. The predicament itself can arise whenever the act of payment and the act of delivery are temporally separated or whenever the quality of goods or services supplied is known to the seller but not evident to the buyer until some time after the point of purchase. Of course, not all cases where one party happens to be vulnerable to another are instances of the reliance predicament. The reliance predicament involves only those cases where A's vul-

Figure 8.2   The Dependence Game

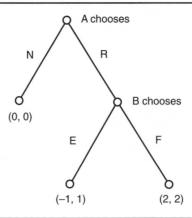

nerability is an object of choice by A (that is, where A can act to reduce his vulnerability) and where it would be rational for the second party to exploit A's vulnerability, in the absence of other considerations.

On this basis we can distinguish the reliance predicament from a somewhat similar interaction that we might term the dependence game, exemplified in figure 8.2. Here, A again chooses first and may render himself vulnerable to B, but in this case it is rational for B to choose F over E, because B's payoff under F is 2, whereas under E, B's payoff is 1. In this game, the equilibrium outcome for rational players is R:F; A chooses to make himself vulnerable to B, confident that B will not exploit that vulnerability. And the equilibrium outcome in this case is also optimal.

In both the reliance predicament and the dependence game, a necessary condition for achieving the optimal outcome is that A makes himself vulnerable to B. But in the reliance predicament, A will not—cannot rationally—do this. The central problem in the reliance predicament is therefore not that there is too much exploitation; the problem is rather that there is too little reliance. We could design a reliance predicament in which, from a strictly utilitarian point of view, it would actually be better if B did exploit—if, say, the payoff at E in figure 8.1 were (-1, 6). But that outcome would also remain inaccessible; given that A is rational, he will always choose N. What we would like to secure in the reliance predicament is more reliance; we would like to convert the reliance predicament into the dependence game. If some way can be found to achieve this conversion, clearly both A and B will be better off.

Figure 8.3   The Modified Reliance Game

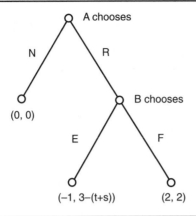

External and Internal Solutions

For expositional purposes, I shall introduce the interaction depicted in figure 8.3. This is either a reliance predicament or a dependence game according to the values of the two parameters t and s, yet to be defined. If $(t+s)$ is greater than 1, then the interaction is a dependence game; A will rationally rely on B and the optimal outcome R:F will be secured. If $(t+s)$ is less than 1, the interaction is a reliance predicament, in which case the suboptimal no-reliance outcome is the equilibrium.

The reason for choosing two parameters, s and t, where algebraically only one is needed, is that I wish to distinguish between routes for making B dependable. One route, associated with the t term (for taxes), involves penalties imposed under direct institutional mechanisms; t operates by changing the objective payoffs to B. The other route, associated with the s term (for subjective), involves B's motivational structure: s operates via B's subjective payoffs. The array of direct institutional mechanisms for solving the reliance predicament is relatively familiar. There may be a posting of bonds or a giving of hostages. The game may be repeated, so that B has incentives to act in a trustworthy fashion in the belief that A will trust B in the future. One further, obvious possibility is the institution of contract enforcement via a state-supported legal system. Indeed, this particular kind of institutional solution is so obvious that one might be forgiven for wondering whether the reliance predicament is really a predicament at all; why can't A simply insist that B sign a contract? If B fails to fulfill, then A can take B to court, ensure that B is appropriately punished, and receive proper compensation. Ergo, B will rationally comply without recourse to courts (the threat is enough), and A can rationally rely on B after all.

Put another way, for the reliance predicament to be interesting there must be some limits to these objective solutions, at least in some cases. For example, all of these objective solutions may be costly, even where they work tolerably well. There is a further issue here, however, that arises specifically in relation to the courts. Courts depend on the reliability of a third party, C (some officer of the legal system), to enforce the original contract rather than, for example, appropriating the resources under dispute for herself. But to assume court reliability is to assume the existence of a trustworthiness (in this case on C's part) that it is the very object of the analysis to explain. This challenge is a primary message of the comparative institutional analysis strand of public choice theory, and I take that message very seriously.

In any event, I want to focus attention here on the possibility of a dispositional solution to the reliance predicament. By a dispositional solution, I mean the possession of a motivational structure by B such that B endures an internal, subjective cost whenever B herself breaks promises—and in particular, whenever B breaks promises made to A not to exploit A's vulnerability in cases where A chooses to rely on B. This subjective cost, s, can be thought of as consisting of two elements: the guilt that B sustains from breaking a promise and thereby causing unfair harm to A, and the loss of esteem that B suffers by virtue of proving untrustworthy.

I have so far abjured the terms *trust* and *trustworthiness* precisely because I wanted to reserve those terms for this dispositional case. And it is specifically the moral connotation—the fact that trustworthiness is normally construed as a virtue—that makes for its usefulness here. The action of fulfillment amounts to an instance of trustworthiness under the dispositional solution because the untrustworthy alternative carries the guilt and shame that are intrinsic to the disposition's effectiveness.

One way of thinking about this dispositional solution is as offering B an additional option in the reliance predicament: the option of making a genuine *promise* that would cost B something if he were to break it. The interaction in each such instance becomes an augmented form of the reliance predicament, along the lines depicted in figure 8.4. I call this augmented form the "trust game." It is characterized by the presence of the pregame move (by B) whether to promise (P) or not promise (M) to fulfill. The former option imposes a genuine—though internal, subjective—cost on B of amount s should B not fulfill the terms of the promise. This formulation makes it possible to specify a measure of B's trustworthiness—namely, the parameter s. The larger is s the more trustworthy is B. For convenience, we here allow t to be zero.

Figure 8.4   The Trust Game

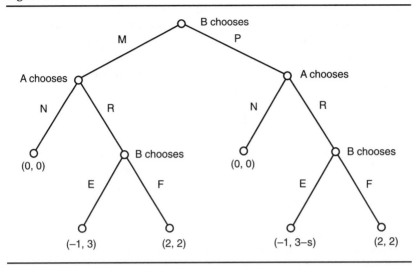

It should be clear that it will be rational for B to adopt the disposi-tion if two conditions are met. First, the parameter *s* must be large enough to make it rational for B to keep his promise (that is, $s > 1$ in figure 8.4); and second, B's adopting the disposition must cause at least some As to *believe* that B will prove trustworthy. The latter ele-ment is clearly crucial. If A has no grounds for believing B to be trustworthy in the sense defined, or if B's actually adopting the dispo-sition makes no difference to A's beliefs, then B's taking up the dispo-sition will not cause A to rely. Within the rational-choice framework adopted here, B's only reason to become trustworthy is that doing so induces A to trust B.

Normally in game theory it is assumed that all players know the payoffs to all others with certainty. That assumption is strained in the trust game. The capacity of A to discern the size of *s* must be limited. We should note, in particular, that it is in B's interests to pretend to be trustworthy; then, once A has chosen to rely, B can exploit after all. In a "perfect information" game among rational players, we would never observe the exploit outcome: if B is untrustworthy, A will not trust B, in which case N is the outcome; and if B *is* trustworthy, A will trust B, in which case F will be the outcome. In the absence of uncer-tainty, there can be no genuine vulnerability, provided B is rational and does not make mistakes.

The degree of uncertainty here must, however, be bounded. On the one hand, if A can identify with certainty whether B has adopted the trustworthiness disposition and whether *s* is big enough in the relevant case ($s > 1$ in figure 8.4), then every rational agent will adopt the trustworthiness disposition and make s appropriately large. At the other extreme, suppose that A cannot tell whether B is more likely to be trustworthy than is some other randomly chosen player (that is, A cannot predict better than randomly whether B has actually chosen P in figure 8.4). Then it will not pay B to adopt the disposition, because so choosing cannot in itself rationally induce A to rely on B and because Bs that don't adopt the disposition won't have to endure the gratuitous cost of s if and when they exploit.

There are a variety of ways of dealing analytically with the uncertainty here. One relatively simple formulation is that A's estimate of the value of s is uncertain but positively associated with the true value for any particular B. The degree of accuracy of A's estimate of B's s-value (trustworthiness) is a measure of the extent of B's translucency in a particular case. Obviously, the higher the level of translucency, the greater the incentive to adopt the trustworthy disposition. Equally obviously, the extent of translucency is a crucial parameter in the whole dispositional story; the more translucent people are on average, the more (rational) trustworthiness there will be and hence the more (rational) trust.

But is this assumption of positive translucency justified? This is an issue of particular relevance to economists, because (notwithstanding the full-information assumptions of game theory) there is a strong behaviorist tradition in economics that asserts the virtually total opaqueness of agents' motives *qua* motives; only action is observable, and only that which is revealed through action can reveal anything authoritative about motivations. In my view, this is a half-truth and can easily be carried too far. For those disposed against any assumption of translucency, perhaps no argument could be convincing, but I am unpersuaded that any particularly elaborate defense needs to be offered. We do routinely make judgments about others' moral character—in the selection of our friends, our confidantes, our spouses. The capacity to make such moral judgments is just an ordinary part of living. And the fact that we do do it must mean that we can do it. Of course, we will sometimes make mistakes. But the rational-actor account provides us with some reason to think that people might develop a capacity to discern tolerably accurately the trustworthiness of their fellows. Those who develop this capacity, other things being equal, will fare better than those who do not. To be sure, trustworthiness in some will typically exist alongside mere expediency in others. And trustworthiness will always be vulnerable to deceptiveness. But deception is parasitic on trustworthiness in the sense that special skills in being deceptive emerge only when there is some trustworthiness to be simulated, and trustworthiness is rational only when the degree of translucency is appropriately large. Being a confidence trickster works only in a world where people are prepared to trust you.

It is worth noting at this point that agents who are trustworthy will have a strong incentive to make their trustworthiness transparent in a reasonably reliable way. Some institutional arrangements may help them to do this. For example, if there exists a costly signal of good faith that it would pay an agent to sustain if and only if he were to fulfill promises over a long period, undertaking that expenditure can be rational for the trustworthy agent. Such an expenditure cannot make it rational for the agent to fulfill promises, because in itself it involves no mechanism to control rational opportunism; but the expenditure can signal the fact that problems of rational opportunism have been dispositionally solved. For example, a firm may undertake a costly advertising program to show that it intends to be in business over an extended future and thereby reveal its long time horizon. A politician may tell the truth when it is electorally costly for her to do and thereby show that she is a trustworthy person. Trustworthiness does not need to hide its light under a bushel.

Given these considerations, it seems to me reasonable to conclude that the degree of translucency is large enough to support the superiority of the trustworthiness disposition over some range. There is, however, an extra dimension to the link between rationality and trustworthiness. This is the question as to whether dispositions as such are available for rational choice.

The difficulty here is connected to the paradox of belief. Consider the following simple example. Suppose that for certain kinds of sickness the time taken to regain good health is positively related to mental state and in particular to attitude to recovery. Specifically, if I believe that I will recover in n days ($n \geq 1$), I will actually recover in (n + 2) days. Accordingly life goes best for me if I believe I will recover in one day. But the reason I believe this cannot be that if I so believe, I will actually recover in three days (as early as possible), because such a reason denies the truth of the belief. It may be that trustworthiness is like this. If the reason I try to become trustworthy is to induce others to trust me, and if I want others to trust me because then I do better (get a higher payoff), then I am particularly susceptible to the temptation to exploit; the reason for being trustworthy is the same reason as the reason to exploit. Such considerations give point to the idea that trustworthiness is made more secure by an independent moral sense—that trustworthiness is a moral notion and needs to be so if trustworthiness itself is to be robust. None of this is to deny the importance of habit—of acculturation to modes of calculation or action—rendering some actions relatively unthinkable or undoable. And it may be that a person can acquire the habit of keeping promises without any particularly moral substructure. But the acquisition of such a habit on rational egoistic grounds seems unusually demanding in terms of the self-deception required.

These difficulties could be finessed, of course, by taking a more evolutionary approach to the question of motivational dispositions. It is clear that given a tolerable degree of translucency, trustworthy types will do better than untrustworthy types over some range; but "doing better" might here be interpreted in terms of survival value specifically. In fact, under tolerably plausible assumptions, it is possible to derive a stable evolutionary equilibrium in which there is a non-negligible proportion of trustworthy types (see for example Güth and Kliemt 1994). The reasoning here presupposes rational action by agents of different types, but the motivational characteristics themselves are chosen by the selection process, not by rational choice over dispositions. Evolutionary models of this kind would explain why rationally trustworthy types (that is, rational agents with the "right" motivations [s-values]) would exist, but such models would not seek to explain the acquisition of the motivations themselves by appealing to a direct rational-choice process.

Accordingly, supposing that there is an appropriate degree of translucency, rational-choice analytics gives us reason to think that trustworthiness as a moral category, and hence rational trust, will emerge in social interactions and will be supported (and perhaps even acquired) by rationally chosen processes of habituation and acculturation. It is important to make this point, because so much of the standard economic account of human motivation assumes that all actors are uniformly opportunistically egoistic. That this motivational assumption is not strictly entailed in rationality axioms has long been recognized. But the idea that rationality at the dispositional level might actually support morality in certain contexts is a more uncommon thought (though it is a predominant theme in Gauthier 1986).

Motivational Heterogeneity and Selection

The analysis so far has established that it may be rational for at least some rational actors to cultivate motivational dispositions, such as the disposition to be trustworthy, that suppress fully rational action at some points in an action sequence. Nothing in our analysis, however, does or should carry the implication that all rational agents will find it desirable to adopt the trustworthiness disposition or be equally trustworthy (that is, exhibit identical s-values). Cultivating a disposition here is best thought of as resembling the acquisition of human capital or an aesthetic sensibility. And as with human capital in the more familiar educational example, there is no reason to believe that all individuals will have identical aptitudes, or indeed that efficiency would require all individuals to acquire human capital in the same quantities, even if aptitudes *were* identical. In other words, we can reasonably expect individuals to be differentially trustworthy.

If they are, and if different activities make different demands on trustworthiness, then one aspect of social organization that will be of considerable importance is the extent to which the scarce resource of trustworthiness is allocated to its socially highest valued uses. This allocation becomes, in particular, a normatively relevant feature of alternative institutional arrangements. That is, institutions not only establish structures of incentives, making some actions relatively more attractive and others relatively less unattractive; they also select particular agents, with particular motivational dispositions, for particular roles. Moreover, the capacity to so select affects the incentives at the dispositional level of choice; it will be more advantageous to become trustworthy if trustworthy persons tend to be allocated to arenas that are well rewarded. (See Brennan 1995 and Brennan and Hamlin 1995 for more detailed discussion.)

Now, some care must be taken in identifying the "highest valued uses" of trustworthiness. It is worth emphasizing that these are not necessarily the areas of greatest vulnerability or dependence. For one thing, some dependence or vulnerability may be unavoidable; there may be no dependence-avoidance strategy available to "first movers" that can lead to untrusting behavior. Trustworthiness in these cases may be desirable to the extent that it reduces exploitation, but it cannot be desirable on the grounds that it elicits more trust. More importantly, perhaps, the personal trustworthiness available can be wasted if it is used in arenas that make too great a demand upon it. Consider specifically two arenas of action, denoted X and Y, and let the relevant payoffs in the trust game in those two arenas be such that the size of s is sufficient to secure fulfillment in arena Y but not in arena X. Then placing trustworthy persons in arena Y will secure trustworthy behavior; they will reliably fulfill, without any additional sanction. But if they are placed in arena X, their degree of personal trustworthiness is insufficient to modify their behavior. There is a kind of moral hernia involved in the X case; the moral strength of agents cannot bear the weight of the temptation to which they are routinely exposed. There is a double case for not allocating trustworthy persons to arena X: First, to do so is to get no return from society's moral capital, which could in other arenas solve the reliance predicament; and second, doing so simply reduces payoffs to second players without any corresponding behavioral adjustment. (That is, trustworthy persons

Figure 8.5   The Hobbesian Dependence Game

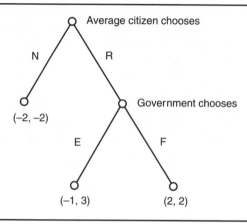

get a lower return when they exploit, by virtue of the shame and guilt they endure, than do untrustworthy persons. Arguably, this lower return is a bad thing.)

To make these points somewhat less abstract, consider the political context as an example. This example will lead to a discussion of *democratic* politics specifically in the following sections, but here I will make several points about government as such. First, it seems clear that citizens are vulnerable to government; governments have the power to harm citizens, and the fate of citizens depends critically on whether government is inter alia trustworthy or not. It would be possible, however, for the relationship between citizens and government to be of the form shown in figure 8.5. Here the payoffs are such that citizens (as first movers) will rationally make themselves vulnerable to government, even if they believe they will be exploited. In this case, the option of not relying on government (Hobbesian anarchy, perhaps) is so terrible that even exploitation is preferable. Of course, citizens will still prefer trustworthy over expedient governments, and to the extend that there is translucency and that the citizens themselves have the power to select their governments, trustworthiness will be rewarded. But the expectation of fulfillment does not induce more trust as such; the level of vulnerability is independent of the probability of fulfillment.

Within the context of this chapter, I shall take it that the standard reliance predicament as depicted in figure 8.1 applies to the political context. That is, I am explicitly rejecting the trust-independent version depicted in figure 8.5. I am taking it that citizens can be more or less trustful of government; they can (rationally) make themselves more or less vulnerable by a variety of constitutional maneuvers, including

Figure 8.6   The Democratic Dependence Game

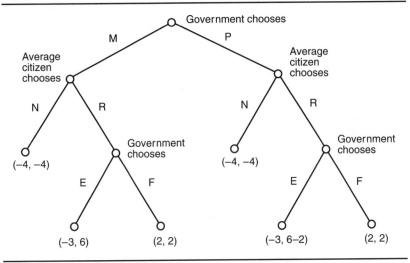

restrictions on the domain of government activity, government's access to information and the internal structure of government (such as checks and balances). But there is a potential cost in so doing; a government made excessively weak by untrusting citizens cannot deliver things that all citizens want. A more trustworthy government can and will induce more (rational) trust, and that increased trust (if it is indeed rationally justified) will be to the benefit of ruled and rulers alike.

A second general possibility is that although more or less vulnerability in politics is conceivable, the extent of trustworthiness available in society is not sufficient to generate rational trust within the political arena. Consider figure 8.6. Here, the value of s (the shame and guilt) is 2, but the exploitation payoff to government is 6, as contrasted with the payoff of 2 if government fulfills. Hence, even relatively trustworthy governments will exploit. Therefore, there are no grounds for allocating trustworthy persons to government; on simple utilitarian grounds, it is better to allocate nontrustworthy agents to government roles, because they do not suffer from the behaviorally irrelevant scruples that the relatively trustworthy do. Of course, trustworthy persons will still be valued in interactions where temptation is less severe. Within the political arena, however, there will need to be considerable reliance on other institutional mechanisms that will reduce the objective payoffs to exploitation—checks and balances, or fragmentation of powers to disperse the rents of exploitation more broadly and hence reduce those rents to all individual B players. In what follows, I shall assume away the case represented in figure 8.6. That is, I shall assume either that trustworthy players are indeed robustly trustworthy (s is sufficiently large) or that other mechanisms are in place to keep the gains from exploitation within tolerable bounds. It is, however, clear that the grammar of the reliance predicament can accommodate the case of extreme political skepticism and explain why it is possible that trustworthiness could be irrelevant in the political setting, even though it is important in other arenas.

A question arises here about the degree of substitutability or complementarity between direct incentive mechanisms and those mediated by dispositional effects. Much of the literature dealing with the question has emphasized the substitutability possibility—that is, the idea that extrinsic rewards drive out intrinsic motivations (see, for example, Titmuss 1970; Hirschman 1985; and, more recently, the interesting work of Frey 1996). My own view is that the complementarity possibility is no less likely, and the case immediately above is one example. In that case, more robust checks and balances make trustworthiness more relevant, not less. For this reason, I tend to identify the dispositional/selection account of institutional operation as a supplement to, rather than a competitor with, the more familiar incentive account. In doing so, however, I do not want to suppress extremely important questions about the possible negative effects of incentive-based institutional mechanisms on dispositions (or "intrinsic motivations," as Bruno Frey [1996] terms them). I simply want to insist that the effects of such mechanisms are not always negative and that there are no obvious grounds for believing the negative case to be the more common one.

Democracy and Impersonal Trust

Within the rational choice tradition, there is a large and rapidly growing literature on the rational trust of democracy as an institution. That literature may not use the language of trust, but the central normative purpose of so-called public-choice scholarship is to identify the extent to which citizens may reasonably rely on the institutions of democracy—and on electoral competition in particular—to produce political outcomes that are generally to their benefit. In this context, democratic institutional arrangements are analyzed by reference to the incentive structures those arrangements embody and assessed by reference to the extent to which those arrangements "bend interests to the service of duty," as Madison put it in *The Federalist*. In terms of the reliance predicament (figure 8.1), the object of institutional arrangements so conceived is to reduce the objective value of B's payoff from exploiting, *ceteris paribus*.

The most obvious mechanism in this regard is electoral competition. Electoral competition is viewed as somewhat analogous to market competition; competing parties and candidates are like rival contenders for a contract, and just as the desire to win the contract induces bidders to offer terms that are attractive to the persons awarding the contract, so the political candidates will be induced to offer to the electorate bundles of policies that they believe will be maximally attractive to voters. And successful candidates will be led to fulfill the terms of such offers because of an analogue to the discipline of continuous tradings—that is, failure to fulfill offers will lead to candidates' being unsuccessful at the next election. At least, all this will be so if electoral competition works well. A critical question, therefore, in the rational-actor analysis of democracy is whether electoral competition does work well in these senses. It is with that question that rational-actor political theory, at least in its normative variant, has been chiefly preoccupied.

There is a subsidiary question to be asked here—namely, how other matters of institutional detail bear on how well electoral competition works. There is a small but growing literature on this aspect, which deals with such questions as whether majority rule or a more inclusive decision rule would generate greater citizen protection (see Buchanan and Tulloch 1962); the effects of bicameral as opposed to unicameral assemblies (see Brennan and Hamlin 1992); the effects of separation of powers (see Brennan and Hamlin 1993); the role of committee systems (Shepsle and Weingast 1981); and a larger literature on federalism, one aspect of which I take up below. (An interesting recent book-length treatment of this material is Mueller 1996.) It is to be emphasised that virtually all this literature is firmly in the homo economicus behavioral tradition. It deals in that sense with impersonal trust, not the personal trust that is the main focus of this chapter.

Although electoral competition is the main focus of the rational-actor analysis of democracy, there is another mechanism that might be looked to as a constraint on government. This is the option of citizens to move from one political regime to another, an option that is institutionalized through the political decentralization characteristic of federal systems. There are two aspects of the argument here. First, citizens who find themselves subject to undue exploitation can limit the extent of such exploitation to the extent that there exists some other jurisdiction where the degree of exploitation is lower; this is the "exit option" as such. But second, to the extent that jurisdictions benefit from population growth (because, for example, persons carry net taxable capacity with them), jurisdictions may actually compete for citizens; jurisdictions there will have an incentive to cater to citizens' preferences. This competitive process may not always exhibit desirable features. For example, it may discriminate excessively between relatively mobile and relatively immobile persons (or tax bases), leading to systematic redistributions toward the former and away from the latter. Nevertheless, political decentralization represents one means of increasing political reliability and becomes a more important means if other mechanisms of constraint in place are less effective.

It should be clear that neither electoral competition nor political decentralization (nor indeed other possible constitutional methods of constraint) as discussed here involve any element of personal trust as I have defined it in the foregoing discussion; the focus within the impersonal trust tradition is entirely on institutional devices and how these affect objective payoffs to citizens and their political agents. This is standard "public choice" analysis and proceeds as if all are rationally egoistic; there is no real trust in any personal sense at all. Now, it goes without saying that democracy as such cannot exhibit personal trustworthiness directly; democracy cannot feel guilt or shame and hence cannot have its performance moderated by the threat of such feelings. Nevertheless, democracy as an institution might connect with personal trust. It might work better in the presence of trust that in its absence, and—an independent possibility—it might serve to support the generation and/or maintenance of political trustworthiness. In what follows, I shall attempt to give an account, consistent with the general apparatus of rational-actor theory, of how it might be that democratic institutions support personal trust more than do other forms of governance. I shall attempt to assess the plausibility of this account at the end of the paper.

Democracy and Personal Trust

As has been described earlier, agents become personally trustworthy by virtue of having internalized a moral disposition under which the breaking of promises (or perhaps the disappointment of reasonable expectations) brings guilt and shame. Collectives such as firms, political parties, or institutions such as Parliament may enjoy more or less esteem and may act in more or less moral ways, but it is only the agents whose esteem is affected by association with those collectives that can be motivated by the threat of loss of esteem or by guilt. Accordingly, personal trust is a mechanism that operates most effectively in a personalized politics—with identifiable agents making real promises or giving real undertakings. In short, personal trust goes most naturally with representative democracy.

Collective decisions can of course, be taken directly under democratic procedures. It is not uncommon for constitutional change to be sought via popular referendum, for example; citizens' initiatives can be put directly on the ballot under many U.S. state constitutions and many decisions in Switzerland are taken under direct democracy. Rational-actor theorists are often attracted by such processes. Direct democracy seems to enroll citizens in an explicit act of choice over political options; it finesses the ad hominem dimension of much representative democracy, with all the dangers of voters being captivated by charismatic leaders. Direct democracy, however, cannot mobilize the resources of trust conceived as a response to dispositional trustworthiness. Only in representative institutions can the issue of the trustworthiness of political agents arise.

The second general point to be made about the connection between representative democracy and trust relates to the account to be given of electoral processes. In the standard rational-actor account of electoral competition, candidates are seen simply as ciphers for the policy platforms the candidates represent. The basic objects of voters' preferences are taken to be the policy outcomes or the states of the world to which the policies offered by various candidates are believed to give rise. It is the process of competition, forcing candidates to modify their policies along electorally favored lines, that is the central disciplinary force. As was noted earlier in the chapter, this story is an incentive-based one, and candidates are essentially incidental players in it.

There is, however, another story that might be told about electoral processes, one in which candidates qua candidates are anything but epiphenomenal. This alternative story is a selectional one. In this account, elections allow voters to select among alternative candidates as such. The role of the electoral process is that of choosing the most competent and trustworthy candidates. A candidate's policies are less to be seen as tenders for office and more as signals of the candidate's general views and moral character. Policies, so the argument goes, should not be treated as choice options, because there is too much uncertainty about the future. Candidates should not totally precommit themselves; they must be left some discretion to respond to contingencies that arise. Even if it were feasible to constrain candidates and parties to their announced policy platforms, it would never be desirable to do so. What electoral processes can do, however, is to allow voters to assign the discretion that representatives inevitably possess to the candidates that voters most trust. And since it is reasonable to suppose that rational actors will have developed the capacity to discern trustworthiness as a routine matter in their private transactions (such a capacity is, after all, privately profitable), it is also reasonable to suppose that voters will more often than not make accurate judgments as to the character of their representatives.

Certainly, it is more reasonable to think this than to think that citizens will have the special skills required to assess the likely consequences of particular public policies. There are, after all, limited private gains from understanding the details of macroeconomic relations or the incidence of alternative policy regimes. The informational demands of detailed policy evaluation are very considerable and the private incentives for voters to acquire that information are minimal. That point is the force behind Anthony Downs's (1957) notion of "rational ignorance." Moreover, the instrumental account of voting offered by the standard incentive story of elections is itself deeply implausible—at least to me (see Brennan and Lomasky 1993; and also Barry 1970; Goodin and Roberts 1975). The most plausible account of truly rational voter behavior, in my view, has the voter supporting electoral options because of what we might loosely call their intrinsic characteristics rather than as a matter of fulfilling the voter's preferences; voting is more like cheering at a football match or filling in a questionnaire than it is like choosing an assets portfolio. In the array of possible intrinsic characteristics that might induce voters to cheer for one candidate rather than another, the candidate's personal character seems no less likely to be relevant than the policy positions he is associated with. Put negatively, it seems implausible that voter support will be attracted to a candidate who is recognized as untrustworthy, however attractive the policies he offers, even if the discipline of other mechanisms (the desire to be elected in the future, for example) were thought to be reasonably reliable.

The idea that democratic elections might serve as a filter to secure representatives of superior moral character and competence—superior trustworthiness—is not at all an unfamiliar one (though it has not, for reasons to be further discussed, had much currency in rational-actor circles). This is, for example, the picture advanced by Madison in *Federalist 57*. As he put it, "The aim of every political constitution . . . ought to be . . . to obtain for rulers men who possess most wisdom to discern and most virtue to pursue the common good of society." Persons selected under popular electoral processes, "as they will have been distinguished by the preference of their fellow-citizens," can be presumed to be "somewhat distinguished also by those qualities which entitle them to [the preference of fellow-citizens] and which promise a sincere and scrupulous regard to the nature of their engagements." Moreover, "there is in every breast a sensibility to marks of honor, of favor, of esteem and of confidence which, apart from all considerations of interests, is some pledge for grateful and benevolent returns." In Madison's view, a person elevated from the common lot is likely to feel obligated to those who so elevated him and to act benevolently to the citizenry accordingly.

There is another aspect of the Madisonian argument that is worth noting. This is that those attracted to political office are those who particularly value the rewards that such office provides: certification of public esteem and confidence. If those who place a high value on such things, even from "motives of a more selfish nature" such as "pride and vanity," are disproportionately represented in public office, then these are persons also likely to be particularly susceptible to the loss of esteem attendant on being proven untrustworthy; the subjective costs of public disgrace are higher for such persons, other things being equal, and hence such persons are more likely to fulfill public expectations of trustworthiness. Persons who place a low value on public esteem will be less likely to be trustworthy, but they will also be less attracted to political careers.

Now, if it is the case that the more trustworthy *are* selected into political agency roles, this is surely a highly satisfactory aspect of the social order, since government is probably an arena in which personal trustworthiness is of high value. I say "probably" here, not because government does not make huge demands on trustworthiness, but because "it may be that" no plausible agents could meet those demands. That is the point of the earlier discussion surrounding figure 8.6. Popular electoral processes will not be wholly reliable in this selection exercise, but they will predictably be more reliable than other possible selection mechanisms—random selection, for example, as recommended by the Marquis de Condorcet (1785) in relation to his "jury theorems," or selection on the basis of birth or wealth. If this line of reasoning is accepted, we might say that representative democracy particularly supports personal trust. All forms of government imply a vulnerability of citizens, and there may be a variety of institutional mechanisms that can directly reduce that vulnerability, but representative democracy gives greater play for the processes of personal trust—play, that is, for greater trustworthiness on the part of political representatives and, *ceteris paribus*, for greater (rational) trust on the part of citizens.

Conclusions

The picture of democratic process presented in the foregoing section may seem unduly heroic to some—and particularly to those in the rational-actor tradition. In that tradition, it has become a kind of methodological axiom that, after all, politicians are no better than the rest of us. Any presumption to the contrary seems to assume away everything that the rational-actor tradition wishes to call into question. It is not for nothing that the rational-actor tradition has as its chief declared enemy the benevolent-despot conception of government. That benevolent-despot model both ignores the very institutional factors (and in particular electoral constraints) that public choice brings to the fore analytically and also assumes the benevolent effect of political processes, which public choice insists is something to be proved. Yet the benevolent-despot conception of government has proven remarkably resilient in policy advice circles. The idea that political agents are in fact engaged in an endeavor to recognize the "public interest" and to devise policies that might promote that public interest must presumably have some connection with political reality. Perhaps that idea is just an elaborate exercise in self-justification— conceivably in self-deception. Perhaps. But here I have put a different view—the view that self-justification is actually demanded by democratic electoral processes and that the moral categories of guilt and shame play a significant role in representative democracy, not only at the level of rhetoric but also within the internal psychology of the main players. Or at least they play a significant role if democracy is working well.

The picture of representative democracy laid out in the last section is intended to support that view. Doubtless the picture can be overdrawn. There is nothing in the discussion to suggest that citizens' trust in their elected representatives may not prove displaced. Nor is there any suggestion that the direct effects of democratic institutions on incentives are unimportant or that institutions that increase impersonal trustworthiness cannot work alongside those that promote personal trustworthiness (as, for example, Madison clearly believed). But personal and impersonal trust in democratic regimes are different; they involve different pictures of electoral processes and tend to appeal to different accounts of human motivations. Both are consistent with variants of the rational-actor model, though they go with different understandings of how the requirements of rationality are to be understood. Simply because models that emphasize impersonal trustworthiness (or untrustworthiness) are currently more common in rational-actor circles, we should not assume that rational-actor arguments do not also lend considerable support to the idea of personal trust or to the feasibility of a democracy in which personal trust plays some non-negligible role.

References

Barry, B. 1970. *Sociologists, Economists and Democracy*. London: Collier-Macmillan.
Brennan, G. 1995. "Selection and the Currency of Reward." In *The Theory of Institutional Design*, edited by R. E. Goodin. Cambridge: Cambridge University Press.

Brennan, G., and A. Hamlin. 1992. "Bi-Cameralism and Majoritarian Equilibrium." *Public Choice* 74(2): 169–80.

———. 1993. "The Separation and Division of Powers." *Journal of Theoretical Politics* 6(3): 345–68.

———. 1995. "Economising on Virtue." *Constitutional Political Economy* 6: 35–56.

Brennan, G., and L. Lomasky. 1993. *Democracy and Decision.* New York: Cambridge University Press.

Buchanan, J., and G. Tullock. 1962. *The Caleulus of Consent.* Ann Arbor: University of Michigan Press.

Condorcet, Marquis de. 1785. *Essai sur l'Application de L'Analyse à la Probabilité.* Paris.

Downs, A. 1957. *An Economic Theory of Democracy.* New York: Harper & Row.

Frey, B. 1996. "A Constitution for Knaves." University of Zurich, Switzerland. Unpublished paper.

Gauthier, D. 1986. *Morals by Agreement.* Oxford: Oxford University Press.

Goodin, R. E., and K. Roberts. 1975. "The Ethical Voter." *American Political Science Review* 60: 926–28.

Güth, W., and H. Kliemt. 1994. "Competition or Co-operation: On the Evolutionary Economics of Trust, Exploitation and Moral Attitudes." *Metroeconomica* 45/2 (June): 155–87.

Hirschman, A. O. 1985. "Against Parsimony." *Economics and Philosophy* 1: 7–21.

Kelman, M. 1988. "On Democracy-Bashing." *Virginia Law Review* 74(2): 199–273.

Madison, J., A. Hamilton, and J. Jay. [1788] 1987. *The Federalist Papers.* Middlesex: Penguin Classics.

Mueller, D. 1996. *Constitutional Democracy.* Cambridge: Cambridge University Press.

Shepsle, K.A., and B. Weingast. 1981. "Structure Induced Equilibrium and Legislative Choice." *Public Choice* 37: 503–19.

Titmuss, Richard. 1970. *The Gift Relationship.* London: George Allen & Unwin.

Chapter 9

Political Trust and the Roots of Devolution

M. Kent Jennings

MERICANS' trust in government underwent a massive decline in the mid- to late 1960s. A modest resurgence during the heart of Ronald Reagan's presidential years proved to be temporary.[1] Virtually all the literature and public discussion treating the sources and consequences of that fall from grace deal with evaluations of the national government. Although this emphasis is understandable, it ignores the fact that individuals are embedded in a multiplicity of governments. Or, from the top-down perspective, it ignores the reality that multiple levels and layerings of government address diverse needs and interests within the citizenry. Federal systems in particular develop layerings and sectors that become objects of demands, locales of interactions, and sources of satisfactions and grievances. These consequences of federalism are perhaps nowhere more evident than in the United States, with its added complexities of strong separation of powers.

While the national government without doubt has the farthest-reaching power of any level of government, especially in its role of providing national security, the states themselves are significant political actors and reference objects.[2] Moreover, in recent times the states have arguably engaged in more innovation than has the national government, and in any event the states are widely perceived by scholars to have undergone a resurgence in the 1980s (see, for example, Gray and Jacob 1996). The increasingly active role of the National Conference of Governors (witness the budget battle of 1996), the spread of direct democracy and term limits, the use of the states as arenas for thrashing out some very divisive social issues (for example, gay rights and environmental protection), and the 1994 election with its Contract with America only served to heighten the salience of the states in the federal system.

Beneath the states resides a varying and often wild profusion of general and ad hoc local governments as well as quasi-public entities. Decades of consolidation efforts have yielded but modest gains, save for sharply reducing the number of rural and semirural school districts.[3] Although nominally creatures of the state government, local governments often have considerable power in their own right and much discretion in their roles as implementers of state and federal programs. The warp and woof of everyday politics, including such topics as schooling, land use, crime, and taxes, frequently reveals itself in the fabric of local governments.

So citizens find themselves, often willy-nilly, in relationships with three levels of government. The different levels touch their lives in different ways. These effects can also differ depending upon an individual's life situation and the particular state of development and conduct characterizing the respective governmental levels. Just as the citizenry has varied over time, so too have governmental functions associated with the various levels of government. Not that the average citizen, or maybe even the average political scientist, can give a completely accurate rendering of his or her relationship to these various levels. Nevertheless, most people have the general notion that there are multiple levels and that they perform different functions.[4]

In this chapter I expand the discussion about the decline of trust in government by chronicling the changes in the faith and confidence accorded the three basic levels of government and the rationales that people develop to justify their judgments. In so doing I hope to provide insight into the expectations and criteria that citizens apply to different levels and that form the basis of their trust levels. I also hope to show how these evaluations and rationales help to explain the contemporary impetus toward the devolution of powers and responsibilities from the federal government to state and local governments.

More specifically, three questions will be addressed, questions typically overlooked in the singular focus on the national government. First, did the state and local governments profit in a relative sense from the steep decline in public approbation accorded the national government? Or, to put it differently, did the national government continue to tower over the other two levels in the esteem of the American people despite its absolute fall from grace? Second, did state and local governments experience the same sort of absolute decline in confidence that befell the national government? Was declining confidence a generalized phenomenon, or was it especially acute at the national level?

The third question arises from the fact that most of the explanations for the shrinking trust in government tend to look at specific causes of the decline (for example, the Vietnam War, the Watergate affair, Irangate, and Congressional scandals) rather than what these events may have symbolized in a larger sense. So the third question is whether the trust positions of the three levels of government, and changes in those positions over time, can be linked to key principles of governance and what people expect from their various governments. In the long run, answering this question may be the most important one in terms of democratic theory. To address these topics I draw on a variety of national surveys covering the period from the mid-1960s to the early 1990s.

Changes in Relative Levels of Trust

Strictly speaking, the absolute drop in trust in the federal government tells us very little about where the federal government stands vis à vis the other two levels. Dramatic though the attrition has been, the national government could still be considered more trustworthy than the two lower levels. In this case, a receding tide could have been lowering all governmental boats while maintaining the national government's relative advantage. As will be demonstrated, that was not what happened.

Fortunately, we have data points that precede the upheavals that commenced in the late 1960s. Data collection on the series of questions began in 1965, with the start of a long-term national panel study of high school seniors, their parents, and their principals and social studies teachers. Three years later it was augmented by inclusion of the questions in the national cross-section sample represented in the 1968 National Election Studies (NES) and in a national survey of school board members and superintendents. Subsequent soundings extending into the 1980s and 1990s were also taken.[5] The root questions began as follows: "We find that people differ in how much faith and confidence they have in various levels of government in this country. In your case, do you have more faith and confidence in the national government, the government of this state, or in the local government around here?" A second question ascertained which level was least trusted. A "why do you feel this way?" question followed each of these lead-in questions.

Despite differences in nuance, I am treating faith and confidence as the equivalent of trust. In addition to the intuitively recognized similarity of the terms, there is empirical support indicating that people

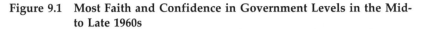

Figure 9.1   Most Faith and Confidence in Government Levels in the Mid-to Late 1960s

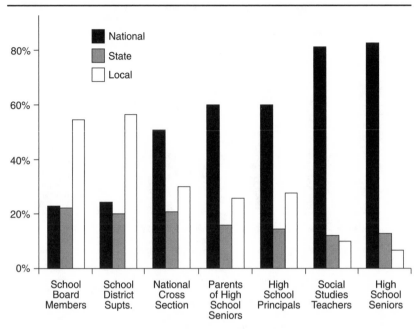

Sources: For school board members, school district superintendents, and national cross section, the National Election Studies. For all others, the Student-Parent Political Socialization Study. All studies conducted by the University of Michigan's Center for Political Studies and Survey Research Center.

equate the terms. Respondents in a 1978 General Social Survey were asked to explain what they had in mind when responding to a series of questions eliciting their "confidence" in a variety of institutions. Over two-fifths of all valid responses included the word *trust* or variants thereof, and well over one-fifth included *faith* or *believe in* and variants thereof (Smith, Taylor, and Mathiowetz 1979, 43–45).

The distributions to the two basic questions are shown in Figure 9.1 and 9.2. I have grouped the samples according to two sets of actors and the kind of relationships they have with each other. The four samples on the right side constitute the socialization set and the three on the left side what might be called the representational or fiduciary set. To some degree the results demonstrate that "where you stand depends on where you sit." Not surprisingly, school board members and superintendents, as members of the local elite, invested local governments with the most trust and the national with the least.[6] All the

Figure 9.2   Least Faith and Confidence in Government Levels in the Mid-to Late 1960s

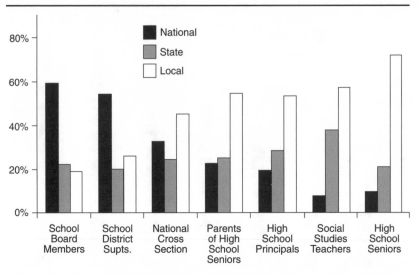

Sources: For school board members, school district superintendents, and national cross section, the National Election Studies. For all others, the Student-Parent Political Socialization Study. All studies conducted by the University of Michigan's Center for Political Studies and Survey Research Center.

other samples placed more confidence in the national government by a wide margin.

Especially important are the high rankings given to the national government by the three most general samples—the national cross section and the high school senior and parent samples. Although the national government's reputation began its descent in the mid- to late 1960s, even as late as 1968 a national cross section would rank it easily above state and local government. This distribution is most likely the kind that would have obtained at least since the emergence of the New Deal, and one that probably peaked during the Second World War and the 1950s. Relief from the Depression, a resounding victory in the Second World War, a flourishing decade of postwar recovery, and an image as the stalwart defender of the West against communism all figured into this superior status for the national government.[7] These images contrasted sharply with the less-than-positive pictures often attached to weak or corrupt state and local governments. Given this background and the very lopsided favoring of the national government by the upcoming generation as represented by the high school seniors, the reasonable expectation was for rank-order persistence.

As it turned out, however, that ordering was to change in an amazingly short period of time, eloquent testimony to the vulnerability of trust attributions. Figures 9.3 and 9.4 add four observations of the general public.[8] The relative status of the national government fell dramatically, with the sharpest movement occurring between 1972 and 1973.[9] The "least faith and confidence" figures are particularly striking. By inference (and as I will show more directly later in the chapter), the emerging Watergate scandal was probably critical in that sudden shift. Nixon's forced resignation seems likely to have solidified the shrinking trust accorded the national government in 1974. By 1976 it was apparent that there would be no quick reversion to the status quo ante. Not only was the national government no longer the repository of the most faith and confidence, but it was also the winner of the dubious title of least trusted. State government and local government picked up the slack in roughly equal amounts.

It might be concluded that these impressive aggregate shifts meant that individual-level changes were almost exclusively in the direction away from confidence in the national government. The reality is more complex, however, as demonstrated by utilizing the panel components contained within the 1972-74-76 NES. For example, an analysis of the 1972 to 1976 two-wave panel respondents (and deleting those respondents declaring "none" or "all"), reveals that some 45 percent of the respondents shifted their first choice from national to either state or local. A much smaller but still significant 19 percent switched from state or local to national. While the net movement tilted decidedly toward the national government, a substantial minority of the populace ran counter to the secular trend. Local conditions and partisan factors loom as the two most likely explanations of this contrariness.

Although the time series for the national cross-section samples does not resume until the 1996 NES survey, the results suggest that the transformation occurring in the mid-1970s stayed in place. The closely bunched rankings for most faith and confidence remained, but a modest shift moved the state level to the highest position (37 percent) with the local (33 percent) and national (30 percent) levels trailing closely behind. What is most significant here is the climb for the state level since 1976, from 28 percent to 37 percent, thus reflecting the increased prominence of state governments. Intriguingly, the least faith and confidence evaluations were almost identical to those for 1976, with the national level easily continuing as the least trusted (48 percent), followed by the local (34 percent) and state (19 percent) levels. There is absolutely no reason to think that mass public surveys during the 1980s or early 1990s would have shown a substantially different picture.[10] Results from wave 3 of the parent-child socializa-

Figure 9.3   Most Faith and Confidence in Government Levels (National Samples)

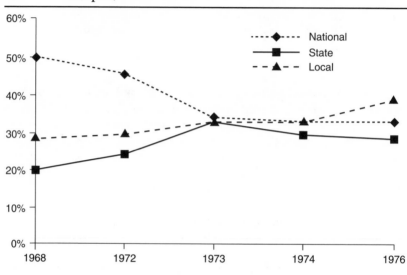

Sources: For all years except 1973, the National Election Studies, conducted by the University of Michigan's Center for Political Studies and Survey Research Center. For 1973, the Omnibus Survey, conducted by the Survey Research Center.

Figure 9.4   Least Faith and Confidence in Government Levels (National Samples)

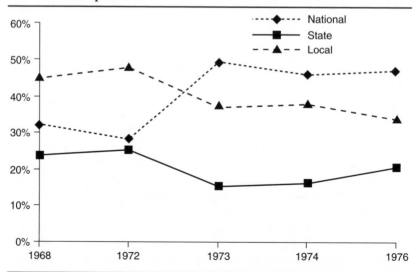

Sources: For all years except 1973, the National Election Studies, conducted by the University of Michigan's Center for Political Studies and Survey Research Center. For 1973, the Omnibus Survey, conducted by the Survey Research Center.

Figure 9.5   Most Faith and Confidence in Government Levels (Parents in Socialization Study)

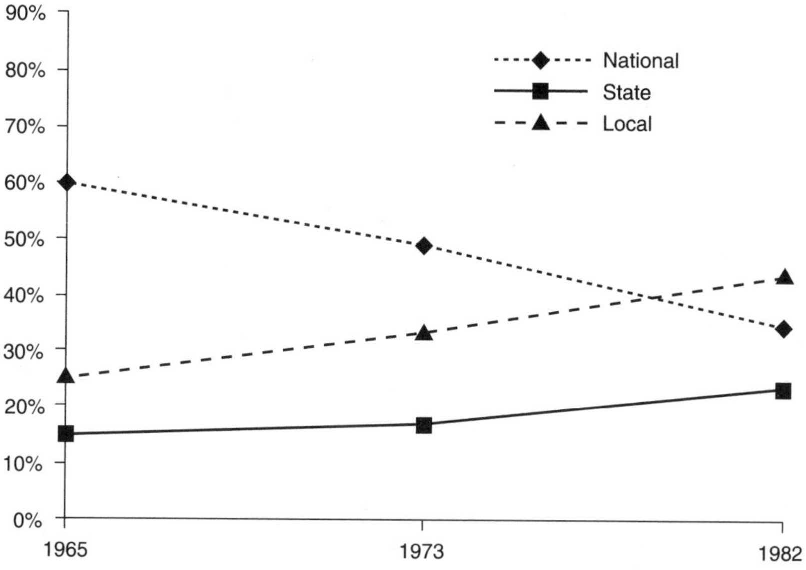

Sources: The Student-Parent Political Socialization Study, conducted by the University of Michigan's Center for Political Studies and Survey Research Center.

tion study, carried out in the spring of 1982, support this view (see figures 9.5 and 9.6). These findings also reveal the precipitous drop in trust accorded the national government by the upcoming generation, especially between 1965 and 1973.

One of the remarkable features of the federal government's free fall relative to the other two levels during the 1970s was its pervasiveness across a variety of important sociopolitical strata. Figure 9.7 to 9.10 show the pattern for most faith and confidence over time according to four characteristics of national cross-section samples. If ever a period effect could be observed with crystal clarity, this would be it. Regardless of region, partisanship, urbanicity, or race, the relative standing of the national government suffered an extraordinarily sharp decline.

That universality notwithstanding, some provocative distinctions can be observed. One is by region. The West went from being the most admiring region in 1968 to the least in 1976. In many ways that regional shift prefigured later developments that seemed to reflect an altered political climate in the Western states. For example, in a lead story in the *New York Times* (March 18, 1979), John Herbers noted the West's growing disgust and impatience with the federal government.

Figure 9.6   Most Faith and Confidence in Government Levels (Offspring in Socialization Study)

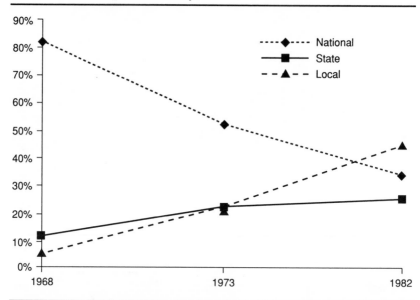

Sources: The Student-Parent Political Socialization Study, conducted by the University of Michigan's Center for Political Studies and Survey Research Center.

Nor is it likely sheer happenstance that the rise in domestic anti-federal (indeed, antigovernment) organizations and law-breaking actions was especially prominent in Western states during the 1990s.

Evaluations of particular governments and officeholders, as distinct from the political system in general, are subject to strong partisan and ideological considerations (Jennings and Van Deth 1989, ch. 11). Trust in the federal government, however, has never rebounded to its apogee of the 1950s and early 1960s, regardless of which party was in power. Indicative of this lowered assessment is the behavior of the Republican respondents portrayed in figure 9.8. Predictably, they experienced a little bounce with Nixon's election in 1972—the 1972 data point occurred in the postelection survey. Nevertheless, Republican evaluations proceeded to fall off the cliff in the 1973 to 1974 period, driven no doubt by the Watergate scandal.

While residents of big central cities continued to have more faith in the national government than did residents of less dense areas, they too shared in the downward plunge. And African Americans, who had looked to and benefited from the actions of the federal government during the 1960s, registered a severe drop in confidence. In

Figure 9.7   Most Faith and Confidence in National Government, by Region

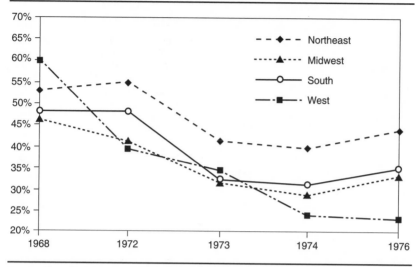

Sources: For all years except 1973, the National Election Studies, conducted by the University of Michigan's Center for Political Studies and Survey Research Center. For 1973, the Omnibus Survey, conducted by the Survey Research Center.

Figure 9.8   Most Faith and Confidence in National Government, by Partisanship

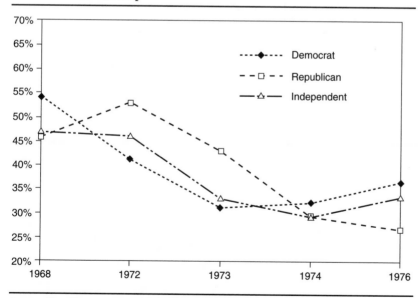

Sources: For all years except 1973, the National Election Studies, conducted by the University of Michigan's Center for Political Studies and Survey Research Center. For 1973, the Omnibus Survey, conducted by the Survey Research Center.

Figure 9.9   Most Faith and Confidence in National Government, by Urbanicity

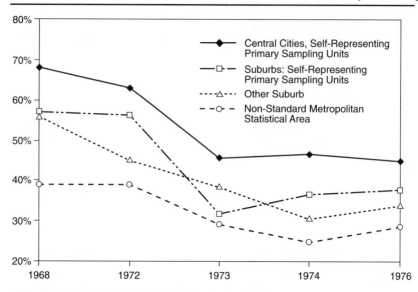

Sources: For all years except 1973, the National Election Studies, conducted by the University of Michigan's Center for Political Studies and Survey Research Center. For 1973, the Omnibus Survey, conducted by the Survey Research Center.

Figure 9.10   Most Faith and Confidence in National Government, by Race

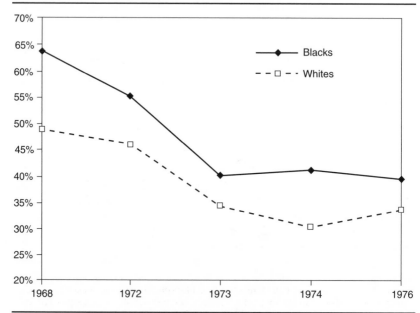

Sources: For all years except 1973, the National Election Studies, conducted by the University of Michigan's Center for Political Studies and Survey Research Center. For 1973, the Omnibus Survey, conducted by the Survey Research Center.

sum, the descent of the national government's standing was wide and deep. Inferentially, the state and local governments now had much greater resources in terms of public support.

Changes in Absolute Evaluations of Levels of Government

A strong reservation can be raised about the inference to be drawn from the changes in the rank orderings just discussed. As the strongest and most visible actor, the national government would be expected to take the brunt of citizens' growing disillusionment. Given the rank-order method used in producing these results, any diminution in appraisals of the national government automatically means that state and/or local governments were improving their status. As has been shown, both levels benefited to some extent. This rearrangement does not necessarily mean, however, that Americans were judging the other two levels more highly in any absolute sense. To benefit because of another's misfortune is not the same as to benefit because of one's own performance. It becomes important to know, then, whether the absolute confidence expressed in state and local governments was undergoing the same erosion as that in the national government, and whether state and locals only looked better in comparison to the shocks being absorbed by the national.

Unlike the rich time series data contained in the National Election Study's political trust battery devoted to "the government in Washington," the data base for absolute evaluations of state and local governments is much thinner. Still, a few questions dealing with all three levels have been asked over time. Perhaps the most convincing of these soundings are the 1972 to 1992 comparisons shown in figure 9.11.[11] The contrasts are startling. Whereas the national government suffered a loss of over 30 percent in terms of trust and confidence, the state level dropped by half that much and local government scarcely at all.[12] Clearly, the tar brush did not sweep with equal vigor across all levels. Disenchantment with the national government did not produce commensurate disenchantment at lower levels. Alternatively, the factors feeding the growing distrust of the federal government did not have as much impact at the lower levels.

Admittedly, the national government had further to fall, even though results based on the standard trust in government items indicate that some decline had already occurred (see, for example, Miller and Traugott 1989, 261–63). Even so, differential attrition resulted in a shake-up in the ordering of absolute trust. In 1972 the national government held a 7 percent edge over state governments and a 10 percent margin over local. In 1992, as a result of the precipitous fall at the

**Figure 9.11   Trust and Confidence in the Three Levels of Government
(Percentage Saying "A Great Deal" or "A Fair Amount")**

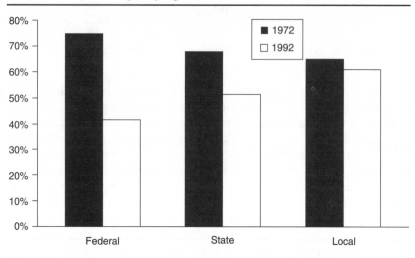

Sources: Opinion Research Center and the Gallup Organization, 1972 and 1992, respectively, as reported in Conlan (1993).

**Figure 9.12   Performance Rating of Three Levels of Government
(Percentage Giving a 5–8 Rating on a 0–8 Scale)**

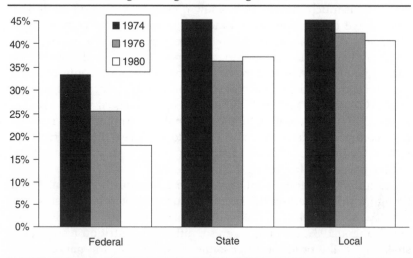

Sources: National Election Studies, conducted by the University of Michigan's Center for Political Studies and the Survey Research Center.

national level and modest to negligible losses at the state and local levels, the national government now trailed the state governments by 9 percent and the local governments by 18 percent, surely a stunning turnaround.

A second set of comparisons (figure 9.12) began in 1974, after Watergate. By this time, and using a performance rather than a trust measure, the absolute ratings of state and local governments had already surpassed those of the national government.[13] Significantly, however, the assessments of the federal government continued to decline substantially in 1976 and 1980 when it was compared with the state and local governments, especially the latter. Thus by 1980 there was an absolute gap of nearly 25 percent between the federal and local levels and 20 percent between the federal and state levels.

A final piece of evidence comes from a series of retrospective questions included in a late 1973 national survey.[14] When asked if they had more, less, or the same confidence in each of the three levels of government now compared with five years ago, 57 percent of the respondents reported "less confidence" in the federal government, compared with 26 percent in the state and 30 percent in the local. Although retrospective questions of this sort are suspect in terms of the absolute values of the resulting responses, the pattern found here dovetails nicely with that from the replicated cross-section surveys.

It is clear, then, that the growing lack of confidence in governments was disproportionately absorbed, if not indeed generated, by the national level. In view of the scope of its actions and the extent of media coverage, it is not surprising that the national level would be hit the hardest. By the same token, it is likely that big positive upsurges in confidence would probably be reflected most acutely in national evaluations.

What Lies Behind the Changes in Trust?

So far I have demonstrated that in the period from the late 1960s to the early 1990s the confidence accorded the national government underwent a monumental decline in both an absolute and a relative sense and that state and local governments fared much better by comparison. I have also noted some of the commonly cited events associated with the national government's fall from grace. But such events do not fully explain why the general public reordered its trust hierarchy so drastically. I would argue that the reordering reflects the expectations and standards that citizens apply to different levels of government. When the standards and expectations are not met, reaction can be swift, dramatic, and durable.

It will be recalled that the follow-up queries to the rank-order faith and confidence questions asked the respondents why they felt that way—that is, why they picked one level as most trusted and another as least trusted. A content analysis of these responses offers much insight into what kinds of criteria people apply to different levels of government and speaks directly to some key aspects of democratic theory. Detailed coding yielded around forty specific categories for each of the follow-up questions. These categories were grouped under two broad rubrics and one smaller one that represent familiar dimensions to students of democratic society.

One such dimension is that of performance. It has to do with how well the government carries out its functions, the caliber of personnel, the range and magnitude of its power, and the kinds of policies adopted and implemented. The second dimension is that of the linkage between the citizenry and the government. Here the emphasis is on the representativeness and accountability of leaders, how much they care about ordinary folks, and how easy it is to understand what the government is doing—its transparency. A third, almost residual dimension is that of probity, the integrity and honesty manifested in the political process and exhibited by key political actors. This dimension could be included under performance, but it is treated separately because, on its face, it has characteristics of both performance and linkage functions and because it has signal importance in affecting the least-confidence rankings during the historical era under consideration.

Table 9.1 shows the distribution of these responses in terms of reasons for most faith and confidence, while table 9.2 does the same for least faith and confidence. The percentage base is the number of responses. Table 9.1 and figure 9.13 make clear that despite the large shift in rank ordering across the years, the rationales advanced by ordinary citizens were remarkably uniform across the decade.[15] By all odds the national government scored highest on the performance dimension, followed by state and then local government. What inspires trust in the national government is its power, competence, and policies.

The linkage function distributions, however, show an opposite pattern. Here, local governments reigned supreme, followed by the state level, and finally the national. Figure 9.14 displays the contrast in graphic form. By this light, the American public was saying that closer is far better for ensuring the representational function. Importantly, the differences in justifications according to governmental level hold in both a relative and absolute sense. For example, not only are proportionately more performance points awarded to the national than to the state and local governments, but the national government's performance points far outweigh its linkage points. Similarly,

Table 9.1 Reasons for Most Faith and Confidence in Three Levels of American Government, 1968 to 1976

	1968				1973				1974				1976			
	Nat'l (%)	State (%)	Local (%)	T (%)	Nat'l (%)	State (%)	Local (%)	T (%)	Nat'l (%)	State (%)	Local (%)	T (%)	Nat'l (%)	State (%)	Local (%)	T (%)
Performance																
Magnitude of power	34	10	3	19	29	9	3	16	31	10	5	14	34	14	6	17
Competence of personnel	22	21	6	17	18	24	7	16	17	15	4	11	16	15	5	11
Policies and programs	4	6	2	4	8	14	11	11	9	14	8	10	13	20	10	14
Subtotal	61	37	11	40	65	48	20	43	58	38	17	35	63	49	21	41
Linkage																
Representativeness and accountability	10	24	35	21	9	19	36	22	15	18	34	24	13	18	39	25
Responsiveness and concern	8	17	13	12	9	19	16	15	9	22	20	18	9	18	16	14
Comprehensibility, transparency	8	16	38	20	11	7	23	14	6	11	24	15	8	6	20	12
Subtotal	27	57	86	52	29	45	75	51	30	51	78	57	30	43	75	52

(Table continues on p. 234.)

Table 9.1 *Continued*

	1968				1973				1974				1976			
	Nat'l (%)	State (%)	Local (%)	T (%)	Nat'l (%)	State (%)	Local (%)	T (%)	Nat'l (%)	State (%)	Local (%)	T (%)	Nat'l (%)	State (%)	Local (%)	T (%)
Politics and corruption																
Honesty, lack of deceit and corruption	12	6	4	8	4	6	4	5	11	9	4	7	6	8	4	6
Electoral and party system	1	—	—	1	2	1	1	1	1	1	1	1	1	1	1	1
Subtotal	13	6	4	8	6	7	5	6	12	10	5	8	7	9	4	6
Total	101%	100%	101%	100%	100%	100%	100%	100%	100%	100%	100%	100%	100%	101%	100%	99%
N	612	249	418	1279	325	363	404	1092	369	375	558	1302	742	652	1005	2399

Sources: For all years except 1973, the National Election Studies, conducted by the University of Michigan's Center for Political Studies and Survey Research Center. For 1973, the Omnibus Survey conducted by the Survey Research Center

Notes: Percentage base equals number of responses for each column. Subtotals and totals may not balance because of rounding.

Figure 9.13   Performance Preferences as Justification for Most Faith and Confidence

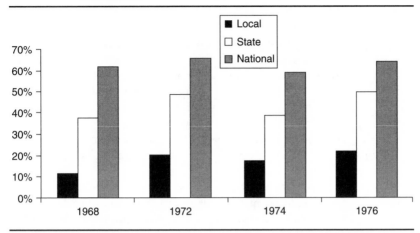

Sources: National Election Studies, conducted by the University of Michigan's Center for Political Studies and the Survey Research Center.

Figure 9.14   Linkage Preferences as Justification for Most Faith and Confidence

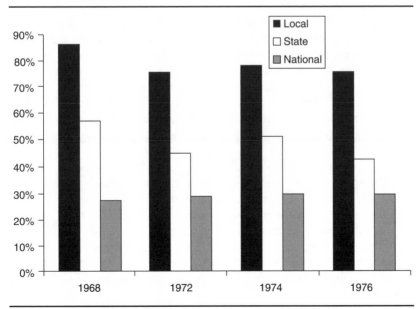

Sources: National Election Studies, conducted by the University of Michigan's Center for Political Studies and the Survey Research Center.

local governments receive proportionately more linkage references than do the other two levels, and such references heavily exceed those garnered for performance.

As is demonstrated in table 9.2, the pattern is not quite so clear-cut with respect to the justifications offered for least faith and confidence. As might be expected, performance references occurred least frequently as the reason for having least confidence in the national government and most frequently with respect to state and local governments. And in 1968 the linkage process was cited most frequently regarding the national and much less so regarding the state and local. All of this mirrors to a great extent the findings for most faith and confidence. Performance and linkage are differentially associated with governmental levels.[16]

A key difference is apparent, however. In 1968, as well as in subsequent years, a substantial number of reservations about state and local governments dealt with politics and corruption, thus echoing the conventional view that lower-level politics and politicians are simply dirtier and more corrupt than those at the national level. Indeed, judging by the low number of attributions of corruptness at the national level in 1968, one would have thought Washington, D.C., was squeaky clean. This image underwent a rude jolt in 1973. References to politics and corruption (mainly the latter) went up sevenfold at the national level, driven in large part by specific references to Watergate and related matters.

From the portion of Figure 9.4 that depicts the sharp increase in lack of trust in the national government it is plausible to argue that the reason for that abrupt jump stemmed in great part from the Watergate affair. Specific references to Watergate declined in subsequent years, but the taint remained, for even by 1976 the references to politics and corruption at the national level were still three times those in 1968. Correspondingly, after a low of 30 percent in 1973, negative references to the linkage function of the national government began to climb.

The foregoing analysis should not be taken to mean that Watergate was the sole or even primary cause for falling evaluations of the national government. As was indicated in the introduction to this chapter, absolute trust in the national government began to erode as early as the mid-1960s. Even without Watergate the trend would most likely have continued. Watergate did, however, almost certainly provide a sharp boost to the trend, raising doubts to a new plateau. That boost, in turn, improved the status of the state and local levels in the eyes of the public.

Combining the results from the rank ordering of trust levels with their accompanying justifications reveals that the public is both malle-

Table 9.2 Reasons for Least Faith and Confidence in Three Levels of American Government—1968 to 1976

	1968				1973				1974				1976			
	Nat'l (%)	State (%)	Local (%)	T (%)	Nat'l (%)	State (%)	Local (%)	T (%)	Nat'l (%)	State (%)	Local (%)	T (%)	Nat'l (%)	State (%)	Local (%)	T (%)
Performance																
Magnitude of power	17	9	13	13	10	8	14	11	10	5	9	9	17	6	11	13
Competence of personnel	5	30	28	21	7	23	23	15	8	27	27	17	8	23	24	16
Policies and programs	10	15	5	9	10	34	15	15	10	19	17	14	14	34	19	19
Subtotal	32	53	47	44	28	65	51	41	28	51	52	39	39	63	54	48
Linkage																
Representativeness and accountability	22	6	4	10	14	6	7	11	21	2	6	15	21	7	9	15
Responsiveness and concern	17	10	7	11	11	11	17	13	13	17	13	13	14	11	16	14

(Table continues on p. 238.)

Table 9.2 *Continued*

	1968				1973				1974				1976			
	Nat'l (%)	State (%)	Local (%)	T (%)	Nat'l (%)	State (%)	Local (%)	T (%)	Nat'l (%)	State (%)	Local (%)	T (%)	Nat'l (%)	State (%)	Local (%)	T (%)
Comprehensibility, transparency	23	12	13	16	5	3	9	6	5	8	6	6	9	6	6	7
Subtotal	62	28	24	37	30	20	33	30	39	37	25	34	44	23	31	36
Politics and corruption																
Dishonesty, deceitfulness, and corruptness	5	15	22	15	11	12	11	11	16	9	17	15	13	11	11	12
Watergate affair	—	—	—	—	28	—	—	15	14	—	—	7	3	—	—	1
Electoral and party system	1	4	7	4	3	3	5	4	3	3	5	4	2	3	4	3
Subtotal	6	19	29	19	42	15	16	29	33	12	23	27	18	14	15	16
Total	100%	100%	100%	100%	100%	100%	100%	100%	100%	100%	100%	100%	101%	101%	100%	100%
N	356	253	496	1104	513	118	347	978	563	144	341	1048	1046	414	678	2138

Sources: For all years except 1973, the National Election Studies, conducted by the University of Michigan's Center for Political Studies and Survey Research Center. For 1973, the Omnibus Survey conducted by the Survey Research Center.

Notes: Percentage base equals number of responses for each column. Subtotals and totals may not balance because of rounding.

able in its attributions of trust and consistent in its application of standards. Malleability does not mean fickleness, for public opinion was obviously responding to external events over the course of the years covered by the various data points reported on here. Yet the rationales advanced for most trust in the three different levels remained virtually constant across that time period. Clearly, the criteria being invoked, the standards by which people are most likely to value one level of government over another, were quite consistent taken in the aggregate. Even what might seem to be an exception in the case of probity concerns expressed as a reason for least trust simply proves the rule. It is highly unlikely that the level of probity expected of the national government suddenly increased in the 1970s. Rather, a widespread belief that those standards of probity had been violated led to disenchantment with the federal government.

Conclusion

What does all this have to do with the recent obsession with devolution? Actually, as pointed out by John DiIulio and Donald Kettl (1995), devolution takes a variety of proposed forms, including privatization and the reduction of government activities at any level. Both of these meanings have sparked considerable public debate and may become even more visible in the future. In the long run these various meanings may, in fact, be pivotal in determining how governments are to function. I use the term here, however, in its more commonly understood sense of shifting resources and responsibilities away from the federal government toward lower levels, a meaning that still marks much of the political rhetoric about devolution, as witnessed by the 1996 presidential campaign.

The groundwork for devolution in this sense was being laid in the late 1960s and the 1970s. Devolution then emerged as a policy cornerstone during the Reagan Revolution, and its cachet has continued unabated into the 1990s. Confidence in the national government is highly contingent on performance, on how well it delivers the goods, whether that be in managing social unrest, ensuring economic well-being, engaging the enemy abroad, or avoiding malfeasance at home. When the national government began to falter in one or more of these dimensions, its support in both an absolute and a relative sense began to erode, and devolution became more attractive.

By contrast, support for local government and to some extent state government derives its strength fundamentally from how well they are seen to provide a link between the citizenry and public officials and decision making. There is no evidence that anything has occurred to vitiate this linkage function—quite the opposite in some ways.

Sunshine laws, open meetings, the resurgence of direct democracy, and term limits have pushed in the direction of enhancing that function, or at least the image of it. While some of these actions could be rightly understood as reflecting a lack of trust in state and local governments, their presence does act to shore up the perception of access, accountability, and responsiveness.

These two dimensions of performance and linkage parallel, in rough fashion, the two psychological models of trustworthiness—instrumental and relational—as discussed by Tom Tyler in chapter 11. In the case of the levels of government, proximity would appear to be a major factor in helping to determine the differential foundations for establishing and maintaining trust. Whereas instrumental components are the most salient ones for trust in the more distant national government, relational elements appear to be most consequential for the more proximate lower levels, local government in particular.

Four further observations about the connections between trust and devolution can be offered. First, the arenas of political contesting have been affected by altered levels of trust. Enterprising politicians and political entrepreneurs in the United States (and seemingly elsewhere) have seized upon this shift in order to wage policy campaigns and to foster and bolster political careers. It is no accident, for example, that the right-to-life movement moved its battleground to the state and local levels, arguing that these levels constitute the more legitimate venues for resolving the abortion issue. Activists with an agenda have not had to work very hard at creating a climate favorable to devolution; it has been there at least since the mid-1970s. The roots of devolution took hold then and eventually yielded a rich harvest in terms of public opinion and at least a moderate crop in terms of public policy.

A second point to make is that the movement toward devolution is not unique to the United States. Western European governments have been under increasing devolutionary pressure in the form of demands for more privatization on one hand and greater authority and resources for subnational jurisdictions on the other. Nowhere has this drive been more pronounced than in Italy, where regional governments have enlarged their governing scope quite substantially since the mid-1970s (see, for example, Putnam 1993, ch. 2) and where the Northern League has, in fact, been pressing for autonomy. In another sense the breakup of the Soviet empire has unleashed its own kind of devolution-inspired stress, manifested most lamentably in the civil wars of the former Yugoslavia. Although declining confidence in the national or superordinate level of government surely does not account for all of the movement toward devolution in other countries, there can be little doubt that such declines have played a role.[17]

Third, the shifting assessments of the federal government provide a textbook example that trust can be a rather fragile commodity, just as it can be at the individual level (see, for example, Dasgupta 1988). From its high-flying days when it held sway over state and local governments as the object of highest trust, the national government suffered a sharp and durable fall. Enduring shifts of this magnitude within a fairly short period of time are relatively rare in public opinion research. Given the fact that people are disinclined to stop trusting that which they have trusted for some time, the change is all the more remarkable. Having once lost its clear advantage, the national government has had difficulty restoring it, thereby suggesting that trust is more easily relinquished than replenished. Frequent performance shortcomings and lapses in behavior at the national level, widely disseminated by a vigilant—some would say rapacious—media corps, have apparently inhibited the rebuilding of faith and confidence in the national government.

Finally, the declining fortunes of the national government and the ensuing devolution movement have made more salient a classic question of democratic theory, namely, what governmental arrangements are most optimal from the citizen's point view. Three decades ago Robert Dahl (1967) wrote an article called "The City in the Future of Democracy." He discussed the optimal unit for a democratic polity in terms that very much resemble my discussion of performance and linkage:

> [Yet] the larger and more inclusive a unit with a representative government, and the more complex its tasks, the more participation must be reduced for most people to the single act of voting in an election. Conversely, the smaller the unit, the greater the opportunity for citizens to participate in the decisions of their government, yet the less of the environment they can control. Thus for most citizens participation in very large units becomes minimal and in very small units it becomes trivial. At the extremes, citizens may participate in a vast range of complex and crucial decisions by the single act of casting a ballot; or else they have almost unlimited opportunities to participate in decisions of no importance. (p. 960)

One solution to this conundrum is simply to say that different levels meet different needs. Let people get their representation and participation kicks out of local politics, and let them have their big needs addressed by the national government—a division of labor to accompany the division of levels. The results presented in this chapter suggest such a division at the aggregate level. Devolution implies a blurring of these functions, however, for the scope of state and local governments would increase along with maintaining the superior linkage functions. Moreover, there is something unsettling about a populace that has less trust in the most powerful level of government. Assuming that at least a modicum of political trust is a desideratum, one formidable challenge lies in trying to achieve some sort of equitable balance between performance and linkage across governmental levels in a way that inspires and feeds on trust.

Notes

1. For documentation on the secular trend see, *inter alia*, Dalton 1996; Erikson and Tedin 1995, 162–65; Ladd 1995, 33; Lipset and Schneider 1983, ch. 1; and Miller and Traugott 1989, 261–63, 272. Some of the most vigorous exchanges about the meaning and measurement of variable levels of trust have involved Arthur Miller and Jack Citrin (Miller 1974a, 1974b; Miller and Borelli 1991; Citrin 1974; Citrin and Green 1986). It should be noted that evaluations of other leading institutions also declined during this period (see, for example, Dalton 1996, 268; Lipset and Schneider 1983, ch. 2).

2. For the sake of variety the terms *national government* and *federal government* will be used interchangeably.

3. Indeed, the number of local governments increased from around 78,000 in 1972 to over 86,000 in 1992. Figures cited in DiIulio and Kettl (1995, 9, n. 13).

4. For evidence at the pre- and young-adult levels, see findings cited in Reeves and Glendening 1975.

5. All the NES studies employed here are available from the Inter-University Consortium for Political and Social Research (ICPSR), University of Michigan. The author was a principal investigator on the school district study and all the political socialization surveys. These studies are also available through the ICPSR.

6. These figures are based on respondents selecting one of the three levels. A small minority of each sample volunteered either "all the same" or "none of them" as responses.

7. It is all too common to view the current era as the blip, when in fact the 1940s and '50s may have been the exception in terms of esteem for the national government.

8. With the exception of 1973, these findings are based on NES surveys. The 1973 data come from an omnibus survey carried out by the Survey Research Center, which also performs the field work for the NES.

9. A small but steady rise in the volunteered response of "none of them" (2 percent to 7 percent) converges with the growing sense of disenchantment directed toward a whole range of American institutions.

10. The decline eventually extended even to the standard of efficiency, as charted by annual national surveys conducted by the Advisory Commit-

tee on Intergovernmental Relations (ACIR). When asked which level of government was the most efficient, the public continued to give the national government the nod until 1989 (as cited in McManus 1996, 184–85).

11. The results are based on surveys conducted by the Opinion Research Center and the Gallup Organization in 1972 and 1992, respectively. Both surveys were commissioned by the ACIR and are cited in Conlan 1993.

12. Two data points do not constitute a trend, of course, but the mountain of evidence showing the fall-off in trust at the national level over time (with only a slight resurgence during the Reagan era), along with other longitudinal observations and evidence to be presented later in the chapter, provide confirmatory evidence.

13. These findings are based on NES surveys. The root question reads: "Now I'd like to ask you how good a job you feel some of the parts of our government are doing. As I read, please give me the number that best describes how good a job you feel that part of the government is doing for the country as a whole." Respondents were presented with a nine-point scale ranging from 0 to 8, with printed labels of "very poor job," "poor job," "fair job," "good job," and "very good job" at intervals of 2. The stimulus objects reported on here were federal government, state government, and local government. (See Miller and Traugott 1989, 259–60).

14. The figures to be presented are taken from Reeves and Glendening 1975 and are based on a Harris Poll survey as reported in "Confidence and Concern: Citizens View American Government," U.S. Senate Committee on Government Operations, Subcommittee on Intergovernmental Relations, Washington, D.C., 1973.

15. Results from the three-wave socialization study, with a last reading of the two generations in 1982, display much the same patterning.

16. The mirror image generated by the two questions is not simply an artifact of individual respondents giving such opposite answers as, for example, that they like the federal government because it is efficient and dislike the local because it is inefficient.

17. Falling and modest levels of confidence have not been confined to the United States, as E.J. Dionne, Jr. reports in the *New York Times*, Feb. 16, 1986 (see also Dalton 1996).

References

Citrin, Jack. 1974. "Comment: The Political Relevance of Trust in Government." *American Political Science Review* 68 (Sept.): 973–88.

———, and Donald Philip Green. 1986. "Presidential Leadership and the Resurgence of Trust in Government." *British Journal of Political Science* 16 (Oct.): 431–53.

Conlan, Timothy J. 1993. "Federal, State, or Local? Trends in the Public's Judgement." *Public Perspective* 4 (Jan.): 3–5.

244   Trust and Governance

Dahl, Robert. 1967. "The City in the Future of Democracy." *American Political Science Review* 61(Dec.): 953–70.

Dalton, Russell J. 1996. *Citizen Politics*, 2nd ed. Chatham, N.J.: Chatham House.

Dasgupta, Partha. 1988. "Trust as a Commodity." In *Trust: Making and Breaking Cooperative Relations*, edited by Diego Gambetta. Cambridge: Basil Blackwell.

DiIulio, John J., Jr., and Donald F. Kettl. 1995. *Fine Print: The Contract with America, Devolution, and the Administrative Realities of American Federalism.* Washington: The Brookings Institution.

Erikson, Robert S., and Kent L. Tedin. 1995. *American Public Opinion*, 5th ed. Boston: Allyn and Bacon.

Gray, Virginia, and Herbert Jacob, ed. 1996. *Politics in the American States*, 6th ed. Washington: CQ Press.

Hibbing, John R., and Elizabeth Theiss-Moore. 1995. *Congress as Public Enemy.* New York: Cambridge University Press.

Jennings, M. Kent, Jan Van Deth, Samuel H. Barnes, Dieter Fuchs, Felix J. Heunks, Ronald Inglehart, Max Koose, Hans-Dieter Klingmann, and Jacques J. A. Thomassen. 1989. *Continuities in Political Action.* Berlin: Walter de Gruyter.

Ladd, Everett Carl, ed. 1995. *America at the Polls: 1994.* Storrs, Conn.: The Roper Center for Public Opinion Research, University of Connecticut.

Lipset, Seymour Martin, and William Schneider. 1983. *The Confidence Gap.* New York: Free Press.

McManus, Susan. 1996. *Young v. Old: Generational Combat in the 21st Century.* Boulder, Col.: Westview Press.

Miller, Arthur H. 1974a. "Political Issues and Trust in Government, 1964–1970." *American Political Science Review* 68 (Sept.): 951–72.

Miller, Arthur H. 1974b. "Rejoinder to 'Comment' by Jack Citrin: Political Discontent or Ritualism." *American Political Science Review* 68 (Sept.): 989–1001.

Miller, Arthur H., and Stephen A. Borelli. 1991. "Confidence in Government During the 1980s." *American Politics Quarterly* 19 (Apr.): 147–73.

Miller, Warren E., and Santa A. Traugott. 1989. *American National Election Studies Data Sourcebook: 1952–1986.* Cambridge: Harvard University Press.

Putnam, Robert. 1993. *Making Democracy Work.* Princeton, N.J.: Princeton University Press.

Reeves, Mavis Mann, and Parris N. Glendening. 1975. "Public Opinion and Levels of Government." Paper presented to the Midwest Political Science Association, Chicago (April).

Smith, Tom W., D. Garth Taylor, and Nancy A. Mathiowetz. 1979. "Public Opinion and Public Regard for the Federal Government." In *Making Democracies Work*, edited by Carol H. Weiss and Allen H. Barton. Beverly Hills, Calif.: Sage Publications.

Chapter 10

Uncertainty, Appraisal, and Common Interest: The Roots of Constituent Trust

WILLIAM T. BIANCO

T HIS CHAPTER deals with the phenomena of leadership in a democracy. My focus is on situations where constituents defer to the judgment of elected officials, allowing them to take actions that are contrary to constituent demands without incurring an electoral penalty. When does this sort of trust arise? More specifically, when can elected officials innovate, changing policy from the status quo or making policy in new areas, without fear of being thrown from office? That is the question addressed here.

Assumptions about trust play a central, if sometimes unacknowledged, role in many of our theories of politics, as both Russell Hardin and Tom Tyler note in chapters 1 and 11 respectively. As I have argued elsewhere (Bianco 1994, ch. 2), any specification of how careerminded politicians pursue reelection, ranging from the descriptive work of David Mayhew (1974) to variables used in models of roll call behavior (for example, Kalt and Zupan 1990) to characterizations of legislators' goals using induced ideal points (for example, Krehbiel 1991; Poole and Rosenthal 1991) is built on assumptions about trust. Similar assumptions about the electorate's willingness to defer to elected officials are prominent in models of executive politics. Finally, assumptions about the electorate's ability (more usually, inability) to make good decisions about trust appear in many normative analyses of democracy, including those addressed to the American case (for example, Bernstein 1989; Page and Shapiro 1992) and elsewhere (for example, Blondel 1973; Converse and Pierce 1986).

The first thing to understand about trust is that decision about whether or not to trust are generally nonobvious. By virtue of their office, representatives are better informed about the policy process. They hold private information about the consequences of enacting policy proposals and the policy implications of procedural choices, and, as a result, they are often in a better position to judge whether a vote serves constituent interests. But deference is not always appropriate; legislators hold policy concerns of their own and are often pressured by special interests or by their party. Constituents cannot accept expertise as a blanket justification for questionable actions. They must develop criteria for making decisions about trust.

How do constituents resolve trust decisions? That is the first question addressed here. The focus is on developing—as Russell Hardin counsels elsewhere in this volume—a micro-level account of where trust comes from. I show that trust depends on perceptions of the act and the agent: what constituents know about the proposal being voted on and what they know about their representative and, in particular, about the probability that the proposal taps interests held in common by the two parties. The next question is where these perceptions come from. How do constituents assess common interest, especially in light of the opportunity costs involved with developing these perceptions? Drawing on results in social psychology, I argue that the typical voter relies on low-cost sources of information, cues or indicators that allow him to form reasonably accurate beliefs about the candidates.

The final section of the paper turns to operationalizing these findings about trust, confirming the intuition that a representative's visible attributes are often imbued with political significance; these characteristics signal policy concerns. Thus, to say that voters want a representative who shares their religious views, their ethnicity, or their race, or a representative who is a war hero, a businessman, or a famous athlete does not imply that they are motivated by cultural forces or extrapolicy goals. Instead, appearance and actions outside politics matter because these characteristics signal motivation, talent, and character and thus provide a basis for resolving trust decisions.

These findings draw on two very distinct modes of analysis, both presented in an earlier work (Bianco 1994). The first is a game-theoretic model of trust decisions, a model that yields predictions about trust as a function of constituents' beliefs about their representative's motives and about the consequences of her actions. These predictions are tested using statistical analysis of data gathered from interviews with ninety-three members of the U. S. House of Representatives. The interviews focused on vote decisions, explanations, and the presence or absence of trust on two proposals, the Ethics Act of 1989 and the Medicare Catastrophic Coverage Act of 1988. Space precludes a full discussion of the empirical analysis; this chapter focuses mainly on the game-theoretic analysis, drawing on the interviews to illustrate the assumptions and predictions.

Modeling Trust

The focus of this section is on a single representative facing a single action, an action that has consequences for constituent welfare. The question for constituents is, should they force the legislator to act as they think best or allow her to act on the basis of her own appraisal of the situation? After describing how rational constituents might resolve this decision—and how rational legislators will act in anticipation of constituent behavior—I set out the conditions under which trust is expected to arise.

The Evaluation Game

The Evaluation Game captures a single interaction involving R and her constituents.[1] R votes on a *policy proposal* (β) that, if enacted, will produce a new *policy outcome*. Afterward, C evaluates R's action. Player C is a stand-in for the set of constituents in R's district who are prepared to make retrospective evaluations of R's vote on β. Since β is considered to be a high-salience issue, this set includes either a high percentage of R's constituents or a smaller but politically significant group. Each player wants R to enact the best possible policy outcome given her policy goal. R also wants to be reelected and considers this goal to be more important than securing good policy. The players pursue these goals under conditions of asymmetric information. R is fully aware of all factors relevant to her decision. C is similarly well informed about most facets of the game, but he does not know two things: what policy outcome will be produced if β is enacted and what R's policy goals are.

Formally, C knows two things for sure: the location of his ideal point (the point in the policy space which summarizes his policy preferences), and the location of the status quo outcome. However, C is uncertain about two things. The first is the location, the outcome that results from enacting β. C is also unsure of the location of R's ideal point—that is, he does not know R's type at R_1. Given these uncertainties, C can be playing one of several games.[2] *The problem is, C does not know which game he is playing—but R does.*

Does enacting β make C better off (that is, yield an outcome that is closer to his ideal point than the status quo), or does it make him worse off? Does R share C's policy concerns or does she hold different concerns? R knows which game describes the situation she and C are in. Thus, she chooses a strategy under full information; C does not. Because of his lack of information, C must base his evaluations on beliefs about which game he is playing—which diagrams are likely to be accurate and which are not.

Trust exists in the Evaluation Game when C is prepared to make a favorable evaluation of R's vote, regardless of how R votes. (This definition is consistent with those advanced by Tom Tyler elsewhere in this volume.) For example, suppose that C believes that enacting β will make him better off. Given these beliefs, C's demand, or his idea about what is best, is that β should be enacted. Therefore trust exists when C, given his beliefs about β, would issue a favorable retrospective evaluation regardless of whether R voted yea or voted nay. That C would approve of a yea vote in this example is no surprise—after all, he thinks enacting β is preferable. The approval of a nay vote, however makes sense only if C believes that R has private information about β, information that indicates, contrary to C's beliefs, that the status quo is preferable given his interests. To say that C decides against trust in this example implies that he will evaluate yea votes favorably and nay votes unfavorably. That is, C will approve of R's vote only if it appears to generate the best possible policy outcome for him.

Beliefs and Explanations

Elected officials spend considerable time and energy offering explanations to their constituents. To paraphrase Richard Fenno's classic work, *Home Style* (1978, 141), explanations involve descriptions, interpretations, and justifications of behavior. They are designed to generate political support and to increase an incumbent's chances of reelection. They occur during face-to-face interactions, such as speeches or question-and-answer sessions with constituents, and through indirect means, such as media coverage or newsletters.

The conventional wisdom is that explanations are a mechanism for persuasion; they alter what constituents think about legislative proposals or about their representatives' policy concerns. For example, Glenn Parker (1989) has argued, "Incumbent congressmen make a point of explaining their votes and policy positions to their constituents when they are called upon to do so. . . . Explanations can be used by members to gain some leeway in their pursuits in Washington" (23). David Austen-Smith's (1992) game-theoretic analysis of explanations and trust makes the link explicit: "Legislators' voting decisions are influenced by the need to justify Washington behavior to home constituents. An inability to offer a satisfactory explanation for some particular vote is perceived as jeopardizing an incumbent's chances of reelection" (68). Both statements convey the idea that explanations are a mechanism for persuasion or conversion. They emphasize the negative aspect; representatives take care to avoid unexplainable votes, votes that will anger constituents regardless of how they are rationalized. But there is a positive angle as well; explanations are thought to be a mechanism that gives representatives room to maneuver, the freedom to deviate from constituent demands without fear of political consequences.

These studies suggest that the Evaluation Game should contain a stage or move where the representative, R, is allowed to make some sort of communication to her constituent, C, which could then be used in C's trust decision. But the game does not contain such a stage. The rationale for its exclusion is an empirical one; the interviews with members of Congress conducted in 1990 suggest that this addition would constitute a misspecification of the trust decision and the behavior surrounding it.

To be sure, the interviews with members of Congress confirm some of the conventional wisdom about explanations. Legislators expect to be asked to explain their votes, and they give considerable thought to how different votes can be explained. The interviews also revealed a serious problem, however; *in the main, members of Congress do not think of explanations as a mechanism for persuasion.* During the interviews, a considerable number dismissed questions along these lines as the product of foolish academic notions, completely out of touch with the exigencies of real-world politics.

The first problem facing would-be explainers is contact. The term *explaining* suggests a forum where constituents assemble to hear their representative. Constituencies typically contain many individuals, however, often scattered across a large area. Even with a maximum effort—sending out newsletters, aggressively courting print and electronic media, speaking before every group who will listen—only a minority of constituents are likely to be exposed to an explanation. On the difficulties involved in contacting constituents, consider what a senior member of Congress said when they were asked if they could explain a vote against the repeal of the Catastrophic Coverage Act:

> It would be difficult. It has to do with my district: because of the low density, I'd have to go to twenty-three media markets and deal with each community on its own. I've got fifty thousand retirees in my district. How do I consult fifty thousand people? It's hard to talk with all those who are affected by a program. It's not that easy. We each represent five hundred thousand people, and we don't have the opportunity to talk with each of them.

A junior representative was asked a similar question about voting for the Ethics Act:

> No, no way. Districts are so huge today, just by sheer logistics there's no way. My district is one hundred and eighty miles north-south and two hundred and fifty miles east-west. I go home and spend four days traveling around. But there's no way to come into contact with all those people, even if that's the only issue to talk about.

This finding is consistent with other analyses. As Fenno (1978) noted, "The more one observes members of Congress at work in their districts, the more one is impressed by the simple fact that people are hard to find" (234). Working from a survey of state legislators, the Malcolm Jewell (1982, ch. 3) concluded that constituents in rural areas are too spread out to contact effectively, while legislators in urban areas cannot get media access when they need it.

Moreover, contact is only the first step in persuasion. Constituents also have to believe what they are told. The message from the interviews was that constituents are reluctant to accept their representative's explanations, however well informed they believe her to be. An explanation designed to persuade is likely to cite information that cannot be verified—private information. And without the ability to verify, constituents cannot be sure whether their representative is telling the truth. This problem supplies a strong incentive for constituents to disregard explanations when making decisions about trust—and an equally strong incentive for representatives to steer clear of explanations as a means of influencing these decisions. For example, when asked how his constituents would react to an attempt to explain a vote in favor of the Ethics Act, a senior legislator replied, "No one but the mothers of members of Congress think that members of Congress would vote for ethics as the objective rather than a pay raise. You have to have a friendly judge to believe that."

In fact, a substantial number of legislators argued that attempts at persuasion only make constituents angry. As one freshman put it:

> I learned during my [first] month in the district not to take on the task of educating the public about the intricacies of an issue like Catastrophic. If you start explaining issues, you have to deal with numerous perspectives and issues. Seniors had been fed a lot of misinformation. Some had rational reasons for opposing Catastrophic, but on the whole if you tried to go down the list and explain, they were so antagonistic that their response was that you were trying to defend it. . . . Trying to analyze it for them so they could make an informed decision put you in hotter water, even though you were doing what they wanted.

Faced with these problems, many representatives apparently steer clear of anything that sounds like persuasion:

> I could tell them that if I vote yea the sun will come up, and if I vote no pestilence will descend. But my biases come in if I do that. So I try to provide them with as much information as I can. Sometimes I say, "Look, I'm biased but here's what I think." I go back home and talk with people, figure out where they are. I try to tell them about some questions they should be asking, answers they should look for. Legislators who try to tell people what the world is about wind up telling more about themselves than about the world.

Thus, while it appears that members of Congress offer explanations, they do not try to persuade, nor do they expect that constituents will be persuaded. Again, this view finds support in the substantive literature. Fenno (1978) has argued that when representatives offer explanations, they do not spend much time trying to educate—persuade—their constituents about policy matters:

> We think of education as an effort to persuade people to change their attitudes when the effort cannot be seen, in the short run anyway, as electorally beneficial. Education is something you do to your supporters—not your nonsupporters. Education involves the willingness to spend electoral capital—votes, even some trust—in an attempt to alter supporter attitudes about member activity in Washington. Few members would deny the importance of "educating your constituents" in the abstract. . . . But if education is a home activity that by definition has to *hurt a little*, then I did not see a great deal of it. (162)

This excerpt suggests that when reading *Home Style*, many scholars have focused on the term *explanation* without considering what Fenno meant by it. It must be emphasized that the legislators *did not* claim that explanations are valueless. Rather, their comments were consistent with Fenno's argument that members of Congress try to appear accessible to their constituents (1978, 131–35). At a minimum, explanations, regardless of who hears them or how they react, appear to be aimed at strengthening this perception. Perhaps representatives are rewarded simply for going home and reporting on their actions or for responding to constituent queries. Explanations might be a mechanism for position-taking (Mayhew 1974, 61). Alternatively, ducking queries about a vote may signal that a representative has something to hide, something worse than a vote against constituent interests. Whatever the reasons, explanations appear to have political value, even if they are not a mechanism for persuasion.

In sum, legislators do not think about explanations in terms of persuasion. They certainly offer explanations when asked, and sometimes volunteer explanations without being asked, but they are under no illusions that their efforts will build trust.[3] Simply put, when a legislator describes a vote as explainable, what he means is that he expects constituents to evaluate the vote favorably, because it is consistent with their demands or because they are inclined to trust his judgment. It does not imply that the legislator expects to be called on to explain, plans to volunteer an explanation, or believes that an explanation, *by itself*, will alter constituents' beliefs or generate trust. Rather, explainability is defined in terms of how constituents will react to a vote, as they assess what their representative has done in light of what they know about his motives and the options before him.

The Level of Trust Decisions

It should be noted, finally, that the Evaluation Game assumes that trust decisions are made one proposal at a time. Many scholars (for example, Parker and Parker 1993) argue that constituents make blanket—overarching—decisions about trust. Often these claims are illustrated using a quote from Fenno:

> When a constituent trusts a House member, the constituent is saying something like, "I am willing to put myself in your hands temporarily; I know that you will have opportunity to hurt me, although I may not know when these opportunities occur; I assume—and I will continue to assume until proven otherwise—that you will not hurt me; for the time being then, I'm not going to worry about your behavior. (1978, 55–56)

While many scholars see this as a reasonable intuition, there is reason to think it suspect. Rather than closing off options, a rational constituent would prefer to make trust decisions as they come up. This suspicion is reinforced by the 1990 interview data. Consider one legislator's initial comments about trust:

> I don't need to poll my constituents to know what to do. The people don't have the information I have. They send you here to listen to the debate and make your own decision based on your judgment.

This comment is consistent with the conventional wisdom. But consider what the legislator went on to say:

> But sometimes you get issues like [The Ethics Act and Catastrophic Coverage], where people depart from that rule. On most things they let you use your own best judgment. Sometimes newspapers pick out

three or four votes and publish them along with the titles of the bills you voted on. People who read those kind of things have to base their judgment of you on the title of the bills. If it had "Pay Raise" in the title, they wouldn't want you to vote for it. It makes you wonder how much they know.

Comments along these lines suggest a different view, that trust decisions involving high-salience proposals are made one at a time rather than in some overarching manner. That is not to say that Fenno's description is incorrect. It may, for example, reflect behavior on low-salience proposals. On high-salience proposals, however, it appears that the assumptions here are by far the more accurate picture.

Where Does Trust Come From?

Proposition 1 in appendix 1 of Bianco 1994 gives the formal game-theoretic predictions about behavior in the Evaluation Game. Drawing on these findings, this section describes the conditions under which rational constituents will trust their representative and shows how expectations about trust enter into a representative's vote decision.

Constituents' Behavior   After their representative votes, constituents must decide how to evaluate her action. Once some initial conditions are met, two factors drive trust decisions: how much constituents know about the proposal—their *level of uncertainty*—and the likelihood that they and the representative have a common interest on the proposal.

Measuring constituent uncertainty about a proposal is straightforward. Saying that constituents know a lot about a proposal, or have low uncertainty, means they can predict with high confidence what kind of policy outcome the proposal will produce if enacted. Along the same lines, saying that they know little about a proposal, or have high uncertainty, means they have only a vague idea what the proposal will do once enacted. To illustrate this concept, suppose that constituents, like C in the Evaluation Game, know that a proposal will produce one of two outcomes if enacted. If they believe that the outcomes are equally likely—from their viewpoint, each could occur with probability .5—they have high uncertainty. Their uncertainty is smaller insofar as they think one outcome is more likely to result than the other if the proposal is enacted.[4]

The effect of policy uncertainty on constituent behavior is simple. Constituents who are confident, who think they know what a proposal will do, have little reason to defer to their representative. Increased uncertainty creates a rationale for deference, as a means of tapping the representative's private information. At the margin, then, constituents should be more likely to trust their representative when they are highly uncertain about a proposal than when their uncertainties are small.

Measuring common interest is somewhat simpler. Given the status quo policy outcome and whichever policy outcome will be produced by enacting a proposal, a common interest exists if the two outcomes are ranked the same way in the preference orderings of a representative and her constituents. (Recall that these orderings are determined by the individuals' policy goals.) Common interest requires only the same relative ranking. The individuals may disagree about the absolute desirability of one or both outcomes, but they must agree on which outcome is relatively better than the other. Thus, when a common interest exists, the players agree on whether a proposal should be enacted or defeated. Under these conditions, a representative can be trusted to act in the interests of her constituents—not out of altruism but because her policy goals are such that she will do exactly what her constituents would want, if they knew what she knows. Similarly, the absence of a common interest implies that a representative and her constituents disagree on what should be done with a particular proposal, implying that trust is not advisable.

The concept of common interest captures exactly what policy-minded constituents should worry about; if they let their representative act as a free agent, what are the chances that she will act in their interest? This question would not be asked in the abstract. Rather, it will be cast in terms of the policy proposal at hand. Nor would constituents be concerned about policy goals their representative might hold that have nothing to do with the proposal at hand. Rather, they should focus on the specific decision the representative has made and the motives she had (or might have had) for making it. This focus makes sense from the perspective of a cognitive miser, but it also makes sense given the nature of trust decisions. To make this decision, constituents do not need to know all their representative's policy goals. They need only consider the goals that might have given her a reason to vote one way or the other. And they need not worry if the representative's policy goals differ from their own, as long as it appears that she had no reason to vote against their interests on the proposal at hand.

Representative's Behavior   When just one proposal is considered at a time, the Evaluation Game suggests that a representative's vote decision is essentially a choice of which goal to maximize, policy or reelection, conditioned on her expectations about trust. A representative who anticipates trust will cast whatever vote secures her preferred policy outcome. If she prefers the status quo to the outcome that will result from enacting a proposal, she will vote nay; if her preference is reversed, she will vote yea. Intuitively, once the representative knows that she will receive favorable evaluations regardless of what she does, policy considerations are the only force driving her decision.[5]

Now consider a representative who believes that constituents are not inclined to grant leeway. Under the conditions assumed thus far, where reelection takes precedence over policy the representative will vote as her constituents desire. If constituents believe that the proposal should be enacted, she will vote yea; if they believe defeat is preferable, she will vote nay.[6] Aside from signaling the representative's willingness to comply with constituent demands, these votes will not have any reputational consequences. They are political votes, uncolored by policy considerations. Thus, constituents, regardless of whether they are stereotype mavens or judicious consumers of signals, should not use them as a source of information about the representative's policy concerns.

What if the representative's political concerns take second place to her interest in good policy? This statement implies that the representative is willing to accept the cost of unfavorable evaluations plus any additional damage the vote causes to her reputation. Under these conditions, constituents lose all influence over their representative's actions. They will continue to make retrospective evaluations, as these judgments help them to assess the representative's performance in office. Moreover, votes cast under these conditions provide a clear signal of the representative's policy concerns. This result is consistent with the theories of stereotyping and signaling; insofar as constituents use votes to assess policy concerns, they will focus on low-salience proposals, where the political consequences are minimal, and on the occasional act of political courage, where a legislator's concern with public policy overrides her interest in getting reelected.

The Conditions for Trust   Figure 10.1 combines the discussion of constituent and representative behavior into a unified prediction about trust. The horizontal axis measures constituent uncertainty about the proposal on a 0 to 1 scale. On the left-hand side, constituents are highly uncertain. Moving to the right, their uncertainty decreases until, at the right-hand edge, they, just like the representative, are fully informed. The vertical axis measures the likelihood of a common interest, with high estimates at the top and low estimates at the bottom.

In the region below the dotted line in figure 10.1, the likelihood of common interest is low relative to the level of constituent uncertainty about the proposal. Thus, compared with the top region, constituents

Figure 10.1   Conditions of Trust

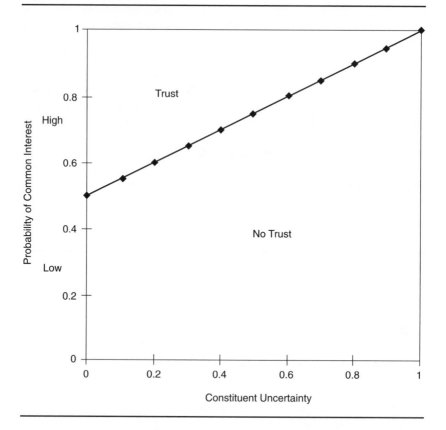

have less reason to defer to their representative, and deference is less likely to produce favorable results. Proposition 1 predicts that under these conditions, constituents will refuse to trust their representative, leaving her the choice of behaving as a delegate or incurring the costs associated with unfavorable evaluations. Assuming that a representative values reelection over policy, she will anticipate this response and comply with her constituents' demands. Of course, the representative's vote may happen to serve her own policy concerns as well as those held by constituents. In addition, votes cast under these conditions will not be read as a signal of the representative's private information. The only thing constituents learn is that the representative is willing to sacrifice good policy in the pursuit of favorable evaluations.[7]

A real-world example of behavior under these conditions is seen in a legislator's comments about his vote against the Ethics Act: "I said it's the right thing to do, but because of my inability to convey that to my constituents or the members of my delegation I decided to vote no. I cast a vote which was not in the interests of good public policy. . . . My constituents understood I had made a political decision."

As the legislator told it, he cast a "political vote"; he did what his constituents wanted, to avoid the political damage that would have ensued if he had done otherwise. There is no hint, however, that the vote had a favorable impact on his reputation. Apparently constituents saw the vote as a response to their demands, not as a signal of their representative's personal concerns. This asymmetry reflects the principle discussed earlier; while politically harmful votes influence a legislator's reputation, politically attractive votes generally do not. Of course, as long as a representative values reelection over policy, as did the legislator quoted here, he will avoid casting such votes in the first place.

In the top triangle in figure 10.1, the likelihood of a common interest is high relative to the amount that constituents know about the proposal. Under these conditions, constituents do best by trusting their representative. This decision may not always yield the best possible policy outcome for constituents, but refusing trust—forcing the representative to vote as constituents think best—is less likely to do so. Thus, given what constituents know, trust is the preferable choice. Under these conditions, the representative's optimal response—again, ignoring reputation effects—is to act as a trustee, voting in line with her policy interests. She will do this regardless of whether policy or reelection ranks first among her concerns. Such a vote will reveal some of the representative's private information to constituents, both about the proposal and about her goals.

One representative's description of his vote against the repeal of Catastrophic Coverage illustrates the conditions for trust depicted in the figure:

> Q. *What did your constituents want?* Originally my constituents were for repeal. . . . [Now] when I tell them what I did they say, "You're absolutely right."
>
> Q. *Why did they change their minds?* First, my poll results indicate that I was and remain enormously popular with senior citizens. I spend time on issues that concern them, we send lots of mail to them, and we are constantly in touch with them. Of my strong supporters, they are the strongest, and they also vote. This vote did nothing to hurt my support. . . . *They sense that I'm on their side on most things.* Also I tell them that I won't cut their Social Security, though I do say that I'll vote for taxing it.

As the representative told it, even though his senior-citizen constituents favored repeal, they approved of his vote to preserve the program. Their change of heart was based on their belief that the representative would vote for Catastrophic Coverage only if he thought it made seniors better off. Seniors did not believe that the representative agreed with them on all issues, such as taxing Social Security benefits. But they perceived agreement on Catastrophic Coverage and reasoned that since the representative voted against repeal, the program must be worth saving. Accordingly, they deferred to their representative's judgment and made a favorable evaluation of his vote against repeal.

Implications of the Leeway Hypothesis

This analysis shows that perceptions of common interest are by far the most important factor in trust decisions. Constituents will always trust their representative if they are sure that a common interest exists. If constituents are suspicious about common interest, they will grant leeway only if they are sufficiently uncertain about a proposal's effects. Below a certain point constituents will never trust their representative, even if they know very little about a proposal. Thus, trust can arise even when constituents know a lot about a proposal; it can be absent even when constituents know almost nothing. Moreover, deference may be the preferable option even when constituents are certain that their representative's policy goals differ from their own, as long as they think their interests coincide on the proposal at hand.

These findings also indicate that retrospective evaluations are insufficient to guarantee delegate behavior—behavior consistent with constituent demands. The threat of unfavorable evaluations will affect a representative's behavior only when her interest in reelection outweighs her policy concerns. When only a few constituents care about a proposal, or when a proposal taps one of a representative's core values, constituents are unlikely to have any real influence over the representative's actions. She may do what they want, but only because of a coincidence between their demands and her policy goals. Conversely, trust does not guarantee trusteeship—it does not ensure that a representative will vote on the basis of private information. Constituents can only offer the opportunity; representatives decide whether to take advantage of it.

Finally, the analysis shows how constituents can learn from their representative even when they ignore—or never hear—any of her statements about the policy process. In situations in which a representative expects trust and ignores reputational concerns and the political consequences of her actions, a representative's vote can reveal some of her private information. No information is revealed, however, if a representative complies with constituent demands, either to gain favorable evaluations or to avoid reputational damage. Thus, a representative can educate constituents, but only by ignoring the political and reputational consequences of her actions. And constituents can induce—but not guarantee—education only by deciding in favor of trust.

How Citizens Assess Common Interest

The previous section argued that constituents' trust decisions hinge on two appraisals, one dealing with the consequences of actions (that is, policy outcomes), the other with the agent's preferences concerning these outcomes. In this section, I consider how constituents form beliefs about their agent's policy preferences as a prelude to their decisions. Since these beliefs play a critical role in trust decisions, any answer to the question, Where does trust come from?, must consider how constituents develop their beliefs.

A Game-Theoretic Picture of Impression Formation

In the context of trust decisions, belief formation is best understood as a front-end or preliminary interaction to the Evaluation Game discussed earlier.[8] Player R holds private information about her policy preferences or type; player C forms beliefs about R's type (policy preferences) as a prelude to his trust decision. In addition to the goals discussed earlier, C wants to form as accurate an appraisal as possible; R wants to have C form whatever beliefs facilitate trust.

Given the nature of the situation, C's assessment can be made up of two kinds of information. First, there is information that C can glean from R's actions, either past actions or actions taken proximate to the trust decision. Such actions can take the form of a direct statement by R or an action that reveals information indirectly. Thus, by giving appropriate signals (taking different actions), R can influence C's beliefs and thereby influence his trust decision. Of course, R may have an incentive to reveal false information or to avoid revealing any information at all. C must therefore take these possibilities into account when deciding how to respond to ostensibly informative signals. The second type of information that C can use to assess R's type consists of information that C brings to the interaction—information available to him prior to viewing any signals by R. Formally, such information is contained in C's prior beliefs about R's type—beliefs that C holds at the beginning of the game.

A more concrete and useful example of a signaling game involving impression formation is David Kreps's (1983, 4) game of beer and quiche.

Party A is one of two types; either he is a wimp, or he is surly. A knows which type he is; at the outset, B assesses the probability that A is surly as .9. Eventually, B must decide whether to challenge A to a duel. If A is indeed a wimp, then B will profit by challenging A, but if A is surly, B will lose by issuing the challenge. Regardless of whether A is a wimp or is surly, A prefers not to duel. Before B must decide whether to duel, B first gets to see a signal that may be informative about A's type. To wit, B observes what A has for breakfast. There are two possible breakfasts, beer and quiche. If A is surly, then A prefers the beer. If A is a wimp, A prefers quiche. But in both cases, the cost to A of having the less-preferred breakfast is less than the cost of having to engage in the duel.

Given this description, the beer-quiche game has player B making a judgment about an unobserved characteristic, player A's type (wimp or surly), on the basis of an observable action (player A's breakfast). It is as though player B operates with two effect-cause links in mind, one saying that wimps prefer quiche, the other saying that surly individuals drink beer. These beliefs enter the description implicitly— player B enters the game with some information about his opponent, that she is surly with probability .9.

Analysis of this sort of signaling game highlights the strategic opportunities for signaling by the sending player (player R, or player A), and the need for the receiving player (Player C, or player B) to adjust his appraisals accordingly.[9] In general, the receiving player is expected to ignore signals that are associated with inferences advantageous to the sending player and that can be taken at low or zero cost. Consider the beer-quiche game. Player A would rather avoid a duel than eat her preferred breakfast—that is, her signal (beer or quiche) can be manipulated at low cost relative to the benefit of not dueling. Her choice should be ignored by player B. Analysis of the game predicts that player A, wanting to avoid a duel, would drink beer regardless of her true preference. Expecting this behavior, player B would ignore the choice. From player B's perspective, player A may be surly and enjoying her beer or be a wimp and drinking beer only to avoid a duel. The choice tells him nothing. As a result, player B is reduced to making his decision on the basis of his prior belief, which is that player A is surly with probability .9. Based on that information, player B's best choice is to avoid a challenge.

Of course, some signals are not cheap talk. For one thing a player's actions can be taken seriously when they are not matters of choice— that is, when information about type is revealed involuntarily. Suppose, for example, that type was related to some immutable aspect of a player's appearance. In this case, appearance would provide reliable (though perhaps not very precise) information about type. Voluntary signals become credible when the cost of misrepresenting one's type is large—large enough that they outweigh the benefit generated by misinforming the receiving player.[10]

Belief Formation and Trust

This discussion of belief formation confirms what students of politics have believed all along, that an elected official's actions and personal attributes are imbued with political significance. But this regularity does not arise because citizens deviate from rational calculation. Rather, these methods of appraisal are sensible, rational, predictable responses to the problem of assessing type. With regard to trust, these findings imply that certain actions or characteristics will separate elected officials who are trusted to resolve some policy question from those who are not. The set of relevant actions and characteristics will be the ones that constituents take to be signals of common interest (or a lack thereof) in light of what they know about their representative, their beliefs about the goals signaled by characteristics and actions, and their beliefs about the proposal.

In the abstract, it is difficult to identify the specific actions and attributes that constituents will use to assess type. Analysis of the Evaluation Game suggests that citizens faced with a trust decision involving a specific proposal will focus their attention on a narrow set of actions and characteristics—those that signal goals that would motivate a legislator to support or oppose the proposal at hand. It is possible that the same actions or characteristics will provide sharp, clear inferences across a range of proposals. Insofar as proposals address different policy questions, it would be no surprise to find that factors that help constituents to assess one set of policy goals are no help on the next.[11]

The set of politically relevant factors is likely to vary over time as voters learn new stereotypes or attributions and discard old ones. A generation ago, divorce or past use of illegal drugs equaled political death for a would-be candidate. Nowadays, absent unusual circumstances, such revelations are no longer politically relevant—or no longer provide sharp inferences about an individual's character. Similarly, the increased activity of evangelical groups in politics may have provided voters with new actions, such as a candidate's membership in the Moral Majority, that can be used for inference.

Moving to specifics, the discussion here highlights the utility of certain kinds of signals, those that are not matters of choice. Precisely because candidates cannot misrepresent their race, or gender, or ethnicity, the strategic considerations noted for the players' choice of breakfast in the beer-quiche game do not apply. For example, Samuel

Popkin (1991) has found that during presidential campaigns, voters focus on a candidate's personal characteristics to the exclusion of the candidate's record in political life. It may be that information about characteristics is less costly to acquire and process, as Popkin argues. But voters may also focus on characteristics because they cannot be the product of calculation and therefore provide a clearer signal of a candidate's policy concerns.

The question of which factors to use to assess type should also depend on the quality of inferences that these generalizations supply. All else equal, voters should favor signals that supply sharp (low-variance) judgments about an elected official's type. Reducing variance is critical, allowing constituents to make better decisions about trust and thus to defer only when a common interest in fact exists. Candidates have a somewhat different preference ordering. Obviously, candidates will try to draw voters' attention to signals that promote favorable (rather than accurate) inferences about their type and damaging inferences about their opponents' types. Within the set stereotypes that yield these types of inferences, candidates will also favor those that generate low-variance inferences, as this condition increases the impact of the resulting inference.

The importance of variance in impression formation also supplies a prediction about nationalistic appeals—situations in which a politician builds support by emphasizing an ethnic or religious characteristic that he shares with his constituents. Presumably such appeals will be made only when a high percentage of constituents hold the characteristic. But the success of these appeals also hinges on the quality of inferences that voters will draw from the characteristic. Suppose, for example, that a high percentage of constituents hold some characteristic (for example, a common ethnic origin). Assume further that constituents believe that individuals holding a particular characteristic all have roughly the same policy preferences—in formal terms, their ideal points in some policy space are clustered about some point. A candidate holding this characteristic would be expected to emphasize his commonality with constituents; insofar as voters use the characteristic to assess type, they will conclude that the candidate can be trusted on all issues large and small. Now suppose a different situation, in which constituents believe that individuals holding the characteristic have a wide range of ideal points. Here the candidate would not be expected to emphasize the characteristic, as it would not signal beneficial, trust-inducing inferences about his type.

With regard to signals that involve matters of choice, the analysis suggests that the inference process will focus on negative aspects of a candidate's record—on politically harmful rather than politically beneficial actions. Beneficial actions are overlooked because voters cannot discern whether these actions were taken for substantive reasons or for their reputational impact. For example, suppose a legislator voted for a proposal, believing that his constituents would be angered by a nay vote, or because he wished to demonstrate that he agreed with his constituents' concerns. Either way, policy goals played no role in the legislator's decision. While the vote may have had policy consequences, it cannot be used to assess the member's policy goals. The only conclusion constituents can draw is that their representative was willing to sacrifice his policy concerns for political ends—the pursuit of reelection or reputation building.

In contrast, actions that are politically damaging, such as actions that are contrary to constituent demands or beliefs, provide a basis for impression formation. To continue the example raised above, suppose the representative voted nay over his constituents' objections. This action suggests that he holds certain policy interests and holds them intensely enough that he will accept costs—negative evaluations and a damaged reputation—in order to achieve them. Constituents could draw similar inferences from actions that, while politically popular, force a representative to incur personal or policy costs that outweigh whatever political benefits the action may generate.

This argument suggests that in political systems such as contemporary American politics, where the reelection goal is ubiquitous, many of a representative's actions are useless for estimating her type. Of course, many of a representative's actions in office will go unnoticed by her constituents. The problem goes deeper than that, however. Consider vote decisions. In general, an interest in reelection will lead a representative to cast votes that are received favorably back home—votes that are the product of political factors, not policy concerns. If so, a representative's voting record, or any transformation of these votes, may not contain any information about her policy goals. This suggestion is consistent with the work of Fenno (1978), who found that when legislators interact with constituents, they spend a great deal of time describing their personal characteristics and their efforts as policy entrepreneurs but give short shrift to their voting record.

Summary

Democratic theory posits that legislators will act in accordance with constituent interests. Yet even a cursory glance through the scholarly literature or the op-ed pages suggests that real-world politics does not match our expectations. Many of these arguments center on the claim that constituents are unable to make good decisions about trust; either they trust too little, or they trust too much. These charges are troubling. Much of our faith in democratic institutions rests on the assumption that democratic theory is a descriptive as well as a normative theory. Continued faith in representative government requires, at a minimum, a response to the charge that constituents cannot take the actions needed to give elected officials the right incentives—the incentives needed to produce fiduciary behavior.

Are these charges true? While the research described here cannot say they are completely false, it shows they are clearly overdrawn. Much of the behavior cited as evidence against democratic theory admits to a different explanation. Even if constituents know very little about policy options, they may do better—better in terms of policy outcomes—by deciding against trust. Similarly, trust may be the preferred option for policy-minded constituents who are well-informed about the policy process. Moreover, trust can be preferable even if constituents are unsure about their representative's policy goals— even if they know that his goals differ from their own. Of course, the ability to identify these alternative explanations does not mean that the critics are wrong. It suggests, however, that the real world is more complex than they appreciate.

Notes

1. For an extensive discussion of the structure of the Evaluation Game, see Bianco 1994.

2. Two auxiliary assumptions are made in this analysis. The first is the *private information* condition. Intuitively, constituents will never trust their representative unless there is some chance that she knows something about the proposal that they do not. In the Evaluation Game, C is sure that R has private information about β. The second assumption is the *lottery condition*. This condition reflects the intuition that C will consider trust only if he is unsure whether enacting β is consistent with his interests. If, despite his uncertainties, C is sure that β will improve on the status quo (produce a policy outcome that is ranked higher in his ordering than the status quo), he will have no incentive to allow R any discretion. The same will be true if C is sure that the status quo is preferable to any outcome that β might produce.

3. These suspicions are confirmed by empirical analysis in Bianco 1994, chs. 5–6).

4. For example, constituents might believe that there is an 75 percent chance of realizing one outcome and a 25 percent chance of realizing the other. At the extreme, where constituents think that one outcome is the near-certain product of enacting the proposal, their uncertainty is low; they are confident that they know what will happen if the proposal is enacted. This characterization would be true if, for example, constituents

believed that one outcome was 99 percent likely, while the chances of seeing the other outcome were only 1 percent.

5. There is one qualification: Votes may function as signals of a representative's policy concerns. A career-minded representative will take these reputational considerations into account when deciding how to vote, given trust. For a discussion, see Bianco 1994.

6. These votes may coincidentally serve the representative's policy goals.

7. If the representative's goals are reversed, she will behave as a trustee under these conditions. Her vote will then signal private information, just as in the top region. Even with this information, however, constituents will punish deviations from their demands.

8. This analysis is cast in terms of game theory. In Bianco, forthcoming, however, I showed that if the analysis of impression formation begins with the same assumptions about motivations and search costs, models drawn from rational-choice theory and from psychology generate the same predictions about the content of voters' impressions of a candidate and their willingness to search for new information. The analysis also identifies several underlying similarities between the two models. Rational actors and motivated tacticians have the same techniques for taking stock of others, one based on nonstrategic processes (that is, prior beliefs or initial categorization), the other on strategic behavior by their target. And while rational-choice and psychology-based analyses typically begin with different characterizations of motives, such differences specify an empirical question, one whose resolution would improve the fidelity of both approaches.

9. For a discussion of these issues, see Banks 1991.

10. For example, suppose player A's penalty from choosing an inferior breakfast exceeded the reduction in payoff caused by dueling. Here player A's breakfast would be a valid indicator of type; a surly player A would drink beer, a wimp player A would eat quiche, and player B would form inferences about player A based on her breakfast choice, dueling with a quiche eater and refusing to duel a drinker of beer.

11. This expectation is confirmed by empirical work in Bianco 1994, especially chapters 4 and 5.

References

Austen-Smith, David. 1992. "Explaining the Vote: Constituency Constraints on Legislative Strategy." *American Journal of Political Science* 36: 68–95.

Banks, Jeffrey. 1991 *Signaling Games In Political Science*. London: Harwood Academic Publishers.

Bernstein, Robert A. 1989. *Elections, Representation, and Congressional Voting Behavior: The Myth of Constituency Control*. Englewood Cliffs, N.J.: Prentice-Hall.

Bianco, William T. 1994. *Trust: Representatives and Constituents.* Ann Arbor: University of Michigan Press.

———. Forthcoming. "Different Paths to the Same Result: Rational Choice, Political Psychology, and Impression Formation in Campaigns." *American Journal of Political Science.*

Blondel, Jean. 1973. *Comparative Legislatures.* New York: Prentice Hall.

Converse, Phillip E., and Roy Pierce. 1986. *Political Representation in France.* Cambridge: Harvard University Press.

Fenno, Richard F. 1978. *Home Style.* Boston: Little, Brown.

Jewell, Malcolm E. 1982. *Representation in State Legislatures.* Lexington: University of Kentucky Press.

Kalt, Joseph P., and Mark A. Zupan. 1990. "The Apparent Ideological Behavior of Legislators: Testing the Principal-Agent Slack in Political Institutions." *Journal of Political Economy* 33: 103–31

Krehbiel, Keith. 1991. *Information and Legislative Organization.* Ann Arbor: University of Michigan Press.

Kreps, David. 1983. "Signaling Games and Stable Equilibria." Stanford University, unpublished paper.

Mayhew, David R. 1974. *Congress: The Electoral Connection.* New Haven: Yale University Press.

Page, Benjamin I., and Robert Y. Shapiro. 1992. *The Rational Public.* Chicago: University of Chicago Press.

Parker, Glenn. 1989. *Characteristics of Congress: Patterns in Congressional Behavior.* Englewood Cliffs, N. J.: Prentice-Hall.

Parker, Suzanne L., and Glenn R. Parker. 1993. "Why Do We Trust Our Congressman, and Why Does It Matter?" *Journal of Politics* 55: 442–53.

Poole, Keith T., and Howard Rosenthal. 1991. "Patterns of Congressional Voting." *American Journal of Political Science* 35: 228–78.

Popkin, Samuel L. 1991. *The Reasoning Voter.* Chicago: University of Chicago Press.

Stroh, Patrick. 1995. "Voters as Pragmatic Cognitive Misers: The Accuracy-Effort Trade-off in the Candidate-Evaluation Process." In *Political Judgment,* edited by Milton Lodge and Kathleen M. McGraw. Ann Arbor: University of Michigan Press.

Zarate, Mark A., and Eliot R. Smith. 1990. "Person Categorizing and Stereotyping." *Social Cognition.* 81: 61–85.

PART IV

TRUST RESPONSIVENESS

Chapter 11

Trust and Democratic Governance

TOM R. TYLER

THIS CHAPTER addresses three issues. The first is the importance of trust. My argument is that trust is an important facilitator of democratic governance. I also suggest that there is a need to distinguish between the influence of trust on deference to authority and the influence of trust on the development of consensus. The second issue is the psychology of trust—that is, the underlying reason that people defer to authorities. I argue that there are two types of trust: trust that is linked to judgments of risk (instrumental trust) and trust that is based upon social bonds and shared identities (social trust). I argue that both forms of trust exist, and that each is important. Finally, I explore the implications of each form of trust for democratic governance.

In addressing each of these issues I will build upon a body of data that I have collected in a variety of studies, all involving interviews with people within organized groups. These studies have in common the exploration of authority as it is experienced by those subject to it—citizens dealing with legal or political authorities, workers dealing with their supervisors, children dealing with their parents, and so on. My approach has been inductive. The interviews with those who have dealt with authorities have been used to identify the factors that actually influenced their reactions to their experiences with group authorities.

Because my work is empirical, I operationalize trust by asking people specific questions about trust. My focus is on their inferences concerning the trustworthiness of authorities. Such trustworthiness is established by asking whether the authority "was genuinely concerned about your needs," "considered your arguments," "tried to take account of your needs," "tried to do what was right for you," and/or "tried to be fair to you." As these questions make clear, trustworthiness is conceptualized in terms of the benevolence of the motives of the authority.

Although my own work on trust is empirical and inductive, it is interesting to see the convergence of that work and the theoretical work of Philip Pettit and Geoffrey Brennan (Brennan and Pettit 1993; Pettit 1995). Their conceptual analysis leads to many of the same conclusions that emerge from my interviews. As a consequence, this interdisciplinary volume illustrates the important degree to which theoretical and empirical work converge on central insights about the meaning of trust.

The Importance of Trust to Democratic Governance

I begin by examining the relationship between trust in authorities and the voluntary compliance with their directives. I will argue that trust is a key component of the willingness to defer to authorities. Such willingness to defer is the central concern in past discussions of the effectiveness of democratic authorities.

I will also argue that trust-based deference should be distinguished from the issue of developing consensus. Governance based upon consensus provides an alternative approach to the traditional concern with deference. The dynamics of governance of this latter type have not been explored; in particular, the role of trust has not been examined.

Behavioral Compliance with the Law

Past discussions of the effective exercise of legal and political authority have focused on the ability of leaders to shape the behavior of citizens. In particular, the ability to secure compliance with decisions and rules, more broadly labeled the ability to be authoritative (Tyler 1990; Tyler and Lind 1992), is widely recognized to be a central characteristic of effectiveness in organizational authorities.

To be effective, legal rules and decisions must be obeyed. They must influence the actions of those toward whom they are directed. As I argued in *Why People Obey the Law*, "A judge's ruling means little if the parties to the dispute feel they can ignore it. Similarly, passing a law prohibiting some behavior is not useful if it does not affect how often the behavior occurs" (Tyler 1990, 19). Hence, "the lawgiver must be able to anticipate that the citizenry as a whole will . . . generally observe the body of rules he has promulgated" (Fuller 1971, 201).

Beyond being able to secure compliance, authorities need to be able to gain *voluntary* acceptance for most of their decisions. Legal, political, and organizational theorists have long recognized that voluntary acceptance of the decisions and rules of organizational authorities is important to the ability of those authorities to function effectively. Within organizational studies, two organizational theorists have made this point. Chester Barnard (1958) argued that maintaining an arena within which subordinates will accept orders voluntarily because of the organizational role of the authority is central to organizational effectiveness, since "an essential element of organizations is the willingness of persons to contribute their individual efforts to the cooperative system" (139). Herbert Simon (1947) similarly proposed that decisions to accept the decisions made by authorities must occur through deference to the organizational role of those authorities and must be made "independently of judgments of the correctness or acceptability of the premise [of their decisions]" (125).

The importance of voluntary compliance is also emphasized by Margaret Levi (1988), who has argued for the need to supplement coercion with "quasi-voluntary compliance" in dealings between citizens and the state. Such compliance cannot be understood as "purely self-interested behavior" (52) and cannot be accounted for solely through an understanding of coercion or positive incentives. In fact, in many cases citizens are "choosing not to free-ride in situations where they are fairly certain of escaping detection" (54). As in my analysis, Levi emphasizes that such quasi-voluntary compliance has a normative base.

Voluntary acceptance is important because, while we often think of legal authorities—such as judges and police officers—and political authorities—such as legislators and members of the executive—as having the power to compel the obedience of citizens, in reality the power of leaders is generally quite limited. When authorities try to shape citizen behavior through the manipulation of rewards and threats of punishment, they typically have at best limited success.

In cases of widespread disobedience with court orders, as has recently occurred in the United States with child support payment orders, the courts have had difficulty securing compliance with threats or punishments. Similarly, in the cases handled in small-claims courts—cases involving landlord-tenant disputes, conflicts among neighbors, nonpayment of bills to businesses for products or services, consumer dissatisfaction with products or services, and other minor disputes—noncompliance is widespread (McEwen and Maiman 1981; Singer 1994).

Threats of punishment have little effect on law enforcement. In a recent review of deterrence research on drug use, for example, psychologist Robert MacCoun (1993) suggested that at best 5 percent of the variance in law-related behavior can be explained by variations in the perceived certainty and severity of punishment, a suggestion consistent with the findings of recent panel studies on law-related behaviors showing that deterrence considerations have, at best, a minor influence on behavior (see Paternoster et al. 1984; Tyler 1990). Despite increasing the size of police forces, enhancing the penalties for drug use, and filling American prisons with drug offenders, the United States has been generally unable to solve its problems of drug use. In the parallel case of drunk driving, sociologist H. Laurence Ross (1982) points out that the level of police enforcement needed to bring the probability of punishment to the level required to deter offenders is prohibitively high.

Because of the limits of coercive power, authorities must depend on voluntary deference to their decisions by most of the population, most of the time. Authorities need to have people take the obligation to obey the law onto themselves and act voluntarily on that perceived obligation. Of course, even when authorities possess the power to reward or punish, they nonetheless benefit from the willingness of people to accept their decisions. Such voluntary acceptance minimizes the need of authorities to explain and justify each decision, as well as to monitor its implementation and to utilize collective resources to facilitate compliance. Hence, efforts to understand the effective exercise of legal authority inevitably lead to a concern with the attitudes toward authorities that exist in the general population, rather than to an exploration of the coercive resources available to legal authorities.

The Role of Trust in Voluntary Compliance

As the previous section has made clear, the legal system is heavily dependent on voluntary compliance. Although the law always involves elements of coercion, the legal system has, at best, a limited ability to compel people to obey the law. Hence, legal and political authorities must be interested in what people are willing to do.

Trust and Legitimacy   Because voluntary acceptance is crucial, the deference model underlying legitimacy theory focuses on people's feeling of obligation to obey the decisions of third-party legal authorities. Irrespective of their judgments about a decision, people obey it if they regard the authority who made the decision as entitled to be obeyed. In particular, judgments about the legitimacy of the judge, mediator, or other legal authorities are an important attitude. Legitimacy is the judgment that legal authorities are competent and honest (*support* or *personal legitimacy*) and that their professional role entitles them to make decisions which ought to be deferred to and obeyed (*institutional legitimacy*). Research suggests that if people believe in either personal or institutional legitimacy they are more likely to obey authorities (Tyler 1990).

Hence, our first concern in considering the role of trust in voluntary compliance should be with whether trust shapes perceived legitimacy. I have explored this issue indirectly by showing that trust shapes procedural justice, which is a key antecedent to legitimacy (see Tyler and Lind 1992). In both managerial and legal settings, trustworthiness is the most important issue people consider when evaluating the fairness of the decision-making procedures used by legal authorities.

I have also addressed the role of trust in an analysis involving six studies of varying types of authority, including parents, professors, work supervisors, local political leaders, and national legal authorities (Tyler 1997). The analysis examined the impact of trust in authorities on evaluations of those authorities, willingness to accept their decisions, and willingness to obey rules. The results of these studies indicated that trust is the most important judgment shaping these reactions to authorities. Trust in the motives of authorities mattered more than did the favorability of one's outcome or one's ability to control those outcomes.

Trust and Deference: The Voluntary Acceptance of Decisions   In part, the importance of the previously outlined influence of trust on procedural justice and legitimacy comes from the influence of procedural justice and legitimacy on behaviors. It has been established that people who regard authorities as legitimate, a judgment that is based strongly upon views about the procedural justice of their actions, are more likely to accept the decisions of authorities and obey the rules they promulgate (Tyler and Lind 1992). This question can also be addressed directly by examining whether trust influences the voluntary acceptance of decisions.

I will consider three studies that examine this question in the context of conflicts involving authorities. These conflicts occurred in managerial, political, and family settings. Study 1, the management study, examined a random sample of workers in Chicago about their recent experiences with their supervisors. In study 2, the political study, citizens of San Francisco were interviewed over the telephone about their views about a local regulatory authority—the Public Utilities Commission—that was charged with enacting water conservation policies during the 1991 California water shortage, the period during which this study was conducted. Study 3, the family study,

Table 11.1   Antecedents of Willingness to Accept the Decisions of
Authorities

	Management	Politics	Family
Instrumental judgments			
Outcome favorability	.37***	.10*	.29***
Control	.07	.07	−.04
Relational judgments			
Trustworthiness	.30***	.47***	.33***
Neutrality	.21**	−.13	.15**
Status recognition	−.12	.01	.11
R^2	45%***	23%***	53%***

Notes: Entries are beta weights and adjusted R-squares.
*$p<.05$ **$p<.01$ ***$p<.001$

asked undergraduate students at the University of California at
Berkeley how recent conflicts with their parents had been resolved. In
each study, the dependent variable was the willingness of respondents to accept the decisions made by the authority in question. (The
details of these three studies are further outlined in Tyler and Degoey
1996.)

Two classes of independent variable were included in the regression analyses: (1) calculative/instrumental judgments, and (2) relational judgments about the behavior of group authorities. The calculative variables included respondents' assessments that the outcome
of the authorities decisions were favorable to them and that they
had some degree of control over the decision-making process (and,
through it, could provide themselves with desired outcomes). Relational judgments included assessments of (1) the trustworthiness of
authorities, (2) their willingness to be unbiased in the decision-making process ("neutrality"), and (3) the degree to which the authorities
treated respondents with dignity and respect ("status recognition"). I
defined trust in terms of feelings that an authority made a good faith
effort, trying to treat the parties involved in the conflict fairly (that is,
with benevolence).

The findings of the three studies are outlined in table 11.1. They
indicate that attributions about trustworthiness were central to the
willingness to accept decisions within all three arenas. In the management setting, trustworthiness and outcome favorability were the most
important factors shaping voluntary decision acceptance (beta = .30
and .37, $p < .001$, respectively), as they were in the family setting
(beta = .33 and .29, $p < .001$, respectively). In the political setting,

Table 11.2   Antecedents of Feelings of Obligation to Obey the Law

	Police	Congress	Supreme Court
Instrumental judgments			
Outcome favorability	.22**	−.04	.14*
Control	.02	−.09	.07
Relational judgments			
Trustworthiness	.28**	.20***	.18*
Neutrality	−.09	.23***	.06
Status recognition	.13	.08	−.07
R^2	6%**	15%***	10%***

Notes: Entries are beta weights and adjusted R-squares.
*$p<.05$ **$p<.01$ ***$p<.001$

trustworthiness was the major factor shaping willingness to accept decisions (beta = .47, $p < .001$).

Trust and Feelings of Obligation to Obey Laws   Three studies examined the question of the influence of trust on people's feelings of obligation to obey rules. All these studies considered the legal/political arena. Study 4 explored the antecedents of the willingness to obey the law among a sample of citizens in Chicago, who were interviewed about their personal experiences with police officers and judges. Study 5 examined feelings of obligation to obey federal laws among citizens of San Francisco who were interviewed about their views on the United States Congress. Study 6 explored feelings of obligation to obey federal laws among citizens of San Francisco interviewed about their views on the United States Supreme Court. (The details of each study were also included in Tyler and Degoey 1996.)

The results of regression analyses on these datasets are shown in table 11.2. They indicate that trust consistently influenced feelings of obligation to obey organizational rules and laws. In the Chicago study, trust significantly shaped feelings of obligation to the police and the courts (beta = .28, $p < .01$), as did outcome favorability (beta = .22, $p < .01$). Trust also shaped feelings of obligation to obey the laws enacted by the United States Congress (beta = .20, $p < .001$). In this case, judgments about the neutrality of Congress also had an influence (beta = .23, $p < .001$). In terms of the United States Supreme Court, trustworthiness and outcome favorability both influenced feelings of obligation (beta = .18 and .14, $p < .05$).

276 Trust and Governance

Trust and Deference to Authority An additional concern in democratic governance is deference to the right of leaders to make authoritative decisions. The importance of trust in generating deference to the right of authorities to make controversial decisions is illustrated by the findings of an analysis of the data included here as study six (Tyler and Mitchell 1984). This study explored the antecedents of legitimacy, willingness to defer, and perceived obligation to obey rules. The results demonstrate that trust was especially important in the case of the willingness to defer to a legal authority—in this case the United States Supreme Court. Trust had more influence on willingness to defer to Court decisions than did judgments about one's influence over Court decisions or about the Court's neutrality.

Trust and Consensus-Based Models of Governance

The findings discussed in the previous section point to a strong, widespread influence of trustworthiness attributions on people's reactions to authorities. This influence is robust across a variety of contexts and groups. In all the settings studied, inferences about the trustworthiness of the motives of authorities had a powerful effect on whether people voluntarily deferred to third-party decisions and to group rules. Hence, a variety of types of evidence suggest that if citizens trust government authorities they are more likely to comply voluntarily with their directives.

Deference Versus Attitude Change The discussion so far has concerned circumstances under which people will allow authorities to dictate their behavior—that is, when citizens follow the directives of authorities because they feel that authorities "ought to be obeyed." This model is the *deference model* of authority. It examines the circumstances under which people are willing to defer to authorities.

Such deference to legitimate authorities should be distinguished from personal attitude change. By deferring to authorities, people are not necessarily indicating that the authorities have convinced them that the course of action taken is right and proper. In Stanley Milgram's famous studies on obedience to authority (1965), for example, those told to shock another person did so, but they did so reluctantly and manifested many signs of stress and emotional anguish. Still, "the experiment required that they continue," and they did so.

So far in this chapter I have not focused on issues of people's attitudes or moral evaluations—that is, on what people want to do or think they should do—hence, I have not considered the ability of authorities to change what people think is right or wrong. This latter type of influence has been referred to as the educative function of the law, the ability of authorities to shape privately held views about what is right and what is wrong. It can also be described as the development of consensus. When people discuss issues and determine a commonly accepted course of action, some, at least, have changed their views about what ought to be done.

The potential limits of the deference model are hinted at in my book on obeying the law, Tyler 1990. That book notes the important role of legitimacy in gaining deference to authorities. It also, however, recognizes the importance of a second, distinct factor in shaping deference—views about the morality of law. In the case of everyday obedience to the law, these two forces overlap. People feel both that lawbreaking is morally wrong and that legitimate authorities ought to be obeyed. We must recognize, however, that these two forces are not necessarily always going to be in harmony.

The distinction between deference to authority and attitude change was examined in a recent study of American's views about abortion (Tyler and Mitchell 1994). That study explained the willingness of citizens who were morally opposed to abortion to defer to the decisions of the United States Supreme Court. It found that citizens regarded the Court as legitimate if it followed fair decision-making procedures. If they regarded the Court as legitimate, they deferred to its decisions, but they did not change their views about the morality of abortion. In other words, the Court did not persuade these citizens that its position was morally correct. There was no consensus reached. Instead, people deferred to the right of the court to make the decision.

The key to understanding the findings of Tyler and Mitchell 1994 has been provided by an analysis of the psychology of authority by Herbert Kelman and V. Lee Hamilton (1989). Kelman and Hamilton explored the circumstances under which subordinates engage in actions they regard as immoral. One psychological force in such circumstances is authorization. In hierarchies, the orders of superiors override standard moral considerations, if the authorities are legitimate and hence "ought" to be obeyed. People focus on obeying orders and do not consider their personal attitudes or moral values. It is not that they change their views but that they no longer consider them relevant. In the situation considered by Kelman and Hamilton, the massacre of women and children by U.S. soldiers during the Vietnam War, the soldiers were not persuaded that their actions were morally right. Rather, they focused on their perceived obligation to their superior officers and "just followed orders."

The Consensus Model   We have documented the importance of trust in the context of deference to authority. The studies outlined suggest that trust is central to the willingness of people to follow the dictates of authorities. If people trust the motives of authorities, they are more likely to view those authorities as acting fairly, to consider them legitimate, and to defer to their decisions voluntarily.

Interestingly, there has been less attention to issues of attitude change, which I will refer to as building consensus through changing what people think is right. The *consensus model* provides an alternative to deference, since achieving consensus leads to a solution that people want to accept, irrespective of the dictates of established authorities. For example, in bilateral bargaining, people freely engage in a search for an agreement that meets both parties' interests. If such an agreement is reached, people freely choose to follow it. They do so because they have made a decision that flows from their own views about what is desirable or right.

A consensus about the appropriate resolution for a dispute may emerge from the discussions and presentations of views that occur during the processes of dispute resolution. This recognition is consistent with the discourse theory proposed by German philosopher Jürgen Habermas (1979, 1987), which seeks to identify the conditions under which discussions among the parties to a political or legal conflict can lead to a true consensus about the appropriate norms to use in resolving the conflict. These conditions include allowing open communication and giving the parties involved opportunities to express their views. Interestingly, this solution focuses upon procedural issues, as does my deference-based work (Tyler 1990).

This consensus perspective emphasizes the convergence of the attitudes of the parties toward a common feeling that a particular solution to a conflict is fair, which is accomplished through discussion and consideration of the views and needs of others. Having reached an agreement, people willingly embrace the decision and voluntarily obey it, because it reflects their own views about what is right and what is wrong. My study (Tyler 1990) found that personal moral views about right and wrong were a stronger influence on law-related behavior than legitimacy, suggesting that a consensus-based society should have especially high levels of compliance with rules.

The Role of Trust   For the purposes of this volume the key question is how a focus on consensus would change the role of trust in democratic governance. I speculate that it would increase the importance of trust. Why? If we consider the literature on persuasion—that is, changing people's attitudes—one key communicator characteristic is trustworthiness. The credibility of a communicator or communication is strongly affected by the degree to which those experiencing the communication trust the motives of the communicator. If recipients feel that the communicator has benevolent intentions, they are much more open to considering his arguments. Conversely, if people distrust the motives of the communicator, they are resistent to considering his arguments (Eagly and Chaiken 1993). Similarly, attributions of intention are central to the ability of parties to reach consensus about how to resolve disputes. If people regard their opponent as untrustworthy, they are less willing to discuss issues openly and to make the types of concessions that lead to settlement. Hence, bargaining is hampered by a lack of trust in others (Pruitt and Carnevale 1993).

It may also be the case that attributions about the trustworthiness of others influence the form of governance that people seek. In other words, the degree to which people want deference-based versus consensus-based governance may depend upon their feelings about the other people with whom they are dealing. People may be more willing to seek consensus if they trust the others with whom they are dealing.

It is possible to draw upon the work of law professors Ian Ayres and John Braithwaite (1992) to argue for a sequential approach to issues of governance. They have suggested that dialogue and persuasion are a first strategy in regulatory situations. When dialogue fails, they advocate moving to a strategy of deterrence. It might be similarly argued that consensus building is a first strategy that might be followed by appeals to deference and obligation. Hence, we can imagine a sequential model of authority, with consensus-based appeals followed by deference-based appeals.

Of course, I do not want to suggest that deference-based and consensus-based trust are in some way mutually exclusive. In fact, they can work together. For example, in a given situation those most likely to support the government are those who *both* think the government is legitimate and think the policy is right. Tyler 1990 found such a situation with everyday obedience to the law. People think they should obey legitimate authorities. They also think that following rules is the morally right thing to do. Hence, compliance is both based on deference and a consensus about what is right.

Finally, the recognition of the distinction between deference and consensus-building raises the broader question of whether consensus-based rules are deferred to for procedural reasons. A key finding of the deference literature, as has been outlined, is that the legitimacy that leads to deference flows from judgments of procedural fairness. People defer to authorities because they think they ought to obey properly made decisions, not because they agree or disagree with those decisions. If people have worked to achieve consensus about the issues involved, however, then substantive consensus may play a larger role in the willingness to accept decisions. People may be more concerned about whether or not a policy is the right one if they have been involved in efforts to resolve a moral or policy dilemma. On the other hand, it is interesting that in the work of Habermas the possibility is also raised that people may assess the value of a consensus by considering the quality of the procedures by which it was reached. If this is true, then procedural evaluations would dominate judgments about both deference and consensus-based trust.

Psychological Models of Trustworthiness

The findings reported in the previous section point to the importance of two types of trust in authorities. But which psychological models explain this importance? The traditional model of the psychology of trustworthiness is instrumental; it suggests that trustworthiness should be linked to individual beliefs about the likelihood of receiving positive outcomes from interactions with authorities. It is thus linked to our judgments about the probable consequences of trusting others—that is, the likelihood that others will behave as they have promised. The other model is relational; it suggests that trust is related to the nature of the social connection to authorities; that is trust is a social commodity and is linked to our social connections with others. My concern in this discussion is with what can be gained by adding the concept of social trust to a framework that already includes the idea of instrumental trust, creating two potentially important forms of trust.

Self-interest and Instrumental Trust

The economic perspective, which has dominated sociology, law, political science, and management, places primary emphasis on individual's calculations of the degree to which their interests are served by the decisions of authorities (Bradach and Eccles 1989; Dasgupta 1988). In the context of cooperative behavior this self-interest model is linked to expectations of reciprocity. For example, whether people will defer their consumption of community resources in a scarcity situation depends upon their judgments about whether others will do so as well.

This argument has also recently been made by economist Oliver Williamson (1993), who suggested that trust may "have the appearance of being noncalculative" (486) but is in fact a response to environmental contingencies. His analysis considers trust as one aspect of rational "risk analysis"—that is, estimations of the likelihood that others will perform a particular action. "When we say we trust someone or that someone is trustworthy, we implicitly mean that the probability that he will perform an action that is beneficial or at least not detrimental to us is high enough for us to consider engaging in some form of cooperation with him" (463). Similarly, Bradach and Eccles (1989) have argued that trust is the expectation that an economic exchange partner will not act opportunistically (see also Dasgupta 1988).

Within social psychology the idea of self-interest underlies social exchange theory (Thibaut and Kelley 1959). One example of this model has been provided in the area of social conflict by the general control model of psychologist John Thibaut and law professor Laurens Walker (1975), which suggests that people trust authorities who are judged to be motivated to share control. In other words, trustworthiness can be viewed from an instrumental perspective as the belief that one will have a reasonable degree of control over outcomes. Trust in control, in turn, is grounded in expectations that desired outcomes will be received.

A similar argument has been developed within the literature on social dilemmas. That literature examines situations in which groups or communities are faced with a scarcity of shared communal resources. Much social dilemma research has focused on developing an understanding of the conditions under which individuals will forgo their short-term self-interests and voluntarily restrain their actions. Widespread evidence suggests that people behave cooperatively when they trust that others will reciprocate cooperative behavior (Brann and Foddy 1988; Brewer and Kramer 1986; Komorita, Chan, and Parks, 1993; Komorita, Parks, and Hulbert 1992; Kramer and Goldman 1988; Kramer, Goldman, and Davis 1989; Kramer, McClintock, and Messick 1986; Messick et al. 1983). In these studies, trustworthiness is essentially viewed as a probability analysis of the likely consequences of acting cooperatively.

Social Bonds and Identity Concerns

In contrast to the calculative or instrumental models of trust that have been outlined, recent approaches to studying authority relations have suggested an alternative perspective, which has been labeled the "relational perspective on authority" (Tyler and Lind 1992). That model proposes that trust is linked to the sense of identity people derive from their relationships with authorities. I will call such trust *social trust*.

The social trust argument has several key suggestions: (1) that people value their social status and social reputations, and those concerns motivate voluntary compliance with group rules; (2) that people's trust in social authorities shapes their judgments of their social status and social reputations; (3) that treatment by social authorities leads to inferences about their trustworthiness; and (4) that the nature of people's identification with society and with political/legal authorities influences the role of trust in gaining voluntary deference to authorities.

The first argument is based upon the premise that people want to have good feelings about themselves. To develop such feelings, people need to acquire information about their identities. One source of such information is one's connection to others. This argument is a core premise of social identity theory (Tajfel and Turner 1979). That theory argues that we use others to help define our social selves, a key component of our feelings of self-esteem and self-worth. In other words, we do not simply interact with others to exchange resources; we also do so to define and develop the social aspects of our sense of ourselves. Because people want to have good feelings about themselves, they want to be positively treated by others (see Baumeister and Leary 1995). This is particularly true of treatment by group authorities, who speak for the group.

One aspect of the information we gather from others involves the meaning of our connections to groups and group authorities. We are concerned about two distinct issues. First, we are concerned about our *social status*. That status determines the *pride* we take in the groups of which we are members. In other words, we are concerned about what we think is the desirability of being a member of the groups to which we belong. Second, we are concerned about our *social reputation*. That reputation reflects the degree to which we think that we are *respected* by others within the group. Pride reflects our feelings about the status of the groups to which we belong, respect our status within those groups. Empirical assessments of these two judgments suggest that they are related, but distinct, judgments about groups (Tyler, Degoey, and Smith 1996).

My core argument is that these identity-relevant judgments have implications for the feelings of legitimacy and obligation to obey rules that have already been outlined. The first aspect of this argument is the suggestion that judgments about pride and respect influence people's conformity to group rules (see figure 11.1).

I have examined this relationship in several studies. The first study is the previously outlined study of citizens in San Francisco (study 2), interviewed about a local political authority (Tyler and Degoey 1996). That study measured both pride and respect and examined the influence of each on deference to local political authority. Pride and respect were found to significantly influence deference ($R^2 = 6\%$, $p < .001$), with both having a significant independent influence (beta for pride $= .12$, $p < .01$; beta for respect $= .18$, $p < .001$).

Figure 11.1   Conceptual Model of Social Trust

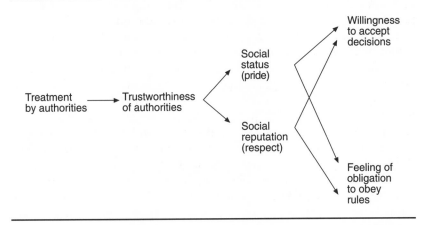

A second study involved a multicultural sample of 305 employees at the University of California at Berkeley, interviewed about a recent experience with their work supervisor (Huo et al. 1996). Employees were asked about their feelings of pride in their work organization and their judgments about how much they were respected by organizational authorities. They were also asked about their voluntary conformity to group rules. An analysis of the data suggests that judgments of greater pride and greater respect increased voluntary conformity to group rules ($R^2 = 15\%$, $p < .001$), with both pride (beta $= .36$, $p < .001$) and respect (beta $= .16$, $p < .01$) independently influencing conformity.

Finally, a third study involving a random sample of Bay Area citizens evaluating the United States government explored the influence of judgments about pride in American society and judgments about one's respect by other Americans on feelings of obligation to obey government rules and laws (the previously outlined study 6). This study found that pride and respect influenced judgments about the obligation to comply with laws ($R^2 = 10\%$, $p < .001$). In this study pride (beta $= .30$, $p < .001$), but not respect (beta $= .08$, n.s.), had an independent influence (Tyler and Degoey 1996).

These three studies in real-world political and managerial settings support the basic proposition that identity-relevant status judgments influence people's conformity to organizational rules. Interestingly, this influence occurred both for local legal political authorities and for national-level authorities. In both cases, assessments of social status and/or social reputation affected people's behaviors.

This suggestion is further supported by other recent findings (Smith and Tyler 1996). In two studies of college students we found that judgments about social status and social reputation affected both voluntary conformity to group rules and voluntary assertive behavior on behalf of the group (such as the willingness to make extra efforts for the group, to work when not required, and to volunteer innovations). Further, our findings suggest that these judgments also directly influence people's self-esteem, as would be predicted by identity-based theories. In other words, people's judgments about themselves affected both their behavior toward the group and their sense of self.

The second question is whether inferences about trustworthiness shape identity-relevant judgments, as depicted in (figure 11.1). In other words, do people use their judgments about the trustworthiness of group authorities to determine their social status and their social reputations? In particular, do those who think that authorities are benevolently motivated toward them (who want to treat them fairly, take account of their needs, consider their opinions, and so on) consider themselves (1) members of a higher status group and (2) more respected members of that group?

We addressed this question using a combined index of relational judgments about authorities which includes assessments of their trustworthiness, neutrality, and willingness to treat people with respect (Tyler, Degoey, and Smith 1996). We found that, across four different studies, treatment by authorities consistently influenced both judgments of social status (pride) and judgments of social reputation (respect). In other words, people do use their judgments about the trustworthiness of authorities to make inferences about their social identity.

The third question addressed is whether treatment by authorities shapes judgments of trustworthiness (see figure 11.1). Addressing this question requires distinguishing between judgments of trustworthiness and judgments of other aspects of treatment. In contrast to the former, judgments about outcome favorability, control, neutrality, and treatment with respect are judgments about what an authority *does*. People use these behavioral observations to infer the motives of authorities. Hence, it is possible to view inferences about trustworthiness as flowing from these other aspects of treatment. We took this approach by separating trustworthiness from other instrumental (outcome favorability, control) and social judgments (neutrality, status recognition) and demonstrated that inferences about trustworthiness are consistently shaped by noninstrumental aspects of treatment by authorities (Tyler and Degoey 1996).

Overall, these findings support the suggestion that inferences of trustworthiness lead to compliance with laws and regulations because they change people's conceptions of themselves. We directly tested this idea and demonstrated through causal modeling that inferences about trustworthiness influence the willingness to accept decisions, compliance with rules, and self-esteem because they change people's assessments of both their social status (pride) and their social reputations (respect) (Tyler, Degoey, and Smith 1996).

A further type of evidence in support of the social trust argument develops when trust in the benevolence of authorities is distinguished from confidence in their competence (Tyler and Degoey 1996). It is trust in character that shapes the willingness to accept decisions. In a regression equation defining trust, the beta weight for competence is 0.24 ($p < .01$), while that for benevolence is 0.38 ($p < .001$). Hence, people's concerns about authorities focus on social aspects of their character rather than on their ability to solve problems.

The fourth implication of the social approach to trust is that trust should vary in importance in response to social, but not instrumental, variables. In particular, people should draw more inferences about themselves from people with whom they share group membership or a common social identity. Hence, people should be more affected by the actions of authorities within their own groups, and they should be influenced by the degree to which they identify with group authorities and institutions.

We tested the degree to which trust becomes an important factor because of identification (Tyler and Degoey 1996). We used three types of analysis, each conducted in a management setting. First, we examined when trust is important. The instrumental model suggests that people will care about trustworthiness when they are dependent on the organization for resources or vulnerable to harm. The relational model suggests that trustworthiness is central when people have a personal connection with authorities (a social bond) or identify with the organization and draw self-relevant information from it. Our findings indicate that people care about trust more when they have social bonds with the authority and when they draw their identity from work. On the other hand, they are not affected by their dependence on the organization. These findings support the relational perspective but not an instrumental orientation.

A similar test was conducted in a political setting (Tyler and Degoey 1995). We examined whether or not people's identification with their community shaped their reliance on relational factors, including trustworthiness, when making decisions about whether to empower government authority. The findings suggest that relational issues are more important when people identify with their community. Similarly, another study demonstrated that people evaluate decisions by Congress in more strongly relational terms if they identify with being

Americans (Smith and Tyler 1996). In both cases, people who do not identify with authorities evaluated government decisions by asking, "How much did I win or lose?" People who identify with authorities evaluated the same decisions by asking, "Do I trust the motives of the decision makers?"

This identity-based model raises the broader question of where identities come from. It is only by understanding how people form their linkages to others that we can understand how authority will function. Identification is a psychological process, and people can identify with a wide variety of groupings—thinking of themselves as being rich or poor, male or female, white or minority, and so on. Hence, it is important to identify factors that lead people to identify with one group versus another. For example, recent discussions of nationalism have emphasized the potential artificiality of nation states as objects of identification (Anderson 1983; Azzi 1994), suggesting the importance of trying to understand how people naturally form identifications with social and political groups (see Tyler, Smith, and Huo 1996).

The importance of identification also suggests a potential limit to the effectiveness of authorities. If people identify more strongly with subgroups, rather than with the superordinate group, they may care more about what they get and less about the trustworthiness of authorities. A study of a multicultural workforce (Huo et al. 1996) supports this position. It found that people who identified strongly with the overall organization (assimilators and biculturalists) judged the decisions of authorities in terms of relational criteria such as their trustworthiness. People who identified more strongly with their ethnic subgroup than with the overall organization (separatists), however, evaluated decisions in instrumental terms ("What did I get?"). This pattern is shown in figure 11.2. It suggests that there are clear boundaries to the situations in which trustworthiness is central to deference to authorities.

Implications of Two Kinds of Trust for Governance

The findings outlined in the previous section suggest that there are two forms of trust: instrumental and social. These forms of trust are not mutually exclusive, and they may exist at the same time. What these findings suggest most clearly is that an explanation of trust that considers only instrumental motives is inadequate. There is also considerable evidence that social trust exists.

As has been noted, democratic governments need trust of one form or another. There must be some basis for long-term commitments to

Figure 11.2   Willingness of Assimilators, Biculturalists, and Separatists to Accept Decisions

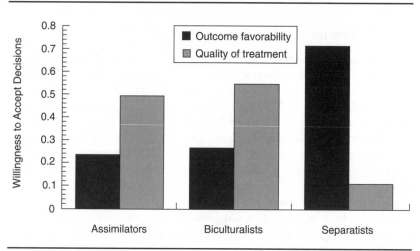

government and government officials, to facilitate cooperative solutions to collective action problems. Hence, trust in one form or the other is an important ingredient in successful societies. My concern here is with the implications of choosing one form over another as the basis for maintaining a political or legal system.

It is also necessary to consider when and where each form of trust will be important. Social trust should be important within existing groups, in which social bonds are in place and people have already internalized group values. Instrumental trust should be more important when dealing with outsiders or strangers. Further, social trust should be important when issues of identity are more salient. People focus on trustworthiness when they share a social bond or sense a shared identity with an authority. Hence, recognizing the nature of the shared identities that people feel they have is crucial to understanding the nature of trust that will be effective within a particular social group. When people are dealing with strangers or outsiders, they will be more instrumental.

Ironically, while these findings point to the importance of both social bonds and internalized values, both may be declining in the United States. The collapse of the sense of community and the increase of contingent contracts in work settings discourage the development of social trust. Further, the declining legitimacy of legal and political authorities discourages the development of identification with superordinate group authorities. Hence, America may be experiencing a decline in the "social capital" needed to sustain the operation of social trust.

Implications for the Maintenance of Trust

The creation and maintenance of instrumental trust has been addressed by rational-choice theorists. For example, Gilson and Mnookin (1994) have recently addressed this issue in the context of declining cooperation among lawyers. They argue that changes in the practice of law have led to declines in the conditions that promote trust. The stability of social networks has declined, and the number of one-shot encounters among lawyers has increased. Because of these changes, lawyers worry less about their reputations for trustworthiness; that is, if they are untrustworthy, others are less likely to know about it. Hence, there is greater advantage to being untrustworthy, and knowing this people are less likely to rely on others. This argument suggests that people's willingness to be trustworthy is linked to their judgment that there will be reputational costs if they are not trustworthy. Conversely, people's willingness to trust others is linked to believing that there are societal mechanisms that lead others to be trustworthy by punishing them when they are not. For example, past studies of lawyers show that they punish those who are untrustworthy be refusing to deal with them (Ross 1980). Thus, untrustworthy behavior has costs.

As this discussion makes clear, the key to an instrumental view of trust is the question of individual costs following from untrustworthy behavior. For an actor, the temptation to take advantage of others' trust is strong in the absence of such costs. Hence, society needs to impose costs. This argument is similar to that already outlined in the case of compliance with law. The instrumental view is that society needs to create a credible threat of punishment to influence people's behaviors. Without it, there is little incentive to comply. For someone considering basing his behavior on trusting others, the problem lies in recognizing temptation in others. Without credible societal mechanisms it is difficult to believe that others will follow through on their promises. Hence, it is unwise to trust. In a social dilemma situation, for example, it is unwise to limit personal consumption of scarce resources in the belief that others will also do so. Better to overconsume while resources are available.

In contrast, trust based upon social bonds and shared identity is linked to an identification with the group. That identification could lead to either a social bond with the group or an acceptance of group values (internalization). In either case, people's sense of self would be linked to acting in compliance with group norms. The difference in the case of social trust is that the motivation for the behavior is internal and is not linked to judgments of risk in the environment. For example, people with social bonds to their community do not base their decisions about whether or not to cooperate with authorities on judgments about the likely behavior of others (Tyler and Dawes 1993). Instead, they are motivated by their sense of ethical commitment to the group. Studies suggest that both social bonds with others (Batson, Batson, et al. 1995; Batson, Turk, et al. 1995) and internalized feelings of moral obligation to rules or authorities (Hoffman 1977) can motivate behavior that aids groups.

The development and maintenance of social trust requires the creation and maintenance of a community, with shared attachments and shared values. In other words, the authoritativeness of leaders is linked to their representation of a social group. Hence, the operation of social trust requires a set of social institutions and social values with which people identify. One source of such identification is socialization in a particular society or group.

Implications for the Operation of Government

From an instrumental perspective, the key to governance is the establishment of a track record of reciprocity, which creates the expectation that desired behavior will be rewarded. Hence, authorities must create the conditions for their own and others' behaviors that will lead trust to be the most cost-effective behavior. Lawyers or politicians who must continually deal with the same adversaries, for example, have an incentive to be trustworthy. They have concerns about social capital. Similarly, lawyers or politicians who know that judges will punish untrustworthy behavior have an incentive to be trustworthy.

In contrast, social trust is linked to creating a commitment and loyalty to the group and to group rules and institutions. Unlike instrumental trust, social trust requires the development of "social capital" in the form of interpersonal connections and feelings of shared identity and/or values. Such social capital is more difficult to create than institutions based upon rewards and punishments, but once created it allows authorities more freedom of action. Discretionary authority is greater if it is based upon social bonds, and authorities can rely on deference to their decisions when it is linked to the shared commitment to society and social bonds.

The problem with instrumental trust is illustrated in the social dilemmas literature. Societies most need the cooperation of citizens in times of difficulty, when the instrumental risks of trusting are high. At such times instrumental trust is not especially effective. In the midst of a social dilemma, when scarce resources are being consumed, it is difficult for an individual to rely on the belief that government can control the behavior of citizens. Government has great difficulty controlling behavior when it can rely only on instrumental means. Hence, I would argue that societies based upon social trust are ultimately more stable and durable.

It is possible that the two forms of trust are independent and can be created or maintained separately. There is a large literature in social psychology that raises questions about this possibility, however, suggesting that a focus on instrumental concerns undermines feelings of personal motivation. I am referring to the literature on intrinsic motivation, which suggests that rewarding people for undertaking behavior undermines their intrinsic motivation to perform that behavior (see, for example, Deci and Ryan 1980). In that study, children who are rewarded for performing a task that they have performed because they enjoyed it are less likely to experience the task as enjoyable in the future. The task has been redefined in instrumental terms.

While the research or achievement motivation focuses on a different context than the one we are exploring, the underlying psychological logic applies. When people think about their motives for acting, having salient instrumental cues undermines the development and maintenance of internal reasons for action. The operation of instrumental mechanisms—either rewarding people for desired behavior or threatening punishment for undesired behavior—will undermine feelings of internal obligation to behave in desired ways. Hence, surveillance creates the need for future surveillance.

An example of the application of these ideas to the arena of government is the work of John Braithwaite on regulation (chapter 14). Braithwaite argues that government creates trust by trusting others. Government must therefore approach citizens with the assumption that they are trustworthy, if it is to reinforce and solidify trust. This approach encourages the voluntary acceptance of government regulations. In contrast, approaching citizens in ways that suggest they are not trustworthy and must be watched decreases trust and lessens voluntary compliance with rules. Similarly, economist Bruno Frey (1993, 1995; Frey and Oberholzer-Gee 1995) has suggested that the application of sanctions "crowds out" the operation of civic virtues. If so, this effect suggests a fundamental antagonism between these two approaches to governance.

Summary

In this chapter I have sought to make two basic points. First, governments benefit from receiving the willing compliance of their citizens. Such willing compliance is encouraged by trust. Although governments may be able to control a population without trust through the use of coercive resources, as the Nazis did in Czechoslovakia and the Communists in Poland, it is difficult to implement the programs of a modern state effectively without the voluntary cooperation of citizens. Control through coercion is costly and unstable. Hence, governments have a great deal to gain by facilitating trust.

In particular, governments gain when social trust exists. Such trust is based upon identification with the group and/or the internalization of group values. Unlike instrumental or calculative trust, which is linked to expectations about the behavior of others, social trust develops from the important role that groups play in helping people to define their own identities. Social trust is linked to people's judgments about their status within society, status judgments that they use to form their sense of self and social identity. How do people know their status? The findings outlined suggest that they draw inferences about status from their treatment by group authorities. If those inferences are favorable and people feel valued by the group, they are more likely to defer voluntarily to decisions made by authorities, as well as to the rules of their group. Hence, social trust is linked to different psychological motives from those that shape calculative trust.

References

Anderson, B. 1983. *Imagined Communities*. London: Verso.

Ayres, I., and J. Braithwaite. 1992. *Responsive Regulation: Transcending the Deregulation Debate*. Oxford: Oxford University Press.

Azzi, A. E. 1994. "From Competitive Interests, Perceived Injustice, and Identity Needs to Collective Action: Psychological Mechanisms in Ethnic Nationalism." In *Nationalism, Ethnicity, and Violence*, edited by B. Kapferer. Oxford: Oxford University Press.

Barnard, C. I. 1958. *The Functions of the Executive*. Cambridge: Harvard University Press.

Batson, C. D., J. G. Batson, R. M. Todd, B. H. Brummett, L. L. Shaw, and C. M. R. Aldeguer, 1995. "Empathy and the Collective Good." *Journal of Personality and Social Psychology* 68: 619–31.

Batson, C. D., C. L. Turk, L. L. Shaw, and T. R. Klein. 1995. "Information Function of Empathetic Emotion: Learning That We Value the Other's Welfare." *Journal of Personality and Social Psychology* 68: 300–13.

Baumeister, R. F., and M. R. Leary. 1995. "The Need to Belong: Desire for Interpersonal Attachments as a Fundamental Human Motivation." *Psychological Bulletin* 117: 497–529.

Bradach, J. L., and R. G. Eccles. 1989. "Price, Authority, and Trust: From Ideal Types to Plural Forms." *Annual Review of Sociology* 15: 97–118.

Brann, P., and M. Foddy. 1988. "Trust and Consumption of a Deteriorating Common Resource." *Journal of Conflict Resolution* 31: 615–30.

Brennan, G., and P. Pettit. 1993. "Hands Invisible and Intangible." *Synthese* 94: 191–225.

Brewer, M., and R. Kramer. 1986. "Choice Behavior in Social Dilemmas: Effects of Social Identity, Group Size, and Decision Framing." *Journal of Personality and Social Psychology* 50: 543–49.

Dasgupta, P. 1988. "Trust as a Social Commodity." In *Trust: Making and Breaking Cooperative Relations*, edited by D. Gambetta. Oxford: Basil Blackwell.

Deci, E. L., and R. M. Ryan. 1980. "The Empirical Exploration of Intrinsic Motivational Processes." In *Advances in Experimental Social Psychology*, vol. 13, edited by L. Berkowitz. New York: Academic Press.

Eagly, A. H., and S. Chaiken. 1993. *The Psychology of Attitudes*. Fort Worth, Tex.: Harcourt, Brace, Jovanovich.

Frey, B. S. 1993. "Shirking or Work Morale? The Impact of Regulating." *European Economic Review* 37: 1523–1532.

———. 1995. "A Constitution for Knaves?" Institute for Empirical Economic Research, University of Zurich. Unpublished paper.

Frey, B. S., and F. Oberholzer-Gee. 1995. "The Cost of Price Incentives: An Empirical Analysis of Motivation Crowding-out. Institute for Empirical Economic Research, University of Zurich. Unpublished paper.

Fuller, L. 1971. "Human Interaction and The law." In *The Rule of Law*, edited by R. P. Wolff. New York: Simon and Schuster.

Gilson, R. J., and R. H. Mnookin. 1994. "Disputing Through Agents: Cooperation and Conflict Between Lawyers in Litigation." *Columbia Law Review* 94: 509–66.

Habermas, J. 1979. *Communication and the Evolution of Society*, trans. T. McCarthy. Boston: Beacon Press.

———. 1987. *Theory of Communicative Action*. 6 vols. trans. T. McCarthy. Boston : Beacon Press.

Hoffman, Martin. 1977. "Moral Internalization: Current Theory and Research." In *Advances in Experimental Social Psychology*, vol. 10, edited by L. Berkowitz. New York: Academic Press.

Huo, Y. J., H. J. Smith, T. R. Tyler, and E. A. Lind. 1996. "Superordinate Identification, Subgroup Identification, and Justice Concerns: Is Separatism the Problem, Is Assimilation the Answer?" *Psychological Science*, 7: 40–45.

Kelman, H. C., and V. L. Hamilton. 1989. *Crimes of Obedience*. New Haven: Yale University Press.

Komorita, S. S., D. K. S. Chan, and C. D. Parks. 1993. "The Effects of Reward Structure and Reciprocity in Social Dilemmas." *Journal of Experimental Social Psychology* 29: 252–67.

Komorita, S. S., C. D. Parks, and L. G. Hulbert. 1992. "Reciprocity and the Induction of Cooperation in Social Dilemmas." *Journal of Personality and Social Psychology* 62: 607–17.

Kramer, R. M. and L. Goldman. 1988. "Expectations That Bind: Group-based Trust, Causal Attributions, and Cooperative Behavior in a Commons Dilemma." Stanford University. Unpublished paper.

Kramer, R. M., L. Goldman, and G. Davis. 1989. "Social Identity, Expectations of Reciprocity, and Cooperation in Social Dilemmas." Stanford University. Unpublished paper.

Kramer, R. M., C. G. McClintock, and D. M. Messick. 1986. "Social Values and Cooperative Response to a Simulated Security Dilemma." *Journal of Psychology* 54: 576–92.

Levi, M. 1988. *Of Rule and Revenue.* Berkeley: University of California Press.

MacCoun, R. J. 1993. "Drugs and the Law: A Psychological Analysis of Drug Prohibition." *Psychological Bulletin* 113: 497–512.

McEwen, C. A., and R. J. Maiman, 1981. "Small Claims Mediation in Maine: An Empirical Assessment." *Maine Law Review* 33: 237–68.

Messick, D. M., H. Wilke, M. B. Brewer, R. M. Kramer, P. E. Zemke, and L. Lui. 1983. "Individual Adaptations and Structural Change as Solutions to Social Dilemmas." *Journal of Personality and Social Psychology* 44: 294–309.

Milgram, Stanley. 1965. *Obedience to Authority.* New York: Harper & Row.

Paternoster, R. , L. E. Saltzman, G. P. Waldo, and T. G. Chicicos. 1984. "Perceived Risk and Social Control: Do Sanctions Really Deter?" *Law and Society Review* 17: 457–79.

Pettit, P. 1995. "The Cunning of Trust." *Philosophy and Public Affairs* 24: 202–25.

Pruitt, D. G., and P. J. Carnevale. 1993. *Negotiation in Social Conflict.* Pacific Grove, Calif.: Brooks/Cole.

Ross, H. L. 1980. *Settled Out of Court.* Hawthorne, N.Y.: Aldine.

———. 1982. *Deterring the Drinking Driver: Legal Policy and Social Control.* Lexington, Mass.: Heath.

Sarat, A. 1977. "Studying American Legal Culture: An Assessment of Survey Evidence." *Law and Society Review* 11: 427–88.

Simon, H. A. 1947. *Administrative Behavior.* New York: Macmillan.

Singer, L. R. 1994. *Settling Disputes,* 2nd. ed. Boulder, Col.: Westview.

Smith, H. J., and T. R. Tyler. 1996. "Justice and Power: Can Justice Motivations and Superordinate Categorizations Encourage the Advantaged to Support Policies Which Redistribute Economic Resources and Encourage the Disadvantaged to Willingly Obey the Law?" *European Journal of Social Psychology* 26: 171–200.

Tajfel, H., and J. C. Turner. 1979. "An Integrative Theory of Intergroup Conflict." In *The Social Psychology of Intergroup Relations,* edited by W. G. Austin and Stephen Worchel. Monterey, Calif.: Brooks/Cole.

Thibaut, J., and H. H. Kelley. 1959. *The Social Psychology of Groups.* New York: Wiley.

Thibaut, J., and L. Walker. 1975. *Procedural Justice.* Hillsdale, N.J. : Erlbaum.

Turner, J. 1987. *Rediscovering the Social Group: A Self-categorization Theory.* London: Basil Blackwell.

Tyler, T. R. 1988. "What is Procedural Justice?" *Law and Society Review* 22: 301–55.

———. 1990. *Why People Obey the Law.* New Haven: Yale University Press

———. 1997. "The Psychology of Legitimacy." *Personality and Social Psychology Review* 1: 323–24.

Tyler, T. R., and R. Dawes. 1993. "Fairness in Groups: Comparing the Self-interest and Social Identity Perspectives." In *Psychological Perspectives on Justice,* edited by B. Mellers and J. Baron. Cambridge: University of Cambridge Press.

Tyler, Tom R., and Peter Degoey. 1995. "Collective Restraint in Social Dilemmas." *Journal of Personality and Social Psychology* 69: 482–97.

———. 1996. "Trust in Organizational Authorities: The Influence of Motive Attributions on Willingness to Accept Decisions." In *Trust In Organizations,* edited by R. Kramer and T.R. Tyler. Thousand Oaks, Calif.: Sage.

Tyler, Tom R., P. Degoey, and H. J. Smith. 1996. "Understanding Why the Justice of Group Procedures Matters: A Test of the Psychological Dynamics of the Group-value Model." *Journal of Personality and Social Psychology* 70: 913–30.

Tyler, Tom R., and E. A. Lind. 1992. "A Relational Model of Authority in Groups." In *Advances in Experimental Social Psychology,* 25, edited by M. Zanna. New York: Academic Press.

Tyler, Tom R., and G. Mitchell. 1994. "Legitimacy and the Empowerment of Discretionary Legal Authority: The United States Supreme Court and Abortion Rights." *Duke Law Journal* 43: 703–815.

Tyler, Tom R., H. J. Smith, and Y. J. Huo. 1996. "Member Diversity and Leadership Effectiveness: Procedural Justice, Social Identity, and Group Dynamics." In *Advances in Group Processes,* vol. 13, edited by B. Markovsky.

Williamson, O. E. 1993. "Calculativeness, Trust, and Economic Organization." *Journal of Law and Economics* 34: 453–502.

Chapter 12

Republican Theory and Political Trust

PHILIP PETTIT

T
HE REPUBLICAN way of thinking about citizenry and government has long given prominence to the notion of trust. We are
told that government is a trust with which the people invest
those in power; this theme is prominent among the "commonwealthmen" (Robbins 1959) who dominated eighteenth-century England
and America and was most explicitly formulated by one of their
heroes, John Locke ([1690] 1965). And we are told that there is no
prospect of decent government unless those in power prove to be of a
trustworthy disposition; this theme recurs in the emphasis among all
republicans, classical and modern, on the need for civic virtue (Burtt
1993).

This chapter outlines and defends a characteristically republican
picture of the role of political trust—that is, trust in government—
connecting that picture with the traditional republican way of thinking. When I speak of the republican way of thinking, I do so with a
degree of idealization. I refer to the distinctive habits of thought
found in the long republican tradition that goes back at least to Cicero
and that encompasses Machiavelli at the time of the Renaissance,
Harrington at the time of the English Revolution, and a wide spectrum of English, American, and French thinkers in the seventeenth
and eighteenth centuries—thinkers as various, for example, as Algernon Sydney and Joseph Priestley, Tom Paine and James Madison, the
Baron de Montesquieu and Jean Jacques Rousseau (Oldfield 1990;
Pocock 1975, Skinner 1983, 1984).

I associate the republican way of thinking, in particular, with habits of thought that are dictated by the view that the point of government is to promote liberty among the citizenry—however narrowly the citizenry is conceived—and that liberty requires, not noninterference, but nondomination (Pettit 1996, 1997). Under this view of liberty, a person will be free just to the extent that no one can interfere at will—no one can interfere on an arbitrary basis—in her affairs. However restrained she may be by a fair rule of law, she can look others in the eye without need of fear or deference.

The chapter is in five sections. First, I distinguish between two sorts of trust, one impersonal, the other personal. Next I argue, in line with the republican tradition of thought, that people have no choice but to trust or distrust, on a personal basis, those in government. In the third section I go on to show that according to traditional republicans this need not be bad news, because the public authorities may well be virtuous and trustworthy. Does that mean that republicans have to have a blind faith in the trustworthiness of the public authorities? I argue not, showing in the fourth section that the tradition identifies a rational, even self-interested form of trust-responsiveness that ought to boost the trustworthiness of those in power. The final section rounds off the chapter with a discussion of something that must seem paradoxical in light of these arguments: the traditional republican emphasis on the need for citizens to be vigilant or distrustful in their scrutiny of government. I argue that this paradox is readily resolved and that republicanism offers us a coherent and appealing perspective on the role of political trust.

Trust, Personal and Impersonal

The word *trust* is used in relation to a great number of phenomena (Pettit 1995). It may be used in relation to relying on people or on things, for example; or to relying on a person or thing to act in a certain way or just to be of a certain sort. In the sense that is relevant to the relation between people and government, it involves relying on people—the authorities—and relying on them to behave in a certain way. Reliance of that kind may be a detached, inductive reliance, of course, or it may be the reliance of someone whose welfare depends on whether the person relied upon does indeed prove reliable. And clearly, once again, the reliance involved in the relationship between people and government is of the involved, vulnerable kind.

But even when we have made such specifications, there remains an important distinction between two different sorts of phenomenon, either of which might pass as the trust of people in their government.

The one sort I shall describe as impersonal trust, the other as personal trust.

Suppose that I am planning a weekend trip to the coast with my family and need to know if the journey will be delayed by roadworks. Suppose, then, that I make a telephone call to the relevant traffic center and take a note of their recorded advice. In such a case I rely on the center personnel to give me the required information, building my plans around the assumption that they will do so. I assume that the personnel have access to the information and are so motivated that they will provide accurate information.[1] And assuming those things, I give over control of certain of my fortunes—or of the fortunes of those with whom I identify—to the center; I bind the welfare of me or mine to their performance.

The sort of trust I exercise in this example will be impersonal in nature if it is grounded in the belief that the agents are so constrained by regulations that they are more or less bound to pass on the information available to them. My reliance on the people involved is not prompted by any beliefs about their person or character, not even by any superficial beliefs of the kind that might be based on how they look or on their color or gender or profession. I rely on the personnel because I believe that such employees are subject to fairly exacting scrutiny and sanctions and that they are unlikely to give inaccurate information.

But the reliance that this example illustrates will involve a personal form of trust if two further conditions are fulfilled. The first is that by my lights it is manifest to the center personnel, if not that I am relying on them, at least that people like me—members of the public—are relying upon them. And the second is that by my lights the evident fact of such reliance is likely to trigger a cooperative disposition—say, their civic virtue—and to increase their reasons for giving accurate information in their recorded messages and in other forms of advice. Not only do I take the fact of reliance to be manifest to them, I also take it to be motivating for them.

It will be more likely that I am exercising personal trust of this kind, of course, if I go further than just telephoning the traffic center and instead drop by to discuss the situation with the personnel at the center. I explain to them that it is particularly important that I not be delayed on the trip—say, because of having a sick child—and I place my faith in their having such a cooperative attitude that they will be motivated by my plea—by the evident fact of my personal reliance— to give me exact and correct information.

In impersonal trust, the reliance that I display is not particularly trusting, in the ordinary sense of that word. I rely on the center personnel because I know the accountability constraints under which they are employed. I rely on them solely because I judge that they are independently constrained to behave in the required fashion. In personal trust, on the other hand, the reliance that I display is distinctively trusting. I see the center personnel as people who have such a cooperative attitude toward me, whether in my individual right or as a member of the public, that my manifesting reliance will strengthen or reinforce their existing reasons to do that which I rely on them to do (see Baier 1986).[2]

What can it mean to believe that the center personnel's reasons for acting in the required way are strengthened or reinforced, if I already believe that there is little or no possibility of their letting me down—say, if I think that they are more or less bound, on pain of dismissal, to give me accurate information? I already believe in such a case that their utility for giving the correct information is higher than the utility they attach to not doing so. But I will be trusting in my attitude toward them if I also believe, on the grounds of their being cooperatively disposed, that the utility they attach to giving the right information increases with the recognition that doing so will serve my purposes.

Someone may say that trusting always means taking a risk and that my account allows that I may trust someone—trust him personally, and also impersonally—to do something even when I have independent reasons to be sure that he will do it; thus they may claim that the phenomena I target do not strictly deserve to be called trust (Hardin 1993). But it is certainly possible for me to trust someone of whose behavior I am independently assured. I may trust a friend in the personal way to do something—A, for example—even though, for any of a variety of reasons, I cannot imagine his doing anything other than A; the reason may be that the law requires that he do A, that doing A is a matter of virtue or honor, that he is indeed a very good friend, or whatever. But though trusting someone may not always mean taking a risk, in the sense of relying on him to do something that I am not sure he will do, it will always mean taking a risk in another sense. It will always require me to make myself vulnerable to the other person in some measure, to put myself in a position where it is possible for the other person, so far as that person is a free agent, to harm me or mine. While I may run no probabilistic risk in relying on someone to act in a certain way, therefore, I must still recognize that he is a free agent and that my welfare is in his free hands.[3]

The example of relying on the personnel at the traffic center enables us to draw the distinction between two different modes of trust, one impersonal, the other personal. In both forms of trust I rely on another to do something. In impersonal trust that reliance is associated with the belief that the agent is independently motivated, perhaps constrained, to act in the pertinent manner. In personal trust it is associated with the belief that the agent, being of a cooperative disposition, will be motivated by my reliance on his mode of action to prove reliable. The associated belief leads me to think in each case that the trustee has a reason that will help to produce or reinforce the behavior on which I rely; and in each case that belief makes it rational, assuming that the costs and benefits are appropriate, to invest my trust in the trustee.

But not only does our example help to bring out the difference between impersonal and personal trust, it also shows that these modes of trust are not exclusive of one another. I may simultaneously trust someone on an impersonal and on a personal basis. I may trust her to the extent of thinking that she is independently motivated to do that on which I rely. And I may trust her to the extent of thinking that she will also find my relying on her motivating; if she is cooperatively disposed, the perception that I am relying on her will raise the utility that she attaches to proving reliable.

While the distinction between impersonal and personal trust has been drawn with reference to a simple, artificial example, it should be clear that it applies more generally. In particular, it should be clear that it applies in relationships between the people and those in power. We may trust our politicians or bureaucrats or judges to behave appropriately on the grounds that they are effectively bound to do so by the disciplines of office. Or we may trust them to behave appropriately on the grounds that they are cooperatively responsive to the reliance of individual people, or of the people as a whole, to their decisions. Or of course we may trust them at once on both sorts of grounds.

People Have No Choice but Personally to Trust or Distrust Government

The main difference between the simple example and the general political case is that when I invest trust in the traffic center personnel, whether on an impersonal or on a personal basis, I have a choice that is often lacking in politics. I may choose to invest trust in those personnel, or I may decide to exit from the situation that requires trust; I may decide against going to the coast. If I make myself vulnerable to how the center performs, as I do when trusting the information they provide, then I assume that vulnerability in a voluntary manner. But in the political case I may have no choice of this kind. Wherever I choose to live, I will find myself subject to a government and in a position of vulnerability to government agents. I may trust or distrust the government, of course, but I have no choice about whether to put myself in a position where those are the only alternatives.[4] And this is true not just for me personally but for every individual and, in effect, for every collectivity of individuals.

There is no incoherence about the idea of exercising trust in a position where the only alternatives are to trust or distrust (Holton 1994). Suppose that I have to take a certain course of action and that what I do depends on the assumption I make about where a particular friend now is. Suppose, furthermore, that the only information available is from a certain witness's report. In that case I will have no choice but to trust or distrust the witness; whether I like it or not I am vulnerable to what she says. And yet it will make perfect sense in such a case to speak of deciding to trust the witness.

But it may be that while I have no choice but to trust or distrust those in government, I am in the happy position of having impersonal grounds for trusting them. There may be sufficient constraints on what the authorities can do, or I may have sufficient control over what the authorities do, for me to be able to be rely confidently on their performance. In that case I will not face the choice of having either to trust the authorities on a personal bias or to distrust them on a personal basis. That choice will not be forced upon me—I may form no particular opinion as to whether the authorities are personally deserving of trust or not—because I will have perfectly good grounds for impersonal trust in government. The next question, then, is whether indeed things could ever be like that, whether things could be such that I do not have to face the choice, in relation to those in government, between personal trust and personal distrust.

Are the authorities capable of being so constrained, then, that there is no need to choose between personal trust or distrust? Or can they be so subjected to my control, or to the control of those in my position, that I can evade that choice? As it happens there are two political positions that claim, respectively, that government can be constrained and that it can be controlled in ways that make it unnecessary to choose between personal trust and distrust. The first can be associated, roughly, with a libertarian approach to politics, the second with a populist approach.

Libertarians argue that those appointed to government can be so constrained, actually or ideally, that there are adequate impersonal grounds for trusting them; there is no need to have to choose between personal trust and personal distrust. In particular they argue that this can be so if government is restricted, as they think it should be restricted, to the nightwatchman jobs of external defense and internal protection (Nozick 1974). The agents of government will have decisions to make, but the rules under which they make them will be so demanding that they will rarely, if ever, have any discretion. Their brief will not leave them any effective leeway in which to interpose their own ideas or interests.

Libertarianism in this sense is not a plausible view of government. No matter how restricted the tasks assigned to government, there are bound to be areas of significant discretion that are left to legislative, executive, and judicial authorities. There will be legislative questions to do with how much defense and protection are adequate; there will be executive decisions on where best to commit the resources made available by the legislature; and there will be significant judicial issues on the interpretation of this or that law, or this or that constitutional clause.

If we admit that government is bound to involve agents who face certain relatively unconstrained choices, then we recognize that, so far, it looks like government has to be a matter of personal trust or personal distrust. But another way of arguing that government does not force this choice on citizens is to hold that government agents need not be given autonomous power in relation to whatever discretion is left them by their briefs. The idea is that wherever there is discretion, then the people individually or collectively can be given the power to direct the government or at least to force the government, if necessary, to reverse any decision it makes; they can be given the power to control the government.

What approaches take this line? The outstanding example is the majoritarian or populist view of government, under which those in government are the servants of the people and are ideally subject to their continuing control. The populist view shares with the libertarian the hope that for all posts that are not elective and that cannot feasibly be made so, those who occupy those posts can be denied any significant discretion. But where libertarians think that all government agents can be deprived of discretion, populists believe that this is not desirable and perhaps not feasible. They hold enthusiastically by the ideal of a government in which the legislators make a large range of unconstrained decisions, as they seek to articulate the will of the people whom they represent. The reason is that in their ideal world legislators are subject to the control of the people. Legislators act on the more or less specific mandates of their electors and if they fail to live up to those mandates on any issue, then they can be called to account in some manner. For example, their decision can be exposed to the judgment of the electorate, as under an arrangement for citizen-initiated referenda.

But the populist picture of the relation between people and government is no more plausible than the libertarian image. It shares the problem raised for libertarians, that even with nonlegislative agents of government it is impossible to eradicate discretion. And it raises two independent problems of its own. The first is that there is no effective possibility of submitting the legislature to the sort of popular control that would mean that the people did not have to choose between personal trust and personal distrust in the legislators. And the second is that even if the people in its collective capacity could exercise the required control—even if electronic technology made it possible, for example, to have government by plebiscite—that would still leave in place a legislature that was uncontrolled from the point of view of individual agents. The legislature would now be the people in its collective identity, not the body of elected representatives, and from the point of view of individual persons that agent would certainly have discretion and power sufficient to force on them the choice between personal trust and personal distrust. Indeed it requires little reflection to see that from the point of view of individual persons the collectivity may look like an agent that is particularly difficult to control, an agent that is as wanton as the wind.[5]

I think that this discussion shows that issues of desirability apart, neither the libertarian nor the populist image of government represents a serious alternative. However government is organized, and to whatever ultimate end, there is no possibility of constraining government agents to more or less uniquely determined choices. Nor is there any realistic possibility, where such constraints fail, of subjecting government agents to the control of those who are governed. Government agents inevitably enjoy such discretion and power that people have no choice but to trust or distrust them on a personal basis.

This point of view fits well with the republican way of thinking. The tradition has been associated with a sustained search for mechanisms whereby impersonal trust in government can be boosted—mechanisms like limited tenure, rotation of office, separation of powers, democratic accountability, bicameralism, and the like. But it is a recurrent theme among republicans that government cannot live by law and regulation alone, that inevitably it presupposes the presence of virtue—the presence of trustworthiness—in the society, particularly among those who hold power. If government will work only to the extent that those in power are virtuous and trustworthy, then the people are in a position where they have no choice but to trust or distrust personally the relevant public officials.

This theme was well elaborated during the renaissance of republican thought in the northern Italian republics of the fourteenth and fifteenth centuries, particularly in the work of Machiavelli (1965): "Just as good morals, if they are to be maintained, have need of the laws, so the laws, if they are to be observed, have need of good morals" (241; see also Rubenstein 1991). This republican emphasis

on the need for trustworthiness among public officials, clearly gives
expression to the idea that the constraints that provide grounds for
impersonal trust are never going to bind with sufficient strength or
scope to drive out the choice between personal trust and personal
distrust. But it also reflects a belief that those in government can
never be subjected adequately to the control of the citizenry, however
broadly the citizenry are conceived.

This latter feature of republicanism may seem surprising. Republicanism is firmly associated with a belief in the power of democracy,
and some commentators have tended, for that reason, to give it a
populist gloss (Arendt 1973). But the populist reading of republicanism is downright mistaken, at least as I understand the tradition.
The central republican focus is always on creating institutions that
will further people's enjoyment of freedom as nondomination, and
while democracy is certainly recognized as an important safeguard
against governmental domination it is never presented as the center-
piece of the republican polity.

The seventeenth-century republican James Harrington (1977) made
particularly clear that for all the importance he gave to democratic
measures, he did not think that populist democracy was at the center
of things: "The spirit of the people is no wise to be trusted with their
liberty, but by stated laws or orders; so the trust is not in the spirit of
the people, but in the frame of those orders" (737). And similar qualifications about populist democracy are found in contemporary republicans such as John Milton, who actively shunned "the noise and
shouting of a rude multitude" (Worden 1991, 457) and, a little later,
Algernon Sydney (1990), who said of "pure democracy . . . I know of
no such thing; and if it be in the world, have nothing to say for it"
(189).

The authors of the *Federalist Papers* thought that representative democracy was important enough to build it into the definition of a
republic (Madison, Hamilton, and Jay 1987; see also Paine 1989). But
they too insisted that democratic representation was only one of a
number of ways of furthering "civil liberty"; like the separation of
powers, they placed it in the catalogue of "powerful means by which
the excellencies of republican government may be retained and its
imperfections lessened or avoided" (Madison, Hamilton, and Jay
1987, 119). Like almost all republican writers, they shrank from any
suggestion that government can be subject to such perfect popular
control that there is no need for the people to have choose between
personal trust and personal distrust in relation to those in power.

The belief that government has to involve giving not fully constrained and not fully controlled discretion to public officials is characteristic of the republican tradition, as I hope these considerations

show. But I should mention that it is also part of contemporary liberal thought. John Rawls has emphasized it, for example, in arguing that if people were to try to assert their democratic or political liberties, they would be cutting off their noses to spite their faces. For fear of giving over control to those in government—in effect, to those who can never be fully constrained—they would be like the passengers of a boat who refuse to give control to the captain; they would be denying themselves access to "the other freedoms that, so to say, define the intrinsic good of the passengers" (Rawls 1971, 233).[6]

The Republican Belief in the Availability of Political Trustworthiness

Why might we trust a particular government agent on a personal basis? The principal ground for personal trust is the belief that those in government are worthy of trust—that they are sufficiently conscientious about their brief, for example, or sufficiently devoted to their people to find the prospect of proving reliable attractive. If people take their politicians or bureaucrats, their police or their judges, to be virtuous in these ways, then they will certainly tend to trust them in the personal mode. They will tend to believe that so far as they saliently rely, individually or collectively, on the authorities' behaving in a particular manner, those agents will be motivated in a corresponding measure to behave in that manner.

The long tradition of republican thought suggests, as we have seen, that if government is to work well, if government is to succeed in securing the freedom of citizens—in particular, their freedom as nondomination—then those in government, and citizens in general, must be possessed of a good deal of civic virtue or civility; they must be trustworthy (Burtt 1993). But it is one thing to say that trustworthiness is required, another to hold that it is available. And now the important thing to see is that the tradition also emphasizes that this essential condition of good government is capable of fulfillment, that there are dispensations where the people have good reason to believe in the virtue and trustworthiness of their rulers and are entitled to have a lot of personal trust in how they will behave.

This republican belief in the availability of trustworthiness comes out in the insistence that it is not utopian to look for civic virtue among those in power. But it comes out also, and perhaps more vividly, in the association that republicans make between the freedom attainable for citizens—freedom as nondomination—and the attitude of confidence and boldness that they expect in such citizens. Being free, as republicans represent it, consists in the condition of not being exposed to the arbitrary interference of any other, including any other in governmental power. And that condition, so they suppose, is more or less bound to constitute a subjective and social status, as it becomes a matter of shared knowledge that one is indeed protected against others—protected both by the external constraints that give grounds for impersonal trust and by the internal constraints provided by the virtue of others. Among these writers, being free is scarcely distinguishable from the status of being able to look others in the eye without fear or deference, being able to walk tall, knowing that one does not live at anyone's mercy.

Consider this remark from Machiavelli (1965), which emphasizes the linkage between republican liberty and confidence: "The common benefit gained from a free community is recognized by nobody while he possesses it: namely, the power of enjoying freely his possessions without any anxiety, of feeling no fear for the honor of his women and his children, of not being afraid for himself" (236). Or consider the gloss, as it were, that Montesquieu (1989) offered over two centuries later: "Political liberty in a citizen is that tranquillity of spirit which comes from the opinion each one has of his security, and in order for him to have this liberty the government must be such that one citizen cannot fear another citizen" (157; see Spinoza 1951).

Where Machiavelli and Montesquieu stressed the confidence that goes with republican liberty, others have stressed the boldness in overtures to others; they have emphasized the intersubjective as distinct from just the subjective aspect of such freedom. John Milton is a good example. "They who are greatest," he said of the "free commonwealth," "walk the streets as other men, may be spoken to freely, familiarly, without adoration" (Worden 1991, 457). This theme assumed rhapsodic dimensions in the writings of Richard Price (1991) and Joseph Priestley (1993). I quote Priestley at length, though his references are unfortunately sexist:

> A sense both of political and civil slavery, makes a man think meanly of himself. The feeling of his insignificance debases his mind. . . . On the other hand, a sense of political and civil liberty, though there should be no great occasion to exert it in the course of a man's life, gives him a constant sense of his own power and importance; and is the foundation of his indulging a free, bold, and manly turn of thinking, unrestrained by the most distant idea of control. Being free from all fear, he has the most perfect enjoyment of himself, and of all the blessings of life. (35–36)

Not only is it going to be necessary, then, for people to be able to trust their government on a personal basis; and not only does every republic have to be a republic of morals as well as a republic of laws.

It is also a recurrent theme in republican writing that the republican image of a confident, bold citizenry is an accessible vision and that people do often have reasons to invest personal trust in those who hold power; in particular, they often have reasons associated with believing in the trustworthiness of the authorities.

The Republican Reliance on the Trust-Responsiveness of Those in Power

The chapter thus far has showed that according to republicans people need to have grounds for personally trusting those in power and that such grounds are often provided by the fact that the authorities are virtuous and trustworthy. Do republicans build their political hopes, then, on blind faith in the availability of trustworthy politicians? We know that they look for institutions that create grounds for imperso-nal as well as personal trust in the authorities, and that fact testifies to a certain realism about human motivation. But do they have any sim-ilarly realistic grounds for expecting the authorities to prove worthy of personal trust? I maintain that they do. Republicans have generally argued that there is a self-interested mechanism available to reinforce and reinvigorate the trustworthiness of those in government. I call it a mechanism of trust-responsiveness (Pettit 1995).

It is a common republican belief that where there is a modicum of trustworthiness in government—in particular, where there is a shared belief that people in power are sometimes trustworthy—then there is going to be a reason for trusting government agents over and above the fact of believing that they are trustworthy. The key idea in this theme is that if there are standards and models in a society that estab-lish what it is to be honorable—say, what it is to be trustworthy—then even those who are not possessed of such virtue will desire to be thought to have it; they will desire to be regarded as honorable. To be regarded as honorable is to be honored, after all, and to be honored—to enjoy the good opinion of others—is one of the primary human goods (Brennan and Pettit 1993; Pettit 1990). Thus the idea is that trustworthiness, an essentially admirable trait, will be boosted by a trait that has no place in the list of virtues—that is, the love of glory or esteem. The love of honor, the love of opinion, will serve as a sort of saving vice; it will serve to ignite the motivation of those in whom virtue proper has stalled.

John Locke ([1690] 1975) offered one of the most striking state-ments of this theme when he argued that the law of opinion offers a most potent means of keeping officials honest.

> For though Men uniting into Politick Societies, have resigned up to the public the disposing of all their Force, so that they cannot em-

ploy it against any Fellow-Citizen, any farther than the Law of the Country directs: yet they retain still the power of Thinking well or ill; approving or disapproving of the actions of those whom they live amongst, and converse with: And by this approbation and dislike they establish amongst themselves, what they will call Virtue and Vice. (353–54)

The incentives of shame and glory are invoked throughout the later republican tradition. Montesquieu ([1748] 1989) is famous, for example, for having argued that in moderate monarchical regimes—including the sort of monarchy that conceals a republic—the spring of all action is honor: "In monarchical and moderate states, power is limited by that which is its spring; I mean honor, which reigns like a monarch over the prince and the people" (30). The incentives of shame and glory appear again in the *Federalist Papers* as one of the two great securities, alongside the possibility of discovery and impeachment, against the abuse of power (Madison, Hamilton, and Jay [1787] 1987). Joseph Priestley (1993) offered a characteristically moderate version of the idea: "Magistrates, being men, cannot but have, in some measure, the feelings of other men. They could not, therefore, be happy themselves, if they were conscious that their conduct exposed them to universal hatred and contempt. Neither can they be altogether indifferent to the light in which their characters and conduct will appear to posterity" (33).

The republican argument implicit in these comments is not exactly straightforward, but it is pretty convincing (Pettit 1995). Assume that appropriate standards of government behavior are established and that the performance of agents in relation to those standards is generally likely to be recognized. Provided that that performance can be plausibly put down to trustworthiness—provided that a regime of personal trust is established in common consciousness—then those in government have a reason supplementary to reasons of trustworthiness for actually complying. As those in power recognize that the citizenry ascribe trustworthiness in explanation of their behaving well—at least at a certain limit—they are given an extra motive for actually behaving in that way; in the event of behaving appropriately they are offered the prospect of being well regarded—of being regarded as trustworthy—by the citizens generally.

The appearance of personal trust among the citizens, then, can actually increase the grounds that people have for feeling trust. For when citizens trust government agents to do that which the citizens apparently have only reasons of trustworthiness to expect, then in reality there are also other reasons for expecting those agents to comply. Those other reasons come of the recognition that the government agents are going to recognize that by complying they can help to win a good opinion for themselves and that by not complying they run the risk of losing that good opinion.

These extra reasons that people have for trusting those in power are not reasons of trustworthiness—they do not come of a belief in the trustworthiness of the officials—but reasons of trust-responsiveness. They come of the belief that even if the agents are not moved by the fact of others' relying on them, in the manner of truly virtuous and trustworthy individuals, they will at least be moved by the fact that those others will think well of them for proving reliable and will think badly of them for proving unreliable. They come of the belief that even if the agents are not trustworthy, in the sense of possessing the cooperative disposition associated with virtue, they are at least trust-responsive; they possess the cooperative disposition associated with caring about the good opinion of the trustees. The lesson of the republican observation about the love of glory is that those who have grounds of trustworthiness for personally trusting those in government may also have grounds of trust-responsiveness for such personal trust. In the more extreme case, indeed, the lesson may be that those who seem to have grounds of trustworthiness for personally trusting those in government may actually have grounds of trust-responsiveness for such personal trust.

One final comment. Although trustworthiness is a morally challenging trait and trust-responsiveness is an aspect of human frailty, the two mechanisms are synergetic; they pull in the same direction. To be trust-responsive, to be desirous of being thought trustworthy and therefore admirable, is to have reason to present yourself as trustworthy—in effect, to prove yourself trustworthy. In particular it is to have reason to present yourself as trustworthy rather than trust-responsive, since in most cases you will win no honor if you are recognized as an honor-hunter. "The general axiom in this domain," as Jon Elster (1983) has said, "is that nothing is so unimpressive as behavior designed to impress" (66). But that means that trust-responsiveness reinforces trustworthiness in a particularly intimate way; it gives a person reason to let impulses of trustworthiness have their way and indeed to try to drum up such impulses. We can think of trust-responsiveness as a force that boosts the motor of trustworthiness, not as an alternative, potentially rival motor.

Republican Vigilance

But the republican story about trust is not so straightforward a narrative as the discussion so far may suggest. For there is another theme that we also find in the republican literature, and on the face of it this theme runs directly counter to the message so far conveyed. The price of liberty is eternal vigilance, according to the traditional republican doctrine, and that suggests that the best way to keep others on track— in particular the best way to keep government agents on track—is never to take your eye off them, never to relax in the manner associated with personal trust. On the contrary, so the lesson goes, the best way to ensure that they prove reliable in the manner of virtuous officials is to subject them to sustained checks and sustained challenges, to insist that they operate under the challenge of always having to prove themselves to an unconvinced and untrusting audience. How otherwise to "keep the bastards honest"? (see Ely 1981).

The doctrine I am describing took a particularly sharp form during the seventeenth and eighteenth centuries in the commonwealthmen tradition. One of the principal messages of the commonwealthman was that people had to keep a continual watch on those in power— power being inherently corrupting—and that they should challenge rulers to explain and justify their behavior on every possible front. "As he never saw much Power possessed without some Abuse, he takes upon him to watch those that have it; and to acquit or expose them according as they apply it to the good of their country, or their own crooked Purposes" (quoted in Robbins 1959, 120).

Like Montesquieu ([1748] 1989), some thought that this sort of vigilance, this sustained manifestation of personal distrust, could be more or less routinized, that things could be organized so that without any tumult, without any hue and cry, those in power were systematically required to vindicate themselves under their reciprocal scrutiny and the scrutiny of ordinary citizens. But others sided with Adam Ferguson ([1767] 1971) when he railed against this restriction of vigilance, arguing that there is no hope for virtue in public life unless ordinary people also remain actively alert to the worst that the powerful can do. The rule of law that Montesquieu found and praised in Britain was fine, for example, so Ferguson said, "But it requires a fabric no less than the whole political constitution of Great Britain, a spirit no less than the refractory and turbulent zeal of this fortunate people, to secure it" (167).

How is one to make sense of this emphasis on distrust of government, given our claim that republicanism takes personal, political trust to be both necessary and available? How can the tradition assume that it is essential and possible to establish personal trust in government and at the same time argue that citizens should never indulge the complacency associated with such trust—on the contrary, argue that it is essential for them to manifest an attitude of downright distrust? Is there an incoherence at the center of republican thinking, assuming that we are justified in speaking of a common republican tradition of thought? I argue that there is not.

The key to my argument is a distinction between having or feeling trust in someone—in particular, personal trust—and displaying or expressing trust in someone.[7] To trust someone in the sense of having trust in him involves confidently assuming reliance upon him. But without feeling and having such trust, I may practice an expressive form of trust or, as we say, perform an act of trust. Without feeling an attitude of confidence in the reliance I have assumed, for example, I may choose to trust someone in the way that leads me to say, "I have decided to trust you in this, and I can only hope that you will not let me down." To trust someone in that expressive sense is not to rely with confidence upon him, or at least not necessarily, but to go through the expressive motions—that is, the behavioral motions—of relying with confidence upon him.

What goes for trust goes, naturally, for distrust—in particular, for personal distrust. I will distrust someone in the ordinary sense of feeling and instantiating distrust to the extent that I feel no confidence that she will prove reliable and do not actually rely upon her—do not build my plans around her proving reliable—or at least not for personal reasons. I will distrust her in the expressive sense—I will perform an act of distrust—just to the extent that I go through the behavioral motions of not relying with confidence upon her. If I have no choice but to rely upon her, for example, I will perform an act of personal distrust to the extent that I insist on external checks or constraints and try to ensure, on an independent basis, that she does not let me down.

There is no tension between the republican belief in a dispensation of trustworthiness and trust-responsiveness on the one hand and the emphasis on maintaining eternal vigilance on the other. For vigilance clearly involves expressive or behavioral distrust. The republican recommendation is that whatever personal and impersonal confidence people have in the authorities, they will have all the more reason to feel such confidence if they always insist that the authorities go through the required hoops in order to prove themselves reliable. To be vigilant in this sense is not to have an attitude of distrust towards the authorities—or at least not necessarily—but to maintain a demanding pattern of expectations in their regard—to insist, for example, that they should abide by certain procedures, for example, that they should accept challenges to their actions in Parliament or in the press, and that they should allow access to information on relevant aspects of their personal lives.

It should be clear why it might make sense to maintain expressive personal distrust—to behave as if one felt distrust—while actually feeling no such distrust. People may have an attitude of personal trust because they believe that the authorities are uncorrupt and that they will reliably behave in the proper manner. But there are good reasons, nonetheless, why they may behave as if they had an attitude of distrust, insisting on the necessity of various checks and constraints. First, it may be that however uncorrupt the authorities actually are, human corruptibility means that in the absence of the checks and constraints implemented in such distrustful behavior, they would begin to develop habits of corruption. And even if that were not so, imposing those checks and constraints should increase people's reasons for impersonal trust in the authorities and reduce the need for personal trust.

Not only is there no inconsistency in having personal trust in the authorities while behaving as if one felt distrust, it is even possible for people to make it clear to the authorities that they are espousing this dual posture. They can quite easily present the routines of distrust as constraints that are required in general and that help to keep the best of agents honest, while communicating the sense that they personally, or they as a group, are actually quite confident of the virtue and good will of the authorities in question. They can go through the established routines of expressive or behavioral distrust and show in other, less-established ways that actually they feel a lot of personal trust in the authorities. This dual posture will often make a lot of sense under our argument. By insisting on expressive distrust people can maximize the grounds for impersonal trust, forcing the authorities to jump a maximal number of hoops. By indicating that this expressive distrust is required only on an impersonal, routine basis, however, and by signaling the existence of personal trust, they can increase the chances of also triggering the trustworthiness and trust-responsiveness mechanisms; they can maximize the grounds available for personal as well as impersonal trust.

The upshot, I hope, is clear. The republican emphasis on vigilance reflects a belief that those in authority must be subjected to quite demanding checks and constraints, that this may be the only way of guarding against corruptibility and of maximizing the grounds available for impersonal trust. But that emphasis is quite consistent with enjoying and generally acting on an attitude of personal trust in the authorities. There is no incoherence at the heart of republican tenets. On the contrary, the allegedly conflicting views fit quite naturally together.

My thanks to John Braithwaite for advice on an earlier version. My thanks also to members of the conference at which this paper was first

presented at the Australian National University, February 1997, especially to Geoff Brennan; he was the one who pressed me to account for
the republican ambivalence. My thanks, finally, to Valerie Braithwaite
and Margaret Levi for their extremely helpful editorial comments.

Notes

1. Or I assume that that is a good bet, or as good a bet as any other available
   to me (Holton 1994).

2. Why do I stipulate that the personnel should have a cooperative attitude
   toward me, should be more or less well disposed? I do so to guard
   against having to say that I trust the personnel in the personal mode
   when I realize that they have been promised a reward by some enemy to
   lure me toward the coast and that that is why my reliance is motivating.
   The notion of being well disposed, the notion of having a cooperative
   attitude, is to be understood in a deflationary manner—in a manner, for
   example, such that I can trust someone in personal mode when I regard
   her, in the phrase I use later, as trust-responsive.

3. Richard Holton drew this point to my attention.

4. There is a difference, of course, between the sort of vulnerability to government that everyone suffers, as a citizen—the sort I have in mind
   here—and the more specific kind that is triggered by a person's looking
   for some government service that is due to him in virtue of his special
   circumstances—say, the sort of vulnerability assumed when I call in the
   police to help me cope with a threatening neighbor, or when I make a
   claim on social security. A person may have a choice as to whether or not
   he should assume this special vulnerability.

5. The one possibility that would give control to individual people is a veto
   over every collective decision. I am assuming that such a "unanimitarian"
   arrangement would clearly be infeasible.

6. In his discussion of the analogy with the captain of a ship, Rawls suggested that the captain is fully constrained by his own wish to get to port,
   even if he is not controlled by the passengers: it is obvious, however, that
   such full constraints—such grounds for impersonal trust—are not generally going to be available.

7. My thanks to Simon Blackburn for a helpful conversation about this.

References

Arendt, Hannah. 1973. *On Revolution*. Harmondsworth: Pelican Books
Baier, Annette. 1986. "Trust and Antitrust." *Ethics* 96: 231–60.
Brennan, Geoffrey, and Philip Pettit. 1993. "Hands Invisible and Intangible."
    Synthese 94: 191–225.

Burtt, Shelley. 1993. "The Politics of Virtue Today: A Critique and a Proposal." *American Political Science Review* 87: 360–68.

Ely, J. H. 1981. *Democracy and Distrust: A Theory of Judicial Review.* Cambridge: Harvard University Press.

Elster, Jon. 1983. *Sour Grapes.* Cambridge: Cambridge University Press.

Ferguson, Adam. [1767] 1971. *An Essay on the History of Civil Society.* New York: Garland.

Hardin, Russell. 1993. "The Street-Level Epistemology of Trust." *Politics and Society.* 21: 505–29.

Harrington, James. 1977. *The Political Works of James Harrington.* Edited by J. G. A. Pocock, Cambridge: Cambridge University Press.

Holton, Richard. 1994. "Deciding to Trust, Coming to Believe." *Australasian Journal of Philosophy* 72: 63–76.

Locke, John. [1690] 1965. *Two Treatises of Government.* Edited by Peter Laslett. New York: Mentor.

———. [1690] 1975. *An Essay Concerning Human Understanding.* Edited by P. H. Nidditch. Oxford: Oxford University Press

Machiavelli, Niccolo. 1965. *The Complete Work and Others.* 3 vols. Translated by Allan Gilbert. Durham, N.C.: Duke University Press.

Madison, James, Alexander Hamilton, and John Jay. [1787] 1987. *The Federalist Papers.* Edited by Isaac Kramnik. Harmondsworth: Penguin.

Montesquieu, Charles de Secondat. [1989] *The Spirit of the Laws.* Translated and edited by A. M. Cohler, B. C. Miller, and H. S. Stone. Cambridge: Cambridge University Press.

Nozick, Robert. 1974. *Anarchy, State, and Utopia.* New York: Basic Books.

Oldfield, Adrian. 1990. *Citizenship and Community: Civic Republicanism and the Modern World.* London: Routledge.

Paine, Thomas. 1989. *Political Writings.* Edited by Bruce Kuklick. Cambridge: Cambridge University Press.

Pettit, Philip. 1990. "*Virtus Normativa* Rational Choice Perspectives." *Ethics* (100): 725–55.

———. 1995. "The Cunning of Trust," *Philosophy and Public Affairs.* 24: 202–25.

———. 1996. "Freedom as Antipower." *Ethics* 106: 576–604.

———. 1997. *Republicanism: A Theory of Freedom and Government.* Oxford: Oxford University Press.

Pocock, J. G. A. 1975. *The Machiavellian Moment: Florentine Political Theory and the Atlantic Republican Tradition,* Princeton, N.J.: Princeton University Press.

Price, Richard. 1991. *Political Writings.* Edited by D. O. Thomas. Cambridge: Cambridge University Press.

Priestley, Joseph. 1993. *Political Writings.* Edited by P. N. Miller. Cambridge: Cambridge University Press.

Rawls, John. 1971. *A Theory of Justice.* Oxford: Oxford University Press.

Robbins, Caroline. 1959. *The Eighteenth Century Commonwealthman.* Cambridge: Harvard University Press.

Rubenstein, Nicolai. 1991. "Italian Political Thought 1450–1530." In *The Cambridge History of Political Thought,* edited by J. H. Burns and M. Goldie, Cambridge: Cambridge University Press.

Skinner, Quentin. 1983. "Machiavelli on the Maintenance of Liberty." *Politics* 18: 3–15.

———. 1984. "The Idea of Negative Liberty." In *Philosophy in History*, edited by R.Rorty, J. B. Schneewind, and Q. Skinner. Cambridge: Cambridge University Press.

Sydney, Algernon. [1698] 1990. *Discourses Concerning Government*. Edited by T. G. West. Indianapolis: Liberty Classics.

Worden, Blair. 1991. "English Republicanism." In *The Cambridge History of Political Thought*, edited by J. H. Burns and M. Goldie, Cambridge: Cambridge University Press.

Chapter 13

Trusting Disadvantaged Citizens

MARK PEEL

F OR SOME observers, there are few more pressing problems in late-twentieth-century political culture than the apparent decline of conscientious citizenship. Contemporary Australian discussions form part of a broader debate about national institutions and national identity, arising in part from the prospect of a republic and an Australian head of state in time for the anniversary of federation in 2001. They have focused to a significant extent on young people and have tended to assume that distrust of politicians and governments stems from declining civic awareness or a lack of civic education. The problem, in other words, lies within the citizen.

While the best of these reports address real concerns about popular awareness of the institutions and possibilities of democratic governance, few pay much heed to the role governments play in citizen distrust and disengagement. Indeed, celebrations of "active" citizenship by Australian state and federal government sit oddly alongside their marginalization of public protest; their hit-and-run attacks on groups and individuals who dare to differ; their shielding of an increasing range of political decisions from the public gaze in the name of commercial confidence; and or their reliance on more or less facile surveys, quick-fire community consultations, and carefully monitored "independent" research as a substitute for democratic decision making (Irving 1995).

Whether or not there is a historical narrowing of active citizenship—and the evidence in Australia is not conclusive—there are certainly good reasons for investigating the ways in which governments *produce* and *maintain* distrust, especially among groups where these feelings form part of the very "social capital" and shared political understandings identified as the solution to citizen disengagement in other accounts. Interviews with around three hundred fifty people living and working in four suburbs commonly ranked among the most disadvantaged in Australia—Adelaide's Elizabeth (E), Brisbane's Inala (I), Sydney's Mount Druitt (MD), and Melbourne's Broadmeadows (B)—suggest that these citizens have good reasons for distrusting a government that, through its agents, so consistently manifests its distrust of them. For disadvantaged citizens, distrust is a rational, critical response to their actual experiences of distrustful and even destructive governance, both in the everyday delivery of welfare services and in larger-scale projects of community development, consultation, and urban renewal.

These shared experiences of being distrusted also generate strong social bonds. In all four suburbs, local identity is grounded in the divisions between "us" and "them," in legacies of inadequate service, and in weary expectations of a situation that will never change: "The government is constantly the enemy, I think, for these folks" (B8, 8).[1] As one Inala activist said, "People are apathetic, simply because for years people knew that no matter what we do, nothing ever gets done; . . . maybe that's not apathy, maybe that's realism" (I1, 9). And these reasons for distrusting public institutions are increasing rather than diminishing as governments explore mechanisms for funding and delivering benefits that stress an ever more punitive surveillance (Cappo and Carlisle 1993).

Residents, activists, and workers in these four suburbs experience a governance based on distrust, ignorance, and an obsession with control. And they stress its costs, especially the suppression of novelty and initiative. The current mania for obedience, they argue, helps create the very lack of initiative and the reliance on social and community workers that are considered deficiencies of the supposed "culture of poverty." The heavy-handed insistence on following rules may be a remedy that actually ends up creating the disease.

Yet in their interviews the people of these four suburbs also emphasized concrete examples in which trust had played a crucial role in promoting better relationships between governments and citizens and had shifted the focus of collective action toward cooperation rather than antagonism. Moreover, disadvantaged people have good reasons for insisting that only governments have the means and the legitimacy to tackle large-scale problems with long-term measures. While they provided an articulate critique of current welfare procedures and programs, they also offered prescriptions for overcoming some of the problems they identified and, perhaps, for transforming the objectives and outcomes of social welfare. Most of all, the stories told by these citizens show that good governance must ultimately stem from—and produce—something other than sullen, fearful obedience.

Four Suburbs

The working-class suburbs of Broadmeadows, Inala, Elizabeth, and Mount Druitt all experienced rapid development in the 1950s and 1960s, much of it in the form of public rental housing. All have since suffered the worst impact of the grinding recessions and fitful recoveries that characterized the Australian economy during the 1970s and 1980s. As I conducted these interviews in 1994 and 1995, another sharp economic downturn had barely lifted. Official adult unemployment rates hovered around fifteen or twenty percent, public housing was more and more a refuge for the victims of industry downsizing, and welfare agencies were struggling to cope with a combination of dramatic increases in need and severe funding cuts.

I spoke with a range of people, including workers in government and nongovernment organizations, longstanding local activists, other residents with a sporadic or recent involvement in specific campaigns, and the users of various community institutions and welfare services. Rather than gathering exhaustive life histories or the accounts of household time and labor budgets common in other studies, I was more interested in hearing what feminist scholar Nancy Fraser (1989, 178) has called "alternative narratives," life histories that describe the world as it is but also picture how it *might* or *should* be. Most stories began with the personal dramas of increasing economic vulnerability; even those people who had kept their jobs and avoided "the welfare" had unemployed sons, daughters bringing up kids on their own, or friends and kin who were suffering and scared and didn't know what to do. Yet the women and men in this study also used the interviews to display their wider knowledge of the world around them, justifying their choices and wryly judging their victories and defeats. They placed their personal accounts within a wider context, appealing to particular normative guidelines and common-sense statements in order to generalize about their neighbors, their community, or their class.

In their study of a disadvantaged housing estate, British investigator Bill Jordan and his colleagues (1992) argued that their interviewees "do not display a *theory* of poverty, how to prevent it or even how to alleviate it, nor do they make social policy prescriptions" (320). Perhaps because my interviews were more focused on how the world *should* be, I think I heard more than that. While the stories of those I interviewed were often dominated by tragedy, despair, and the legacy of "years of frustration and inability" (MD9, 12), they also spoke of occasional victory and of the important social welfare experiments and changes in which they had participated. They were articulate and passionate about change, and their stories showed imagination, not just indignation.

Certainly, the majority of the local residents I spoke to were or had been involved in some kind of local activism; these conversations were shaped by their stories of agency, as well as by my objectives. By and large, I spoke to people I empathize with, people whose knowledge I value and who knew that I wanted to carry that knowledge into public view. I was helping particular kinds of people produce a particular kind of story.[2] This does not mean there were no surprises. Nor does it mean that my respondents simply endorsed what I said and offered no challenges to my interpretations. Indeed, as the interviews progressed, they changed what I needed and wanted to say. I had not imagined that being distrusted would play so central a role in their stories. I had not predicted that trust would so consistently anchor their accounts of victory and achievement. Nor had I predicted that they would focus so consistently on how governance could be improved; on small, practical changes; and on the importance of actions that told people that governments trusted their stories, their interpretations, and their ideas. And if much of what I heard was the frustration of "old hands" and seasoned activists, then this is surely even more significant. If the hopeful are losing hope, and if those who have always helped their neighbors through the thickets of rules and regulations can see no reason to keep on explaining the inexplicable and defending the indefensible, then the problems of governance in these disadvantaged communities will only get worse.

Distrust and Individual Compliance

While my research focused on collective experiences and activism, it also confirmed that individual welfare beneficiaries have little faith in governments' ability to address or even understand their needs (Weatherly 1993). Unlike more affluent citizens, of course, they are compelled to remain in a close relationship with government agencies. It is difficult to withdraw from the last resort of public housing and welfare or from compulsory relationships with parole officers or rehabilitation services. Many residents, especially women, also perform voluntary work in a range of state-sponsored services, such as neighborhood houses, child care centers, and schools (Peel 1995b). And when they have to, people use government in other ways, deploying its punitive power—the police, tenancy officers, and social workers—against those who threaten the security of the home, the street, or the neighborhood. When there is no money for private transport, private housing, private security, or private health, people have little option but to rely upon government.

Yet having to use government services and benefits does not imply consenting to government's interpretations and prescriptions. Most people view government as a ponderous structure of unreasonable obligations and irrational sanctions, represented by people who ask a lot of stupid questions and rarely come up with the right answers: "People get sick of telling their life story in half a dozen places to achieve one end. It's demoralizing having to do that. . . . You've got to go through the story over and over and over again" (B16, 7). Disgruntled compliance is mixed with frequent expressions of powerlessness, fears about inadvertent rule breaking, a culture of "dobbing" and distrust among beneficiaries, and the feeling that the insensitivity of punitive decision making justifies various forms of evasion. Most feel that they can't win; urged to avoid dependency, they nonetheless find that independence, especially as it is reflected in the skills involved in managing low income, is interpreted as using the system, rule breaking, or noncompliance.

While most people are cynical about the state's competence, their most common complaint is its expectation of stupidity or fraud. They resent rules and regulations that expect standards of budgeting and self-control few well-off people could manage and administrative practices—like home visits and patronizing interviews—that seem to predict that their first impulse is to lie, defraud, and cheat. They also resent having to accept passively someone else's interpretation of their problems, when they are henceforth excluded from the definition of *their* needs and *their* situation:

I've had a terrible run-in with them just recently, when I said to them, "What do you want from me, tell me what you want, because I am giving you everything I possibly can, but obviously it's not the right stuff." They cannot tell me. They won't tell me, and then they send me another form for me to fill in. . . . I screamed, you know, they're wasting my time, making me full of anxiety, they won't give me an answer because they were told they weren't allowed to tell anyone anything. I said, "Can I have a look at my file?" "Oh no, you've got to go through the Freedom of Information Act to see your file." That's my file. I snatched it off the poor lady. I grabbed it, and I looked through it, and she didn't know what to do with me, so she raced out and got someone else, who demanded it back, so I said, "No, it's my file, I'm going to read it, because I want to know what you people are doing, this is my life, I want to know what you are saying about me." (B7, 17)

The indignity of the investigative and decision-making process is much more important than the insufficiency of the outcome (Tyler and Degoey 1996). Most significantly, valued workers and services are not those who have the most to give or who give without question, but those who shape their relationships with clients around trust and respect: "I mean, it's not the good ones who say 'the tenants can have everything'; that's not what we're looking for. We want a fair go. . . . All we're asking for is . . . [to be] treated with respect . . . not treated as 'that lower-class person'" (MD10, 9).

Most people also have very low expectations of public welfare services. They are unwilling, in Russell Hardin's (1993, 517) phrase, to "test interactions," because their aggregate experience is such that even if their immediate needs for cash or emergency relief are fulfilled, there is a strong prospect of losing not only self-respect but also the power to control their own stories and their own definitions of problems. There is little to celebrate in victory and much to lose from the round of small defeats and indignities: "They've lived their lives constantly being put down, so you get to the point where [they think] 'here comes another one'" (MD4, 7).

It is also clear that distrust is not simply a matter of bad personal experience. Personal and collective histories are gathered into shared scripts that mythologize the distrusting state: "They seem to think we're a certain type, or a certain class, or whatever it is they've got in their little minds, and that we're bereft of brains, we don't know how to express ourselves, we have no rights, we shouldn't speak up" (B13, 18). Distrust is learned, and all too often it is proved. People share stories of misunderstanding, ignorance, and occasional brutality: the indignities at the front counter, the police raid on the wrong house, the mother who killed herself when the welfare took her kids away. These ready-made interpretations infect every interaction, especially with the police and social workers, who form most people's daily experience of governance. People take on the identity of a suburb besieged: "What they do now, the government, is that they keep us poor to keep us at a certain level . . . they keep Broadmeadows down, so you're not living, you're just surviving" (B2, 4). In some urban renewal projects, consultation teams have been surprised to discover that local residents spread inaccurate stories about forced removals and people being taken away in trucks. They are exasperated by people's credulity, when surely the more troubling fact is that local people are *able* to believe such stories.

Even achieved trust remains "a fragile commodity" (Dasgupta 1988, 50) that is easy to destroy (Levi 1994). Workers in state agencies commonly refer to a "one step forward, two steps back" problem; an incremental gain is undone by an insensitive remark, a poorly explained decision, the perception of unfair procedure. Gaining trust is a very slow process and accordingly even more vulnerable to disruption: "I wrote in the daybook yesterday about one particular woman who's been scouting around the edges the whole time, you know, and she actually asked yesterday if she could do something for the center. That's been a long time. It's been about a year's work" (MD6, 3). As another community worker put it, "It takes time to be accepted [and] . . . to win the approval of the people. They test you, they really test you" (B8, 12).

Moreover, if mistrust of government is common sense, the evidence of change needs to be impressive and consistent (Hardin 1993). As one worker said, "It's very difficult to get over that mistrust. I'm sure it's going to take time, and some positive experiences, before they feel able to play a part in consultation processes and trust the outcomes of them" (I3, 8). The great difficulty for government-based workers, too, is that they must prove themselves both trustworthy and trusting in a situation where neither is predicted and neither is expected to last. Moreover, they often find themselves the brunt of frustrations and antagonisms they played no part in, or the focus of a collective animosity about outsiders and "do-gooders" they have spent years overcoming in their own ethical dealings with clients.

Finally, the research confirmed that complaints and apocryphal stories are not really about the quality of services so much as the adequacy of official interpretations of problems and possible solutions. Disengagement from government measures normative resistance, not simply dissatisfaction with outcomes. Assertions of personal and collective ability, and the insistence on telling their own stories in their own way, are the surface manifestation of a much deeper resistance at the level of beliefs (Fraser 1989). Like the war of words traced by anthropologist James Scott (1985), these stories begin "close to the ground, rooted firmly in the homely but meaningful realities of daily experience" (348). They concern visible injustices, perpetrated by real people. And at their core is a personal refusal to accept or condone the rules of the welfare game. As Scott argues, people use their own words in order to maximize their sense of rights, minimize their dependence on a system they do not control, and maintain a conversation about justice and equity largely unrecognized by those defining those concepts from above.

Activism and Civil Society in Disadvantaged Suburbs

Recent reforms in welfare services generally address only the relationships between government agencies and individual citizens. Some have proved successful in overcoming distrust, usually by allowing workers more flexibility and allowing clients to play an active role in defining solutions. The JET Program for single parents is a case in point, though there is little that even good casework can do about entrenched labor-market disadvantages for single mothers.[3]

Relationships between governments and the institutions of civil society in disadvantaged suburbs have received much less attention, even though building better relationships between government agencies and local community organizations might reinforce attempts to overcome the legacies of distrust among individual beneficiaries. In any event, entrenched disadvantage, the continued inflow of newly impoverished people into cheap public or private housing, and shrinking funds for public agencies mean that governments will continue to rely on local activist groups and nongovernment services to provide information and to deliver and manage a variety of services in all these areas. Governments and local organizations will continue to share a close bond.

These organizations are certainly diverse. As in more affluent places, some groups are sparked into life by specific protests, though in these poorer suburbs few survive without some kind of outside funding. Most groups rise and fall on the back of particular issues or seek to grow through securing public funds for new programs. There are all the nongovernment institutions characteristic of low-income areas: the church missions, the emergency relief centers, the desperately overworked advocacy groups and welfare rights organizations, their postered walls reminding everyone of rallies for demands that have still not been fulfilled. Some of the larger bodies cut across ethnic and cultural divides, though new migrant groups like the Vietnamese and the Latin Americans still tend to generate their own advocates and services. Aboriginal and Torres Strait Islander people, too, have built parallel organizations, while another division is expressed by the large number of youth services.

These groups have a variety of relationships with government, depending upon the service they provide and the extent to which they seek general or specific funding. Some rely on a mix of federal and state government money for different activities or to pay for particular workers; others rely more heavily on volunteers for general community work and seek funding only for specific services (language training, community arts, tenant participation or parenting education, for example). A few rely entirely on contributions or are attempting to become self-funding—by marketing local art and design, for instance.

At the same time, governments have directly created other welfare and community centers. While they remain government sponsored and fully dependent on direct funding, these organizations nonetheless play an important part in local civil society. Finally, there are the regional offices of government departments and the "community liaison" units of the police force. Their social and community workers provide direct services, coordinate liaison with other agencies, and sponsor new groups among public housing tenants and others.

Certainly, antagonism towards government is a first principle in most organizations, however much they depend on public money. It could be little different for the local advocacy groups that originated in attempts to shame government departments into accepting responsibility for often appalling lags in the provision of such basic services as sewerage and schools. Yet more recent organizations, often developed out of government initiatives, tell similar stories of distrust and frustration. These stories are widely shared, because even relatively secure residents in these suburbs have always relied on public services rather than expensive private ones and have often had a hand in demanding and then building or managing a day care center, school, health center, or sportsground. Many have also been dependent on welfare benefits at some stage in their lives. Certainly, few would dispute the conviction that governments have not treated their suburb well and are run by and for "people who aren't like us."

The most consistently and strongly cited evidence of this distrust is that the state neither listens nor learns: "They don't have any trust in the community. We talk about the community not having any trust in them, but they don't have trust in people at the local level" (MD1, 8). The history of governance in all these suburbs is of yet more research, yet more stupid questions about problems and needs, yet more inaction and unfulfilled promises. Governments consistently ignore and mistrust reasonable argument, justified complaints, and carefully collected evidence:

Most of them [suggest outcomes], but then the funding runs out and nothing's ever done with it. You do the research, you've got the papers, and the government chucks it. You have to go back then, in a few years' time, to resurvey, because things change, and people just get fed up with it. . . . Until people see things being done from the research that's happening, you're not going to have very sympathetic audiences as far as your questions go. They're just not interested any more. They want to see results. (E2, 14)

Some workers certainly do listen, but the system as a whole simply does not trust the initiatives of its own employees, let alone the knowledge and ideas of disadvantaged people themselves. As a Western Sydney migrant worker put it, "[This] disenfranchises a substantial number of people, and it becomes a top-down approach towards providing a solution to a problem that *they* see, the problem as *they* see it" (MD3, 5).

In all four suburbs, people talked about a worsening relationship between local organizations and government. In the 1950s and 1960s, there was the authoritarianism of unforgiving social workers and draconian inspectors, and church-based agencies tended to add insult to injury with the tattered remnants of "moralizing" charity. During the 1970s and 1980s, however, community development perspectives helped push welfare and social-work practice toward a more productive, trusting engagement with local people and local problems. Unfortunately, the trend in community services and welfare administration in the 1990s is precisely in the opposite direction, away from collaboration and trust and toward closer surveillance and control.

Defining Needs and Delivering Services: Managerialist Welfare

The residents and workers I interviewed all described the rapid emergence and solidification of a "managerialist" welfare model based on delivering predefined services, a more careful targeting of resources, and competition between agencies in the name of efficiency: "It's all about unit costing and direct service, bums on seats and numbers through the doors. It's about 'quick through-put,' quick fix, come in, we'll fix you up, and after six weeks you're gone, it doesn't matter about the past thirty years" (B9, 5). Few would argue that some efficiencies were overdue, especially in the area of interagency coordination to prevent duplication of services. And the impact and extent of these changes varies widely between areas of federal and state jurisdiction, which often overlap in one organization or agency. Politically and electorally vulnerable departments like community services and housing are particularly susceptible to the managerialist approach, while within other departments, like those servicing health, the easiest targets are either community-based initiatives or services rarely used by the well-off, such as free dental care.

According to those at the receiving end, managerialism basically means cutting costs, mostly by delivering services from the top down at the least possible expense. Meaningful client participation is sacrificed to short-term perspectives. Ever more complex policing strategies and unworkable rules surround the definition and use of each service or benefit. Another key motive of managerialism is avoiding risk, which usually means an obsession with controlling funds. Avoiding risk, of course, also means avoiding innovation, while the insistence on control at all costs only creates more control costs. Still, with the victory of a conservative coalition—even more deeply imbued with economic rationalism than its Labor opposition—at the federal election in March 1996, managerialism is now even more entrenched. The rhetoric of social justice has disappeared, to be replaced by a much more powerful commitment to combating welfare fraud and a new assortment of ill-conceived measures to ensure that help reaches only the "truly needy" and "deserving."

The most important faults of the managerialist paradigm stem from its profound distrust in the ability of either local workers or those actually suffering disadvantage to define needs and to carry out programs for addressing them. Increasingly strict accountability and fund management criteria almost seem to expect fraud, ignorance, and poor finanical skills and force workers to spend large amounts of time in record keeping and performance appraisal:

> They're shitting themselves about accountability, to the extent that they're going to extremes which make workers totally robotic in their approaches to things. They're so scared of issues' being taken up by the media and blown out of proportion that they put in accountability mechanisms which basically leave you no time to do work, because you're too busy filling out forms. . . . They are going to the extent of being totally paranoid about their accountability, about wasting resources. Besides that, they've cut resources to the bone. (B10, 14)

Shorter budgeting periods create instability; having satisfied accountability criteria, workers spend even more hours on the cycle of proposal writing, reporting back, and seeking new sources of funding. The world of community organizations reliant on government funding is becoming a world of reports and flow charts, strategic planning exercises and outlandish record keeping requirements, where the conversation about "what would work" is being overpowered by "what does it cost": "It's like talking to an accountant, I suppose; they think with this really pragmatic, rational approach, and you're trying to justify a community development project, something that you think has real benefits for health, but you can't, there's no argument because you never meet on any plane" (MD10, 11). And it is becoming a world ruled by fear, whether government's fear of fraud or residents' fears of getting something wrong:

> I think communities do have to be accountable . . . [but] you spend hours of your time just filling in forms. That would take up sixty to

seventy percent of a worker's time . . . with the neighborhood house people, they spend so much of their time being accountable. It's always a balancing act, but people have just gone over the top. It's become obsessive. Once you have fear, fear will not drive change. You will never have change, because fear will not make change. (B4, 8–9)

In one sense, that fear has made government departments devolve all the hard work of accountability outwards, while pulling money, ultimate responsibility, and powers of definition in toward the center. It is a mix that produces compliance without trust or any sense of worthwhile engagement. Resentment comes from the assumption that people and workers in local organizations are not already accountable, to each other and to the communities in which they embed themselves. Nervous accountability may achieve some set outcomes, but no surprises or innovations: "There's a difference between planning and administering, and ministering and discerning. . . . One is much messier than the other, much harder" (MD1, 5–6). Most telling is the common argument by local residents and workers that the programs that are most effective in drawing new people into groups and services, developing links between different cultures, and meeting new and unexpected needs are precisely those less specific and longer-term activities that fall afoul of managerialist criteria. The cooking classes, play groups, informal language classes, and sports teams are much less threatening to new and isolated residents because they are not issue-based and do not force people to acknowledge "a problem" publicly. Yet they are increasingly hard to defend on "core business" grounds.

There is strong pressure on workers to make needs fit already available services or to specify needs to fit funding criteria. To defend a generalist program, they must predict outcomes and performance measurements that may not be met, while others, invisible at the beginning, may come to be much more important. Because the best proposal wins—and the best proposal uses the language of managerialism—user participation in defining procedures, writing proposals, and managing eventual programs becomes a risk few groups can take:

I think this is getting much harder, and it's getting more professionalized and . . . the community is losing the ability to actually be involved. . . . Apart from lack of time, my committee members were just attending so many meetings to try and keep things together. They're voluntary workers, they're unpaid, why should they be slogging over pages of bloody submissions and stuff? (B18, 11)

Local activist groups are made responsible and accountable for precisely the wrong sorts of tasks—large-scale fundraising, accounting and financial management, and the delivery of specific predetermined and prepackaged programs—while the flexibility and initiative at which they might excel are being removed.

These pressures on worker-resident relationships are intensified by the call for increased competition between agencies in the name of "better client outcomes": "We've got to run around saying 'we're better than that organization over there' so that we can get our money, and they've got to do the same to us" (B16, 5). Leaving aside the bizarre juxtaposition between demands for one-on-one competition and calls for more effective interagency cooperation, competition creates a series of powerful human dilemmas: "You've got the most disadvantaged fighting with one another for meager, meager resources" (B12, 10). Or, as one Inala resident put it, "Departments coming into a community blunder in, and they couldn't give a shit what happens" (I5, 13). And in Western Sydney, attempts at regional cooperation fall afoul of shrinking funds:

> It could be the case that to obtain a worker in a place like Mount Druitt might well mean that one gets defunded in Fairfield or Liverpool. . . . It just means that somebody shows a greater need and bang, that's where the money goes. The fact is that a lot of these areas have a very great deal of need, and to start ranking them, to me, is really quite wrong. (MD7, 5)

Asking people in need how they would like a few thousand dollars carved up between dozens of equally deserving agencies is a cavalier perversion of "self-determination."

Certainly, if the goal of managerialist welfare is to reduce dependency, it is difficult to see how it will achieve this end (Jamrozik 1991; Travers and Richardson 1995). Efficiency is achieved by enforcing the passive consumption of services and rendering participation meaningless. The emphasis on *delivering* services also assumes that social welfare bureaucracies have already interpreted and properly defined the needs and problems each local agency should meet (Fraser 1989). Despite government's stated interest in client involvement, that involvement is restricted to where, how, and when services are accessed, rather than the nature of those services or why they are presumed to be more efficient and appropriate than other options. In addition, the increasing sophistication of targeted delivery mechanisms ignores more crucial questions. For instance, how are services to be managed so they can respond quickly to changing needs and circumstances? How can novel methods or definitions of need emerge, either from experience or from making mistakes, when everything is ruled by service contracts, prepackaged programs, and performance quotas?

Clients—and many workers—become outsiders to the definition of needs and practices and are brought back in only as consumers or clients or service deliverers. This is a careful, politically safe logic, dedicated to counting effectiveness by people in seats and tailored to simplistic "temporary" solutions to complex problems:

> They're too keen to give a clear definition. You're dealing with people who aren't in order anyway. Their lives are dysfunctional. Money will often go the "wrong way," but at the time that's totally appropriate. . . . And that, I think, is the simplistic approach in what this government's on about, you know, that you only sort of "hit" the welfare scene once. . . . I think they want a quick return for very little investment (B5, 4–5).

This delivery approach gives people little chance to challenge or even affect the definitions of need and strategy developed somewhere above their heads: "They come in . . . with preset programs; like Daleks [robots] . . . they come in to 'save Inala'" (I1, 4). Or, as a veteran of Mount Druitt's running battles with state agencies argued:

> What are the outcomes, what are your throughputs? It's not measurable. I mean, with most things, it takes you three or four years to get on the drawing board, to get to the starting line and get funded. By the time you get funded, the need that you've actually applied for has shifted considerably. Then you get funded, and when you should not be funded, they can't stop. I've watched that dynamic, observed it, for a long time. It's extraordinary. You're not supposed to stop, you see, nor are you supposed to change, move one degree from your objectives and all that stuff and your target groups. All those games you play about your stats. It's just too much. It's hard to get on, it's hard to get off, and you can't change. (MD1, 13)

Asking Without Listening

Managerialism clearly privileges "monological, administrative processes of need definition" (Fraser 1989, 156). Under this rubric, people do not use benefits; they simply "have" them, ready-made and delivered. They are filled up, to the appropriate level, with transferred income or access to specified services that they "truly" need. Any remaining anomalies—for instance, who is going to create and guarantee the expanded opportunities disadvantaged people are promised—are matters for technical and administrative fine-tuning (Jamrozik 1991). This is a conception of social welfare and citizenship that is about accepting rather than making decisions and that disengages people from the very process of deliberation and dialogue about the future that engenders a sense of responsibility and agency. For the people on the receiving end, it becomes a lot easier to sink back and accept someone else's diagnosis and someone else's prescription. Some just pull away, or worse:

> Anything that's laid down is either a quick fix, a touch-and-go model, or a very efficient, computerized accountability thing, where kids go off the dole, on the dole. . . . And in the end you ask yourself, well, the young people tell you very plainly, that you're not on the ball at all, government or nongovernment. That's what it's about, and it's directed at us too. You know, a lot of our young people have died, they're gone, they've actually given up. They've just packed it in, got out of it. (MD1, 6)

Yet at the same time governments insist that they are interested in client participation. If Labor's favorite theme was community consultation, the conservative government uses a quite bizarre rhetoric of "customer input" and "customer service," which pretends that what the customers say actually matters. However frequently and enthusiastically expressed, and for all the hard work being done on the ground or at the front counter, these are hollow promises. In the area of community participation, what citizens get is the showcase public meeting. This isolated opportunity for speaking assumes that the community can find and articulate its authentic voice in a couple of hours and that community consensus is never more than another convincing speech or community education project away. It feels meaningless: "They come to people like me, ask you to put in some recommendations, and if they've had their coffee that morning, they might say 'Yeah, we'll pick up a bit of that,' but if they haven't, they'll probably throw it in the bin. If they're going to have *consultation*, then that is what it's got to be" (B7, 26).

And most residents know the place of consultation in the hierarchy of decision making. In Queensland, the excitement of the "community action planning days," at which the local citizenry were encouraged to try their hand at building a new Inala in plasticine and crepe paper, couldn't hide the fact that the government was much more interested in showy infrastructure and quick returns than in a careful community process. The people of the suburbs can see a facile consultation process from a mile away. They are well versed in workshops— which some rather unkindly describe as "encounter groups" for planners—and the public meeting has become one of their favorite spectator sports: "It's fun, especially if it's a pie in the sky thing where you know you could ask for the world and you're getting nothing" (B11, 10).

They, and many of the people who consult them, know how difficult a job community consultation really is. The expectation that a community can be consulted always raises hard questions about who actually speaks and who actually gets heard. But many planning projects expect that not only can a community be consulted, but it can be consulted quickly. Here, community consultation is actually a means of telling people what is going to happen whether they like it or not. And what is often lost in the process is both valuable knowledge and the chance for a meaningful participation next time:

> I still don't think they really take note of what they have to offer. The ordinary Mum and Dad, the housewife: it is amazing what they have got to offer when you sit and give them the opportunity to express. It really is. It always amazed me then and even now. . . . But it often turns a lot of those people into cynics, because they soon realize that having spent all this time and contributed all this, they realize that it was more a public relations exercise than a real consultation. (B1, 5)

Indeed, people in these areas have every reason to ask why they are still being consulted about problems that haven't changed and solutions they know won't work:

> People are saying "Well, why do we need people knocking on the door when we really want a better bus service, and how many people do we have to tell, and what do they do with it anyway when we tell them?" It's an issue a social planner confronts, because as soon as you go to a place and say, "What are some of the needs?" there's this floodgate that opens, people saying "Well, don't you know? . . . We keep saying it and it appears nobody knows." (MD7, 14)

It is usually all too obvious that "they only want consultation if you tell them what they want to hear" (MD5, 16). Far too many community consultations are poisoned by their effective function of idealizing and legitimating what has already been decided.

Of course, agencies' desire to consult communities repeatedly and to redo the research one more time springs in part from legitimate concerns about structures of leadership and representation in these suburbs. These concerns are real enough in places that not only experience a high degree of population turnover but are among the most culturally diverse places in the nation. Divisions based on culture, generation, and length of residence are important in disadvantaged areas, and they are also easily exacerbated by workers in a careless language, which unwittingly confirms ideas about places "under siege" from criminals and youth gangs (Peel 1996) or a perception that some groups—especially racial minorities—have somehow "won" while other groups have lost. There is always a danger of allowing participation to empower exclusive ideas and derogatory alliances (Young 1990).

At the same time, there is ample evidence from well-designed and well-conducted programs that problems of representation can be addressed, that cooperation and trust are not ruled out by difference, and that truly deliberative consultation processes can accommodate and indeed productively bring out conflicts of culture and belief; as the philosopher Iris Young (1990) argues, "To say that there are differences among groups does not imply that there are not overlapping experiences" (171). And overcoming this danger should not mean limiting the scope of active citizenship. Governments must instead promote a politics of inclusion—a language of "us too" rather than "why them"—through ensuring the presence and participation of different groups and providing a clear and honest statement of its principles and capabilities. The point might be to locate common projects—perhaps small in scale and scope at first—on which everyone can agree, all the while ensuring the voice and presence of smaller constituencies.

Again and again, residents in these suburbs speak of their respect for and trust in those projects that were actually honest about what could be done and that actually listened to what was being said. They do not expect endless possibilities, nor promises of the world made over. As one youth worker suggested:

> [They want] more open communication, and to be told the truth. None of this Band-Aid stuff or anything like that, or pie in the sky, or "by the year 2000 this will happen." They want to be told the truth; if things are bad, tell them that things are bad, but tell them why things are bad and how things are going to be improved for them. (E1, 5)

Indeed, stupid promises actually destroy trust and a sense of engagement, because those involved in them know they will fail. In a truly participatory process, people are not just heard; they are listened to, asked questions, debated, challenged. And they are shown respect for their honesty and integrity.

Nothing I heard in my interviews implied that citizens are always right. There was no argument for reducing the role of government in society. Nor was the reduction of "bureaucracy" favored; much of the energy, and many of the ideas and initiatives people value, emerged *from* that bureaucracy. Nor did anyone suggest that everyday understandings of justice or needs should be somehow immune from challenge and debate. The problem is not inexpert, apathetic citizens. The problem is a top-down model for defining needs, delivering welfare, and consulting customers that stems, in turn, from a model of citizenship aptly described by Australian writer Michael Salvaris (1995) as "constipated" (38).

People in these suburbs—whether they are recipients of welfare

benefits or activists or both—do not trust government, because it neither listens to nor trusts their interpretation of problems and solutions
and because its ways of guaranteeing efficiency and accountability
destroy initiative, flexibility, and meaningful participation. When people have no right to choose their own way or to make the mistakes
that propel reform, the key component of active citizenship—some
degree of self-determination—is ruled out from the beginning. And
even if the function of social welfare is defined very narrowly—reducing dependence and fostering self-reliance, for example—it is difficult to see how current approaches will deliver even those objectives. The most likely outcome of a managerialist perspective that
avoids risk, limits innovation, and dictates specific outcomes is *more*
disengagement, *more* apathy, *more* dependence, *less* active citizenship,
and an ever stronger conclusion that government just never listens.

Building Trust

Yet while activists and local workers in these four suburbs stressed
the injuries of distrusting governments, they also provided examples of
change and improvement drawn from specific programs. Of course,
there are major differences between the four suburbs in this respect.
In both Mount Druitt and Inala, the regional programs and outer suburban initiatives of the Whitlam Labor government (1972 to 1975) are
remembered, and its legacies—community health centers, footpaths,
streetlights, community theater, and legal aid services—are memori-
als to the "last time the government gave a damn about this place"
(I4, 1). In Broadmeadows, the burst of activity around progress associations and neighborhood organizations is traced to churches in the
early 1970s and to the neighborhood house, tenant participation, and
regional planning programs that accompanied the state Labor government into office in the early 1980s. Residents in Mount Druitt described the Western Sydney Area Assistance Scheme and the Housing
Department's revamped tenant participation program as 1980s victories, while in Inala, people pointed to the breaking of the conservative
doldrums in the late 1980s with the Housing Department's Area Improvement Scheme. The chronologies of migrant and Aboriginal
groups differ according to the funding rhythms of their respective
federal and state departments. In Elizabeth, distinguished by the
quality and quantity of its original public facilities and its prosperity
under the guidance of an anxiously paternal state housing authority,
the story is one of lost ground until the highly successful Social Justice Project of 1992 to 1993 (Peel 1995a).
    Indeed, what impresses most workers in these suburbs is how
these memories of better relationships encourage local people to bat-

tle on and to continue investing time, energy, and scarce resources in activism. Despite claims ignored, expectations thwarted, and struggles wearily renewed, people use the tales of occasional success to assert their obligation to their suburb and to others, especially to children, and to defend their principled belief that the rights of common citizenship do matter: "We're the same as everyone else," "we deserve what everyone else has," or "we don't want handouts, we deserve a chance." If one lesson of this shared past is that much good work comes to nothing, another is reflected in the urge to find opportunities for cooperation and to locate agencies and workers with whom trusting and cooperative relationships are known to occur or can be anticipated.

The activist mothers of these suburbs, in particular, maintain the energetic work that some community organizations and welfare agencies helped draw into public activism during the 1970s and 1980s (Naples 1991, 1992; Peel 1995b). The frenetic world of the neighborhood house or the government-run community center offers the best possible proof not only that local people are skilled and knowledgeable participants in social welfare systems (Lewis 1994) but also that they are still willing to risk the investment of trust and time in some public institutions. They are not distrustful of every relationship or interaction; they are, from hard experience, careful and economical in their allocation of trust and commitment. They will risk trust, if only because they know that government is the only institution powerful enough to provide them—and especially their children—with the means to a better life. To believe otherwise is to accept that things will never get better. It is a crucial judgment that divides the activist from the cynic and the hopeful from the hopeless. People's stories accordingly focus again and again on the projects that helped, on workers who really made a difference, on a struggle that made some people's lives better.

The most important outcomes are long-term; in these four suburbs, the rewards of active citizenship can certainly be counted in new facilities, a school saved, a service funded. But they are more often remembered in the concrete relationships and problem-solving experiences of what political scientist Jane Mansbridge (1994) has called "ideal deliberation" (157). Well-designed community projects can bring into the open the kinds of heterogeneous, participatory publics described by Iris Young (1990). Indeed, it is those opportunities for cooperation and self-determination that stick in the minds of the participants. What they also remember is the combination of relatively successful concrete outcomes and a participatory public process that not only respected local definitions of need but supported initiative, encouraged advocacy, and strengthened local cooperation. Most of all, they are regarded as having belonged to the community. They are not, by and large, remembered as delivering victory to particular groups or interests, nor as having spent large amounts of money, but as forums in which different interests were expressed, debated, and—crucially—listened to. They drew on existing activism and carried the voices of local people into the policy-making process. And they trusted the people they claimed to be working for.

The lesson of these successful projects and collaborations for governments, meanwhile, is that trust proffered is trust repaid, and that an expectation of trustworthiness, capacity, and useful knowledge *can* transform the outcomes of welfare and social programs into something other than sullen compliance. Practices that encourage and nurture trust and active participation also give governments better access to the often untapped resources of activism, knowledge, and commitment among local citizens. The benefits of trust might therefore extend well beyond increased compliance with and respect for government agents and programs. A trusting and cooperative approach to the problems of disadvantage might also generate better solutions.

In other words, trusting disadvantaged citizens—expecting trustworthiness, showing confidence in people's ability to be trustworthy, and working within a mutually defined structure of accountability and obligation—might have a transformative function. A reasonable expectation that ideas will be listened to, that engagement with governments will yield positive long-term returns, and that activism will be respected might help empower those active citizens and rehabilitate that spirit of participation we endorse and rely upon in conceptions of healthy democracy.

How, then, might distrust and disengagement be reduced? Are workers who rely on "all that self-determination jazz" (I5, 12) simply fooling themselves? Are there institutional designs and practices that might nurture participatory, heterogeneous publics, or civic communities of strong horizontal bonds? These are difficult questions, but my informants provide useful ideas. First, it is important that greater trust be placed in the priorities, solutions, and ideas of people suffering disadvantage and in their ability to use their knowledge to improvise, innovate, and form their own judgments. There needs to be room for surprises—even mistakes—and there needs to be a recognition that the most effective ways of reaching particular objectives might not be obvious at the beginning. No one could have planned the children's play group that turned into a support group for women leaving violent relationships, the cooking and sewing circle that transformed itself into a language class for Turkish women, or the open-house display of new public housing units that was allowed to become a public discussion day about urban renewal. In fact, careful control and direction would have guaranteed that nothing of the sort would have happened.

Second, trust is best seen as a construction over time, for which evidence must be sustained. It is important to build and rebuild confidence, and one particularly good way of doing that is for governments to take action, without prevarication and without stringent assessment, when citizens point out obvious deficiencies. Such projects would not necessarily be expensive; all disadvantaged suburbs stand in crying need of things that more affluent areas take for granted: better lighting in the shopping center, a new or more frequent shuttle bus service that takes in the senior citizens center or the community health complex, ten new computers for the local high school. Just as important is quick attention to procedural matters: rewording a pamphlet that doesn't make sense, responding quickly to a complaint, judging in favor of a beneficiary who, in the absence of hard evidence to the contrary, is *presumed* to be telling the truth. It is these small victories, perhaps minor in themselves, that build engagement and create confidence that government actors are listening and willing to risk trust.

I would argue that such actions could also build a reservoir of citizen confidence in government that might help overcome the "one step forward, two steps back" problem. It is already possible for people to explain occasional disappointments with "Oh well, they tried their best" or "It'll come good in the end." Indeed, many workers expressed their surprise that residents often show "anger in very specific terms about particular things, rather than the system" (MD2, 5); in other words, people are willing to believe that the system as a whole *can* work. Concrete evidence of trust and faith might generate similar interpretations of government actions in general. Further, investments in local groups must attend to the development of competence and independence over time. It is ridiculous to propose that long-term or secure funding creates dependence and inertia among disadvantaged people when it apparently carries no such risk for middle-class beneficiaries.

Third, if funding for community organizations promotes citizens' ability to participate directly in the construction of proposals, it must explicitly recognize their desire to be accountable and to be good managers. It must also recognize their planning and evaluative abilities:

The kids have just done a complete evaluation of the entire youth project here, and it was an evaluation not only of the project but an evaluation of themselves as well. That'll be coming out in the next week or so. They did it warts and all. Picked out the good points and picked out the bad points, identified areas where they think we're going wrong. Instead of the adults sitting back and saying "This is what we're going to do, this is how we're going to do it," we're actually getting the kids to do it, and they did a damn good job of it. . . . They haven't pulled any punches; as I've said, we've been trying to instill into them that if they want truth from other people, they've got to be prepared not to put a cover over something. If they've got something to say, say exactly what you mean, and that's what they've done with the evaluation. . . . They were critical of themselves, they were critical of themselves as a group as well as individuals. (E1, 8–9)

It might be useful to remember, too, that the careful management of money is one of the most prized skills among people living in poverty, and that for all the brouhaha about welfare fraud, there is little evidence that it involves more than a tiny minority of welfare recipients. In any event, those most likely to have the knowledge and the means to perpetrate major fraud are unlikely to be poor. There is no need to remove the sanctions against criminal fraud or other grave misdeeds, or to shield the financial and administrative practices of organizations from scrutiny; what might work even better is to provide each nongovernment body or organization with direct assistance in budgeting, accounting, and funds management.

Of course, the question of how to judge who should receive funding is complex, especially when there are potential new participants or needs to consider. Governments have no reason to offer perennial support to organizations that purposefully exclude people on illogical criteria, pursue antagonistic agendas against other groups, or persistently mismanage their funds. While the tactic of subjecting community funding to a show of hands at a public meeting is inappropriate, there could perhaps be some element of collective deliberation, perhaps through a small grant or tax credit to be used by citizens (following John Braithwaite's example in chapter 14), or public forums to allocate a proportion of the funding. There is also scope, perhaps, for including "nonaligned" outsiders with some knowledge of the area in the mix of decision making.

Fourth, the funding, controlling, and guiding of programs should be managed so as to avoid placing pressure on the trusting relationships built between different groups of residents and between workers and residents. The differences between outsiders who want to control and those who want to participate are very clear:

So much of the experience of people in Broadmeadows and equivalent sorts of places is people coming in with incredible value judgments and saying, "Oh, we've got to do this, this and this." You just have to be a part of the place. It's about life, just being friends with people, just getting to know people. (B12, 14)

Changing and managing programs should not imply a succession of upheavals, new regimes, and sudden changes. Established, informal practices of information sharing, mentoring, and cooperation should be protected from competitive pressures and from unwieldy and insensitive rationalizations, which usually end up costing rather than saving money.

At the same time, government departments need to recognize conflict and diversity, and especially to realize that people are unlikely to want or be able to speak with one voice. Citizens must be able to exhibit their differences as well as their similarities and to make claims grounded in their particular experience (Young 1990). Simplistic competition for needs-based funding, where groups are forced to manufacture their difference in oppositional terms, will make this process more difficult, not less. In the first instance, the point is to avoid practices that exacerbate opposition; as one community worker said, "It's about the departments' knowing what exists in a community, and in fact avoiding some of that conflict, or the *creation* of competition between services" (I5, 14).

Fifth, government agencies need an imaginative approach to the problem of allowing entry to new participants. Again, noticing the perspectives relayed by workers in funded organizations or by the state's own employees is a good start. In the short term, special funding or attention to some groups has to be made and it must be explained on the grounds that an inclusive and participatory public demands different treatment for some groups at some times. The example of the Elizabeth-Munno Para Social Justice Project (Peel 1995a) shows that public advocacy can generate a variety of competing demands, an improved recognition of potential conflicts, and compromises based on discussion and debate.

Sixth, government language must include positive endorsement of what these communities are, as well as what they might become. One might, for instance, hope that politicians could put aside the electoral temptations of magnifying supposed welfare fraud, dependency, and criminality. The idea that poor people need to be saved or that poor places need to be subjected to wholesale renewal must be rejected. When I talked with senior administrators in a major redevelopment project, they indicated that their most difficult strategic problem was how to "market" the suburb. They simply had no idea what might be good about the place. Yet the people of these suburbs have confronted and managed the most profound social changes of the last fifty years: an incredibly diverse immigration intake; the urban movement of Aboriginal people; the restructuring of industry and jobs; numerous experiments in social welfare, education, and urban development; a profound challenge to received gender identities; and so on.

There may be much to celebrate in their ability to handle those challenges without much overt conflict and with a good deal of inventiveness and cooperation. The last thing they need is romanticization, but there are achievements here from which the rest of Australia has benefited and from which something might be learned.

Finally, addressing these changes will mean accepting the risks of trust and of an active, dynamic, and possibly quarrelsome citizenship. In other words, there must be some investment in active citizenship as a positive good and some agreement to take it seriously because it will yield better results: "The relationship of trust is probably of paramount importance. If that never happens, then there are real problems, not least communication problems, [because] you never get to hear the real dilemmas" (B18, 13).

One might predict that the risks involved in trusting ordinary citizens will be less than those involved in trusting small-time entrepreneurs and corporate high-fliers with large amounts of public money. Certainly, investing in the future of Inala, Broadmeadows, Mount Druitt, and Elizabeth will mean investing in debates about different futures. It will mean accepting the risks of innovation, disagreement, and discord as the various groups that make up these communities speak to each other, try things out, strike out on their own, and build bridges of their own devising. Most difficult of all, perhaps, it will mean accepting not just their right to speak but their right to be heard and even to disagree.

Arguing for Citizenship

Explanations of a supposed "civic deficit" that begin from the proposition that disadvantaged people are uninterested or incapable not only miss the point but might generate counterproductive remedies. Educating people in their civic rights and responsibilities will seem incongruous when governments simultaneously undermine those same rights and responsibilities. Insisting that government listens will seem ludicrous when experience and common sense tell people that it rarely does. And urging more informed participation when participation leads nowhere may well create more apathy and more disillusionment (Irving 1995).

In all the talk of citizenship and participation, there is precious little indication that those living with disadvantage will be trusted to determine their own best future. The problem is not the apathy of disadvantaged people. Nor is it the inadequacy of what I have called the everyday meanings of social justice (Peel 1994). The problem is the failure to allow people the wisdom of their own explanations, to trust their ideas about problems and solutions, and to accept that when we listen to people who suffer injustice, our conception of justice may have to change.

Listening and trusting are the most important triggers for productive, long-term change. Certainly, they are risky, at a time when avoiding risk dominates decisions about welfare and social services. Governments have much to lose from decisions that don't work out, especially with fearless protectors of the "public interest" in the media sniffing around. In the long term, the suppression of innovation, the cultivation of frustrated compliance and dependency, and the undermining of participation in ways that exacerbate existing distrust will all prove far more costly than small amounts of fraud. But these consequences are hard to see and to sensationalize.

Arguments for trust and arguments about citizenship must therefore go beyond badgering hard-pressed government bureaucrats, demanding that they break rules they didn't invent and maybe don't like, or insisting that they manage their affairs as if this were already a perfect world. On a broader front, we need discussion and debate about how to argue for active citizenship, how to talk about social justice, and how to stress the obligations that come with sharing a society. We must, in other words, also attend to the bonds of citizenship, which are also fractured by distrust and disdain, and revive the sense of public responsibility that takes seriously the rights and needs of *unspecified* people, not just ourselves (Goodin 1985). That will mean constructing a language describing the rights and obligations of shared citizenship without endorsing the communitarian fallacy of homogeneity (Plant 1992; Young 1990) or, conversely, pretending that "difference" equates with an individual or collective right to act without regard for others. Clearly, reviving imaginative government will rely as well on reviving imaginative and empathetic citizenship. Neither can survive without the other.

Most importantly, these arguments cannot be based on a fear of the disadvantaged, because as governments come and go, the only measures their successors will retain will be the cheap, the politically safe, or the punitive. Nor, as sociologist Kevin McDonald (1995a) argues, can they be grounded in the pursuit of invulnerability and difference, or in a personal escape from disadvantage or oppression. Perhaps the crucial point to make is that, for most of us, disadvantage and disaster are only a retrenchment, an accident, or a bad decision away. This might be the place to begin speaking about social justice not as the prevention of bad judgment or bad planning nor as the elimination of differences but as making sure that their costs and implications are less drastic than they are now. We might mobilize through empathy and imagination, rather than through fear. As McDonald (1995a) suggests, a democratic citizenship "ultimately requires of our culture a capacity to name what we share and to explore [our common] vulnerability" (48).

The task, in those terms, is to revive a sense of responsibility and empathy in the abstract, a capacity to imagine injustice that builds from the stories and perspectives of those who know it best. It is to recognize that governments have a crucial role to play in asserting their responsibility and their capacity not only to take action in the interests of justice but to represent these stories and perspectives in the public realm. Advertising distrust of the disadvantaged—which includes implicit endorsement of recent media attacks on "work-shy" unemployed youth, scheming single mothers, and a supposed crisis in welfare fraud—is an irresponsible form of governance (McDonald 1995b). It undermines the willingness of other citizens to recognize their bonds with the poor and is likely to increase rather than decrease the perception that governments are incapable of doing anything about fundamental social problems.

Unfortunately, almost every message citizens now receive from cost- and debt-conscious governments is that people must now look after themselves, that self-interest is a benefit even if it becomes selfishness, that the powerful and the wealthy can be trusted but the powerless and the poor cannot, that "public" means substandard and backward, that those with everything are under no obligation to share what they don't want to give. Governments more frequently assert their incapacity than their capacity. Ultimately, then, the task is to rehabilitate our notions of governance to focus on what it is that only collective means can achieve and prevent. That is why I am arguing for trust, for investing in the initiative and strength of disadvantaged people, for listening to their voices. Telling the stories of these hundreds of people is, I hope, some way of building that sense of imaginative connection, empathy, and trust that is crucial to effective governance and to real social welfare. It means saying again and again that the poor are "us," not "them," that they are strong, resilient, and capable people, coping in a world of rocks and hard places, and that they are among the best of us, not the worst.

I wish to thank the participants in the Trust and Governance workshop for their comments on the preliminary draft. Margaret Levi, Graeme Davison, and the two reviewers of the manuscript provided written comments that were invaluable in reshaping this paper.

Notes

1. Because individual respondents have not been able in all cases to authorize the use of their words, interview transcripts are referred to by a number and an identifying letter (B = Broadmeadows, E = Elizabeth, I = Inala, and MD = Mount Druitt) and the relevant page.

2. There is a further complication; because I grew up in Elizabeth and published a book on its history during these interviews, my position in regard to my respondents was neither simple nor straightforward. People in all four suburbs, traditionally and understandably wary of outsiders and "experts," would always want to know my story. In Elizabeth, I am known and responded to as someone who shared part of this past; in the other suburbs, I think my past allowed people to bring into their speech assumptions about shared understandings of the world, shorthand expressions and narrative structures laying out "the world as it is" that I was expected to comprehend more easily. I was not an insider; even in Elizabeth, the fact that I had left for good at the age of seventeen meant that I was no longer really a local. But neither was I a real outsider. The role of memory and place and of my ambivalent status as insider/outsider is discussed in Peel 1995a.

3. The Jobs, Education, and Training (JET) scheme was jointly managed by the Department of Social Security and the Commonwealth Employment Service. It provided intensive counseling and support for sole supporting mothers and allocated each client to one worker who managed all aspects of the client's involvement in training, further education, and job placement (Evans 1993). The conservative government elected in 1996 is trying to privatize and streamline employment services, and the JET approach seems likely to disappear.

References

Cappo, D. and C. Carlisle. 1993. "Citizenship, Rights and Privileges: A Shift in Welfare Policy." *Journal of Australian Studies* 39: 1–8.

Dasgupta, Partha. 1988. "Trust as a Commodity." In *Trust: Making and Breaking Cooperative Relations*, edited by Diego Gambetta. New York: Basil Blackwell.

Evans, Patricia. 1993. "Work Incentives and Sole Mothers: Comparing Australian Policy." *Australian Journal of Social Issues* 28: 318–33.

Fraser, Nancy. 1989. *Unruly Practices: Power, Discourse and Gender in Contemporary Social Theory*. Cambridge: Polity Press.

Goodin, Robert E. 1985. *Protecting the Vulnerable: A Reanalysis of our Social Responsibilities*. Chicago: University of Chicago Press.

Hardin, Russell. 1993. "The Street-level Epistemology of Trust." *Politics and Society* 21: 505–29.

Irving, Helen. 1995. "The Virtuous Citizen." *Arena Magazine* 15: 19.

Jamrozik, Adam. 1991. *Class, Inequality and the State: Social Change, Social Policy and the New Middle Class*. Melbourne: Macmillan.

Jordan, Bill, Simon James, Helen Kay, and Marcus Redley. 1992. *Trapped in Poverty? Labour-Market Decisions in Low-Income Households*. London: Routledge.

Levi, Margaret. 1994. "Trust, Credibility and Consent." Administration, Compliance and Governability Program, Australian National University. Unpublished paper.

Lewis, Jane. 1994. "Gender, the Family and Women's Agency in the Building of 'Welfare States': The British Case." *Social History* 19: 32–55.

McDonald, Kevin. 1995a. "Leeching the Meanings of Human Experience." *Arena Magazine* 17: 44–8.

———. 1995b. "Morals is All You've Got." *Arena Magazine* 20: 18–23.

Mansbridge, Jane. 1994. "Public Spirit in Political Systems." In *Values and Public Policy*, edited by H. J. Aaron, T. E. Mann, and T. Taylor. Washington: Brookings Institution.

Naples, Nancy. 1991. "'Just What Needed to be Done': The Political Practice of Women Community Workers in Low-Income Neighbourhoods." *Gender and Society* 5: 478–94.

———. 1992. "Activist Mothering: Cross-Generational Continuity in the Community Work of Women from Low-Income Urban Neighbourhoods." *Gender and Society* 6: 441–63.

Peel, Mark. 1994. "Everyday Meanings of Social Justice." Administration, Compliance and Governability Program, Australian National University. Unpublished paper.

———. 1995a. *Good Times, Hard Times: The Past and the Future in Elizabeth.* Melbourne: Melbourne University Press.

———. 1995b. "The Public World of Women and the Private World of Men: Gender and Disadvantage." Paper presented to the Urban Planning and Urban History Conference, Australian National University, Canberra (June 26–30).

———. 1996. "Fearing Los Angeles: Australia's Postmodern Urban Nightmare." *Political Expressions* 1(2): 1–20.

Plant, R. 1992. "Citizenship, Rights and Welfare." In *The Welfare of Citizens: Developing New Social Rights*, edited by Anna Coote. London: Institute for Public Policy Research.

Salvaris, Michael. 1995. "Privatization, Citizenship and the Public Interest." *Just Policy* 4: 37–43.

Scott, James. 1985. *Weapons of the Weak: Everyday Forms of Peasant Resistance.* New Haven: Yale University Press.

Travers, Peter, and Susan Richardson. 1995. "The Elusive Quest for 'Those Most in Need.'" *Australian Journal of Social Issues* 30: 335–49.

Tyler, Tom R., and Peter Degoey. 1996. "Trust in Organizational Authorities." In *Trust in Organizational Authorities*, edited by Roderik M. Kramer and Tom Tyler. Beverly Hills: Sage.

Weatherley, Richard. 1993. "Doing the Right Thing: How Social Security Clients View Compliance." *Australian and New Zealand Journal of Sociology* 29: 21–39.

Young, Iris Marion. 1990. *Justice and the Politics of Difference.* Princeton, N.J.: Princeton University Press.

Chapter 14

Institutionalizing Distrust, Enculturating Trust

John Braithwaite

W E HAVE all experienced how distrust can sour interpersonal relationships, how heavy-handed managerialist distrust can destroy a work environment. Yet the more trust there is in the world, the greater the opportunities for its breach. Corporate crime (Shapiro 1987, 1990), abuse of state power (Finn 1993; Grabosky 1989), and the abuse of women and children in families (Widom 1989) are preeminent examples of the centrality of breach of trust to the biggest problems contemporary societies face. This chapter explores how we might structure distrust into contemporary societies to protect against violation of trust. The idea is that if we can structure distrust deeply enough into our institutions, then in day-to-day life we can be maximally nurturant of trust; in short, we would institutionalize distrust so we can enculturate trust.

While citizens have good reasons for distrusting business and government, recent scholarship has helped us better understand how trust increases the efficiency of both (Casson 1991; Fukuyama 1995; Putnam 1993). Trust is undersupplied in contemporary societies, particularly in those that suffer from the deepest problems of poverty and corruption. How then do we maximize the benefits of trust while limiting the extent to which we fall victim to it? We will not resolve this dilemma by killing interpersonal trust with distrust, since that would deprive us of the benefits of trust. Moreover, I will argue that trust is the most important resource for combating breach of trust.

The solution proposed to the dilemma is to institutionalize distrust while seeking a culture that maximizes interpersonal trust and thereby sustains a viable level of citizen trust in business and government. Institutionalizing distrust does not mean cultivating distrust of institutions; it means deploying sound principles of institutional design so that institutions check the power of other institutions. Both timidity about maximizing interpersonal trust and failure of robust institutionalization of distrust are paths to poverty, corruption, and maladministration.

A common mistake is to institutionalize distrust by making certain institutions weak because they are judged untrustworthy. When all the key institutions of a plural democracy are strong—state institutions, market institutions, and institutions of civil society—they are best able to nurture trust and exercise countervailing power against abuse of trust within other institutions.

The plan of this chapter is first to juxtapose two conceptions—trust as obligation and trust as confidence. I show that these are mutually constituting. As a result of the positive correlations among different types of trust, disaggregating them is not always analytically strategic, and in nonexperimental research, it is methodologically difficult. I then argue that trust, conceived both in the aggregate and in its various disaggregated forms, is undersupplied in contemporary societies. Finally, I discuss how interpersonal trust can be maximized while distrust is institutionalized behind the backs of actors.

Two Conceptions of Trust

Legal conceptions of trust are strangely peripheral to the social science literature. The most important of these legal conceptions is of trust as a moral obligation of power: directors as trustees of shareholders, legislatures as trustees of the people (Finn 1993). Trustworthiness is the social science conception that comes closest to this legal conception. But trustworthiness is for most social scientists a thin concept. Trustworthiness can be a mere statistical probability that the trust we place in the trustee will be honored, excluding any notion of obligation or duty, which is included in the law's thicker conception. I call the legal conception trust as obligation. I take trustworthy actors to be those who cognitively accept that they have obligations and who act to honor them.

The dominant social science conception is of trust as confidence, as opposed to trust as obligation. In its thin version, trust as confidence means little more than the expectation that someone will do what we want. In its thicker versions, trust as confidence attributes goodwill, social solidarity, even shared group identity to the trustee (see, for example, Tyler and Degoey 1996). Again, I propose that these thicker conceptions of trust as confidence are positively correlated with thin trust as confidence, because social solidarity or friendship builds bare confidence (thin trust) in others, while breach of confidence undermines friendship (thick trust). It is useful for certain analytic purposes to disaggregate trust into thicker and thinner conceptions, because thick and thin trust do perform different kinds of work in enabling social and economic systems to function. This chapter, however, is about the analytic advantages that can be secured by aggregating the competing conceptions of trust.

Trust as obligation and trust as confidence are mutually constituting. This is the claim I now flesh out. Both conceptions of trust have cognitive and behavioral counterparts. I can believe I should honor an obligation, or I can honor it behaviorally without believing it to be an obligation. I can be confident in my cognition that a person is worthy of trust, or I can act as if I trust him even though I do not believe that trust is justified. Both the cognitive and the behavioral counterparts of trust as obligation and trust as confidence are of empirical significance, as will be seen in the following exploration, under three propositions, of how one kind of trust constitutes the other.

1. *Trustees who honor their trust as obligation increase trust as confidence among their trusters.*

The City of London became a major financial center because investors could have confidence in the sense of obligation of chaps who went to the right schools and belonged to the right clubs (Clarke 1986). Its financial institutions were built by people who had been enculturated in these schools and clubs to believe in their obligations and to act on them. Conversely, in the 1980s when corporate crime scandals enveloped Australian entrepreneurs such as Alan Bond, investment confidence in Australian companies dropped for a time.

Trustworthy trustees are more likely to be trusted by trusters. An experimental psychology literature supports this hypothesis (Merluzzi and Brischetto 1985; Messick et al. 1983; Schwartz and Bless 1992), particularly studies of promise keeping in prisoner's dilemma games (Gahagan and Tedeschi 1968; Ayres, Nacci, and Tedeschi 1973; Schlenker, Helm, and Tedeschi 1973).

2. *Trusters who communicate trust as confidence in trustees will thereby increase trust as obligation among trustees.*

Toni Makkai and I found empirical support for this claim in research on nursing home regulation in Australia (Braithwaite and Makkai 1994). Nursing homes are fiduciaries for our most vulnerable, least powerful citizens. As Joel Handler once said, even prisoners can riot, but nursing home residents have neither muscle nor voice and rarely have effective power to vote with their feet by moving to another facility. In the worst cases of abuse of this trust, residents are tied up, drugged to keep them quiet, physically maltreated, and allowed to die from neglectful care. The trusteeship of nursing homes is held accountable by government inspections; Australian proprietors are required to comply with thirty-one quality-of-care standards, including standards about empowering and respecting the rights of residents.

One of the important findings from our multivariate analyses of compliance with these standards by 410 Australian nursing homes concerned trustees' believing that they are trusted. When chief executives of nursing homes believed that they were treated as trustworthy by inspectors, their nursing homes experienced a significant improvement in compliance with the law during the two years following that inspection (Braithwaite and Makkai 1994). These were chief executives who agreed with the attitude statement "[The inspectors] treated me as a person who could be trusted to do the right thing." Conversely, when chief executives agreed that "[The inspectors] treated me as someone who would only do the right thing when forced to," their compliance with the law was reduced. We found that trust as confidence increased compliance even after controlling for what we assessed to be the objective trustworthiness of nursing homes. This finding generalizes to trust as *self-confidence*. My colleague Anne Jenkins (1994) found that managers with high self-efficacy—that is, high confidence in their own ability to meet the standards—are more likely to actually meet the standards, after other influences on compliance are controlled. We concluded that trust by others and self-trust build cognitive capacity to meet fiduciary obligations to nursing home residents. The psychological theory our research team draws upon here is the social cognitive theory in Albert Bandura's *Social Foundations of Thought and Action* (1986).

3. *When trust as confidence increases among trusters, trust as obligation is increased after the trusters themselves become trustees.*

All of us participate both in roles where we trust others and in roles where we are trusted by others. Child abuse is a simple illustration of what can happen when trust as confidence is crushed. When parents abuse their trust as parents through violence against their children, those children are much more likely themselves to become violent adults (Dodge et al. 1990; Dutton and Hart 1992; Widom 1989). So a cycle of parental abuse of trust is passed from generation to generation, particularly among males. John Scholz, in chapter 6, reports compliance with tax law to be higher among upper-middle-class New Yorkers who agree that "we can trust the government." I trust therefore I pay. This is also a message in Margaret Levi's historical analysis of tax compliance and resistance in twentieth-century Australia, republican Rome, renaissance France, and elsewhere (Levi 1988). Scholz found high tax compliance not only when the government was perceived as trustworthy but also when other taxpayers were perceived as trustworthy. When citizens believe that other citizens can be trusted to pay their taxes honestly, they are more likely to be honest taxpayers themselves.[1] These findings are an obverse of the nursing home results, which show that trust *by* the state increases citizen trustworthiness; the tax results show that trust *of* the state increases citizen trustworthiness.

To summarize so far, the social science literature provides a variety of kinds of evidence that trust as confidence increases trust as obligation, and vice versa, and that the trustworthiness of trustees increases the trustworthiness of trusters, and vice versa. These findings lead in turn to a general characteristic of trust that distinguishes it from most other assets studied by social scientists: Trust is not a resource depleted through use. In fact, trust is depleted through not being used (Gambetta 1988, 224–25; Hirschman 1984, 91–92). There are important qualifications of this general claim; these arise from the fact that in an environment of low trust as obligation, while trust as confidence still increases trust as obligation, trust as confidence is more likely to be crushed when the trust as confidence is proved to be misplaced. I argue, however, that we can protect trust as confidence from sliding to a low-trust equilibrium by sensible institutionalization of distrust (as well as by nurturing trust as obligation).

The proffering of trust can transform what looks to the rational-choice theorist like a low-trust equilibrium into a high-trust equilibrium. As Valerie Braithwaite explains in chapter 3, citizens have multiple selves. In contexts where people's untrustworthy or exploitative selves are to the fore in an encounter, switching tactics are available to persuade them to switch to a trustworthy or public-regarding self. Trust as confidence is a most important switching tactic. The more it is transparent that an exploitative self dominates in a particular situation, the more trust as confidence will be seen as an act of grace. Turning the other cheek can be conceived as a switching technique for reversing a situation that is spiraling toward a low-trust equilibrium. The most fruitful research strategy on trust is to study situations with the lowest possible levels of trust—a meeting between a mugger and his victim, for example—to discover the conditions for rituals that flick the switch from tracking down to low trust to tracking up to a high-trust equilibrium. This search has been at the center of our research on nursing home regulation and conferences for criminal offenders and victims (Braithwaite and Mugford 1994).

The most important mechanism for enculturating trust is deadly simple; it is to trust others. Societies do better with an interpersonal associational order that provides venues for the proliferation of this interpersonal mechanism. This means a rich civil society. We learn to trust and be trustworthy by being trusted in families, schools, churches, community groups, sporting clubs, and institutions of civil society generally (Putnam 1993).

It follows from this perspective that trust should be seen as a virtue. Our presumption should be to trust until others give us reason not to. Institutions such as families, schools, and clubs enculturate trust by teaching our culture's stories about trust as a virtue. But more important than teaching us the story of the prodigal son, they enculturate trust simply by extending trust to us as we grow.

The Undersupply of Trust

The previous section has showed how both trust as confidence and trust as obligation can contribute to controlling the abuse of power, be that tax cheating, child abuse, traders failing to honor their word, or the neglect of vulnerable nursing home residents. A feature of most standard means of controlling abuse of power is that they reduce power and involve a cost. Auditors-general and courts tackle the abuses of bureaucrats by limiting their power; they are also an expense to taxpayers. Trust differs from such institutions because trust increases both power and wealth as it does the work of controlling abuse of power.

For example, trust increases the power of traders in markets. You will become an influential trader if you are trusted by others who give you power. London continues to be a center of financial power out of proportion to the economic and military might of its host state because of the fabric of trust of the City. Lloyd's of London might have experienced shaky times, but Lloyd's is in fact a good example of a nuanced, informal architecture of trust that could not be erected at all in Moscow or New Delhi. We should wonder less at why its foundations have been shaky at times, more at how it can work at all. It is a miraculous thing to stand on the Lloyd's trading floor and observe within a matter of minutes the reinsurance of something as risky and massive as an off-shore oil rig, efficiently transacted on the floor through a process in which people who trust the signature of fellow agents agree to share huge risks. I trust you to be a "respected lead" underwriter on oil-rigs; you trust me to be a "respected lead" on oil tankers.

Japanese corporations may have a comparative advantage in the modern world because intra-corporate and intra-keiretsu trust have deeper cultural roots than elsewhere.[2] Equally, many Third World businesses may be hindered in the acquisition of power because, although trust works well in their cultures among kin or tribal affiliates, it does not work when those affiliations are lacking (Gambetta 1988, 229; Hart 1988). Hence, Kenneth Arrow (1972, 357) contended: "It can be plausibly argued that much of the economic backwardness in the world can be explained by the lack of mutual confidence" (357)—that is, the undersupply of trust. Lord Vinson has cited as one of the ten commandments of his successful entrepreneurship; "Trust everyone unless you have a reason not to" (*The Economist*, Jan. 7, 1994, 93). Yet prior to the emergence of merchant codes of trustworthiness in eighteenth-century England, this may have been bad advice to the English entrepreneur.

John Maynard Keynes understood the importance of trust (Barbalet 1993, 235–38). In *The General Theory of Employment, Interest and Money* (Keynes 1936), he lamented the theoretical neglect of confidence, and the discipline of economics has perpetuated this neglect by ignoring this aspect of the *General Theory*. Keynes's theory of the marginal efficiency of capital turns on subjective expectation of yield, which renders confidence critical to the propensity to invest. It follows from Keynes that economic growth depends in part on a rationality based on trust rather than on certainty of calculation—"spontaneous optimism rather than on a mathematical expectation" (Keynes 1936, 161). Yet contemporary economics is about mathematical expectation, leaving the study of business confidence to journalists and political practitioners. Sociologist Jack Barbalet (1993) thinks economics must grapple with how architectures of trust generate emotions and cognitions of confidence that enable actions like investment. As we recover from the deregulatory excess of the 1980s, which was a myopia of mathematical expectation, we now see once again that prudential regulation is about prudence, that securities regulation is about security. Regulation is partly about mooring emotions like panic against the turbulent currents of the market.

Transition in Eastern Europe has also helped us see what social scientists had been blind to in the West. A tragedy of Communism was that it set out to destroy the institutions of civil society—all those institutions intermediate between the individual and the state. It is in these institutions—professions, industry associations, unions, self-regulatory organizations, business schools, churches, families—that the fabric of trust is woven (Krygier 1996). When we destroy the institutions of civil society, trust and many other forms of civility are destroyed. Once the fabric of trust unravels, a society suffers in two ways—from abuse of power and from a want of the confidence necessary for a flourishing economy.

Put more optimistically, by nurturing institutions of trust we can simultaneously contribute toward controlling the abuse of power and promoting economic growth. Trust does more than enable efficiency and investment in business; when we have a more trust-based society, we can enjoy the benefits of a more efficient public sector as well. When politicians win elections in societies where trust works, they can get on with the job of governing without distracting their energies into ensuring that the military does not reverse the election result. When judges make decisions in western Germany, litigants normally accept them; when judges make decisions in eastern Germany, the decisions tend not to be accepted, because judges are not to be trusted. As Niklas Luhmann (1979) argues, the benefits of trust progressively increase during modernity as the world becomes more complex and uncertain—a risk society, as the German sociologists say (Beck 1992).

Economist Mark Casson (1991), in a book that does not cite Keynes, has reached the same conclusion from a game theoretic analysis. Casson says that transaction costs are the largest costs in a modern economy and are increasing: "Overall economic performance depends on transaction costs, and these mainly reflect the level of trust in the economy" (1). John Wallis and Douglass North (1986) have shown empirically that transaction costs in the U.S. economy have increased from 25 percent in the late nineteenth century to 45 percent in the late twentieth century. Moreover, changes in the nature of postindustrial work and trade mean that more people are involved in endeavors that are difficult to monitor. Hence, the information asymmetry that makes trust superior to monitoring becomes progressively more profound. This information asymmetry is that people know their own plans and actions better than others do, conferring a decisive advantage for self-discipline over discipline by others.

With a broad historical sweep, Douglass North has contended that secure property rights and trust nurtured by merchant codes of behavior enabled a striking decline of interest rates in the Dutch capital market of the seventeenth century and then in the English capital market in the early eighteenth century (North 1990, 43). There is an open debate, however, over whether it was the moral force of such codes or the monitoring and use of sanctions they enabled that were the more important influence (Greif 1989). With equal sweep, Robert Putnam (1993) has shown that fabrics of trust arising from rich traditions of civic engagement characterize the regions of Italy that have flourished economically. Furthermore, the more economically backward regions, where distrust dominates, are also the regions where political corruption festers. Putnam has been able to show that the direction of historical causality operating here is not that economic success generates a trust-based culture but that a strong fabric of trust, woven in strong institutions of civil society, has economic benefits. Putnam's results are the most tantalizing empirical evidence we have that resilient trust simultaneously limits the abuse of power and expands economic growth.

Putnam's work shows how we can be both freer from want and freer from organized crime and corruption when trust is in plentiful supply. Yet, undersupply is standard, unfortunately, because we all have an interest in free riding on the efforts of others who work to build a rich civil society. Trust creates more wealth to tax and causes people to pay their taxes more honestly. Trust, for Putnam, is the most important resource for social capital—features of social organization that facilitate coordination to solve collective action problems. Putnam (1995) has also shown across thirty-five nations a strong positive correlation between "social trust" and "civic engagement" (the density of associational membership). Networks of civic engagement are where trust and norms of reciprocity and cooperation are learned and enculturated. Enculturating trust is the only technique for controlling abuse of power that not only averts a major drag on economic efficiency but actually increases efficiency. We want more trust as obligation because it both controls abuse of power and increases trust as confidence. We want more trust as confidence because it increases both efficiency and trust as obligation.

The Regulatory Pyramid

There are grave dangers in following the advice of Thomas Hobbes ([1641] 1949) and David Hume ([1875] 1963) and designing institutions that are fit for knaves, based on distrust. The trouble with institutions that assume that people or business organizations will not be virtuous is that they destroy virtue. The research discussed earlier in the chapter was illustrative: treat nursing home managements with distrust, and they do become less virtuous in discharging their care of vulnerable people.

But what about when citizens *are* knaves, or just rational calculators, rather than virtuous citizens? Trust will be abused; vulnerable victims will suffer. Like Philip Pettit in chapter 12, Ian Ayres and I have argued for the development of dynamic regulatory institutions to confront this problem (Ayres and Braithwaite 1992). By dynamic regulatory institutions, we mean institutions that try to effect change through dialogue and persuasion as a first strategy. One rationale for this approach lies in the strong body of empirical evidence that dialogue increases trust, particularly through increasing a sense of "we-ness," a preference for collective welfare over individual welfare (Messick and Brewer 1983; Dawes, McTavish, and Shaklee 1977; Orbell, van de Kragt, and Dawes 1988). When experience proves this trust to be misplaced, the strategy changes from assuming that the regulated actor is a virtuous citizen to assuming that she is a rational calculator (see also Kagan and Scholz 1984). At that point a deterrence strategy—such as the imposition of fines—might be mobilized. Often, however, the rational-actor assumption will prove just as flawed as the virtuous-citizen assumption. For example, it might be incompetence that is the cause of noncompliance (perhaps the firm's environmental engineers lack knowhow). Deterrence will not cure incompetence, but a consultancy strategy, or a transfer of technology, might. In the worst cases of incompetence, incapacitation from further lawbreaking may be required; production lines may have to be shut down, or a license to operate a nursing home may have to be revoked.

This is the basic idea of the regulatory pyramid: Trust first, and thereby get the efficiency benefits of trust in most cases, but motivate trust as obligation by signaling very clearly a preparedness to escalate intervention to progressively less trusting interventions when trust is abused. The paradox of the pyramid is that by signaling a willingness to escalate to draconian strategies of total distrust (such as corporate capital punishment for nursing homes—license revocation), one can increase the proportion of regulatory activity that is based on trust. Desire to avoid severe sanctions channels more of the regulatory game down to the base of the pyramid (see figure 14.1).

These principles apply as much to private firms regulating other private firms, or to environmental groups regulating other organizations of civil society, as they do to states regulating such actors. The regulatory pyramid is a general model of how civil and state actors can move toward a more trust-based culture because fail-safe regulatory mechanisms swing into play when trust is abused. It is a strategy that assumes the motives that underlie abuse of power are diverse— sometimes failure to understand why the law is important, sometimes calculative utility maximization, sometimes incompetence, sometimes irrational resistance to reason (as with a psychopathic murderer). The weaknesses of the trust model are covered by the strengths of the rational-actor model, the weaknesses of the rational-actor model by the strengths of the incapacitation model. But the trust model is privileged in time and through coordination of the other strategies so as to maximize channeling into trust-based problem solving.

Institutionalizing regulatory pyramids institutionalizes distrust; a culture that nurtures interpersonal trust as a virtue educates its citizens to persevere with trust at the base of the pyramid until they are given reason to escalate to deterrence or incapacitation. In other

Figure 14.1   Three Types of Actors and Three Strategies, Ordered in a
Regulatory Pyramid

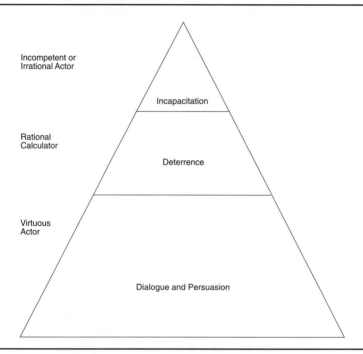

words, the pyramidal institutionalization of distrust cannot work without an enculturation of trust that persuades citizens to prefer starting at the base of the pyramid.

The Republican Architecture of Trust

Civic republicanism is one body of political theory that helps us to think more clearly about how to move toward a culture that takes trust more seriously. A clue is found in the fundamental tenet of republicanism that a parliament should not be viewed as sovereign over the people. The empirical claims made in the first part of this chapter concerning the reciprocal relationships between trust as obligation and trust as confidence undermine any hierarchical architecture of trust such as A. V. Dicey's ([1895] 1960) parliamentary sovereignty, in which a regulatory authority can be conceived as guarding citizens, a minister guarding the regulatory authority, and parliament the minister (see figure 14.2).

Figure 14.2   Formal Models of Two Conceptions of Trust

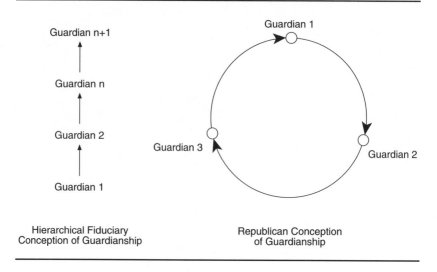

Hierarchical Fiduciary
Conception of Guardianship

Republican Conception
of Guardianship

The hierarchical conception of guardianship, represented on the left side of figure 14.2, is trapped in its own logic. Guardians such as auditors are recruited to catch abuse of trust. But what if the guardians are untrustworthy? The only answer can be another layer of guardianship above them. In the hierarchical model, the only check on abuse by an nth order guardian is an $n+1$th order guardian. But then if the $n+1$th order guardian is corrupt, the whole edifice of assurance can collapse. We see the practical manifestation of this regress with police departments that, like fish, tend to rot from the head down. Figure 14.2 shows a simple solution to the puzzle. Arrange guardians in a circle and there is no infinite regress. The logical structure is that everyone becomes a guardian of everyone else. In the most redundant guardianship design possible, all the arrows will point in both directions and arrows will also cut across the circle. The degree of redundancy needed for any given risk of abuse is a matter for contextual judgment. Each guardian can consider an enforcement pyramid such as in figure 14.1 in respect of each other actor for whom they have a guardianship obligation.

Arranging guardianship in a circle is one view of how the constitution of a republican democracy is different from that of a liberal representative democracy. The institutional embodiments of circular guardianship in business regulation, for example, are multiparty (that is, including community groups), dialogic regulatory institutions in which the actions of those in the circle are transparent and contestable from outside the circle (Ayres and Braithwaite 1992). These can be seen in some, but not most, American and Australian nursing home regulation. Government regulators sit down with representatives of nursing home management, staff, and the residents' committee in an open problem-solving dialogue that leads to negotiated solutions to regulatory problems. Threat and the politics of distrust are rarely necessary in such negotiations. Management more often than not responds in a trustworthy way to the climate of trust, because managers can see that the very process of dialogue empowers the other participants with dangerous knowledge they could use against management. Management is not confronted with a residents' committee that threatens them with litigation by an advocacy group lawyer, but even though that threat may be neither made nor thought by the residents' committee, management can look behind the trusting demeanor of the committee to see that such a capability exists; it is a structural fact of the empowerment of the residents' committee by the knowledge gained from participation in dialogic regulation and the existence of competent advocacy groups at their disposal outside. By getting the structural conditions of republican regulation right, it is possible for regulatory encounters to be based on trust, with deterrence always threatening in the background but never threatened in the foreground (Ayres and Braithwaite 1992, 49–51). Of course, such an accomplishment will always be fragile, and regulatory institutions must therefore be dynamic, responsive to their own histories of misplaced trust.

I am suggesting that there are two civic republican answers to the question of who guards the guardians: (1) communities of dialogue in which each participant is recursively accountable to every other—dialogue that, without threatening distrust, naturally exposes abuse of power to community disapproval; and (2) civic virtue nurtured by trust—trust as obligation nurtured by trust as confidence. Promising strategies can be seen in practice for empowering Aboriginal communities in the regulation of the police, residents' committees and advocacy groups in nursing home regulation, environmental groups in environmental regulation, worker representatives in occupational health and safety regulation, consumer groups in the regulation of banks, women's groups in affirmative action regulation, even the Australian Shareholders' Association in securities regulation.

Civic republicanism is about increasing the trust we place in citizenship, in the institutions of civil society. It is about defending the institutions of representative democracy, the strong democratic state, at the same time as it is about the pursuit of a richer, deeper democracy. When one argues from republican premises (see Braithwaite and Pettit 1990), one ends up with a political theory package that is distinctive in the way it takes seriously plural sources of order for underwriting freedom. Republicans cannot be sympathetic to the libertarian view that we should trust the market, that the state should be kept weak because it poses a threat to individual freedom. They walk away from socialist views that the market order should be weakened because it is exploitative or that the rule of law should be rejected because law is a tool of ruling-class interests. Republicans must be unsympathetic to the views of some liberals that associational orders (unions, industry associations, for example) should be kept weak because they threaten individualism with a range of communitarian pathologies, like oligarchy. Equally, there is no sympathy for neo-corporatist views that direct community participation in the democratic life of the nation should be discouraged in favor of democratic participation that is funneled through privileged associations such as unions.

Republicans have reason to believe in strong individuals, a strong state, strong markets, a strong associational order, strong communities, and a strong judiciary enforcing the rule of law. The ideal is of a separation of powers where each source of power is strong; it rejects the notion of weakening some in order to strengthen others. Republicans believe in strong foundational institutions that exert countervailing power, each checking abuse of power by the other. Freedom is at risk in societies where individuals are weak, where difference is crushed, where the state is too weak to control vested interests, where consumers are forced to take whatever monopolies dish up to them, where trade unions are not strong and free, where community participation is muted, or where the rule of law can be ignored by a strong state and powerful corporations.

A society that is strong on all these countervailing fronts is structurally able to be strong on enculturating trust. The foundation of an architecture of trust is the idea of separation of powers. Dynamic, responsive regulatory pyramids that nurture trust while checking power can be erected on such foundations.

Checking Strength with Strength

The paradox of the pyramid discussed in the last section is that without a strong state capable of credible deterrence and incapacitation, you cannot channel regulatory activity down to the base of the pyramid, where trust is nurtured. In the section before that, I argued that strong institutions of civil society constitute the trust that makes for economic efficiency and civility. If the theory of the regulatory pyramid is right, the trust (as obligation and confidence) enabled by a strong state and vigorous institutions of civil society is what controls abuse of trust.

Obversely, interpersonal trust is important to constituting strong institutions of civil society, a strong state, and strong markets and strong individuals as well. Trust in institutions of government or civil society is obviously conceptually different from interpersonal trust, but as with the foregoing conceptual differences among types of trust, lumping together interpersonal trust and trust in institutions is not necessarily an error, because the two are mutually constituting. One reason we trust an institution of government or civil society is that we have experienced interpersonal trust with the various agents of that institution whom we have encountered (see Philip Pettit's discussion of personal and impersonal trust in chapter 12). And interpersonal trust with those agents is constituted in part by the trust we have in the institution they represent. It is not a particularly desirable objective to maximize the trust citizens have in their institutions, but it is a desirable objective to seek a culture that nurtures interpersonal trust (while checking individual abuse of that trust with regulatory pyramids). One reason this is a desirable objective is that it will constitute a level of citizen trust in institutions that enables those institutions to secure a decent social order and to create wealth. Where interpersonal trust is localized to a limited kin or ethnic circle, interpersonal trust is prevented from building the institutional trust necessary for a rule of law to underwrite fully flourishing markets (Wong 1991). We need enough trust in institutions to secure these benefits. My hypothesis is that we can secure it by maximizing interpersonal trust. Yet we need enough distrust in institutions for the vigilance presumed in figure 14.2 to work. Whatever we do, this required level of distrust will usually exist; it is difficult to conceive of a sociologically possible world where absence of distrust is a problem. The problem is getting people to act on their distrust, the democratic challenge of channeling distrust into active citizenship.

Obviously, the reason it is undesirable to maximize citizen trust in institutions is that institutions are concentrations of power with the potential for great evil. This is why it is better to maximize interpersonal trust while institutionalizing distrust. Consider the state. Under most political theories, up to a certain point the state is viewed as a good thing. Anarchism is perhaps the only major political theory that does not allow for a relationship between the strength of the state and the public interest of the form modeled in figure 14.3. A liberal who believes in no more than a nightwatchman state will see further growth of the state as harmful (to liberty) at quite a low level of state strength. A civic republican who believes that a strong state is necessary to constitute liberty as nondomination (Pettit 1997), to combat some of the forms of domination that the liberal is happy to leave to

Figure 14.3   Political Ideals of State Strength

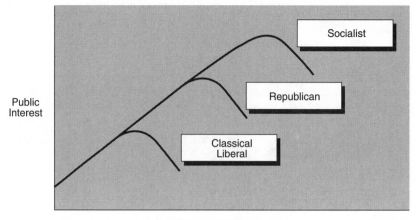

market forces, nevertheless fears the state's becoming so strong as to be totalitarian. Yet even a Stalinist, who does believe in a totalitarian state, does not want the state to take over everything, down to the feeding of children.

The "public interest" on the vertical axis of figure 14.3 that concerns a civic republican is freedom as nondomination (Pettit 1997; Braithwaite and Pettit 1990, 66–67); for the liberal it is freedom as noninterference. I have said that a way to institutionalize distrust is to check the power of one strong institution with other strong institutions. The republican dilemma is that while a stronger state risks bigger abuses of trust and has more power with which to crush freedom, a stronger state can also do more to increase freedom. The bigger the state budget, the more it can disperse to combat the unfreedom of poverty, for example. Strong states, strong markets, and strong civil society (especially strong families) are simultaneously the greatest resources we have for building freedom and the greatest threats to it. The challenge of institutional design is to realize fully their potential for building freedom while maximally controlling their potential for destroying freedom.

The republican perspective is that we can trust the state to be stronger when there is a robust separation of powers, Montesquieu's complex scaffolding of restraint (Krygier 1996, 12). A state where the judiciary is independent and the rule of law is strong can be more powerful than one where they are not; a state with strong institutions of civil society to exercise countervailing power against the state can

Figure 14.4   State Strength and Freedom

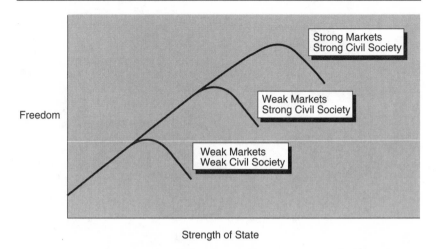

Freedom

Strong Markets
Strong Civil Society

Weak Markets
Strong Civil Society

Weak Markets
Weak Civil Society

Strength of State

be stronger than one where such institutions are weak. A state can be stronger where trust within strong families constitutes strong individuals capable of standing up to unjust authority; a state can be stronger where markets are strong enough to contest monopolies of state provision.

Eighteenth-century American republicans, particularly the anti-Federalists (Ketcham 1986, 329), were against states' having a standing army, preferring instead an armed citizenry capable of forming militias. From the perspective of Western history, this now seems a quaint and misplaced concern (given the problems an armed citizenry now poses to the United States). From another perspective, most Western democracies acquired powerful standing armies only when other institutions of democracy—most importantly the rule of law—had become strong. Consequently, few Western democracies suffered military coups. In contrast, the new nations of the twentieth century (except Costa Rica) all acquired standing armies before countervailing democratic institutions had become strong. Consequently, almost all suffered military coups (Hobsbawm 1994, 347–50). Basically, the eighteenth-century American republican argument about the separation of powers and a standing army was not quaint but right.

Figure 14.4 illustrates a simplified model in which are considered only the strength of the state, civil society, and markets. When both markets and civil society are strong, we can trust the state to do more; growth of the state can continue to increase freedom up to a higher turning point of state strength. To say this is not to deny that to the

Figure 14.5   Market Strength and Freedom

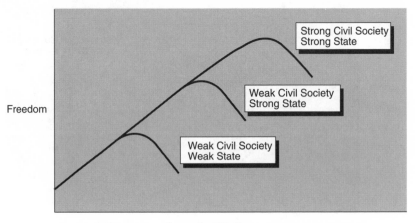

Strength of Market

left of this turning point there will be state expenditures that reduce freedom. For example, there will be some police districts that are overly oppressive because they are overstaffed. There will be some police functions that are oppressive at any level of staffing and therefore should be eliminated. If the elimination of this state function occurs to the left of the turning point of the curve in figure 14.4, freedom can be increased by devoting the resources from the elimination of one function to beefing up an underresourced function. When there are more overresourced state functions that have become a drag on freedom than there are underresourced, freedom-enhancing state functions, the society is past the turning point of figure 14.4.

This republican analysis of how we can strengthen the state is mirrored in the analyses of how we can trust strong markets and civil society. Figure 14.5 suggests that we can allow markets to rule over more domains of resource allocation when state regulatory capacities are strong. A common myth is that privatization and deregulation go together. They have not tended to do so either historically or as a matter of policy coherence (Ayres and Braithwaite 1992). When Baroness Thatcher privatized facets of health care, she had to increase state regulatory capacity in the health domain; when she privatized telecommunications, she had to set up a new telecommunications regulatory agency, and so on. Unregulated private markets for, say, nursing home care will allow the most horrific exploitation of vulnerable people. It is quite possible that allowing private competition where state monopolies of nursing home care have prevailed will increase

Figure 14.6   Strength of Civil Society and Freedom

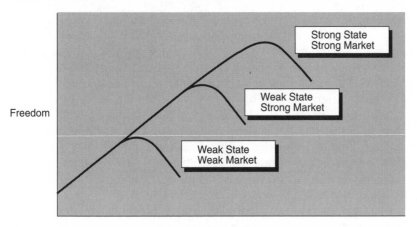

Freedom

Strong State
Strong Market

Weak State
Strong Market

Weak State
Weak Market

Strength of Civil Society

freedom for citizens by expanding their choice and giving them a means of escape when they feel the state system is oppressing them, but freedom will be increased by a private market for health care only when that market is effectively regulated by the state. Otherwise, what will be increased will be domination of the infirm by those enabled to profit from their infirmity.

Similarly, we can better trust markets to provide nursing home services when advocacy services for the aged are strong in civil society and when extended families are interested in checking the quality of institutional care their loved ones are getting and in protesting when state regulation is captured or corrupt. When civil society is strong, the jeopardy to freedom from what Jürgen Habermas (1985, 305–96) called "the colonization of the lifeworld" is checked. A danger of rampant markets is the commodification of things that better constitute freedom when they take a noncommodified form. Education and research are good examples. Art is perhaps a more controversial one, given the impetus markets have so often given to artistic innovation. Even so, it seems clear that we can be much more relaxed about market encroachments on art when elements of civil society that nourish the arts are strong. So long as local folk clubs continued to meet and play in little pubs and cafes, we did not need to worry about Peter, Paul, and Mary being in the Top 40.

Figure 14.6 shows that we can trust civil society to be strong when the state and markets are strong. A strong civil society is by no means always constitutive of freedom. Perhaps no institution does more damage to freedom than the domineering, engulfing family. As another example, consider Southern U.S. civil society in 1960.[3] While the prime countervailing power against this dominating civil society also came from civil society—from black churches and white college campuses—a strong attorney general and a strong president of the United States, who stood in the firing line, were also critically important.

We can trust families to be strong only when the state is willing to intervene in families where women and children are brutally dominated. In comparatively egalitarian capitalist societies, where family monopolies of socialization are contested by a state education system and markets for information in the media, and where job markets give women economic opportunities to escape, strong families are not quite as worrying as they are in feudal or tribal societies where markets allow no exit, no countersocialization.

Similarly, there were good reasons to worry about the threat of the church to freedom when markets were so weak and the church so strong that it could dictate who could get employment and who should be denied it on the basis of religious belief. Today, we need not fear another Inquisition, because the power of the church to punish is so much more effectively checked by the separated powers of the state.

Public interest groups are less likely to become neo-corporatist oligarchies when states require them to be run democratically and to respect human rights. Environmental groups are less likely to be captured or corrupted by the very business and state institutions against which they should be exerting countervailing power if their seats at negotiating tables with business and government are contested by competing environmental groups (Ayres and Braithwaite 1992, 54–100).

Constituting Strength with Strength, Trust with Strength

In the foregoing discussion, the institutionalization of distrust was simplified to a consideration of how a strong state, strong markets, and a strong civil society can mutually check abuse of trust. In fact, we should aspire to a much more variegated institutionalization of distrust than this—for example, one where strong international institutions check the power of the state from above, strong individuals are able to stand up to it from below, and a strong judiciary, ombudsmen, auditors, and parliamentary committees are able to check state power from within, a fourth estate of independent media from without. Most critically, as Margaret Levi points out in chapter 4, we should and will trust government more when it can be thrown out of power for breach of trust. At all these levels, the republican ideal is of strong institutions helping to constitute other institutions as both strong and autonomous—autonomous so they are able to check the very power that helped create them. Thus, the state provides salaries that guarantee tenure to judges; the judiciary thereby enjoys an autonomy that enables it to check abuse of trust by the legislature and executive. The state helps constitute markets as strong by providing legal infrastructure such as enforceable contract law and secure property rights; it prevents cartels from weakening markets by enforcing antitrust laws.

Some contemporary states do a better job than others at constituting strong markets and a robustly autonomous judiciary and rule of law. All contemporary states fail to do enough to constitute strong institutions of civil society. The realization that robust markets and stable democracy have proved hard to establish in the old communist societies because their states had crushed civil society has led in turn to the recognition that markets and democracy could be even stronger in the West if we had not only refrained from corroding civil society but actively nurtured it. As I have argued earlier in the chapter, interpersonal trust is undersupplied in contemporary societies, and strong institutions of civil society are the most important resource for constituting it.

Strength in civil society is undersupplied because we all have an interest in free riding on the contributions of others to civil society. Parents have an interest in free riding on the work of their partners in child-rearing (a temptation to which men succumb more than women). Since quality child-rearing to build strong, trusting, and trustworthy individuals is undersupplied in civil society, we all have an interest in the state's regulating business to give time off to workers with family responsibilities. When we are young, we all have an interest in free riding on the work of others to provide advocacy services for the infirm that we may rely on when we are old. We want the rainforests to be saved, but we want someone else to do the work of confronting private logging interests. We are better off when we live in a locality where civility reigns, and so we want local community organizations to flourish, but we breathe a sigh of relief at the community meeting when we are not nominated to be treasurer. Undersupplied civil society is one of the biggest collective action problems of the modern world.

The state is well placed to solve this collective action problem. It could force all of us free riders on the benefits of civil society to support chronically underfunded organizations of civil society through our taxes. Indeed, fewer of us might be free riders if tax dollars were available to replace the dreadfully inefficient work of raising money through fetes, raffles, and cake sales. Putnam's (1993) data suggest that riches of civic engagement translate not only into a richer democracy but also into monetary riches, because civic engagement constitutes the trust that lubricates the creation of wealth. Taxes to support civil society might then be self-liquidating through social capital formation.

Of course, most Western democracies already use tax dollars to support all manner of underresourced agencies in civil society and also make donations to them tax deductible. But in no Western democracy is this support so generous as to change the fact that civil society is massively underresourced. Activating civil society requires more than just resourcing it; it calls for a strategy that will solve both the chronic underresourcing and the lack of active citizen interest in civil society.

One approach to tackling both these problems would be to shift the greater part of existing state subsidies to civil society (including foreign aid), plus supplementary tax dollars, into a tax credit. Every citizen would have a tax credit of, say, $500. These dollars would have to be allocated to institutions of civil society to solve the collective action problem. But the citizen would be empowered to choose the institutions that they would like to get their dollars. In effect, citizens would be authorized to write checks up to $500 in value to support institutions of civil society of their choosing, so long as those organizations did not seek to endanger basic human rights (ideally as defined in the Constitution). Control over foreign aid would shift from the state to organizations like Community Aid Abroad. This strategy would enhance citizen interest and political interest in institutions of civil society. Suddenly, citizens would be empowered to vote taxpayers' funds to organizations of their choosing. These organizations would then have to lobby for this new kind of citizen support. In the Australian context, one might envisage umbrella organizations like the Australian Council of Social Services producing slates of recommended allocations of the tax credit to ensure that no important social service organizations were denied satisfactory support. Other umbrella bodies would produce competing slates, and this process might generate lively debates on the values and effectiveness of different organizations. Umbrella bodies would also solicit some tax dollars for investment funds, so that interest could be used to smooth uneven flows of money to organizations overlooked in the uncoordinated allocations of tax credits.[4]

Consider the problem—described by Mark Peel in chapter 13—of local community organizations hamstrung and demoralized by the distrust in which they are held by the state. Why not abolish all the extraordinary accountability mechanisms imposed on local community and Aboriginal groups (retaining universal mechanisms such as the criminal law of fraud) and trust the allocations of local citizens from their tax credits? There might be a case for assuring a fixed proportion of the tax credit for neighborhood organizations, with the amount of the tax credit being higher for people who live in poorer areas.[5] The accountability mechanism would then be that citizens who did not like the service provided by a community organization would not allocate them any tax money the following year.

Thinking Contextually About Institutionalizing Distrust

Contrary to the prescriptions in this chapter, as parents we need to be active in persuading our children to distrust strangers who offer them lifts in cars. Fortunately, however, the exceptions where we need to teach our children to distrust in potentially dangerous encounters are not large in number. Through consumer education to foil con-artists and personal safety education to foil sexual predators, we can teach the need for contextual distrust while preserving a predisposition to trust (unless given special reason not to).

Theories of institutional design are useful as metaphors that supply competing ways of imagining changes in direction for social policy. They are rarely useful in supplying eternally true sets of propositions. The world changes too quickly for that, and science too slowly. Sound thinking about democratic governance is therefore contextual. It involves acquiring a nuanced understanding of policy possibilities through imagining the policy problem as many things at once, applying multiple metaphors supplied by different theories of institutional design.

Is the theory in this chapter useful to such an enterprise? My colleagues and I have found it so. In fact, the theory has largely been generated inductively from our work with governments and institutions of civil society on problems such as the design of criminal justice institutions (Braithwaite and Pettit 1990; Braithwaite 1995a, Braithwaite 1995b; Fisse and Braithwaite 1993); ensuring that workplaces are safe and healthy (Braithwaite and Grabosky 1985; Braithwaite, Grabosky, and Fisse 1986; Ayres and Braithwaite 1992); competition policy ("trust-busting"!) (Ayres and Braithwaite 1992); and in a review of all Australia's laws and administrative practices affecting business costs (Office of Regulation Review 1995). Consultancy work for the Australian government since 1987, when it took over responsibility from state governments for improving the quality of nursing home care, has provided the most sustained opportunity for testing the usefulness of these metaphors on new terrain (Braithwaite et al. 1993).

These studies have led us to doubt state monopolies of service provision and to confirm this doubt when we found that some of the new frontiers in quality of care were being pushed forward in private-sector provision for the rich (Braithwaite et al. 1990, 131–34). We also found empirically that the general quality of for-profit provision was lower than that of nonprofit, nongovernment providers such as churches (Jenkins and Braithwaite 1993). While a strong private sector increases choice and innovation, it also increases the need for well-resourced government regulation. This intensive regulation seems to have worked in the Australian context (Braithwaite et al. 1993).

A strong state can do more than guarantee the availability of an essential service like nursing home care to all who need it, constitute a plural (private-charitable-state) market for that provision, and regulate its quality. The state can also promote the competitiveness of the market by improving the information available to consumers on the quality of nursing home care in different facilities. One way to do so is to require that state assessments of the quality of nursing home care be posted on notice boards at the entrance to facilities or in some other prominent place. These can then be published in magazines like *Choice* (the Australian equivalent to *Consumer Reports*). In Australia, the state has also played a central part in funding aged-care advocacy organizations, which in turn have had an important role in preventing the state from being captured by the industry in specific regulatory encounters. In this particular domain, therefore, the metaphor of a strong market, a strong state, and strong civil society that mutually constitute institutional autonomy and strength has proved useful in the intricate work of imagining how to weave a policy fabric. Designing regulatory pyramids that institutionalize distrust in a way that nurtures interpersonal trust between inspectors and nursing home management also seems to work. A relatively trusting nursing home regulatory culture has been accomplished in Australia, if not in the United States (Braithwaite 1994), and where this trust is greatest, quality of care improves most (Braithwaite and Makkai 1994). Yet the very idea of a dynamic regulatory pyramid is that there is no enduring truth about what works. What works depends on histories of the success and failure of past strategies, histories that define the credibility of future ones. There is no escape from continually rethinking the contextual relevance of policy metaphors like institutionalizing distrust.

Conclusions

A widespread mistake in political theory is to assume a hydraulic relationship between the strengths of different institutions. When one is increased in strength, another decreases at its expense. Of course, it is sometimes empirically true that such hydraulic relationships exist. Quite frequently in history strong states have destroyed the vitality of markets or civil society (Gellner 1988), as under communism and fascism. But an objective of normative political theory should be to discover a political program by which the virtues of one institution can nurture the virtues of other institutions while also controlling their vices. It is simple-minded of communitarians to argue for "shifting the balance" from an emphasis on individual rights to communal responsibility (see, for example, Fukuyama 1995). There is no inconsistency in advancing a political program that is both strong on individual rights and strong on community responsibilities (Sunstein 1995; Engel and Munger 1996). Equally, some feminists are mistaken when they assume that community necessarily destroys difference in the pursuit of a community consensus (which may be a male consensus).[6] There is no incoherence in a political program that simultaneously seeks to be strong on community and strong on difference. The first-wave women's movement slogan of "unity within diversity" is testimony to the political wisdom of this second position,[7] as is the partially successful policy of a multicultural yet unified Australia. Feminists who want to weaken families for fear of family violence make the same mistake as libertarians who want to weaken trade unions, women's groups, and environmental groups because they see them as a threat to a free market. It is the mistake of weakening institutions that build freedom in some respects because in other respects they threaten it.

The challenge is to institutionalize distrust in these institutions so that their various pathologies can be checked by the strength of other institutions. To the extent that these other institutions are strong, their countervailing power to check abuse of trust by the institution of concern will be enhanced. To the extent that the institution of concern is trusted to be strong, it will be able to help constitute strength in the countervailing institutions and to deliver on its own potential for enhancing human freedom.

Similarly with interpersonal trust. Fear of abuse of trust can counsel caution about building a trusting culture. This is not wise counsel. Trust is the most powerful weapon we have for fighting abuse of trust. If our institutional designs arrange guardians in republican rather than hierarchical relationships (figure 14.2), then breach of trust at one point in the circle can be healed by the strength of trust around the rest of the circle. By seeking to maximize interpersonal trust within circles of accountability, we maximize capacities to reform a circle that has been broken by a breach of trust. When circles of accountability overlap, so that guardians guard more than one circle, the strength of weak ties also enhances detection and control of breach of trust (Granovetter 1973). While hierarchical conceptions of guardianship heighten risks that our institutions will rot from the head down, republican conceptions of guardianship heighten prospects that rotting institutions will heal from the healthy tissue that surrounds them. This healthy tissue is networked circles of guardianship.

The conclusion is to nurture a trusting culture that may, just as in Putnam's (1993) empirical findings about the regions of Italy, leave us wealthier, less infested with corruption, and more ennobled by civility and enriched in our democracy. In this nurturance, thicker trust as obligation/friendship and thinner trust as bare confidence are both desirable, because they help constitute each other and because they do different kinds of valuable work. Thicker trust holds families together in ways that forge strong, independent individuals; lack of it disintegrates them, inducing untrusting, coercive child-rearing that produces weak, dominated individuals. Thinner trust holds markets together and enables the civility of a street life where minor incidents do not escalate to violence.

It is behind the backs of circles of interpersonal civility that we should want to institutionalize distrust. As Melancton Smith said in debating the U.S. Constitution in 1788, "Checks in government ought to act silently, and without public commotion" (Ketcham 1986, 353). Giving local citizens tax credits to bestow on or withdraw from neighborhood organizations may be a better way of institutionalizing distrust than central bureaucratic oversight; yet it seems not to be an institutionalization of distrust because its outward appearance, indeed part of its reality, is of trust in local people.

Charles Sabel (1986, 137) was led to the same basic insight when he confronted as "the central dilemma" of economic growth "reconciling the demands of learning with the demands of monitoring." The dilemma is that economic actors need to trust each other to learn by sharing know-how, while they must distrust each other by monitoring that the gains from the shared know-how are also shared in the agreed way. In Sabel's view, economic success flows from the design of discursive institutions that make discussion of know-how inextricable from discussion of apportioning gains or losses. Mutual dependence can resolve the paralyzing fear of deceit by allowing both scrutiny and learning to be natural consequences of a joint enterprise. A fusion of identities (for example, in families) means that untrustworthiness by one member causes other members to share the shame of the breach of trust while all share the joy of others' learning. Both learning and monitoring are products of discursive problem solving and partial fusing of identities in joint ventures (see also Powell 1996).

When we put twelve citizens on a jury instead of one, through numbers we institutionalize distrust that some jurors are corruptible. But this institutionalization of distrust is quite impersonal, routinized, normal, and therefore in no way insulting to the jurors, just as double-entry bookkeeping is not insulting to treasurers. Centuries ago wise designers of the jury institutionalized distrust in a way that is quite behind the backs of contemporary jurors. Similarly, the republican designers of the separation of powers in the U.S. Constitution were quite explicit in the *Federalist Papers* that their enterprise was about institutionalizing distrust (Madison, Hamilton, and Jay [1788] 1987). It is at this level of the design of institutions where we must structure distrust into society. Because such distrust is in the background rather than the foreground of here-and-now disputes, it is unlikely to undermine the cultivation of interpersonal trust. These arguments can be summarized as thirteen propositions.

Propositional Summary

1. Distrust is best institutionalized behind the backs of actors; trust is best consciously nurtured through interpersonal action.

2. Institutionalizing distrust makes it easier to trust others interpersonally.

3. The most important mechanism for enculturating trust is to trust others; trust as obligation and trust as confidence are mutually constituting.

4. A central strategy for institutionalizing distrust as we enculturate trust is to privilege trust temporally ahead of distrust in dynamic regulatory strategies. In standard regulatory encounters, trust is therefore foregrounded, distrust backgrounded.

5. Institutional designs that organize distrust hierarchically destroy trust; circular, recursive institutionalization of distrust is more robust and more able to background distrust while trust is foregrounded.

6. Enculturating trust is the means of controlling abuses of power such as violence, environmental destruction, and political corruption, with an economic benefit rather than a cost.

7. The crucial challenge of institutional design is to discover how to encourage a strong economy, a strong state, and strong civil society to be mutually constituting yet autonomous (the separation of powers). Trust is a crucial cultural resource for all three to be strong.

8. When civil society and markets are strong, we can trust a stronger state to do more to increase our freedom.

9. When civil society and the state are strong, we can trust stronger markets to do more to increase our freedom.

10. When the state and the market are strong, we can trust civil society to do more to increase our freedom.

11. Civil society is the most crucial arena for the constitution of trust as confidence and trust as obligation, for social capital formation. Trust is encultured in civil society through the educative stories of families and schools on the virtues of trustworthiness, through the actual granting of more trust to children as they grow, and through nurturing pride in virtue by honoring trust as obligation.

12. While there are plenty of actors with an interest in the growth of strong markets and strong governments, we all have an interest in free riding on the virtue of those who build a strong civil society. Governments therefore need to be strong enough to impose special measures such as tax credits to deliver a level of social capital formation that makes civil society and the economy as strong as they can be.

13. Civil society is also the arena with the most scope for creative improvement in the institutionalization of distrust—women's, Aboriginal, youth, and gay groups to check the power of the police or of markets; environmental, consumer, shareholder, and civil liberties groups to check the power of business and its state regulators; and so on. Within state institutions and the institutions of business as well, contextual creativity is needed to construct variegated separations of powers. Private and public sector ombudsmen and auditors, independent arbitrators and judiciaries, professional societies, a free press, and international institutions can all be important to nuanced institutionalization of distrust.

Thanks to Andrew Brien, Ann Daniel, Nathan Harris, Susanne Karstedt, Martin Krygier, Kathy Laster, Ian Marsh, Brenda Morrison, Christine Parker, Marian Sawer, David Soskice, Tonia Vincent, and participants at the two ANU/Russell Sage Workshops and the Academy of Social Sciences in Australia Conference on Trust for helpful comments on a draft of this chapter.

Notes

1. These findings are consistent with experimental psychological studies that have found that trust as confidence in other players increases the trustworthiness of players in modified prisoners' dilemma games (see, for example, Loomis 1959). Thomas Wright and Afshan Kirmani (1977) found that female but not male students who were low trusters on the Rotter Interpersonal Trust scale were more likely to shoplift.

2. This is not to say that these cultural roots constitute a generalized cognitive bias to trust. Rather, as Toshio Yamagishi and Midori Yamagishi (1994) suggest, Japan enculturates committed relationships that deliver "assurance," a perception of an incentive structure that leads to cooperative interaction.

3. I am indebted to Philip Pettit for this example.

4. Residual state funding could also be used to remedy the effects of the reduced coordination from a tax-credit regime.

5. I am indebted to Leanne Steadman for this thought.

6. For an interesting discussion of this question, see Young 1995.

7. This was the motto of the General Federation of Women's Clubs in the United States.

References

Arrow, K. J. 1972. "Gifts and Exchanges." *Philosophy and Public Affairs* 1(4): 343–62.

Ayres, I., and J. Braithwaite. 1992. *Responsive Regulation: Transcending the Deregulation Debate.* Oxford: Oxford University Press.

Ayres, L., P. Nacci, and J. Tedeschi. 1973. "Attraction and Reactions to Noncontingent Promises." *Bulletin of the Psychonomic Society* 1: 75–77.

Bandura, Albert. 1986. *Social Foundations of Thought and Action: A Social Cognitive Theory.* Englewood Cliffs, N. J.: Prentice-Hall.

Barbalet, J. M. 1993. "Confidence: Time and Emotion in the Sociology of Action." *Journal for the Theory of Social Behaviour* 23(3): 229–47.

Beck, U. 1992. *Risk Society: Towards a New Modernity.* Newbury Park: Sage.

Braithwaite, John. 1994. "The Nursing Home Industry." In *Beyond the Law: Crime in Complex Organizations,* edited by M. Tonry and A. J. Reiss, *Crime and Justice: A Review of Research* 18: 11–54.

———. 1995a. "Corporate Crime and Republican Criminological Praxis." In *Corporate Crime: Contemporary Debates,* edited by Frank Pearce and Laureen Snider. Toronto: University of Toronto Press.

———. 1995b. "Inequality and Republican Criminology." In *Crime and Inequality,* edited by John Hagan and Ruth D. Peterson. Stanford: Stanford University Press.

Braithwaite, John, and Peter Grabosky. 1985. *Occupational Health and Safety Enforcement in Australia*. Canberra: Australian Institute of Criminology.

Braithwaite, John, Peter Grabosky, and Brent Fisse. 1986. "Occupational Health and Safety Guidelines." *Report to the Victorian Department of Labour*, Melbourne.

Braithwaite, J., and T. Makkai. 1994. "Trust and Compliance." *Policing and Society* 4: 1–12.

Braithwaite, J., T. Makkai, V. Braithwaite and D. Gibson. 1993. *Raising the Standard: Resident Centred Nursing Home Regulation in Australia*. Canberra: Australian Government Publishing Service.

Braithwaite, J., T. Makkai, V. Braithwaite, D. Gibson, and D. Ermann. 1990. *The Contribution of the Standards Monitoring Process to the Quality of Nursing Home Life: A Preliminary Report*. Canberra: Department of Community Services and Health.

Braithwaite, John, and Stephen Mugford. 1994. "Conditions of Successful Reintegration Ceremonies: Dealing with Juvenile Offenders." *British Journal of Criminology* 34: 139–71.

Braithwaite, J., and P. Pettit. 1990. *Not Just Deserts: A Republican Theory of Criminal Justice*. Oxford: Oxford University Press.

Casson, Mark. 1991. *The Economics of Business Culture*. Oxford: Clarendon Press.

Clarke, Michael. 1986. *Regulating the City: Competition, Scandal and Reform*. Milton Keynes, England: Open University Press.

Dawes, Robyn M., Jeanne McTavish, and Harriet Shaklee. 1977. "Behavior, Communication and Assumption About Other People's Behavior in a Common Dilemma Situation." *Journal of Personality and Social Psychology* 35(1): 1–11.

Dicey, A. V. [1895] 1960. *Introduction to the Study of the Law of the Constitution*. London: Macmillan.

Dodge, Kenneth A., John E. Bates, P. Pettit, and S. Gregory. 1990. "Mechanisms in the Cycle of Violence." *Science* 250(4988): 1678–1685.

Dutton, Donald G., and Stephen D. Hart. 1992. "Evidence for Long-Term, Specific Effects of Childhood Abuse and Neglect on Criminal Behavior in Men." *International Journal of Offender Therapy and Comparative Criminology* 36: 129–37.

Engel, David M., and Frank M. Munger. 1996. "Rights, Remembrance and the Reconciliation of Difference." *Law and Society Review* 30: 7–54.

Finn, Paul. 1993. "Making Our Governors Our Servants." Cunningham Lecture. Canberra: Academy of Social Sciences in Australia.

Fisse, Brent, and John Braithwaite. 1993. *Corporations, Crime and Accountability*. Cambridge: Cambridge University Press.

Fukuyama, Francis. 1995. *Trust: The Social Virtues and the Creation of Prosperity*. New York: Free Press.

Gahagan, J. P., and J. T. Tedeschi. 1968. "Strategy and the Credibility of Promises in the Prisoner's Dilemma Game." *Journal of Conflict Resolution* 12: 224–34.

Gambetta, Diego. 1988. "Can We Trust?" In *Trust: Making and Breaking Cooperative Relations*, edited by D. Gambetta. Oxford: Blackwell.

Gellner, Ernest. 1988. "Trust, Cohesion and the Social Order." In *Trust: Making and Breaking Cooperative Relations*, edited by D. Gambetta. Oxford: Blackwell.

Grabosky, Peter. 1989. *Wayward Governance: Illegality and its Control in the Public Sector*. Canberra: Australian Institute of Criminology.

Granovetter, Mark S. 1973. "The Strength of Weak Ties." *American Journal of Sociology* 78: 1360–80.

Greif, Avner. 1989. "Reputation and Coalitions in Medieval Trade: Evidence on the Maghribi Traders." *Journal of Economic History* 49(4): 857–82.

Habermas, Jürgen. 1985. *The Theory of Communicative Action, Vol 2: Lifeworld and System* (trans. T. McCarthy). Boston: Beacon Press.

Hart, K. 1988. "Kinship, Contract and Trust: The Economic Organization of Migrants in an African City Slum." In *Trust: The Making and Breaking of Cooperative Relations*, edited by D. Gambetta. Oxford: Blackwell.

Hirschman, Albert O. 1984. "Against Parsimony: Three Easy Ways of Complicating Some Categories of Economic Discourse." *American Economic Review* 74(2): 89–96.

Hobbes, Thomas. [1641] 1949. *De Cive*. New York: Appleton-Century-Crofts.

Hobsbawm, Eric. 1994. *The Age of Extremes: The Short Twentieth Century, 1914–1991*. London: Michael Joseph.

Hume, David. [1875] 1963. *Of the Independency of Parliament. Essays, Moral, Political and Literary*, vol.1. London: Oxford University Press.

Jenkins, A. L. 1994. "The Role of Managerial Self-Efficacy in Corporate Compliance." *Law and Human Behaviour* 18(1): 71–88.

Jenkins, Anne, and John Braithwaite. 1993. "Profits, Pressure and Lawbreaking." *Crime, Law and Social Change* 20: 221–32.

Kagan, Robert A., and John T. Scholz. 1984. "The Criminology of the Corporation and Regulatory Enforcement Strategies." In *Enforcing Regulation*, edited by K. Hawkins and J. Thomas. Boston: Kluwer-Nijhoff.

Ketcham, Ralph, ed. 1986. *The Anti-Federalist Papers and the Constitutional Convention Debates*. New York: Mentor Books.

Keynes, J. M. [1936] 1981. *The General Theory of Employment, Interest and Money*. London: Macmillan.

Krygier, Martin. 1996. "Virtuous Circles: Antipodean Reflections on Power, Institutions and Civil Society." Collegium Budapest Discussion Paper Series. Budapest: Collegium Budapest.

Levi, M. 1988. *Of Rule and Revenue*. Berkeley: University of California Press.

Loomis, James L. 1959. "Communication and the Development of Trust and Cooperative Behavior." *Human Relations* 12: 305–15.

Luhmann, Niklas. 1979. *Trust and Power*. Chichester: Wiley.

Madison, James, Alexander Hamilton, and John Jay. [1788] 1987. *The Federalist Papers* , edited by I. Kramnick. New York: Penguin.

Merluzzi, T. V., and C. S. Brischetto. 1985. "Breach of Confidentiality and Perceived Trustworthiness of Counsellors." *Journal of Counselling Psychology* 30(2): 245–51.

Messick, David M., and Marilyn B. Brewer. 1983 "Solving Social Dilemmas: A Review." In *Review of Personality and Social Psychology*, edited by L. Wheeler and P. Shaver. Beverly Hills: Sage.

Messick, D. M., H. Wilke, M. B. Brewer, R. M. Kramer, P. E. Zemke, and L. Lui. 1983. "Individual Adoptions and Structural Change as Solutions to Social Dilemmas." *Journal of Personality and Social Psychology* 44: 294–309.

North, Douglass. 1990. *Institutional Change and Economic Performance*. Cambridge: Cambridge University Press.

Office of Regulation Review. 1995. *A Guide to Regulation Impact Statements*. Canberra: Office of Regulation Review.

Orbell, John M., Alphonso J. C. van de Kragt, and Robyn M. Dawes. 1988. "Explaining Discussion-Induced Cooperation." *Journal of Personality and Social Psychology*, 54(5): 811–19.

Pettit, Philip. 1997. *Republicanism: A Theory of Freedom and Government*. Oxford: Oxford University Press.

Powell, Walter. 1996. "Trust-Based Forms of Governance." In *Trust in Organizations: Frontiers of Theory and Research*, edited by R. M. Kramer and T. R. Tyler. Beverly Hills: Sage.

Putnam, Robert D. 1993. *Making Democracy Work: Civic Traditions in Modern Italy*. Princeton, N. J.: Princeton University Press.

———. 1995. "Bowling Alone: America's Declining Social Capital," *Journal of Democracy* 6: 65–78.

Sabel, Charles. 1986. "Learning by Monitoring: The Institutions of Economic Development." In *The Handbook of Economic Sociology*, edited by Neil J. Smelser and Richard Swedburg. Princeton, N. J.: Princeton University Press

Schlenker, B., B. Helm, and J. Tedeschi. 1973. "The Effects of Personality and Situational Variables on Behavioural Trust." *Journal of Personality and Social Psychology* 25(3): 419–27.

Schwartz, N., and H. Bless. 1992. "Scandals and the Public's Trust in Politicians: Assimilation and Contrast Effects." *Personality and Social Psychology Bulletin* 18(5): 574–79.

Shapiro, Susan. 1987. "The Social Control of Impersonal Trust." *American Journal of Sociology* 93: 623–58.

———. 1990. "Collaring the Crime, Not the Criminal: Reconsidering the Concept of White-Collar Crime." *American Sociological Review* 55: 346–65.

Sunstein, Cass R. 1995. "Rights and Their Critics." *Notre Dame Law Review* 70(4): 727–68.

Tyler, Tom, and Peter Degoey. 1996. "Trust in Organizational Authorities: The Influence of Motive Attributions on Willingness to Accept Decisions." In *Trust in Organizational Authorities*, edited by R. Kramer and T. Tyler. Beverly Hills: Sage.

Wallis, John J., and Douglass C. North. 1986. "Measuring the Transaction Sector in the American Economy, 1870–1970." In *Long-term Factors in American Economic Growth*, edited by S. L. Engerman and R. E. Gallman. Chicago: University of Chicago Press.

Widom, Cathy Spatz. 1989. "Child Abuse, Neglect, and Violent Criminal Behavior." *Criminology* 27: 251–71.

Wong, Sui-lun. 1991. "Chinese Entrepreneurs and Business Trust." In *Business Networks and Economic Development in East and Southeast Asia*, edited by G. Hamilton. Hong Kong: Centre of Asian Studies, University of Hong Kong.

Wright, Thomas L., and Afshan Kirmani. 1977. "Interpersonal Trust, Trustworthiness and Shoplifting in High School." *Psychological Reports* 41: 1165–66.

Yamagishi, Toshio, and Midori Yamagishi. 1994. "Trust and Commitment in the United States and Japan." *Motivation and Emotion* 18(2): 129–65.

Young, Iris. 1995. "Communication and the Other: Beyond Deliberative Democracy." In *Justice and Identity: Antipodean Practices*, edited by Margaret Wilson and Anna Yeatman. Wellington: Bridget Williams.

Conclusion

Valerie Braithwaite and Margaret Levi

W HEN AND how trust affects actions of citizens and government officials depends on the assumptions that are made about motives, cognitions, and emotions. This volume represents a variety of perspectives on trust, ranging from trust that is rationally grounded to trust that springs from shared identity and emotional connectedness.

In the more rationalist approach, individuals are assumed to be rational, and trust is a form of encapsulated self-interest. For these theorists, trust is responsive to data, to beliefs about the trusted, and to likely outcomes from the trusting relationship. Its sources include familiarity, reliable information, generalizations based on experience with similar actors, on-going interactions, and confidence in the constraints provided by institutions. Russell Hardin, Margaret Levi, Martin Daunton, Susan Whiting, Kent Jennings, and William Bianco all emphasize trust as a phenomenon of this sort. Although these authors differ in the weightings they attach to various kinds of beliefs, norms, and knowledge, they share the view that citizens and government officials will trust each other when there are benefits to each in doing so.

Others in the volume—Simon Blackburn, Valerie Braithwaite, Geoffrey Brennan, Philip Pettit, Tom Tyler, Mark Peel, and John Braithwaite—define trusting and trustworthiness as desirable qualities that may enter into rational calculations but that acquire value outside self-interested discourse. Trusting and trustworthiness are virtues, moral standards, or gifts given and received. Giving, honoring, and betraying trust are linked not only with cognition but also with the emotions of pride, shame, guilt, and anger. Such emotions can disrupt rational calculations. They are not simply additive terms in a subjective utility model; they are moderating factors, framing the selection of relevant information and affecting the form that the subjective utility model will take.

In spite of differing understandings of human motivation, the contributors agree that the effects of the act of trust are normatively ambiguous. Trust may be good when it leads to socially productive cooperation, but it can equally lead to exploitation of the trusting by the trusted, confirm a person's sense of inability to make good judgments, or produce support for unjust or morally retrograde rulers. We approve when government facilitates the social trust that enables residents to walk their neighborhoods without fear of attack from their neighbors. We tremble when trust among one group of neighbors leads them to act collectively but illiberally and violently against others who reside in their community.

For all the contributors, these two faces of trust pose an institutional design challenge: how to attain the social advantages of trust while avoiding its undesirable effects. The authors nonetheless diverge in their perceptions of the importance of trust to good governance.

Among the rationalists, Hardin is the most skeptical about how essential trust is to the maintenance and performance of government. He argues forcefully that trust is most likely among individuals who have considerable information about each other or about the effectiveness of institutional constraints, information that is unattainable about distant officials. Others offer a somewhat broader definition of the informational requirements of trust and argue that trust is crucial to good governance. It may ease coordination by citizens with each other and with government actors, reduce transaction costs, increase the probability of citizen compliance with government demands, and contribute to political support of the government. Whiting uses Hardin's notion of encapsulated self-interest to show how local Chinese officials can win the trust of private investors and bring economic prosperity to their region. Levi and Daunton develop dynamic models of trust; government builds trust by making credible commitments and showing good faith with the citizenry, and citizens reciprocate by demonstrating willingness to contribute to public goods and comply with law.

Maintaining trust requires work on the part of government officials, and failure to meet performance standards brings an erosion of trust, as Jennings illustrates with survey data tracking loss of confidence in the U.S. government over a thirty-year period. The process of building and retaining trust, however, may not be as labor intensive as the discussion so far implies. Scholz points out how individuals compensate for poor information with a trust heuristic, which fluctuates with the perception of the favorability of tax law, the pervasiveness of a sense of civic duty, and the estimate of the compliance of others. Bianco argues that citizens can reduce their calculation costs by relying on stereotypes of officials as those who share common interests with constituents and those who do not. A belief in common interest becomes the heuristic for trust.

In the second conception of trust, individuals are motivated to give and honor trust without deliberation over outcomes. Trust is socially valued as a symbol of social-emotional connectedness. The argument of these contributors is that trustworthiness is generated through the communication to the other that one is trusted. Trust is responsive to the attribution of trustworthiness. For Blackburn and Brennan, the relationship between trusting and trustworthiness is direct. For Pettit, it may be direct for those who are virtuous, or it can be mediated by the desire for esteem and glory, the desire to be thought trustworthy. Tyler posits a more complex explanation of this form of trust. A trust relationship between government and citizens creates a shared social identity that gives citizens both respect and pride in their group. The rewards gleaned through membership in the group lead citizens to defer to the authority of government, even when it acts in ways that are counter to the self-interest of individuals.

Trust of both kinds appears to exist and to have legitimacy among the citizenry. Jennings describes these basic types as performance and linkage trust and notes consistency of usage among American voters over a long period of time. Valerie Braithwaite identifies similar standards in Australia but defines them as exchange and communal trust norms, based on the enduring societal values of security and harmony. Both Jennings and Braithwaite produce data to show that different types of trust relationships exist between citizens and government in different contexts.

By and large, the papers in this volume suggest that rational and communal trust offer comparable benefits—that is, reduced transaction costs, the control of abuse of power, support for government, and compliance. Communal trust theorists, however, especially Tyler, John Braithwaite, Peel, and Valerie Braithwaite, argue for an additional benefit. Trust that entails social-emotional ties creates a collective identity, engages citizens in the community, facilitates cooperation, and engenders a willingness to forgo self-interest.

This particular benefit is a double-edged sword that communal theorists carry and rationalists avoid. Rational trust entails continuous collection and assessment of data to justify trusting. The risks of trust are a function of poor information collection, inappropriate generalization, or the transmission of misinformation. Communal trust involves a willingness to allow oneself to believe, regardless of the performance information one has. Bearers of communal trust are particularly vulnerable to those who seek advantage through breaching trust.

What kinds of institutions can be set in place to protect against these vulnerabilities? Levi, Bianco, and Brennan see the institutions of democracy as vital to the enterprise of ensuring the trustworthiness of elected representatives. Making credible commitments by setting performance goals, facilitating transparency, and ensuring accountability to the citizenry have been shown effective by both Levi and Daunton. Whiting demonstrates how certain kinds of markets secured trust between Chinese government officials and private investors, in spite of a legal-political framework that might have concealed common interest.

But do the institutions that support rational trust also support communal trust, or can one undermine the other? Peel raises concerns about imposing performance standards and accountability mechanisms on a community that is suspicious of government. In this case, rational trust offered by the in-group to the out-group magnifies divisions between community and government. Tyler's work suggests that when groups see themselves as in-groups and out-groups, communal trust is likely to be in short supply, leaving rational trust as the most viable means of doing business.

How to turn a culture where rational trust dominates into one that fosters communal trust is the question that drives the empirical work reported by John Braithwaite. He advocates trusting as a moral imperative, fully recognizing the implications for risk that this course of action brings. His response is an elaborate institutional infrastructure to come down hard on those who take advantage of the gift of trust they have been offered. His regulatory pyramid and circles of guardianship are designed not only to detect abuse of trust but also to punish, with sanctions escalating in severity for those who act with persistent disregard for cooperation in the trust game.

Similarly, Pettit and Brennan rely on heavy institutional artillery to reinforce the value of trustworthiness in the community. Communal trust relies on the normative properties trust has acquired through the socialization process. As such, it may be a fragile commodity. Thus, Pettit argues for institutionalized impersonal trust in society, where vigilance and performance requirements are knit into the fabric of daily life. Against this fabric, an individual can distinguish herself by being singled out as a trustworthy person and, in turn, behaving in a trustworthy fashion. Brennan presents a case for rewarding trustworthiness. Those who have demonstrated their trustworthiness should be recognized by being elevated to positions of trust in society. He also raises the concern that trusting and trustworthiness will lose their currency as symbols of virtue if institutions are too directive in channeling performance in certain directions. Institutions that virtually guarantee performance may constrain choice in such a way as to deny individuals the discretion to be virtuous or not. Without practice and recognition, virtue falters.

To ensure that rational and communal trust do not undermine each other, some contributors such as Blackburn, Brennan, Pettit, and John Braithwaite have favored institutional designs that bring each into play at a different level of social functioning. Trust as gift giving dominates in personal contexts and first encounters, while rational trust operates in impersonal contexts or when the gift of trust is abused. Institutional designs that accommodate communal and rational trust at different levels offer opportunities for achieving three seemingly conflicting objectives: (1) a strengthening of an individual's motivation for trustworthiness, (2) elevation of trustworthiness as a virtue above self-interest, and (3) an overarching regulating infrastructure that identifies and contains risk when trust falters.

The relationship between rational and communal trust is addressed by a number of contributors but is far from resolved. To many of the more rationalist theorists, such a relationship is beside the point. Both Hardin and Levi argue that trustworthiness is a virtue, yet they see no benefit—and much danger—from encouraging trust as a virtue. Fairness, respect, and acceptance of norms are important in the models of Scholz and Levi, but they play informational and institutional roles rather than normative ones. On the other hand, Tyler regards communal trust as more fundamental to stable government than rational trust. John Braithwaite also gives priority to the role of communal trust but regards different kinds of trust as mutually constituting. Valerie Braithwaite shows that where rational trust is strong so is communal trust; she argues that each can serve as a corrective for the weaknesses of the other. Jennings suggests that the two kinds of trust operate at different levels of government.

In spite of the considerable differences among the authors and in spite of the many puzzles and issues still unresolved, this volume has achieved its purposes. It creates the basis for an intellectual exchange and shared agenda among scholars of various disciplines, and it lays the groundwork for a more systematic investigation, both logical and empirical, of the relationship between trust and governance. By making explicit the differences among good scholars looking at similar evidence, we hope we have revealed new insights and arguments concerning the institutionalization of both rational and communal trust and the role both play in good governance.

Index

Anti-Federalists, 14, 359
Aristotle, 21
assurance, 80
attitudes: changing, 276–77; as clusters of beliefs, 48
authority: ability to change people's attitudes, 276–77; based on social bonds, 289; deference model of, 276; obedience to, 276

behavior: influence of democracy on citizens', 94–96; norms as standards of, 48–49; patterns produced by trust heuristics, 159–60; representing communal trust norms, 58–60, 65–66; signaling trustworthiness, 307
beliefs: about values, 48; based on expectations, 23; deceiving oneself into trusting, 38–41; exchange and communal trust norms as, 54; influences on, 37–38; value as enduring, 48. *See also* Pascal cases.

citizens: in democratic dependence game, 209–10; factors in trustworthiness of, 347; influence of democracy on behavior of, 94–96; involvement in policy making process, 92; personal trust among, 307–8; rational expectations related to government, 12; relations with different levels of government, 219; skepticism in democracies of, 96; trustworthiness

for trust-based compliance, 138; vulnerability to government, 208–9
citizens, disadvantaged: building trust in government for, 332–38; distrust of government, 316–32
citizenship: arguing for, 338–40; channeling distrust to, 357
civil society: British income tax system within, 121; civic republicanism in, 355–56; in disadvantaged suburbs, 322–24; strong, 359–62; trust in institutions of, 348–51, 356
coercion
as signal of a state's fairness, 90
collective action: compliance as problem of, 135–37; trust heuristics as strategy for, 158–60; undersupplied civil society as problem of, 363
commitment: credible, 86–88, 175; credible commitment of government, 175; as means to create trust, 80
common interest: citizens assessment of, 259–63; concept of, 254; as factor in trust decisions, 258; probability of constituent-legislator, 255–58
commonwealthmen tradition, 309
communal norms, 53–54
communal trust norms: behaviors representing, 58–60, 65–66; defined, 54; link to harmony value system, 54–55, 61–65